D1616743

China's Rise in Asia

China's Rise in Asia

Promises and Perils

ROBERT G. SUTTER

ROWMAN & LITTLEFIELD PUBLISHERS, INC.
Lanham • Boulder • New York • Toronto • Oxford

ROWMAN & LITTLEFIELD PUBLISHERS, INC.

Published in the United States of America
by Rowman & Littlefield Publishers, Inc.
A wholly owned subsidiary of The Rowman & Littlefield Publishing Group, Inc.
4501 Forbes Boulevard, Suite 200, Lanham, Maryland 20706
www.rowmanlittlefield.com

P.O. Box 317, Oxford OX2 9RU, UK

British Library Cataloguing in Publication Information Available

Library of Congress Cataloging-in-Publication Data

Sutter, Robert G.
  China's rise in Asia : promises and perils / Robert G. Sutter.
    p. cm.
  Includes bibliographical references and index.
  ISBN 0-7425-3906-7 (alk. paper)—ISBN 0-7425-3907-5 (pbk. : alk. paper)
  1. China—Foreign relations—1976- I. Title.
  DS779.27.S86 2005
  327.51'009'051—dc22   2004028708

Printed in the United States of America

♾™ The paper used in this publication meets the minimum requirements of American National Standard for Information Sciences—Permanence of Paper for Printed Library Materials, ANSI/NISO Z39.48-1992.

Contents

Contents

List of Abbreviations

Anti-Ballistic Missile Treaty (ABM)
ASEAN Regional Forum (ARF)
ASEAN-China Free Trade Agreement (ACFTA)
Asia-Europe (ASEM) meetings
Asian Cooperation Dialogue (ACD)
Asian-Pacific Economic Cooperation (APEC) forum
Association for Relations Across the Taiwan Strait (ARATS)
Association of Southeast Asian Nations (ASEAN)
Boao Forum for Asia (BFA)
Cambodian People's Party (CPP)
Chinese Communist Party (CCP)
Commonwealth of Independent States (CIS)
Confidence-building measure (CBM)
Democratic Progressive Party (DPP)
East Asian Economic Caucus (EAEC)
European Union (EU)
Exclusive Economic Zone (EEZ)
Group of Seven (G7)
Intermediate Nuclear Forces (INF) treaty
International Monetary Fund (IMF)
Joint Cooperation Committee (JCC)

Legislative Yuan (LY)
Liberal Democratic party (LDP)
Line of Actual Control (LOAC)
Liquefied natural gas (LNG)
Memorandum of understanding (MOU)
Ministry of Foreign Affairs (MOFA)
Ministry of Foreign Trade and Economic Cooperation (MOFTEC)
Missile Technology Control Regime (MTCR)
National People's Congress (NPC)
National United Front for an Independent, Neutral, Peaceful,
    and Cooperative Cambodia (FUNCINPEC)
Nationalist Party (KMT)
New Security Concept (NSC)
North Atlantic Treaty Organization (NATO)
Overseas development assistance (ODA)
Partnership for Peace (PFP)
People First Party (PFP)
People's Republic of China (PRC)
Peoples Liberation Army (PLA)
Republic of China (ROC)
Republic of Korea (ROK)
Severe Acute Respiratory Syndrome (SARS)
Shanghai Cooperation Organization (SCO)
State Peace and Development Council (SPDC)
State Planning Commission (SPC)
State Economic and Trade Commission (SETC)
State-owned enterprise (SOE)
Straits Exchange Foundation (SEF)
Theater missile defense (TMD)
Union of Soviet Socialist Republics (USSR)
United Nations (UN)
Weapons of mass destruction (WMD)
World Trade Organization (WTO)

Acknowledgments

This book benefited from a research grant from the Smith Richardson Foundation. Special thanks go to Mr. Allan Song of the Foundation for excellent guidance and support. The staff of the Atlantic Council of the United States, where I held a position as a nonresident Senior Fellow, was also very helpful in the project, and special thanks go to Banning Garrett and Lyn Soudien for their support.

My 2004 trip to China and surrounding countries benefitted greatly from arrangements and support provided notably by the Chinese Association for International Understanding, the Bureau of Public Diplomacy of the U.S. Department of State, and the Institute for Peace and Conflict Studies (New Delhi). Special thanks go to Chris Siefken of the State Department.

I reviewed the findings of this study with numerous government and academic groups in the United States and abroad in 2003-2004 and benefited greatly from the comments and suggestions at those meetings. Especially useful were international conferences at the University of Denver in October 2003 and at George Washington University in December 2003; presentations to groups of specialists at People's University in Beijing, Seoul National University in South Korea, and the National University of Singapore; roundtable discussions with foreign ministry and intelligence officials in Singapore, foreign and defense ministry groups in Japan, and Asian affairs specialists at the Australian National University and Griffith University, as well as foreign ministry and intelligence agency groups in Australia; and a weeklong series of presentations to groups in New Delhi arranged mainly by the Institute for Peace and Conflict Studies.

Important research assistance was provided by Hyon Joo Yoo. As with other recent books with Rowman & Littlefield, I benefited greatly from the guidance of editorial director Susan McEachern and the anonymous review of the manuscript she arranged. Also repeating a pattern of previous books was the timely and excellent manuscript preparation work by David Hertzberg.

Introduction

The rapid rise of China's military and economic power prompts a steady stream of analysis and debate about China's motivations and objectives toward the United States and U.S. interests, especially in areas along China's borders in Asia. While most analysts agree that China does not intend and is not able to directly challenge the United States on a global scale, there is no consensus regarding China's policy in its Asian periphery. For example, there is disagreement among specialists on how significant and long lasting the current U.S.-China modus vivendi in Asia is likely to be. Looking to the future, some optimists foresee continued improvement in China-U.S. cooperation in Asia,[1] while skeptics take fuller account of the many deeply rooted differences that Chinese and U.S. leaders will continue to grapple with in the years ahead. For the latter, China's position as a "locomotive" of Asian economic growth, a growing web of China-centered trade and political arrangements with Asian partners, and the rapid buildup of Chinese military power reinforce these arguments.[2]

Below the surface of current U.S.-China amity, these skeptics point out, lie an array of contentious security, political, economic, and other difficult issues that make the U.S. bilateral relationship with China by far the most contentious and complicated U.S. relationship in Asian or world affairs.[3] There is no guarantee that the conditions that came to hold those differences in check and gave rise to the positive path of U.S.-China relations in 2001-2004 will continue, or that third parties outside U.S. and PRC control (e.g., North Korea, Taiwan) might not intervene in ways that

1

will disrupt U.S.-China relations. Thus, it seems prudent to be wary of predicting any long-term or fundamental positive change in China-U.S. relations over Asian affairs or other key issues. Among the many differences that characterize Sino-American relations is the stark reality that China remains the sole large power today building military forces to attack Americans if the United States were to intervene militarily in the Taiwan contingency. At the same time, U.S. forces are being enhanced to deal with such contingencies.

A central argument of this study is that China's approach to foreign affairs after the Cold War is strongly influenced by and related to China's approach to the United States. The behavior and commentary of Chinese leaders in the post-Cold War period gives pride of place to relations with the United States in Chinese foreign policy.[4] Asia is the region where China exerts greatest influence and where its most important foreign policy interests are located. Chinese leaders consistently view the United States as the greatest power in Asia and the most important power affecting Chinese interests in the region.

For much of the post-Cold War period, Chinese officials and other elites viewed the United States in contradictory ways—as the main international danger to the survival and development of China's Communist regime, and as China's critically important partner in economic modernization and in sustaining stable international conditions advantageous for China's economic growth and political stability. Managing these kinds of contradictions was difficult and led to periods of aggressive Chinese action against the United States in Asia and elsewhere, and periods of close cooperation with the United States on regional and other issues. At bottom, the Chinese approach to the United States in Asian and world affairs has appeared contingent, depending on how Chinese leaders weighed costs and benefits for China in the evolving circumstances as Asian and world affairs developed into the twenty-first century.[5]

China's Evolving Approach to Asia

Part of the problem in resolving analytical differences and divisions over China's foreign policy in Asia and its implications for the United States is that scholars and specialists over the years have had a hard time discerning a coherent Chinese policy toward Asia and its implications for the United States. In the post-Mao period, China multiplied its political and cultural relations with both developed countries and the Third World, expanded its participation in the international economic system, and played a more active role in the United Nations and other international organizations. But even though China grew into a position of a global political actor, its foreign policy was still concerned predominantly with Asia. China's security concerns focused on Asia, and its military power did not extend much beyond the region. China's political and cultural influence was strongest in Asia, and the largest proportion of its foreign trade was conducted with Asian neighbors.

As Steven Levine pointed out in the 1980s,[6] Chinese leaders rarely thought at a conceptual level about foreign policy in regional terms, even though the bulk of Chinese interests and activities rested in Asia. Chinese leaders tended to approach their relations with their neighbors either on a purely bilateral basis, or else on the basis of a set of global policies that Beijing endeavored to apply to all countries in a universal way. If China's actual international undertakings—whether support for revolutionary movements and insurgencies or emphasis on conventional diplomatic relations with established governments—wound up being directed mainly at Asia, this was dictated by distance and geography, not doctrine or intent.

Further illustrating a duality of Chinese actual interests versus foreign policy design, China on the one hand was preoccupied with issues close to home: nurturing friendly neighbors, border security, recovery of lost territory, assertion of claims to maritime jurisdiction, concern for overseas Chinese, and support for client communist parties and their insurgencies. Heading the list was ensuring that hostile powers did not establish dominance around China's periphery. On the other hand, when Chinese leaders discussed these issues they insisted on doing so in a global context, with China positioned as a world leader. Thus, China's conflict with Vietnam was seen as part of the world struggle against Soviet expansionism, and support for Malaysian and Indonesia claims to the Straits of Malacca was defined as part of a broader Third World resistance to superpower maritime hegemonism. Chinese opposition to U.S. policies in Taiwan and South Korea was part of worldwide opposition to American imperialism, and China's trade with the Association of Southeast Asian Nations (ASEAN) was portrayed as an example of South-South cooperation in the face of an unfair international trading regime dominated by the developed nations. Levine concluded such tension between China's regional stature and its global ambitions complicated assessing China's "Asian" policy, as China at the time was "a regional power without a regional policy."[7]

Things did not get easier at the end of the Cold War when the collapse of the great power competition in the U.S.-Soviet and Sino-Soviet relationships during the Cold War seemed to reinforce fluidity in Asia and made assessing Chinese regional policy appear more difficult. Denny Roy in 1998 saw no coherent Chinese regional policy in Asia.[8] What he saw was a collection of distinct bilateral relationships with a highly diverse group of countries. There were seen to be Chinese incentives for cooperation with most countries in Asia, such as economic opportunities, an interest in resisting perceived U.S. pressure in several Asian countries, and divisive issues such as territorial disputes and security concerns. In some ways, China was seen as a supporter of the regional status quo, but regarding other aspects it is seen as a challenger.

Despite these analytical difficulties and complications, however, one can discern overarching imperatives that have evolved in the post-Mao and post-Cold War period and that help to define a distinct Chinese policy throughout China's periphery evident in recent years. They include the strong concerns of Chinese leaders to promote the legitimacy of their continued rule through domestic economic growth and political stability dependent on active economic exchange and an open door to economic globalization and modernization. Chinese leaders have been seen to remain concerned about trends and power relations in Asia that could enhance or disrupt their modernization efforts and other core interests, notably ensuring China's territorial integrity and the return of Taiwan. Their policy toward the region has appeared to be driven heavily by Beijing's overall concern to deal effectively with the policies and influences of the United States and other influential Asian powers.[9]

Jiang Zemin and the successor generation of Chinese leaders led by President Hu Jintao have endeavored to emphasize China's multidirectional, good neighbor policy in recent years. They have played down China's global ambitions and adopted a relatively low profile on most international issues not directly bearing on China's interests in Asia. They have come to terms, at least for now, with U.S. dominance of many key international regimes and regions, so long as the United States does not infringe on core Chinese interests. Thus, although China has become increasingly reliant on imported oil from Southwest Asia, China, along with other major importers, continues to rely without serious objection on the U.S.-military supported security order for the smooth flow of oil to its ports. As Michael Yahuda has argued,[10] China may be said to have benefited in the post-Cold War period from both American primacy and from the effects of globalization. The former provided the peaceful international environment and the international public goods that have enabled the Chinese to focus on an export-led strategy of rapid economic development and the latter has facilitated China's integration into the regional and international economies. As a result, China has become less of a challenger to the status quo in Asia and more of a net contributor to regional order—at least for now.

Based in part on a New Security Concept launched in 1997[11]—based on the Five Principles of Peaceful Coexistence, the mainstay of phases of moderate and conventional Chinese diplomacy since the 1950s—Chinese leaders have applied the concept in an array of unprecedented active interchange throughout China's periphery. Taken together with the growth and spread of the Chinese economic power and interchange with Asia, and the expansion of Chinese military capabilities, China has improved its standing with almost all of it neighbors in recent years, with exceptions being Taiwan and possibly Japan.

The progress China has made in expanding its influence in Asia has coincided in the past three years with the most significant improvement in China-U.S. relations in more than a decade.[12] The comparatively smooth and businesslike U.S.-China relationship has witnessed greater cooperation in Asia, notably in the war on terrorism and in dealing with North Korea's provocative nuclear weapons development. It has appeared to reinforce Chinese incentives to sustain a cooperative and relatively moderate approach to Asia. Optimists argue that the recent upswing in U.S.-China relations and concurrent constructive Chinese policy and behavior in Asia will continue to gain momentum.[13] They point to the wide variety of mutual interests of the United States and China regarding promoting international stability and prosperity, and working with international organizations to find common solutions to transnational issues like terrorism, drug trade, health issues, and environmental problems. In this view, the stated Chinese foreign policy approach of building common ground while reserving differences would work over time. Common ground would grow, and differences would seem less important and would be more likely to be settled in a mutually beneficial way.

The reasoning behind predictions of greater Chinese cooperation with the United States and others in Asia is strong and sound. It tends to give heavy emphasis to Chinese leaders' focus on continued and deepening economic interaction with the United States, Japan, the developed economies of Asia, and elsewhere as they endeavor to strengthen their political standing and legitimacy through effective modernization and conventional nation building. These tasks require a peaceful international environment especially around China's periphery, which necessitates a protracted modus vivendi with the United States and others important in Asian affairs. They provided a foundation for the Chinese formula, announced in 2003-2004, concerning China's "peaceful rise" in Asian and world affairs. Chinese leaders said that this peaceful Chinese approach to development and expanded international influence for China would be a strategic one, lasting well into the new century.[14]

China appears to have little to gain from aggressive or assertive actions against the United States and others in the region. Its greater embrace of globalization means that the Chinese leadership has come to a more sophisticated view of U.S. power and Asian affairs, recognizing how China benefits in the face of U.S. global leadership in Asia and other U.S. policies, many of which until very recently had been seen as fundamental challenges to Chinese interests and concerns. According to the argument, as Chinese leaders "learn" more about the benefits for them in accommodating the prevailing order in Asia and in relations with the United States, the prospects for greater cooperation with the United States and others over Asian affairs will grow.[15] A concurrent trend that facilitates this process is the perceived shift in the U.S. George W. Bush administration from a posture that appeared to focus on China as a strategic adversary to one that sought broadening common ground and accommodation.[16]

This study duly acknowledges the positive trends noted above, but it does so with a clear recognition of deeply rooted problems and important negative trends that point to a future Chinese posture in Asia that could revert to a more assertive and disruptive stance against the United States or others, if conditions were to change. To support this judgment, introduced in the next chapter are a wide range of issues that continue to bedevil the U.S.-China relationship and influence China's approach to the United States and its allies and associates in Asia. Also reviewed there are the prevailing negative Chinese elite and popular attitudes toward the United States and its approach to Asia and how these are likely to influence China's approach toward the region, and the long-standing Chinese priority to secure China's periphery from the presence and pressure of the United States or other perceived antagonistic powers. Chapter 3 assesses the relative importance of China's policy toward Asia and the United States in Asia in the context of recent Chinese leadership policy priorities. Subsequent chapters review Chinese interaction with all the main powers around China's periphery. The conclusion assesses the implications for China and the United States of Chinese policies and behavior in Asia, including the

Chinese leadership's emphasis in 2003-2004 on China's intention to "rise" and develop peacefully, and makes brief recommendations for U.S. policy.

The analysis in this study gives strong emphasis to the role of the United States as a key determinant in China's continued moderate approach to the Asian region.[17] A key finding is that without the United States pursuing a firm and effective policy toward China, avoiding challenge to core Chinese interests while making clear boundaries China should not cross, Chinese leaders would be more likely to be impelled by long-standing ambitions, domestic political forces, and realist power considerations to adopt a more assertive and likely more disruptive stance in Asian affairs.

Overview

The Chinese leadership has been developing a relatively pragmatic approach to China's Asian neighbors for over twenty years.[18] Beijing has worked to sustain regional stability and has sought greater economic advantage and political influence, without compromising core Chinese territorial, security, or other interests. Chinese regional policy generally has been a secondary priority to Chinese leaders focused on managing more important domestic priorities and dealing with such salient international developments as the fall of Soviet power and the rise of American power that were widely seen among Chinese officials and specialists as significantly affecting important Chinese interests and ambitions.[19]

During the 1990s, the leadership broadened international contacts and increasingly met international requirements and norms regarding market access, intellectual property rights, and other economic issues, eventually becoming a member of the World Trade Organization (WTO). They moved to settle a number of outstanding border issues and use security confidence building measures with neighboring states. Chinese leaders remained sensitive on matters of national sovereignty and international security issues close to home. But they adjusted to world pressure when resistance appeared detrimental to broader Chinese concerns. Examples of this adjustment included Chinese cooperation with the international peace settlement in Cambodia in 1991, willingness to join the Treaty on Non-proliferation of Nuclear Weapons and to halt nuclear tests by the end of 1996 under an international agreement, willingness to abide by terms of the Missile Technology Control Regime, and efforts to help the United States reach an agreement with North Korea in October 1994 over the latter's nuclear weapons development program. Beijing also endeavored to meet international expectations on other transnational issues, such as policing drug traffic, curbing international terrorism, and working to avoid further degradation of the global environment.[20]

China's continued hard line against outside criticism of China's political authoritarianism and poor human rights record graphically illustrated the limits of China's accommodation.[21] China continued to transfer sensitive military technology or dual use equipment to Pakistan, Iran, and other potential flash points, despite criticism from Western countries. Furthermore, Chinese political and military leaders used rhetorical threats or demonstrations of military force to intimidate those they believed were challenging China's territorial or nationalistic claims in sensitive areas such as Taiwan, the South China Sea, and Hong Kong. In the early 1990s, China's assertiveness regarding disputed territories and its bellicose posture during the Taiwan Strait crisis of 1995-1996 alarmed its neighbors.[22] Chinese leaders continued the practice of the past when they tended to exaggerate the threats posed by actions of the United States, the Soviet Union, and their associates when they intruded on key Chinese security and sovereignty interests along China's periphery.[23]

Chinese leaders tended to view China's influence as growing but far from dominant in Asian and world affairs. External and internal factors limited China's assertiveness, and Chinese leaders sought to calm concerns by neighbors and associated powers, notably the United States, about the implications of China's growing stature.[24] By far the most important nation in Chinese foreign policy, the United States posed major opportunities and challenges. In the 1990s, Chinese leaders and specialists, as reflected in official comment, believed the world was becoming multipolar, with the United States as the single superpower but increasingly less able to exert its will as other countries and regions opposed U.S. initiatives. This view changed sharply in the latter 1990s, owing to the striking disparities between U.S. economic performance and that of other major powers, and to U.S. leadership in the Balkans crisis, U.S. policy on missile defense, the U.S. war on terrorism, and other issues.

The Chinese more recently concluded that the world will be unipolar in the near term, with the United States exerting greater influence than Beijing had originally calculated. Chinese leaders often perceived that this influence might not be benign vis-à-vis China's core interests, notably Taiwan and the perceived use of U.S. and allied power in Asian and world affairs contrary to Chinese concerns. They were sharply critical of U.S. policy in the 1990s. However, Chinese officials came to the view since 2001 that for the time being China could do little to counter U.S. influence, particularly as Russia, India, Japan, and other potential power centers generally chose to cooperate with rather that confront U.S. power. Chinese officials were explicit in private conversations since 2001 in noting that China did not want to be in a position of confronting U.S. power alone, and that China would seek to avoid this situation unless its core interests, mainly involving Taiwan, were seriously challenged by the United States.[25]

Jiang Zemin and China's Current Regional Strategy

Coincident with the decline and death of Deng Xiaoping, Jiang Zemin led Chinese officials in pursuing a more active foreign policy that has focused important attention on gradually improving China's influence throughout its periphery. In particular, 1997 saw the transition of Hong Kong to Chinese rule, the reconfiguration of Chinese leadership and policy at the Fifteenth CCP Congress, and the Sino-U.S. summit.[26]

Subsequent policy priorities were led by an ambitious multiyear effort to transform tens of thousands of China's money-losing state-owned enterprises (SOEs). Beijing also embarked on programs to promote economic and administrative efficiency and protect China's potentially vulnerable financial systems from the 1997-1998 Asian economic crisis and subsequent uncertainties.[27] Foreign affairs generally remained an area of less urgent policy priority. Broad international trends—notably somewhat improved relations with the United States—supported the efforts by the Chinese authorities to pursue policies intended to minimize disruptions and to assist domestic reform endeavors. The government remained wary and often sharply critical of the real or potential challenges posed by a possible renewed economic crisis, by Taiwan, by efforts by Japan and the United States to increase their international influence in ways seen as contrary to Beijing's interests, by India's great power aspirations and nuclear capability, and by other concerns. For a time, the PRC voiced special concern over the implications for China's interests of U.S. plans to develop and deploy ballistic missile defense systems in East Asia, and a national missile defense for the United States. Chinese officials also voiced concern over the downturn in U.S.-China relations at the outset of the George W. Bush administration, but appeared determined to cooperate with the U.S.-led antiterrorism campaign begun in September 2001.[28]

Giving priority to domestic economic development, political stability, and seeking to avoid major confrontation or controversy in foreign affairs, China's approach to Asia and other world affairs shifted into a more active posture. An emphasis on a new security concept ran in tandem with Chinese leaders' efforts beginning in 1996 to establish "partnerships" or "strategic partnerships" with most of the powers along China's periphery (e.g., Russia, ASEAN, Japan, and South Korea) as well as other world powers. Those partnerships and other high-level Chinese interaction emphasized putting aside differences and seeking common ground. Beijing also stressed more the importance of the United Nations and other multilateral organizations in safeguarding world norms supported by China and as a check against hegemonism and power politics.[29]

Other features of Chinese policy included a very active schedule for Chinese political and military leaders in meeting visitors from Asia and in traveling there. Regarding regional organizations, Chinese officials were instrumental in the establishment in 2001 of the Shanghai Cooperation Organization, including also Russia, Kazakhstan, Kyrgyzstan, Tajikistan, and Uzbekistan, and they worked assiduously to improve China's relations with ASEAN, proposing an ASEAN-China Free Trade Agreement and Chinese security arrangements with ASEAN and the ASEAN Regional Forum (ARF) that appeared at odds with U.S.-backed security efforts in Southeast Asia. China also worked closely with Japan and South Korea as well as ASEAN in the so-called ASEAN Plus Three dialogue that emerged around the time of the Asian economic crisis.[30]

The greater Chinese involvement with regional and other multilateral organizations represented a significant change in Chinese foreign policy. Previously, Chinese officials generally were wary of many international organizations. They were concerned that such groupings might be influenced by powers opposed to Chinese interests, might require costly commitments of Chinese resources, and might constrain Chinese maneuvering in pursuit of important Chinese interests. These suspicions waned in the 1990s as Chinese officials became more adroit in working constructively with Asian and other multilateral organizations in seeking goals that benefited China. Chinese influence in Asian organizations grew in tandem with the growth of the Chinese economy and the even more rapid growth of Chinese trade with Asian economic partners. China's increasing economic and strategic importance saw Asian leaders seek closer Chinese involvement with regional groupings, and Chinese leaders saw such organizations as consistent with their foreign policy goals emphasizing regional stability and favorable economic exchanges.

Chinese leaders also saw Asian regional groups as useful means to constrain the United States and possibly other powers that might be inclined to take actions contrary to Chinese interests in the prevalent order in Asia. Chinese officials and specialists made clear in consultations in mid-2004 that Chinese leaders viewed deeper Chinese involvement in Asian multilateral organizations as providing a defense against possible revival of U.S. efforts to pressure or contain China. The ever growing webs of Chinese connections with an increasing array of Asian multilateral organizations and groups provided the basis of a sort of Gulliver strategy that would tie down and impede possible U.S. efforts to engage in sharp pressure or containment of China.

A review of Chinese relations with neighboring states and recent in-depth consultations with Chinese foreign policy planners and specialists show that Chinese leaders seem more confident of China's power and influence but they also are keenly aware of and sober minded about the continued predominance of the United States in Asian and world affairs—a dominance that probably will continue for the foreseeable future.[31] They acknowledge that China has been constrained to deal with the reality of U.S. power and influence through less confrontational tactics than those that applied up until 2001, finding their earlier approach on balance counterproductive. They endeavor to deal with U.S. power and influence in the current period through, among others, multilateral and cooperative approaches designed to steer U.S. policy and actions in directions not adverse to core Chinese interests. They also seem anxious to find ways that China's rising influence in Asia and world affairs not be seen as a challenge to U.S. power and influence—a challenge that is not in Chinese interests because of the great difference in Chinese and U.S. power and influence. This reasoning lies behind China's emphasis in 2003-2004 on Chinese leaders' determination that China's development be seen as "peaceful" and not be seen as a threat to its neighbors and other concerned powers, notably the United States.[32]

China's relations with most neighboring powers have made advances in recent years. It is hard to measure exactly how much actual influence this allows Beijing to exert in Asia, especially as China's approach seeks common ground with neighbors and generally does not ask them to do things they are not already inclined to do. China is clearly more popular and the target of less suspicion than in the past among many Asian governments, elites, and popular opinion, and its economic importance as an engine of Asian growth has increased. By and large, Asian governments and elites have remained focused on promoting economic development and related concerns as they seek to build their national wealth and power in a period of international economic interdependence, competition, and globalization. China's approach to its neighbors has a geoeconomic emphasis that seems to mesh well with the prevailing priorities of Asian leaders. This convergence appears to add to China's growing influence in Asia. On balance, there is no question that an image of China's rising influence has been important, particularly in Southeast Asia and Korea, where Chinese relations have improved markedly. The Chinese government also is playing the key mediating role in dealing with the North Korean nuclear crisis of 2002-2004.

In sum, the greater Chinese activism in and clearer focus on Asia reflect multifaceted and long-term objectives:[33]

1. They help to secure China's foreign policy environment at a time when the PRC government is focused on sustaining economic development and political stability
2. They promote economic exchange that assists China's internal economic development.
3. They support PRC efforts to isolate Taiwan internationally and to secure the flow of advanced arms and military technology to China despite a continuing Western embargo on such transfers.
4. Increased Chinese contacts act to calm regional fears and reassure Asian neighbors about how China will use its rising power and influence.
5. Greater Chinese influence around China's periphery boosts China's regional and international power and influence and helps to secure an ambiguous world order; Chinese leaders seem more confident of China's power and influence but they also remain wary of and work against U.S.-led or other regional efforts seen as contrary to China's interests.

The U.S. Role in China's Regional Policy

American specialists and other outside observers seem to have little disagreement over the above Chinese objectives except for the last. In regard to the latter, some specialists say China's primary long-term regional goal is to push the United States out of Asia and assert regional dominance. Their analysis gives U.S. policy a primary role in determining Chinese policy in the region. It forecasts a generally negative outlook for the United States and the region—predicting more friction as China's rise puts it in conflict with the United States for influence in Asia.[34]

Other specialists point to a more confident Chinese leadership approach to Asia. Chinese leaders over time have embraced economic interdependence and globalization as providing great benefits to them as rulers of China. They also have come to accept some of the benefits of U.S. primacy in world affairs. These specialists forecast a generally positive outlook for the region and U.S. interests in Asia, as Chinese leaders see their interests best served by a cooperative stance that over time adds significantly to Chinese wealth and power.[35]

A third group of specialists, including this writer, tries to find a middle ground but in the end sees continued anti-U.S. tendencies in Chinese policy that currently are held in check by circumstances, especially the effective use of U.S.-predominant power and influence in Asia. China's strategy in Asia is seen as contingent and U.S. power and polices play a big role in determining Chinese policy in the region. There has been change in Chinese leaders' attitudes toward economic interdependence and willingness to work with U.S. primacy in many areas in the post-Cold War world, and China has spread influence incrementally throughout the region. But these analysts are heavily influenced by an assessment of factors that appear to make China's recent stance tentative. Chinese leaders seem wary of pressures and events that could compel them to shift to different and perhaps more hard-line positions in Asian affairs. As the acknowledged dominant power in the region, the United States is seen to loom large in these Chinese leadership calculations.[36]

Contingent policies based on pragmatic cost-benefit analyses developed during the post-Mao period as a central feature of Chinese leaders' decision making over foreign policy, especially regarding important issues along China's periphery in Asia.[37] A review of the record shows that for two decades, from the late 1960s to the mid-1980s, the strategic focus of Chinese leaders was guarding and maneuvering against expanding and threatening Soviet power, especially military power, throughout China's periphery. This involved changing degrees of Chinese cooperation with the United States and its allies and associates, depending on variables including changing Chinese perceptions of the Soviet threat, the extent of U.S. resolve, and the assessed utility of alignment with the United States to counter the USSR.[38]

The end of the Cold War and the collapse of the USSR improved China's security situation. However, U.S.-led Western reaction to the Tiananmen crackdown, stronger emphasis on nationalistic themes by Chinese leaders, and perceived adverse separatist trends in Taiwan backed by the United States headed the list of reasons why Chinese leaders came to see the United States and its power and influence in Asian and world affairs as the new "hegemon," striving to pressure, intimidate, and hold back China's rise in Asia. Deng Xiaoping advised Chinese leaders to try to avoid confrontation, to "bide time," working to take advantage of developing international opportunities in order to build up China's "comprehensive national power" and secure a more advantageous world leadership position over the longer term. Chinese leaders continue to reaffirm commitment to Deng's maxims.[39]

Throughout the 1990s, and arguably up to the present, the main obstacle to China's rise has been seen in Beijing as the United States and its allies and associates, notably Japan and Taiwan, but also India, NATO, and other international organizations and groups where the United States plays a leadership role in ways seen as adverse to Chinese interests. U.S. opposition and "containment" have been clearly evident to Chinese leaders in the clusters of security, economic, political, and other differences that have made the U.S.-China relations the most complex U.S. bilateral relationship with any power after the Cold War. Particular Chinese grievances have focused on U.S. resolve to continue support for Taiwan, to remain the leading power in Asian and world affairs, and to promote change in China's political system.[40]

China's negative views of the United States are grounded in deeply rooted suspicions of the United States on the part of Chinese elites, even Chinese academic and government specialists on U.S. affairs. These are reinforced by a national education system and media network that have conditioned broader Chinese opinion to think of China as a long suffering target of depredations and pressures from outside powers, with the United States as the leading oppressor in the recent period. Following the Tiananmen crackdown and the collapse of international communism, Chinese leaders gave greater salience to such nationalistic conditioning, having an impact on the sharp deterioration on Chinese popular views of the United States after the Cold War.[41]

The George W. Bush administration has employed U.S. incentives and disincentives from a position of overall strength in persuading Chinese leaders to pursue cooperative and moderate policies toward the United States, its allies and associates, and others in Asian and world affairs. U.S.-China relations are multifaceted, businesslike, and broadly cooperative, despite the U.S. government's advances in support for Taiwan, missile defense, security relations with Japan, NATO expansion, sanctions on Chinese weapons proliferation actions, U.S. unilateral and militarily aggressive policies in Iraq, and other measures long sensitive to, and until recently sharply criticized by, China.[42]

China's Moderation toward the United States in Asia—Tactical or Strategic?

Among the various Chinese moves in recent years toward greater moderation and accommodation in Asian and world affairs, perhaps the most striking has been the abrupt falloff in mid-2001 of the wide ranging and often very harsh Chinese public criticism of U.S. policy that prevailed throughout the previous decade. For years and with varying degrees of intensity, the United States was portrayed as the "hegemon," the focal point of a world wide struggle fostered by Chinese polemicists and officials. Asia was the focus of Chinese charges centered on alleged U.S. efforts to contain China's rise, to split and weaken the country through interference in Chinese internal affairs, support for Taiwan and Tibetan separatists, and strategic alignments and deployments around China's periphery involving Japan, NATO's Partnership for Peace program in Central Asia, India, and Southeast Asian states.

Authoritative official Chinese comment reached several high points of invective, notably when *People's Daily* "Observer" articles equated the U.S. military campaign against Yugoslavia in 1999 with the Nazi advances in World War II and compared President Clinton with Adolph Hitler.[43]

The Chinese decision to stop this public campaign has markedly improved the atmosphere in recent U.S.-China relations. The decision raises an important question among U.S. and other analysts as to whether this shift represents a basic change in China's approach to the United States in Asian and world affairs. Those who see a more confident Chinese leadership in the twenty-first century tend to believe that there indeed has been a fundamental shift toward "new thinking" in Beijing.[44] Chinese leaders are seen as markedly less concerned and less prone to react sharply and negatively to U.S. policies and practices that in the recent past would have set off strident Chinese invective and other assertive actions. As a newly "responsible" international player, China is assumed to have put aside its until very recently strong efforts to work against U.S. influence and power in nearby Asia.

In contrast are those including this writer who find this argument unconvincing for several reasons. First, they see U.S. policies and behavior as markedly *more* hegemonic and offensive to long-standing Chinese sensitivities under the Bush administration in such areas as Taiwan, missile defense, U.S. defense ties with Japan, U.S. sanctions against China, and U.S. military posture in Iraq, Central Asia, and Southeast Asia. They find it hard to believe that the long-standing and deeply rooted negative and suspicious Chinese elite views of U.S. policy in Asian and world affairs could change so quickly. Indeed, Chinese specialists duly acknowledged that the U.S. actions add to deep-seated Chinese suspicions of U.S. policy intentions toward China.[45] Under these circumstances, more likely in the view of these skeptical U.S. and other foreign analysts, is a Chinese administration decision to mute anti-U.S. rhetoric and assertiveness for tactical reasons involving China's need to maintain a cooperative relationship with the United States and other reasons, rather than any fundamental change in China's opposition to many aspects of U.S. policy in Asia and elsewhere.[46] As noted earlier, Chinese officials carried out a reevaluation of China's strategy against the United States in 2000-2001 and concluded that China did not want to be in a position of confronting alone the U.S. superpower. U.S. military and other strengths backed by the Bush administration's clear willingness to use them against opponents appeared as additional factors that have shown the serious costs for China if it continued a confrontational approach toward the United States. These circumstances favored muting differences for now and following Deng's maxims to bide time and await opportunities while continuing to develop greater national wealth and power.

Indeed, the Bush administration officials privately warned Chinese counterparts in early 2001 against continuing strident anti-U.S. Chinese rhetoric.[47] As the United States seemed to be determined to confront its enemies and likely to remain the dominant power for some time, other power centers, even Russia, were reluctant to confront or seriously challenge U.S. leadership. Under these circumstances, Chinese officials recognized that China was in no position on its own to challenge the United

States and to try to balance U.S. power, even in nearby Asia. This effort would attract few allies and would endanger core Chinese interests in maintaining stability and promoting economic development.[48]

Second, reflecting clear limits on China's accommodation with the United States in Asia, Chinese policy continues to work over the longer term to weaken the predominant U.S. role around China's periphery. In the lead-up to the Iraq war, China continued to straddle the fence, privately pledging not to block U.S. military action but siding publicly with France and others in calling for protracted inspections. Beijing's work to resolve the crisis over North Korea's nuclear program still falls short of U.S. expectations in seeking more concrete pressure on the North. Chinese officials also told U.S. media of their impatience with U.S. demands for support on Iraq and North Korea, without any change in U.S. policy where it matters most to China—that is, Taiwan. A more forceful U.S. stance on North Korea would alarm China, which very likely would take strong measures to block the U.S. pressure.[49] The day-to-day interface of U.S. and Chinese military forces along China's periphery has not been without significant incident, even as the two powers endeavored to resume more normal ties after the April 1, 2001, EP-3 episode. Perhaps of most importance, deep U.S.-China divisions continue to be seen in the continuing clash of long-term U.S.-China interests in the region—particularly the continued PLA buildup targeted at Taiwan and U.S. forces that might help Taiwan, and U.S. military preparations to deal with Taiwan contingencies. They suggest that a major breakthrough toward strategic cooperation is unlikely.[50]

Third, theories regarding learning and change in international relations[51] show that Chinese leaders, deeply influenced by nationalistic feelings and anti-American conditioning, will have great difficulty "learning" a more broadly cooperative approach to the United States in Asia. The leaders also may have difficulty refraining from the long-standing tendency to exaggerate the perceived threats posed by U.S. or other outside pressures.[52] Imbued with such a suspicious mind-set regarding the United States, Chinese leaders are unlikely to change their minds unless some major defining event causes them to do so. It is difficult to see such an event in recent Chinese foreign policy.

Fourth, there remains plenty of evidence that Chinese leaders continue to oppose U.S. policy in many areas, notably U.S. support for Taiwan and U.S. strategic leadership on a number of sensitive issues in Asian and world affairs. While much less public after mid-2001, the opposition is seen in a variety of venues and materials. A book based on files of Chinese leadership deliberations shows graphically and repeatedly that suspicion of and opposition to U.S. policy in Asia remains a driving force in Chinese policy. Typical of the private negative leadership views of U.S. intentions was Hu Jintao who said:

"[The United States has] strengthened its military deployments in the Asia-Pacific region, strengthened the U.S.-Japan military alliance, strengthened strategic cooperation with India, improved relations with Vietnam, inveigled Pakistan, established a pro-American government in Afghanistan, increased arms sales to

Taiwan, and so on. They have extended outposts and placed pressure points on us from the east, south, and west. This makes a great change in our geopolitical environment."[53]

To deal with these adverse trends but avoid confrontation with the United States, Chinese leaders have settled on a longer term approach that for now tries to balance real or potential adverse U.S. power and influence in nonconfrontational ways, often coming in "under the radar" of U.S. decision makers and Asian leaders and thereby avoiding adverse consequences for Chinese interests. The competitive and antagonistic aspects in China's stance toward the United States in Asia show more in some areas of Asia than others. Key determinants seem to include the degree of U.S. and Chinese sensitivity, and their respective influence, in particular parts of Asia.

Chinese foreign policy leader Qian Qichen endeavored to explain the evolution of China's more flexible and cooperative approach to the United States while continuing to oppose U.S. policies and behavior seen as adverse to Chinese interests. In an assessment of international trends and U.S.-China relations after September 11, 2001, Qian urged his colleagues to adopt a more cooperative approach toward the United States with a full awareness of the need to deal resolutely with continuing major differences in China-U.S. relations. He alluded to the long-standing Chinese practice of dealing with the perceived U.S. "two hands" approach to China—the hand of engagement and the hand of containment, by China adopting the hand of cooperation and the hand of struggle. He said, "It is insufficient to have only the hand for struggles. The hand of cooperation is equally important. Cooperation itself is an important constraint on the anti-China forces in the U.S."[54]

In this context, he also said in reference to a continuing skeptical and wary Chinese leadership view of the United States and its intentions toward China: "First, the foundation for cooperation between China and the United States does not change; second, the foundation for contradiction between China and the United States does not change; and third, the two-faced nature of Washington's China policy does not change."[55]

Suggesting a long-term Chinese approach to deal with China's complicated relationship with the United States, Qian added: "When we handle the Sino-American relations . . . the starting point is our basic national interests. While we should firmly grasp the initiative of Sino-American relations, we must make it a contest of wits and courage, but not that of temper; seek not the gratification of a moment; and pursue not the victory of a day."[56]

In conclusion, the pattern of post-Cold War Chinese strategy in Asia emphasizes conventional nation building and gradually strengthening China's influence by a Chinese leadership more focused on domestic issues than expanding foreign power. It reflects greater Chinese confidence, seen in more moderation on territorial issues and more initiatives involving bilateral ties and multilateral arrangements.

China's approach of emphasizing common ground with neighbors provides limited concrete evidence of how much increased influence China actually exerts in Asia—something that would be clearer were China to get neighboring countries to follow policies China favors and they do not. China's economic power and influence as a growing engine of Asian growth seems very important; China's "soft" power also appears to be growing, especially as the elite and popular view of China moves in a positive direction in some Asian areas, notably Southeast Asia and South Korea. It is evident that China's geoeconomic emphasis in Asia coincides with the priorities of Asian government leaders. The latter are concerned with economic development and related nation-building tasks in a period of strong international economic interdependence and competition. China's rise as a focal point of regional trade and investment looms ever larger in the nation-building strategies of these leaders, posing both opportunities for greater growth and competitive dangers. As a result, Asian leaders increasingly take Chinese considerations into account as they formulate their national policies and goals.

Meanwhile, Chinese officials appear to remain highly sensitive to the policies and power of the United States and U.S.-backed allies and associates, especially Taiwan and Japan. North Korea represents another source of uncertainty independent of the United States. The overall rise of U.S. power and assertiveness in post-Cold War Asian and world affairs has many drawbacks for long-standing Chinese interests in Asia. China has viewed negatively or with suspicion greater U.S. support for Taiwan and Japanese military activism, U.S. ballistic missile defense, strengthened U.S. military deployments and closer military cooperation in Central, South and Southeast Asia, and closer U.S. military and foreign policy cooperation with India and Russia.

Chinese leaders have learned after considerable debate over the last twenty-five years that economic globalization is in China's interests, and they have come to embrace it. On political and security issues, however, the prevailing pattern is to deal with these questions on a case-by-case basis, taking account in each instance of the costs and benefits for Chinese interests. In this regard, China is less a "responsible" power—fully embracing international norms in security and political affairs—and more a "responsive" power, carefully maneuvering to preserve long-standing interests in changing circumstances.

In particular, Chinese leaders have concluded that public and vocal efforts in the recent past to oppose and resist adverse U.S. policies and trends have become counterproductive, especially given the Bush administration's power and firmness against adversaries and the strong opposition by Asian governments to great power contention. Nonetheless, Chinese officials continue to oppose U.S. dominance in Asia and world affairs, and to work against adverse trends involving the United States in more subtle and indirect ways. At the same time, they seem to believe that the overall growth of Chinese power and influence in Asia over the long term will secure Chinese interests in opposition to contrary actions and interests of the United States.

Looking out, Asian actors like governments in Taiwan, North Korea, or possibly elsewhere now have the ability to take provocative actions that could change the course of China's moderate and cooperative approach in Asia. Of more long-term importance are U.S. power, policy, and behavior, which is likely to remain a key determinant in China's regional stance. A more hard-line U.S. posture involving sensitive issues like support for Taiwan, military deployments, or closer strategic cooperation with Japan could prompt a reassessment and more harsh Chinese reaction affecting overall Chinese Asian strategy. Chinese officials and specialists warned privately in May 2004 that if the United States did not respond constructively to the moderate Chinese stance toward U.S. interests seen in the recent emphasis on China's "peaceful rise," unspecified "hard liners" will reassert influence in Chinese decision making and shift Chinese foreign policy in a negative direction against the United States and its interests in Asia.[57] A weakening of U.S. power through failure in Iraq, a change of administrations, or U.S. economic decline also could prompt more Chinese pressure against U.S. interests, probing to roll back recent advances in U.S. support for Taiwan or other recent U.S. initiatives that have worked against Chinese interests.

Carefully managing the U.S.-China relationship from an overall position of U.S. confidence and strength would appear to provide a good means to hold in check long-standing Chinese tendencies to assertively challenge U.S. interests and perceived adverse Asian developments. Those tendencies appear to be held in check at least for the time being as Chinese leaders accept U.S. global and regional leadership and seek to avoid confrontation and build cooperation with the United States under the recently emphasized effort to promote China's "peaceful ascendancy" in Asian affairs.

Of possible concern for U.S. policy makers, the rise of Chinese power and influence in Asia in recent years notably has affected the ability of the United States to resort to pressure or other coercive approaches toward China. In general, Asian countries now derive much positive benefit from China's recent positive and moderate approach to the region and are reluctant to risk the negative consequences for their interests by choosing to line up with the United States in a confrontational stance against China. However, these governments had long been disinclined to join in a possible U.S.-led coercive approach to China out of fear of provoking a sharp and aggressive Chinese response. As a result, the rise of China in Asia may not have too much overall effect on U.S. policy interests in this regard. Given that Asian governments have long been loathe to choose between the United States and China, U.S. policy would appear better served by a more active effort to build U.S. power and influence in the region from the existing position of U.S. regional leadership.

There is an alternative U.S. approach to China that does not require as much emphasis on carefully managing U.S.-China relations from an overall position of strength. The United States over time may move away from its long-standing and recently stressed insistence on maintaining the dominant strategic position in Asian and world affairs. This could set the stage for a different kind of Sino-American accommodation where the United States pulls back strategically from Asia as China rises to regional leadership.

Notes

1. Joseph Kahn, "Hands Across the Pacific," *New York Times*, 11 November 2002 (Internet version); Elaine Kurtenbach, "China Emerges as a Possible U.S. Partner," *AP*, 21 October 2003 (Internet version); Ye Zicheng, "Adopting a Diplomatic Strategy that Adapts to Change in the Environment," *Xiandai Guoji Guanxi* no. 11 (20 November 2002): 24-25; Yoichi Funabashi, "China's 'Peaceful Ascendancy,'" *Yaleglobal*, www.yaleglobal.yale.edu (accessed 19 December 2003); Nailene Chou Wiest, "Beijing Presents a New Face in an Innovative Year for Diplomacy," *South China Morning Post*, 2 January 2004, 1.

2. John Pomfret, "In Its Own Neighborhood, China Emerges as a Leader," *Washington Post*, 18 October 2001; Jane Perlez, "China Races to Replace U.S. as Economic Power in Asia," *New York Times*, 28 June 2002; U.S.-China Security Review Commission, *Report to Congress*, www.uscc.gov/anrp02.htm (July 2002); Eric Eckholm and Joseph Kahn, "Asia Worries About Growth of China's Economic Power," *New York Times*, 24 November 2002; Thomas Woodrow, "The New Great Game," Jamestown Foundation *China Brief* III, no. 3, (11 February 2003); Lu Baosheng, "World Multipolar Trend Develops in Meanders," *Jiefangjunbao*, 1 September 2003, 11; Fang Ning, Wang Xiaodong, and Qiao Liang, *Quanqiuhua yinyang xia de Zhongguo zhi lu* (Beijing: Chinese Academy of Social Sciences Press, 1999), 47.

3. Kerry Dumbaugh, *China-U.S. Relations*, Washington, D.C.: Library of Congress, Congressional Research Service, Issue Brief 98018, 16 September 2002. Kerry Dumbaugh, *China-U.S. Relations: Current Issues for the 108th Congress*, Washington, D.C.:Library of Congress, Congressional Research Service, Report RL 31815, 15 September 2003.

4. Consultations with Chinese officials and specialists, November-December 2003. Jiang Zemin and his senior foreign policy adviser Qian Qichen devoted extraordinary efforts in order to maintain an appropriate policy toward the United States. Jiang actively sought summit opportunities with U.S. President George W. Bush, capping his tenure as party leader and president with a meeting with the U.S. president at his ranch in Crawford, Texas, in October 2002. Such visits were reserved for those foreign leaders who had worked closely with the United States on important foreign policy issues. Recently installed President Hu Jintao and Premier Wen Jiabao also devoted close attention and care in dealing with U.S. policy, endeavoring to cooperate closely with the United States and expressing appreciation for U.S. policies in line with Chinese interests regarding Taiwan, U.S.-China trade, and other key issues. Bonnie Glaser, "Sustaining Cooperation: Security Matters Take Center Stage," *Comparative Connections*, www.csis.org/pacfor (accessed June 15 2003); Bonnie Glaser, "Wen Jiabao's Visit Caps an Outstanding Year," *Comparative Connections*, January 2004; Denny Roy, "China's Reaction to American Predominance," *Survival* 45, no. 3 (Autumn 2003). See also Tao Wenzhao , "Changes and Drivers in Sino-U.S. Relations," replayed in *China Strategy* vol. 3, www.csis.org (accessed 20 July 2004).

5. Zhang Yunling and Tang Shiping, "More Self-confident China Will Be a Responsible Power," *Straits Times*, 2 October 2002, www.Taiwansecurity.org (accessed 4 October 2002); Zheng Bijian, "Strategic Opportunities: This is the Fourth Opportunity in Modern History," Hong Kong *Wen Wei Po* (Internet version), (accessed 13 March 2003); Shi Yinhong, "Old Grudges of History and the Principle of Strategic Concentration," Hong Kong *Ta Kung Pao* (Internet version), (accessed 9 June 2003); Pang Zhongying, "Developing an Asian Partnership," *Xinhuanet*, 4 November 2003; Alan Tonelson, *A Necessary Evil? Current Chinese Views of America's Military Role in East Asia* (Washington, D.C.: Henry Stimson Center, May 2003); Denny Roy, "Rising China and U.S. Interests: Inevitable vs. Contingent Haz-

ards," *Orbis*, 47:1 (2003): 124-43; Wu Xinbo, "Future U.S. Military Presence in Asia" (paper presented at a conference in Washington, D.C., October 2003); Shi Yinhong, "The 15 Years of Chinese Diplomacy and Strategy Toward the United States" (paper presented at a conference in Vail, Colorado, November 2003); Yang Yi, "Improving U.S.-China Relations in the New Global Context" (paper presented at a conference in Vail, Colorado, November 2003). Jia Qingguo, "Comments on Bush's National Security Strategy" (paper presented at a conference in Vail, Colorado, November 2003).

6. Steven Levine, "China in Asia," in Harry Harding, ed., *China's Foreign Relations in the 1980s* (New Haven, Conn.: Yale University Press, 1984), 109-14.

7. Levine, "China in Asia," *China's Foreign Relations* , 107.

8. Denny Roy, *China's Foreign Relations* (Lanham, Md.: Rowman & Littlefield, 1999), 158.

9. Andrew Nathan and Robert Ross, *The Great Wall and the Empty Fortress* (New York: Norton, 1998), 121-22.

10. Michael Yahuda, "China's Win-Win Globalization," *Yaleglobal*, www.yaleglobal.yale.edu (accessed 19 February 2003).

11. David Finkelstein, *China's New Security Concept* (Alexandria, Va.: The CNA Corporation, April 1999).

12. David M. Lampton, "The Stealth Normalization of U.S.-China Relations," *The National Interest* 73 (Fall 2003); Michael Swaine, *Reverse Course? The Fragile Turnabout in U.S.-China Relations*, Policy Brief 22, Carnegie Endowment for International Peace, February 2003; Thomas Christensen, "China," in Richard Ellings and Aaron Friedberg, eds., *Strategic Asia 2003-2004* (Seattle, Wash.: National Bureau of Asian Research, 2003), 53-80; Robert Sutter, "U.S.-China Relations After the 16th Party Congress," *Journal of Asian and African Studies* 38, no. 4-5 (December 2003): 447-63.

13. Kahn, "Hands Across the Pacific." "The Rise of China—A Threat or an Opportunity," *People's Daily*, 22 December 2002 (Internet version); Zhang Yunling, "The Process of East Asian Cooperation," Beijing *Qiushi*, 16 December 2002, no. 24 (Internet version); "Beijing to Take an Amiable Approach in U.S.-China Diplomacy this Year, *Wenweipo news*, 28 January 2004; Zheng Bijian, "New Path for China's 'Peaceful Rise,'" Shanghai *Wen Hui Bao*, 21 March 2004 (Internet version); Li Zhaoxing, "Open New Prospects, Build Up a New Image," Beijing *Foreign Affairs Journal* 70 (December 2003): 1-5; Zhou Wenzhong, "Vigorously Pushing Forward the Constructive and Cooperative Relationship between China and the United States," Beijing *Foreign Affairs Journal* 70 (December 2003): 6-13.

14. Speech by Premier Wen Jiabao in New York City, www.fmprc.gov.cn/chn/zxxx/t55972.htm (accessed 9 December 2003); Zheng Bijian, "Globalization and the Emergence of China," opening remarks at a conference hosted by the Center for Strategic and International Studies, Washington, D.C., 13 November 2003. See also Zheng Bijian, "New Path."

15. Evan Medieros and Taylor Fravel, "China's New Diplomacy," *Foreign Affairs*, November/December 2003 (Internet version); Chou Wiest, "Beijing Presents a New Face," 1; Yahuda, "China's Win-Win Globalization;" Liang Xing-guang, "China's New Peace Strategy," *Japan Times*, 17 November 2002 (Internet version).

16. Glaser, "Wen Jiabao's Visit."

17. Wang Jisi, *China's Changing Role in Asia* (Washington, D.C.: The Atlantic Council of the United States, January 2004), 1-5, 16-17; Pan Zhenqiang, "China's National Defense Policy into the 21st Century," Beijing *Foreign Affairs Journal* 70 (December 2003): 35; Wou Songling, Chi Diantang, "Southeast Asia and Central Asia: China's Geostrategic Options in the New Century," Beijing *Dangdai Yatai*, no. 4 (15 April 2003): 9-15; Shi Yinhong,

"Basic Trials and Essential 'Platforms' for China's Peaceful Rise," Hong Kong *Ta Kung Pao* 14 March 2004 (Internet version); Zhang Zhiming, "First Two Decades of the 21st Century," Beijing *Foreign Affairs Journal* 67 (March 2003): 3; in interviews with the author (November-December 2003, May 2004), Chinese officials and specialists repeatedly emphasized the central role played by the United States and U.S. policy in determining China's approach to the Asian region.

18. Suisheng Zhao, *China's Periphery Policy* (Taipei: Cross Strait Interflow Prospect Foundation, 25 September 2001).

19. David M. Lampton, ed., *The Making of Chinese Foreign and Security Policy* (Stanford, Calif.: Stanford University Press, 2001); Tony Saich, *Governance and Politics of China* (New York: Palgrave, 2001); Robert Sutter, *Chinese Policy Priorities and Their Implications for the United States* (Lanham, Md.: Rowman & Littlefield, 2000).

20. Elizabeth Economy and Michel Oksenberg, *China Joins the World* (New York: The Council on Foreign Relations, 1999); Alastair Iain Johnston, "China's International Relations: Political and Security Dimensions," in Samuel Kim, ed., *The International Relations of Northeast Asia* (Lanham, Md.: Rowman & Littlefield, 2004), 65-100; Thomas Moore, "China's International Relations: The Economic Dimension," in Kim, ed., *The International Relations of Northeast Asia*, 101-36.

21. Andrew Nathan, "China and the International Human Rights Regime," in Economy and Oksenberg, eds., *China Joins the World*, 136-60; Bates Gill, "Two Steps Forward, One Step Back: The Dynamics of Chinese Nonproliferation and Arms Control Policy-making in an Era of Reform," in Lampton, *Chinese Foreign and Security Policy*, 257-88.

22. Roy, *China's Foreign Relations*, 143-44, 184-93.

23. For background on this tendency, see Robert Ross and Jiang Changbin, *Re-examining the Cold War* (Cambridge, Mass.: Harvard, 2001), 11-12, 19-21.

24. Wu Xinbo, "Four Contradictions Constraining China's Foreign Policy Behavior," *Journal of Contemporary China* 10, no. 27: 293-302; "China's Peripheral Diplomacy Carries a Heavy Weight," *People's Daily*, www.english.peoplesdaily.com.cn/200312/18/eng200312-18/ 130696.shtml (accessed 20 December 2003); Pang Zhongying, "Asian Partnership"; Mei Zhaorong, "The International Strategic Situation After the Iraq War," Beijing *Foreign Affairs Journal* 70 (December 2003): 50, 52; Fu Ying, "China and Asia in New Period," Beijing *Foreign Affairs Journal* 69 (September 2003): 1-7; Fu Ying, "Strive to Open New Prospects in China's Periphery," Beijing *Foreign Affairs Journal* 70 (December 2003): 19-24. See also Qin Zonghe, "Distinguishing Features of the Asia-Pacific Situation in 2003," (Beijing) *International Strategic Studies* 71:1 (January 2004): 18-24; Wang Jisi, "Impact of U.S. Strategic Adjustment on Sino-U.S. Relations," (Beijing) *Xuexi Shibao* (16 August 2004), Internet version, translated by U.S. Foreign Broadcast Information Service (FBIS).

25. Johnston, "China's International Relations," in Kim, ed., *The International Relations of Northeast Asia*, 75-77; interviews with Chinese officials, 2001-2004. Among the best observers of the ebb and flow of Chinese elite views of U.S. power and prospects for a multipolar world, see the quarterly reviews of U.S.-China relations done by Bonnie Glaser in *Comparative Connections*, Honolulu CSIS, Pacific Forum, www.csis.org/pacfor. On Chinese views of multipolarity, see Zhang Yunling, ed., *Huoban haishi duishou I tiaozheng zhong de Zhong Mei Ri E guanxi* (Beijing: Social Sciences Documents Press, 2000); Zhu Feng, "Zai lishi gui yi zhong bawo Zhong Mei guanxi," *Huanqiu Shibao Guoji Luntan*, www.interforum.xilubbs.com (accessed 28 February 2002); Yong Deng, "Hegemon on the Offensive: Chinese Perceptions on U.S. Global Strategy," *Political Science Quarterly* 116, no. 3 (2001): 343-65; David Finkelstein, "Chinese Perspectives of the Costs of Conflict," in Andrew Scobell, ed., *The Costs of Conflict: The Impact on China of a Future War*

(Carlisle, PA: Strategic Studies Institute, October 2001), 9-27; Denny Roy, *China's Pitch for a Multipolar World*, Honolulu Asia-Pacific Center for Security Studies 2, no. 1 (May 2003); Mei Zhaorong, "The International Strategic Situation," 50, 52; Shi Yinhong, "Basic Trials."

26. Sutter, *Chinese Policy Priorities*, 18.

27. Barry Naughton, "China's Economy: Buffeted From Within and Without," *Current History* (September 1998): 273-278; Joseph Fewsmith, "China in 1998," *Asian Survey* 39, no. 1: 99-113.

28. Dumbaugh, *China-U.S. Relations*; Swaine, "Reverse Course?" *Carnegie Endowment*, February 2003.

29. Reviewed in Sutter, *Chinese Policy Priorities*, 193-96.

30. Robert Marquand, "Central Asian Group to Counterweigh U.S.," *Christian Science Monitor,* 15 June 2001 (Internet version); Ho Khai Leong, "China and ASEAN in the Coming Decades," *Journal of Contemporary China* 10, no. 29 (November 2001): 683-694; Susan Lawrence, "Enough for Everyone," *Far Eastern Economic Review*, 13 June 2002 (Internet version); Wang Jisi, *China's Changing Role in Asia*; Xiao Ren, *Dongya Hezuo Yu Zhongguo* ("East Asia Cooperation and China") at *Zhongguo Guoguan Zaixian*, www.irchina.org/xueren/china/view.asp?id=631, which originally appeared in *Taipingyang xuebao* (Pacific Journal) 2003, no. 3. See also Pang Zhongying, "Developing an Asian Partnership," *China Daily*, 4 November 2003, (Internet version).

31. Mei Zhaorong, "The International Strategic Situation," 50, 52; Shi Yinhong, "Basic Trials"; Li Jianying, "U.S. Stepping Up Efforts for Hegemony by Force," Beijing *Foreign Affairs Journal* 67 (March 2003): 26; Shen Qiang, "Impact of U.S. Strategic Adjustments on International Relations," Beijing *Foreign Affairs Journal* 67 (March 2003): 54; Zhang Zhiming, "First Two Decades of the 21st Century," Beijing *Foreign Affairs Journal* 67 (March 2003): 3; Roy, "China's Reaction"; Adam Ward, "America and China: Trouble Ahead?" *Survival* 45, no. 3 (Autumn 2003): 35-56; Satu Limaye, "Weighting for China, Counting on the US: Asia's China Debate and U.S. Interests," in *Asia's China Debate* (Honolulu: Asia Pacific Center for Security Studies, December 2003), chapter 16; G. John Ikenberry, *Strategic Reactions to American Preeminence*, U.S. National Intelligence Council Conference Report, www.odci.gov/nic/confreports_stratreact.html (accessed 28 July 2003). The author conducted in-depth interviews and consultations with twenty Chinese foreign policy planners and specialists in November-December 2003, and with fifty such specialists in May 2004. See also Wang Jisi, "Impact of U.S. Strategic Adjustment on Sino-U.S. Relations"; "Foreign Minister Li Zhaoxing's Press Conference," *People's Daily*, 7 March 2004, (Internet version).

32. Yoichi Funabashi, "China's 'Peaceful Ascendancy'"; Willy Wo-Lap Lam, "China Aiming for 'Peaceful Rise,'" at www.cnn.com (accessed 3 February 2004); speech by Premier Wen Jiabao in New York City, www.fmprc.gov.cn/chn/zxxx/t55972.htm (accessed 9 December 2003); Zheng Bijian, "New Path"; Zheng Bijian, "Globalization"; Wu Xinbo, "Future U.S. Military Presence in Asia," paper presented at a conference in Washington, D.C., October 2003; Shi Yinhong, "The 15 years of Chinese Diplomacy and Strategy toward the United States," paper presented at a conference in Vail, Colorado, November 2003; remarks of Foreign Minister Li Zhaoxing at the second session of the 10th National People's Congress, *Renmin Ribao*, www.people.com.cn/GB/paper464/11481/1035897.html (accessed 7 March 2004); Pang Zhongying, "China's rise promotes peace," *China Daily*, www.chinadaily.com.cn/english/doc/2004-04/09/content_321789.htm (accessed 9 April 2004); Shulong Chu, "U.S. and China in the Early 21st Century: Cooperation, Competition

or Confrontation?" www.irchina.org/xueren/china/view.asp?id=628 (accessed 20 May 2004);
Yang Yi, "Improving U.S.-China Relations"; Jia Qingguo, "National Security Strategy";
consultations with Chinese foreign policy specialists in Beijing and Shanghai, May 2004;
"China's 'peaceful rise': A Road Chosen for Rejuvenation of a Great Nation," *People's
Daily*, www.peoplesdaily.com (accessed 28 February 2004).

 33. Robert Sutter, "China's Recent Approach to Asia: Seeking Long-term Gains," *NBR
Analysis* 13, no. 1 (March 2002): 20-21; Zonghe Qin, "Distinguishing Features of the Asia-
Pacific Situation in 2003," *Guoji Zhanlüe yanjiu* (International Strategic Studies, English
Version), 71, no. 1 (January 2004): 18-24; Fu Ying, "China and Asia," *Foreign Affairs
Journal*, 1-7; Fu Ying, "China's periphery," *Foreign Affairs Journal*: 19-24; Johnston,
"China's International Relations," *The International Relations of Northeast Asia*, 65-100.
Asia Pacific Center for Security Studies, *Asia's China Debate*, December 2003,
www.apcss.org (accessed 30 December 2003); Alastair Iain Johnston and Robert Ross, eds.,
Engaging China (London: Routledge, 1999); Kenneth Allen, "China's Foreign Military
Relations with Asia-Pacific," *Journal of Contemporary China* 10, no. 29 (November 2001):
645-62; Herbert Yee and Ian Storey, *The China Threat: Perceptions, Myths, and Realities*
(London: Routledge, 2002).

 34. Michael McDevitt, "The China Factor in U.S. Defense Planning," in Jonathan
Pollack, ed., *Strategic Surprise?* (Newport, R.I.: U.S. Naval War College, 2003), 149-58;
Bruce Klingner, 'Peaceful Rising' Seeks to Allay 'China threat,'" *Asia Times Online*, 12
March 2004; Richard Sokolsky, Angel Rabasa, C. R. Neu, *The Role of Southeast Asia in U.S.
Policy Toward China* (Santa Monica, Calif.: Rand Corporation, 2000); Pomfert, "China
Emerges"; Perlez, "China races"; Pang Zhongying, "Asian Partnership"; U.S.-China Security
Review Commission, *Report to Congress*; Eckholm and Kahn, "Asia Worries"; Woodrow,
"The New Great Game."

 35. For variations on this perspective, see Yahuda, "China's Win-Win Globalization";
Kahn, "Hands Across the Pacific"; Medeiros and Taylor Fravel, "China's New Diplomacy";
Kurtenbach, "China Emerges"; Fu Ying, "China and Asia," *Foreign Affairs Journal* (Septem-
ber 2003): 1-7; Zheng Bijian, "Globalization"; Zheng Bijian, "New Path."

 36. Yong Deng, "Hegemon on the Offensive"; Zhang Zhiming, "First Two Decades of
the 21st Century," *Foreign Affairs Journal* 67 (March 2003): 3; Roy, "Rising China"; Robert
Sutter, "China Remains Wary of U.S.-led World Order," *Yaleglobal*,
www.yaleglobal.yale.edu (accessed 8 June 2003). Author's consultations with twenty Chinese
foreign policy planners and specialists, November-December 2003, and fifty such individuals
in May 2004.

 37. Lampton, *Chinese Foreign and Security Policy*, 1-36.

 38. John W. Garver, *Foreign Relations of the People's Republic of China* (Englewood
Cliffs, N.J.: Prentice Hall, 1993), 70-110; Michael Yahuda, *Towards the End of Isolation*
(New York: St. Martin's, 1983); Robert Sutter, *Chinese Foreign Policy: Developments After
Mao* (New York: Praeger, 1986), 10-13.

 39. Saich, *Politics of China*, 274; Yong Deng, "Hegemon on the Offensive," 359; Chou
Wiest, "Low Profile on Foreign Affairs Set to Continue," *South China Morning Post*, 24
December 2003. Consultations with Chinese government and nongovernment foreign policy
specialists, Beijing and Shanghai, May 2004.

 40. Dumbaugh, *China-U.S. Relations*; Sutter, *Chinese Policy Priorities*, 46-58; Zhang
Zhiming, "First Two Decades of the 21st Ccentury," *Foreign Affairs Journal*: 67, 3.

 41. Joseph Fewsmith, *China Since Tiananmen* (Cambridge: Cambridge University Press,
2001), 132-58; Rosalie Chen, "China Perceives America," *Journal of Contemporary China*,
12, no. 35 (May 2003): 239-64; Suisheng Zhao, "A State-led Nationalism: The Patriotic

Education Campaign in Post-Tiananmen China," *Communist and Post Communist Studies* 31, no. 3 (1998): 289; Suisheng Zhao, "Chinese Nationalism and Its International Orientations," *Political Science Quarterly*, 115, no. 1 (spring 2000): 5.

42. Swaine, "Reverse Course?" Robert Sutter, "Bush Policy Toward Beijing and Taipei," *Journal of Contemporary China* 12, no. 36 (August 2003): 477-92.

43. *People's Daily*, 27 May 1999, 22 June 1999.

44. For variations on this perspective, see Yahuda, "China's Win-Win Globalization"; Kahn, "Hands Across the Pacific"; Medeiros and Taylor Fravel, "China's New Diplomacy"; Kenneth Lieberthal, "A New Face on China's Foreign Policy," *Business Week*, www.businessweek.com/magazine/content/03 31163844142.htm (accessed 4 August 2003).

45. Jianfei Liu, "*Danbianzhuyi dui Meiguo tongyang weixian*" ("Unilateralism Is Equally Dangerous to the United States"), www.irchina.org/xueren/china/view.asp?id=559 (accessed 30 June 2003). Li Jianying, "Hegemony by Force," 26; Wang Yusheng, "Latest Manifestation of Terrorism and Hegemonism," Beijing *Foreign Affairs Journal*, 67 (March 2003): 35-40; Shi Yinhong, "The 15 Years of Chinese Diplomacy"; Yang Yi, "Improving U.S.-China Relations "; Jia Qingguo, "National Security Strategy"; Wang Jisi, *China's Changing Role in Asia*. See also Wang Jisi, "Impact of U.S. Strategic Adjustment on Sino-U.S. Relations."

46. For a comprehensive assessment of recent China-U.S. relations, see Christensen, "China," *Strategic Asia*, 53-80; Sutter, "U.S.-China Relations," 447-63.

47. Consultations with Bush administration Asian affairs policy makers, Washington, D.C., March 2001.

48. Consultations with Chinese foreign policy officials and specialists, 2001-2004; Li Zhongjie, "Background Report on the 16th CCP Congress: How to Deal with the Current International Strategic Situation," Beijing *Liaowang*, 3 June 2002, 3-9. Li Shaojun, "Where Do Opportunities Lie?—Viewing Future Great Power Relations," Beijing *Shijie Zhishi*, 1 January 2003, 8-10; Gu Dexin, "The U.S.-Iraq War and China's National Security," Beijing *Xiandai Guoji Guanxi*, no. 4 (20 April 2003): 20-22; Shi Yinhong, "Old Grudges of History."

49. David Shambaugh, "China and the Korean Peninsula, *Washington Quarterly* (spring 2003), 43-56; Sutter, "China Remains Wary."

50. Robert Sutter, "China's Rise in Asia," *PACNET 11A*, www.csis.org/pacfor (accessed 7 March 2003).

51. Robert Jervis, *Perception and Misperception in International Politics* (Princeton, N.J.: Princeton University Press, 1976), 217; Dan Reiter, "Learning, Realism and Alliances," *World Politics* 46, no. 2 (July 1994): 493.

52. Ross and Jiang, *Re-examining the Cold War*, 19-21.

53. Andrew Nathan and Bruce Gilley, *China's New Rulers: The Secret Files* (New York: New York Review Book, 2002), 207-9.

54. Qian Qichen, "The Post-September 11 International Situation and Sino-U.S. Relations," *Xuexi Shibao* (Study Times) (Beijing: Central Party School, October 2002), 6. I am indebted to Professor Chong-Pin Lin for calling my attention to and providing the translation of these excerpts.

55. Qian Qichen, "Sino-U.S. Relations," 4.

56. Qian Qichen, "Sino-U.S. Relations," 8.

57. Consultations, Beijing and Shanghai, May 2004.

Chapter 1

Salient Determinants of China's Recent Approach to Asia and its Implications for the United States

This and the following chapter provide some relevant background for the subsequent chapters that deal with China's recent policies and behavior toward its Asian neighbors and the United States. Chapter 2 reviews issues and attitudes that sustain competitive and antagonistic features in the Chinese leadership approach toward the United States in Asia and balance to some degree the publicly prominent manifestations of U.S.-China cooperation seen in recent years.[1] Positive perspectives on China's policy in Asia, China's "peaceful rise," and its constructive implications for relations with the United States are duly considered throughout this book, notably in the introduction, chapter 3, and the conclusion. The emphasis in chapter 2 on competitive and antagonistic aspects of China-U.S. relations is designed to support the argument that these elements remain important in determining Chinese behavior in Asia and toward the United States in Asia in particular. In effect, it is argued that China's approach to the United States in Asia and elsewhere remains a mix of cooperative, competitive, and antagonistic tendencies.

Chapter 2 also highlights Chinese maneuvers against the USSR and the United States in Asia in the post-Mao period. Throughout the Cold War, China faced serious threats to its national security posed by the United States and the Soviet Union, their forces along China's frontiers, and their alignments with China's neighbors. This national security threat declined with the end of the Cold War and the collapse of the Soviet Union. Nonetheless, it was followed by strong Chinese leadership concern to preserve Communist rule and China's territorial integrity, and to promote the development of China's regional power, against perceived enhanced U.S.-led efforts to contain China's rise and undermine Communist rule there in the years following the Tiananmen incident and the collapse of the USSR. Chinese leaders' concerns with U.S. containment and pressure remained high throughout the 1990s. They arguably declined as the September 11, 2001, terrorist attack on America and U.S.-led wars in Afghanistan and Iraq diverted U.S. strategic attention away from China. However, U.S. policies in Taiwan and North Korea headed the list of Chinese leadership concerns regarding U.S. power and influence along China's periphery being used in ways possibly contrary to Chinese interests. Overall, the record shows strong Chinese concern still relevant today—to free China's periphery as much as possible from potentially hostile and debilitating presence of great powers. It is argued that this objective remains important in determining China's contemporary approach to Asia and its implications for the United States.

Chapter 3 assesses recent determinants of Chinese leaders' policy priorities in domestic and foreign affairs, in order to clarify the relative importance of Chinese initiatives and policies in Asia for the current Chinese leaders.

China-U.S. Differences

While acknowledging important cooperation and moderation in recent U.S.-China relations, it is still relatively easy to see major weakness in the assessments of those who argue that China's recent cooperative relations with the United States and others in Asia will continue unabated. In particular, such optimistic arguments were made at various times during the post-Cold War period when U.S.-China relations seemed to be improving, only to see relations deteriorate into confrontation and acrimony as a result of a crisis or persisting differences.[2]

Indeed, the record of U.S.-China relations since 1989 seems to favor a less rosy perspective. The less optimistic perspective takes account of the many deeply rooted differences that Chinese and U.S. leaders continue to grapple with. As noted earlier, there is no guarantee that the conditions that came to hold those differences in check and gave rise to the positive path of U.S.-China relations in 2001-2004 would continue, or that third parties outside U.S. and PRC control (e.g. North Korea, Taiwan) might not intervene in ways that disrupt U.S.-China relations. Thus, it has appeared advisable to be cautious in predicting any long-term or fundamental change in China-U.S. relations and related Chinese policies in Asia.[3]

The most important differences in China-U.S. relations have included:

Taiwan. For a time, cross-strait economic exchanges and the weaknesses of the administration of Taiwan President Chen Shui-bian, who is viewed with deep suspicion by Chinese leaders, were sources of optimism for Beijing. But separatist political sentiment continued to grow in Taiwan and the PLA military buildup opposite Taiwan also continued. U.S. strategists saw this as a threat to the United States as well as Taiwan and responded by strengthening Taiwan and U.S. forces in the region. The Bush administration in late 2003 began a parallel effort to constrain actions by Taiwan leaders that would seriously disrupt cross-strait relations and run the risk of conflict there.[4]

Asia. China's leaders had long viewed China's rise in power and influence as over time displacing U.S. military power around China's periphery, but at the start of the twenty-first century U.S. superpower influence and military deployments grew around China's periphery to the point where the United States appeared more powerful in Asian affairs than at any time since before the Vietnam war.[5]

CCP Legitimacy. Though the Bush administration appeared to accept the legitimacy of CCP rule in China, strong forces in the U.S. government, Congress, media, and various nongovernment interest groups continued to work to change China's political system—a goal in direct opposition to the core interest of China's leaders.[6]

U.S. World Leadership. Though more reluctant to confront U.S. world leadership, particularly when Russia and other world powers were joining more closely with the United States, China remained opposed to U.S. "hegemonism" and sought to use international organizations and multilateral groups to constrain U.S. power, leading over time to a diminution of U.S. power and a multipolar world.[7]

Regarding important bilateral U.S.-China differences, they could be viewed as clusters of issues in security, political, and economic categories. Apart from Taiwan, bilateral *security disputes* involved U.S. complaints over China's proliferation of weapons of mass destruction (WMD) and China's large defense budget increases, China's complaints and concerns over U.S. military actions and pressure including the negative implications for China of U.S. missile defense programs, expanded U.S.-Japan security cooperation, NATO expansion, and stepped-up U.S. military deployment throughout China's periphery.[8]

A key security flashpoint in 2004 was North Korea. China worked with the United States to seek to curb North Korea's nuclear weapons program. At the same time, Beijing was reluctant to follow the U.S. lead and apply significant pressure on North Korea. Many specialists argued that China would work against any U.S. effort to use force or serious economic pressure against North Korea because China had a much stronger interest than the United States in preserving North Korea as a viable state and avoiding the disruption that greater pressure on Pyongyang would cause. China also sought to diminish international attention to China's role in assisting North Korea's nuclear enrichment and other WMD development efforts. There were continued U.S. charges that China contributed to WMD production in North Korea, and indirectly helped to supply nuclear enrichment technology to North Korea via Pakistan.[9]

The interface of U.S. and Chinese military forces along China's periphery was not without significant incident, even as the two powers endeavored to resume more normal ties after the April 1, 2001, crash between a Chinese jet fighter and the U.S. surveillance plane, the EP-3. An unarmed U.S. Navy surveillance ship was harassed and rammed by Chinese boats in waters off the Chinese coast in 2002. U.S. surveillance aircraft along China's periphery routinely encountered Chinese fighters, sometimes at close quarters. U.S. government support for the Dalai Lama and continued criticism of Chinese policies in Tibet were seen by Beijing as challenging China's territorial integrity. When combined with U.S. support for Taiwan and criticism of Chinese repression of dissent in Xinjiang, U.S. actions regarding Tibet appeared to some in China as part of a broader longer term U.S. effort to break up China.[10]

Political concerns focused on powerful forces in the United States and China that inclined toward harder line policies that would exacerbate differences in U.S.-China relations. The wide range of U.S. interest groups that favored a tougher U.S. stance to China was well demonstrated during congressional and media debates over U.S. China policy in the 1990s. The U.S. preoccupation with the war on terrorism and major crises dealing with Iraq and North Korea curbed the attention these groups gained after 2001, but the groups remained active and ready to pursue their agendas under more advantageous circumstances. In China, prevailing nationalistic emphasis of Chinese education and media coverage taught that China had been victimized by outside powers seeking selfish domination and "hegemony" over the past two centuries. The United States was portrayed as one these powers. As the dominant world power in the recent period, the United States became a focal point of this long-standing Chinese resentment and opposition.[11]

Economic issues centered on the friction arising from asymmetrical growth in U.S.-China trade and commercial relations. U.S. businesses worked hard to invest in and benefit from China's position as a manufacturing base for U.S. and world markets,
and hopefully for the Chinese market. They sometimes were frustrated with conditions in China or lack of Chinese openness to their products. A greater U.S. concern was registered by U.S. labor and other groups who saw the burgeoning U.S. trade deficit with China—the largest U.S. trade deficit with any country—as a threat to U.S. jobs and economic well being. China for its part resented strong U.S. pressures for greater market opening, Chinese currency revaluation, and other measures that could lead to more serious unemployment and economic dislocation, undermining social and political stability in China. Chinese officials chafed at U.S. restrictions on high technology transfers to China, while U.S. officials warned that such transfers increased China's ability to pose a national security threat to the United States and its interests.[12]

Chinese Elite and Popular Views of the United States in Asia

Chinese elite and popular opinion is conditioned by many years of government controlled education and media instruction that reinforce a strong sense of nationalism emphasizing unfair treatment of China by foreign powers including the United States. The conditioning often stresses the need to speed China's drive for comprehensive national power to ensure China's rightful interests in the face of U.S. and other foreign pressures. At times of cooperative China-U.S. relations, Chinese government authorities play down the anti-U.S. stance, but it emerges often with surprising vehemence at times of Sino-U.S. friction. Thus, Beijing followed its relatively benign public treatment of U.S. issues during the important summit meetings with President Clinton in 1997 and 1998 with scathing attacks in the weeks following the U.S. bombing of the Chinese embassy in Yugoslavia in 1999 denouncing the U.S. president and U.S. policy allegedly designed to "hold back" China's rise. Authoritative Chinese media at that time equated President Clinton and his government to that of Adolph Hitler and the Nazi regime. It called for a national crusade to oppose U.S. "hegemonism" and alleged U.S. efforts to contain China in Asian and world affairs.[13]

U.S. and other specialists who have taken a thorough look at Chinese elite and popular attitudes toward the United States policy and behavior in Asia tend to come up with assessments underlining Chinese opposition and a desire to work against and protect China from many perceived negative aspects of U.S. policy and behavior toward China and its periphery. A 1991 assessment by David Shambaugh concluded that many of China's specialists dealing with U.S. affairs had a strong prejudice toward viewing the U.S. as a hegemonic power driven by the desire for world dominance.[14] A 2000 assessment by Phillip Saunders following the Shambaugh study argued that the end of the Cold War exposed underlying weaknesses in Chinese understanding of the United States. Though overall knowledge of the United States had improved over the decade, many Chinese analysts had a tendency to interpret China's ongoing disputes with the United States as evidence of an American strategy to "contain" China. China's American affairs specialists were said often to disagree with the conclusion that the United States sought to contain China, though they tended to be reluctant to challenge the view publicly. The prevailing consensus among elite opinion was that U.S. policy had elements of containment and elements of engagement, and China was able to influence the mix.[15]

Later assessments by U.S. and other China specialists have reinforced the judgment that Chinese officials and the experts who advise them continue to view U.S. external policy and behavior with a great deal of suspicion. As a result, these Chinese elites tend not to trust U.S. motives given their perception of American hegemony. Although they see China benefiting greatly from and heavily dependent on economic and other ties with the United States, they continue to fear American manipulation of China in international strategic terms, exploitation in economic terms, and subversion in political and ideological terms.[16]

In the Chinese view, the U.S. approach to China and China's periphery in Asia is defined and follows U.S. global strategy. After the Cold War, Chinese assessments shifted from a prevailing view of likely imminent U.S. hegemonic decline to a view that U.S.-dominated unipolarity would likely continue well into the twenty-first century. Tending to see a consistent and often malign U.S. strategy of global domination, Chinese expert assessments and official commentary assumed a predatory U.S. hegemony in Asia. In the first half of the 1990s, views that suggested that U.S. domination would be a short duration were widespread in China. It had become clearer by the mid-1990s, however, that the world was not moving as quickly toward multipolarity as Chinese specialists had earlier supposed. Chinese analysts then tended to characterize the world power alignment as "one superpower, many great powers." By 1996, one observer remarked, "the superpower is more super, and the many great powers are less great."[17]

The U.S. decision to ignore Chinese warnings and allow Taiwan's president to visit the United States in mid-1995 not only resulted in a major military crisis in the Taiwan Strait but also reinforced a strongly negative view of U.S. policy intentions on the part of Chinese officials, intellectuals, and other opinion leaders.[18] The view articulated in public pronouncements and private discussions by Chinese government officials, military officers, think tank experts, media representatives, and other opinion leaders held that U.S. government officials were basically opposed to the rising power of China under Beijing's communist system and were taking a variety of measures in various policy areas, including Taiwan and other areas around China, in order to "hold back" China's power. Events at the time cited by Chinese officials and other opinion leaders to support their view ranged from U.S. statements on the security environment in East Asia and on the situation in the South China Sea that were seen as directed at China, to pressure being brought by the United States against China's trade policies, human rights practices, and proliferation of weapons of mass destruction.

In general, Chinese officials and opinion leaders maintained that despite lively debate in the United States over many issues in policy toward China, U.S. policy makers had reached a consensus that China's growing power posed a threat to the United States that needed to be countered by weakening China's strength through security, economic, political, and other measures. Presumably because senior PRC leaders were as yet unwilling to confront the U.S. leadership directly on this issue, the top Chinese officials tended to refrain from directly accusing the United States of this conspiratorial intent. Nevertheless, Chinese officials and intellectuals repeatedly affirmed in private conversations with U.S. observers that senior Chinese leaders did indeed harbor such sinister views of U.S. intentions.

Many Chinese officials and intellectuals traced the alleged U.S. desire to weaken and hold down China to the reevaluation of U.S. policy toward China following the 1989 Tiananmen massacre and the concurrent collapse of the Soviet empire and the end of the Cold War. At that time, they claimed that U.S. leaders took a number of measures in the form of economic, military, and political sanctions against China that were designed to help to bring down Beijing's communist system.

U.S. leaders at this time were not seen as fearful of China's power under Beijing's communist rule; rather, they expected the Chinese regime in a few years time would be swept away by the same forces of history that had just removed their ideological comrades in Europe and elsewhere.

This did not happen as anticipated and the PRC began to grow at a remarkable rate of economic development beginning in 1992 and continued into the next decade. Chinese economic development was accompanied by greater military power, successful expansion of China's foreign relations, and greater self-confidence and assertiveness by Chinese leaders both at home and in Asian and world affairs. In response, the Chinese claimed that the United States began to step up its efforts in a wide range of areas to curb the growth of China's power. Alleged evidence of such U.S. efforts included:

- Stronger U.S. support for Taiwan, Tibet, and Hong Kong as entities separate of PRC control. U.S. support for the Taiwan president's visit and provisions showing support for Taiwan, Hong Kong, and Tibet in U.S. foreign policy legislation were viewed as designed to keep the PRC preoccupied with tasks of protecting China's sovereignty and territorial integrity and less able to exert influence elsewhere.
- Pressure on Chinese trade and other economic practices. The mid-1990s saw strong U.S. efforts to press Beijing to observe intellectual property rights, to open its markets to outside goods and services, and to meet strict conditions before gaining entry into the WTO. Chinese leaders apparently saw these steps as being designed to help to keep the PRC economically weaker and less influential than it otherwise would be.
- Restrictions against military-related and other high technology to China and pressure on China to restrict its sales of technology and equipment that could be used for weapons of mass destruction. For example, the United States maintained technology restrictions against China and warned others (e.g., Israel) about the dangers of military or military technology sales to China—steps interpreted by Beijing as designed to keep China from becoming militarily stronger.
- Warnings against Chinese assertiveness in Asia. The Clinton administration's February 1995 statement about the security environment in East Asia was seen in Beijing as implicitly critical of China's assertiveness and lack of transparency in flexing its military power in the region. At the same time, the U.S. administration articulated a security approach to the region that gave renewed emphasis to Japan as the center of U.S. attention in the face of regional uncertainties—a stance also viewed with some suspicion in China. In May, 1995, the administration came out with a stronger position about U.S. interests in the South China Sea—a statement coming after China had caused serious concerns in the region by taking unilateral military action in South China Sea islands claimed by others. Meanwhile, Congress at that time was considering legislation that took aim at China's assertive actions in the South China Sea. Some in Congress

added that the United States should move ahead with full diplomatic relations with Vietnam as a way to counter PRC expansion.

The views on the enduring and predatory nature of U.S. hegemony were reinforced after the U.S.-led NATO military intervention in Yugoslavia and particularly by the bombing of the Chinese embassy in Belgrade by a U.S. aircraft during the 1999 war. They coincided with a growing acknowledgment by Chinese experts that U.S. unipolarity would endure for some time. There was much less confidence that multipolarity would emerge any time soon. Chinese official statements still insisted that the process toward multipolarity continued, but they described an increasingly drawn-out process.[19]

Though China was reluctant to confront or challenge the United States, the logic of Chinese views of U.S. power held decidedly negative implications for China and the world order. Concentrated power without counterbalancing was seen as dangerous as unchecked unipolar hegemony was viewed as prone to abusive use of power. China emphasized its new security concept, based on the five principles of peaceful coexistence, as the appropriate norms for international relations in the post-Cold War environment that opposed the "power politics" and "Cold War thinking" allegedly prevalent in U.S. policy and behavior.

Chinese analysts maintained that to pursue supremacy, the United States acted unilaterally and disregarded the Anti-Ballistic Missile (ABM) Treaty in developing missile defense systems targeted against North Korea but also seen as designed to counter Chinese ballistic missiles. In their view, the revitalized U.S. security alliance with Japan as well as U.S. forward deployed forces in the Western Pacific partly targeted China's rising power. Chinese commentators accused the United States of attempting to dominate and control international organizations and regimes in order to legitimate U.S. aggressive acts against other countries; when such control efforts met resistance, the United States was seen to disregard international bodies and norms in seeking ad hoc coalitions to pursue coercion and the use of military force in accord with narrow U.S. interests.[20]

At the start of the twenty-first century, the list of Chinese charges and grievances against U.S. hegemonism was long and involved many issues of direct concern to China and nearby Asia. They included the large and growing U.S. defense budget; a strong tendency to use coercive measures in U.S. foreign policy; allegedly wanton disregard of international institutions and rules when deemed inconvenient; an aggressive liberal agenda in promoting Western values; unilateral decisions to build missile defenses; endeavoring to restrict high-technology information to China and others; arrogant violations of other countries' sovereignty; unjustified expansion of U.S. alliances in Europe and Asia; and determination to contain emerging powers, notably China.[21]

To American policy makers and others interested in better U.S. relations with China, the clear tendency of Chinese leaders to exaggerate the negatives in the U.S. approach to China and to highlight the threat the United States posed to the core interests of the Chinese Communist Party leadership were a major obstacle to improved relations. Remedying this tendency was difficult. Part of the problem was the deeply rooted inclination of leaders in China (and the United States) to exaggerate the power and influence—usually seen as negative—posed by the other side.[22]

Chinese strategists throughout the Cold War tended to focus on how the United States and/or the Soviet Union could use "power politics" and outright coercion to force China to compromise over key interests. The exaggerated Chinese claims of the United States seeking to split up, hold back, and contain China in the 1990s echoed the Chinese leadership approach to its prime strategic enemies during the Cold War. Adding to the tendency was the long-standing Chinese leadership practice of analyzing world politics in terms of "contradictions" derived from Marxism-Leninism and developed by Mao Zedong. The Chinese international strategy and worldview thus had a clear emphasis on focusing on the "main enemy" or danger to China and its interests. U.S. imperialism played this role in the 1950s and 1960s; the USSR was the main enemy in the 1970s and much of the 1980s. Despite China's strong need to promote advantageous economic and other relations with the United States, Chinese elite thinking and behavior in the 1990s showed that the United States also became the main target of Chinese international concern—that is, China's main "enemy."

In order to mobilize domestic and international forces to deal with the main danger, Chinese leaders tended to portray the adversary in starkly negative terms. Often associated with this kind of international outlook was a policy of united front that involved Chinese efforts to win over other powers to assist in the focused Chinese efforts to counter the danger posed by the main adversary. China's post-Cold War approach to the United States in Asian and world affairs clearly reflected this long-standing tendency to exaggerate the strategic threat to China, posed in this period by the United States, and to foster a united front against it. Of course, China's dealing with the United States in the 1990s was not as clear cut as its dealing with the Americans and the Soviets in the Cold War. The United States was not seen only as an adversary; it also was a competitor and a partner whose cooperation was essential to Chinese modernization. Thus, Chinese leaders endeavored to sustain a balanced approach to the United States that preserved a working relationship—especially economic relations—with the United States, while continuing to view U.S. power as threatening many core Chinese interests.[23]

It is also worth noting that Chinese leaders were not alone in continuing Cold War practices in exaggerating perceived threats. U.S. elite attitudes toward China swung wildly in the post-Cold War period. At first, it was widely assumed by many in the United States that the Chinese communist regime would collapse like the communist regimes in Europe. When Chinese leaders seemed to restore their power based on remarkable economic growth and attendant military modernization, a clear tendency among many U.S. officials and opinion leaders was to exaggerate the possible negative implications for U.S. interests pose by "rising" China.[24]

Popular Chinese attitudes toward the United States over the past decade showed the influence of a resurgence of Chinese nationalism that reinforced the negative implications for China's approach to the United States in Asia and elsewhere posed by Chinese elite views of U.S. hegemony. The trauma of Tiananmen followed by the collapse of communist systems in Eastern Europe, the USSR, and elsewhere led for a time to resurgence in "leftist" thinking associated with more traditional ideological Marxist thinkers. Subsequent tensions in U.S.-China relations were seen to have enhanced this line of thinking that not only viewed U.S. global and regional policies with great suspicion but also had serious reservations about China's accommodation to U.S.-backed economic norms and growing economic interdependence and globalization. Concurrent with this trend was broad disillusionment with the West, especially the United States and Japan, reflected in public opinion surveys and popular media.[25]

Populist and nativist attitudes also rose in the overall nationalistic atmosphere of the 1990s as the Chinese Communist regime fostered popular enthusiasm for nationalism in a bid to shore up leadership and party stature, at a time of obvious weakness in communist ideology, as a bulwark of regime power and control. While there were mixed currents in popular attitudes toward engagement with the United States, the rise of populist and more nativist attitudes posed dilemmas for the regime as it saw a continued need to pursue economic engagement with the United States and others and further opening to international economic interchange. Notably, the Chinese leaders were subjected to broad criticism and popular pressures when they endeavored to keep relations with the United States, Japan, Taiwan, and some others on a sound basis on account of China's economic and other stakes in these ties, as popular sentiment at various times of China-U.S., China-Japan, China-Taiwan, or other friction appeared to favor a much tougher Chinese stance.[26]

The Chinese leaders had a strong ability to manage such difficulties and channel public opinion on these issues into appropriate paths provided the leaders remained unified on the issues at hand and difficulties with the United States, Japan, Taiwan, and others had not led yet to popular mobilization. In studying the interaction of public opinion on Chinese policy toward the United States in Asia and elsewhere, Joseph Fewsmith and Stanley Rosen in 2001 found that in 1995-1996—a period of major crisis with the United States over Taiwan, leading to the first U.S.-China military face-off in the Taiwan Strait in decades, Chinese elite conflict coincided with an increase in Sino-U.S. tensions to generate a wave of popular nationalism that arguably inclined Chinese leaders to more militant actions in the Taiwan Strait crisis. In 1996 to 1998, a reduction of elite conflict and an improvement in China-U.S. relations tended to calm public attitudes and make public opinion less important in driving China's policy. This calm ended with aborted China-U.S. negotiations over China's entry into the WTO and the bombing of the Chinese embassy in Belgrade in 1999 that unleashed a new wave of nationalistic emotion and set off a new round of elite conflict. At this time, popular attitudes clearly drove Chinese policy in a harder direction against the United States in Asian and world affairs.[27] A similar upswing followed the EP-3 episode in April 2001, though subsequent careful managing of China-U.S. disagreements by the leaders of both countries, and broader concerns over the war on terrorism and other issues, damped public outbursts pressing for a harder Chinese line against the United States.[28]

Chinese Opposition to Superpower Dominance in Asia

The record of Chinese policy and behavior in Asia shows repeated maneuvering to keep China's periphery as free as possible from hostile or potentially hostile great power pressure. This trend has persisted along with the growing Chinese economic integration and increasing political and security cooperation with the region. It has underlined continued Chinese efforts to work against U.S. power and influence in Asia in the recent period.

Available scholarship, including an important work on Chinese foreign policy decision making,[29] makes clear that Chinese decision making regarding issues like future Chinese policy in Asia is only partly constrained by economic or other interdependence. PRC leaders could decide at some point to put aside their current moderation and pragmatism for a more assertive and disruptive policy directed against U.S. interests and leadership in Asia. The scholarship shows a growing acceptance by PRC leaders of interdependence in international economic relations, but political and security concerns present a different picture.

In treating China's recent approach toward key security issues in Korea in his chapter in the above mentioned volume, Samuel Kim judged, "The making and implementing of China's Korea policy is best understood as an ongoing process of choosing among competing options rather than any finalized decision, even as Chinese central decision-makers, situated strategically between domestic and international politics, are constrained simultaneously by what the two Koreas will accept and what domestic constituencies will ratify. The making and execution of a foreign policy decision requires that China's decision-makers engage in 'double-edged' calculation of constraints and opportunities in both domestic and international politics in order to achieve international accord and secure domestic ratification."[30]

Moreover, scholarship shows that it is still too early to know if Chinese leaders are genuinely internalizing and embracing global norms and values that would argue for greater stability and moderation in Asian affairs, or if they are merely adapting to global norms to derive tactical benefits, biding their time to exert greater pressure and force to achieve Chinese goals when future circumstances are more advantageous. While Chinese leaders have moved over time to see their interests best served by full engagement with international economic norms, Chinese leaders are seen to follow a case-by-case approach, doing cost-benefit analysis in making key foreign policy decisions. Interdependence with and moderation and accommodation toward the United States in Asia prevail in part because the costs of a more assertive posture more consistent with Chinese nationalistic and prevailing attitudes toward the United States, Japan, Taiwan and others outweigh the benefits.

Meanwhile, consultations with Chinese foreign affairs specialists in 2003-2004 regarding the purpose and scope of China's emphasis on China's determination to "rise peacefully" underline the importance of U.S. cooperation with China's newly flexible and moderate approach to the United States in Asia. Were the United States to fail to reciprocate Chinese moderation, some of these specialists argue, more "hard-line" tendencies would prevail in Chinese policy toward the region. At the same time, the Chinese specialists also readily admit that China's initiatives in Asia, while designed to promote cooperation with the United States, also strengthen Chinese ability to offset possible U.S. efforts to pressure or contain China. Thus, they acknowledge that China's interest in multilateralism in Asia, and improvements in Chinese relations with key regional states like South Korea and those in ASEAN, ensure that if the United States reverted to a hard-line or containment policy toward China, U.S. efforts would be constrained. They would be constrained particularly by the "Gulliver" effect of multilateral organizations tying down U.S. power, and by China's improved relations with key Asian states who would be less than willing to cooperate in a containment posture toward the PRC.[31]

Chinese foreign policy in the Maoist period strongly opposed U.S. and Soviet power and pressure, especially along China's periphery. Moscow's persisting military buildup and search for greater political and military influence around China's periphery became the strategic center of gravity for Chinese foreign policy in Asia and China's overall approach to world affairs in the late 1960s. Top-level Chinese leaders of whatever background or ideological inclination were forced by Soviet actions to focus their foreign policy on the fundamental question of how to deal effectively with the Soviet military threat and political intimidation, without compromising Chinese security and sovereignty or mortgaging aspirations for independence and development. Initially, Chinese leaders came up with strikingly different approaches, leading in the late 1960s to the most serious dispute over foreign policy in the history of the People's Republic.[32]

The death of Defense Minister Lin Biao and the arrest and purge of a large segment of the Chinese military high command markedly reduced the political importance of Chinese leadership differences over how to deal with the Soviet Union. From that time on, China developed a fairly consistent strategy, at first under the leadership of Premier Zhou Enlai and Chairman Mao Zedong, and later under Deng Xiaoping. It attempted to use East-West differences pragmatically to China's advantage. The Chinese leaders recognized that only at tremendous cost and great risk could China confront the Soviet Union on its own. It relied heavily on international counterweights to Soviet power, provided mainly by the United States, and its allies and associates in Asia and elsewhere. As the United States reevaluated its former containment policy directed against China, and no longer posed a serious military threat to Chinese national security, Chinese leaders maintained a collaborative relationship with the United States and the West as a key link in its security policy against the USSR.[33]

Of course, the most significant development in Chinese policy, including foreign policy, after the Maoist period was the Chinese leadership focus on economic development and modernization. Strong Chinese leadership attention to economic development, reform, and opening up to economic opportunities outside China impelled Chinese foreign policy to focus ever more strongly on closer economic relations with the United States, Japan, and other more developed Western and Asian countries well integrated into the Western dominated international economic system.

The United States, Japan, and other noncommunist-developed countries in Asia and elsewhere had the markets, technology, managerial expertise, and financial resources that were crucial in speeding and streamlining China's troubled modernization effort so as to increase material benefit to the Chinese people, and thereby help to sustain their political loyalty and support for the Chinese Communist Party-led regime.[34]

The primary concerns of Chinese leaders were to guarantee Chinese national security, maintain internal order, and pursue economic development. Especially after the death of Mao in 1976, the highest priority was to promote successful economic modernization. This development represented the linchpin determining their success or failure. Thus, officials geared China's foreign policy to help the modernization effort.

In order to accomplish modernization, as well as to maintain national security and internal order, Chinese leaders recognized the fundamental prerequisite of establishing a relatively stable strategic environment, especially around China's periphery in Asia. The alternative would be a highly disruptive situation requiring much greater Chinese expenditures on national defense and posing greater danger to domestic order and tranquility. China did not control this environment. It influenced it, but the environment remained controlled more by others, especially the superpowers and their allies and associates. As a result, China's leaders were required repeatedly to reassess their surroundings for changes that affected Chinese security and development interests. The result was repeated Chinese adjustments to take account of such changes.[35]

At the same time, Chinese leaders had nationalistic and ideological objectives regarding irredentist claims (such as Taiwan) and a desire to stand independently in foreign affairs as a leading power among "progressive" nations of the Third World. These goals struck a responsive chord politically inside China. Occasional leadership discussion and debate over these and other questions regarding foreign affairs sometimes had an effect on the course of Chinese foreign policy. In the late Maoist period, for example, leaders sometimes allowed these nationalistic and ideological objectives, and other questions of political debate, to jeopardize seriously the basic security and development interests of the nation. China's move toward greater pragmatism in foreign and domestic policy after the late 1960s did not develop smoothly. It was accompanied by often very serious leadership debates over which foreign and domestic policy goals should receive priority. However, after the death of Lin Biao and the purge of his collaborators and later the Gang of Four, the debates became progressively less serious, at least until the leadership impasse in the late 1980s setting the stage for the Tiananmen crisis and crackdown of 1989. Of course, that leadership crisis focused mainly on domestic issues, and China's foreign policy orientation toward strengthening national security and development was not altered fundamentally.[36]

Thus, the two decades after the violent phase of the Cultural Revolution saw China's top foreign policy priority remain the pragmatic quest for a stable environment needed for effective modernization and development. Chinese leaders since the late 1960s saw the main danger of negative change in the surrounding environment posed by the Soviet Union. At first, Chinese leaders perceived Soviet power as an immediate threat to its national security. Over time, it came to see the USSR as more of a long-term threat, determined to use its growing military power and other sources of influence to encircle and pressure China into accepting a balance of influence in Asia dominated by the USSR and contrary to PRC interests.[37]

China's strategy against the Soviet threat was both bilateral and global. Bilaterally, China used a mix of military preparations and tactical political moves to keep the Soviet Union from attacking it. Globally, China's strategy focused on developing—either implicitly or explicitly—an international united front designed to halt Soviet expansion and prevent the consolidation of Soviet dominance abroad.

As the most important international counterweight to Soviet power, the United States loomed large in Chinese calculations. Because the United States under terms of the Nixon Doctrine announced in 1969 seemed determined to withdraw from its past policy of containing China in Asia, and thereby end a perceived threat to China's national security, the PRC was prepared to start the process of Sino-American normalization. The process was complemented by China's strong interest in the post-Mao period in pragmatic economic modernization, which emphasized the importance of technical and financial help from the West and access to Western markets.

Closer Chinese ties with the United States continued to be complicated by Chinese nationalistic and ideological concerns over Taiwan and Third World questions, as well as by fundamental differences between the social, political, and economic systems of the United States and China. Most notably, U.S. support for Taiwan was seen as a continued affront to China's national sovereignty. But Chinese leaders differentiated between substantive threats to China's national security, posed by the USSR, and threats to their sense of national sovereignty, posed by U.S. support for Taiwan.

In short, Chinese leaders worked hard to ensure that China's strategic environment around its periphery in Asia, threatened mainly by Soviet expansionism, remained stable, so that China could focus on economic modernization. The USSR was seen as having a strategy of expansion that used military power relentlessly but cautiously in order to achieve political influence and dominance throughout the periphery of the USSR. China long held that the focus of Soviet attention was in Europe, but that NATO's strength required Moscow to work in other areas, notably the Middle East, Southwest Asia, Africa, and East Asia, in order to outflank the Western defenses. China was seen as relatively low on Moscow's list of military priorities, although Chinese leaders clearly appreciated the dire consequences for China should the USSR have been able to consolidate its position elsewhere and then focus its strength to intimidate China.

China's strategy of deterrence and defense, therefore, aimed basically to exacerbate Soviet defense problems by enhancing the worldwide opposition to Soviet expansion in general, and by raising the possibility of the Soviet Union confronting a multifront conflict in the event it attempted to attack or intimidate China in particular. Chinese leaders saw their nation's cooperation with the United

States as especially important in strengthening deterrence of the Soviet Union and in aggravating Soviet strategic vulnerabilities. Chinese leaders also encouraged anti-Soviet efforts by so-called Second World, developed countries—most of whom were formal allies of the United States—and by developing countries of the Third World. At the same time, Chinese leaders used a mix of political talks, bilateral exchanges, and other forms of dialogue to help manage the danger posed by the USSR.

Within this overall strategy to establish a stable environment in Asia, Chinese leaders employed a varying mix of tactics to secure their interests, depending on international variables, such as the perceived strength and intentions of the super-powers, and Chinese domestic variables, such as leadership cohesion or disarray. For example, when Chinese leaders judged their strategic surroundings were at least temporarily stable, they had less immediate need for close ties with the United States, and thus felt freer to adopt more insistent policies on Taiwan and other nationalistic issues that appealed to domestic constituencies but offended the United States. This type of calculus was in part responsible for China's tougher approach to the United States over Taiwan and other issues in 1981-1983. But when the Chinese leaders judged that such tactics risked seriously alienating the United States and thereby endangered the stability of China's environment, they put them aside in the interest of preserving peaceful surroundings. Such reasoning undergirded China's moderation in approach toward the United States in 1983-1984.[38]

Cold War Maneuvering

Chinese foreign policy maneuvering against mainly Soviet and to a much less degree U.S. pressure and power along China's periphery in the twenty-year period to the end of the Cold War can be divided into three subperiods.

Balancing the Superpowers, 1969-1976.[39] As China was beginning to emerge from the violent domestic conflict and international isolation caused by the Cultural Revolution, the Soviet military buildup and the border clashes between China and the Soviet Union prompted a major reassessment in Chinese foreign policy that now focused on countering the Soviet threat to Chinese security. Given the concurrent U.S. pullback militarily from Asia, Chinese leaders saw an opportunity to work with the United States, its former adversary, against Soviet hegemonism, especially in Asia.

Chinese officials used the opening to the United States to support a broader effort to gain international recognition and to isolate Taiwan. Beijing's entry into the United Nations in 1971 was a high point in this effort. China-U.S. agreements in the Shanghai Communiqué, signed during President Nixon's visit to China in 1972, said that both sides opposed the efforts of an unnamed third party (presumably the Soviet Union) to establish "hegemony" in Asia. Subsequently, China cited this understanding to encourage worldwide efforts to block the expansion of what China called "Soviet hegemonism." China was sharply critical of any moves by the United States or others that it perceived as efforts to accommodate or "appease" Soviet expansion.

While Chinese leaders were generally supportive of the gradual U.S. withdrawal from Vietnam set under the terms of the Agreement Ending the War and Restoring Peace in Vietnam signed in Paris in January 1973, China was alarmed by the rapid collapse of pro-U.S. regimes in South Vietnam and Cambodia in 1975. Deng Xiaoping toured Southeast Asia, China rapidly normalized diplomatic relations with some noncommunist Southeast Asian states, and Chinese officials showed deep concern that expanding Soviet power and a unified Vietnam strongly backed by the USSR would fill the power vacuum left by the United States. Chinese pronouncements encouraged the United States to remain actively involved militarily, economically, and politically in Asia, and pointedly warned Asian countries to beware of Soviet and Soviet-backed efforts to fill the vacuum created by the U.S. pullback.

The China-U.S. accommodation that emerged during this period was restricted largely to strategic factors. Because of ongoing leadership struggles, China remained unwilling to break away from Maoist development policies emphasizing Chinese "self-reliance." China also remained very cautious in developing educational, cultural, and technical contacts with the outside world that might be called into question by the ideologically rigid members of the so-called Gang of Four—the Maoist radicals who along with their entourage had significant influence over policy at this time.

Domestic Reform and External Outreach, 1977-1980.[40] This period began with the death of Mao, the purge of the Gang of Four, and the rehabilitation of more pragmatic leaders led by Deng Xiaoping. Deng and his reform-minded colleagues began a major economic and related political reform effort designed to end the ideological struggles of the past and to improve the material well-being of the Chinese people. In foreign affairs, they broadened the basis of China's interest in contacts with the West and the rest of the developed world from common anti-Soviet strategic concerns to include greater economic, technical, and other exchanges.

Foreign policy initiatives supported the new quest to achieve economic modernization by helping to promote economic contacts with the various countries in Asia and elsewhere that could benefit China's modernization and by helping to maintain a stable and secure environment in Asian and world affairs that was conducive to Chinese modernization efforts. Chinese leaders put aside past ideological, political, and other constraints in order to seek beneficial economic and technical interchange with a wide range of industrialized and developing nations. They halted or cut back support to Maoist insurgencies and political groups in Southeast Asia and elsewhere in the Third World that would impede smooth economic exchanges with existing governments and states; they sharply reduced Chinese foreign assistance to the Third World, seeing it more as a drain on resources needed for China's modernization; and they showed an increased willingness to play down past Maoist pretensions to change the world in China's image.

Chinese leaders focused foreign policy concerns on establishing a "peaceful environment" (that is, a balance of power) around China's periphery in Asia. China could not, on its own, safeguard its interests in this region, which remained heavily influenced by the Soviet Union and the United States. China continued to see the main danger of instability and adverse development in Asia as coming from the Soviet Union and its allies and associates. Thus, Chinese leaders were particularly concerned by the Soviet-Vietnamese strategic alignment that allowed Vietnam in late 1978 to invade Cambodia, overthrow the Chinese-backed Khmer Rouge regime there, and successfully resist the subsequent Chinese military incursion into Vietnam in 1979.

These economic and strategic imperatives helped to explain China's decision to normalize diplomatic relations with the United States in 1978 and to sign the Peace and Friendship Treaty with Japan on August 12, 1978. They also help to explain China's highly vocal effort at the time to encourage a worldwide "anti-hegemony front" to contain the expansion of the Soviet Union and its proxies in Asia and elsewhere in the Third World. As it was in the 1969-1976 period, the Chinese government was especially critical of perceived efforts by the United States or other powers in the West to accommodate or "appease" perceived Soviet or Soviet-backed expansion in the interest of U.S.-Soviet arms control or other concerns. Chinese leaders also were supportive of the continued effort by the United States and its allies to maintain a firm military and diplomatic position against Soviet expansion in Asia and elsewhere.

Reassessment and an Independent Foreign Policy, 1980-1989.[41] Throughout the 1980s, Chinese leaders were generally supportive of the strong U.S.-led international response to the Soviet invasion of Afghanistan in December 1979. The election of Ronald Reagan and the buildup of U.S. military strength in the early 1980s were seen by Chinese commentators and officials as complementing similarly strong efforts against Soviet expansion by U.S. allies in Europe and Asia. China remained active in facing off with Soviet forces along the Sino-Soviet border, in confronting Vietnam along its border with China, and in supporting Khmer Rouge and other armed resistance against the Vietnamese- and Soviet-backed regime in Cambodia. China worked with the United States and others in clandestine efforts to arm the resistance to the Soviet occupation in Afghanistan and publicly demanded the Soviet Union withdraw its forces from Mongolia and other areas around China's periphery. Encouraged by the upswing in U.S. and Western resolve against the USSR, Chinese officials came to view Soviet expansion to be held in check for the first time in more than a decade. They also saw this international resolve against Soviet expansion likely to continue along with a deepening economic malaise and serious leadership succession issues in the USSR. The result would be an overall decline in the danger China saw posed by the Soviet Union in the 1980s.

Meanwhile, Chinese leaders reassessed for a time China's close alignment with the United States in light of President Reagan's early strong statements in favor of greater U.S. support for Taiwan. In 1981-1982 China opted for an "independent" posture in foreign affairs that publicly pulled away from the previous close de facto alignment with the United States; showed some ostensible willingness for greater interchange with the USSR; and gave renewed emphasis to Chinese interest in cultivating relations with Third World nations, communist and socialist parties, and other "progressive" international groups that had received relatively low priority in Chinese foreign policy during the immediate post-Mao period. The new independent posture also struck a favorable chord among Chinese intellectuals and others who sought a foreign policy consistent with Chinese Communist ideology and nationalism and chafed under the perceived excessive pragmatism and utilitarianism seen in China's reliance on the United States and the West in the immediate post-Mao period.

Nevertheless, the ailing Leonid Brezhnev and subsequent Soviet leaders were unwilling to reduce Moscow's military forces around China's periphery or to reduce support for Asian countries, such as Vietnam and India, which served as local counterweights to Chinese influence. Moreover, Chinese leaders also clearly recognized the importance of their newly developed economic ties with the United States, including U.S. leadership in international financial institutions then providing increasing amounts of funding and technical support to China's economic modernization. After two years of political crisis in China-U.S. relations that saw tough negotiations and public disputes with the Reagan administration over U.S. arms sales to Taiwan and other issues, Chinese leaders set limits on China's independent foreign posture. They compromised on heretofore sensitive disputes and consolidated ties with the United States during Reagan's visit to China in 1984. The U.S. government facilitated this change by increasing the flow of U.S. technology to China and by minimizing public U.S. references to differences with Beijing over Taiwan and other issues.

In the mid-1980s, with the rise to power of Mikhail Gorbachev and his reform-minded colleagues in the Soviet Union, China and the Soviet Union slowly moderated past differences and appeared determined to improve political, economic, and other bilateral concerns. Chinese and Soviet leaders focused on internal economic and political reforms, and expressed interest in fostering a stable, peaceful international environment conducive to such domestic change. Ideological, territorial, and leadership differences between Beijing and Moscow were deemed less important. However, the two sides remained divided largely over competing security interests in Asia. Gorbachev gradually began to accommodate China's interests in this area by starting to pull back Soviet forces from Afghanistan, Mongolia, and other places around China's periphery. Concurrently, Chinese military planners began to revise substantially China's strategic plans. They downgraded the danger of Soviet attack and allowed for a major demobilization of Chinese ground forces.

The Soviet initiatives also reduced Chinese interest in cooperating closely with the United States and its allies and associates in Asia in order to check possible Soviet expansion. But China's growing need for close economic and technical ties with these countries compensated to some degree for its decreased interest in closer security ties with them. Chinese officials also wished to improve relations with the

Soviets in order to keep pace with the rapid improvement in Gorbachev's relations with the United States and Western Europe. Otherwise, Chinese leaders ran the risk of not being consulted when world powers debated international issues important to China. The agreement marking the Soviet withdrawal from Afghanistan was reached without China playing an active role in the negotiations, for example.

During this period, the United States and its allies found the Soviet Union more accommodating than China on matters of interest to the West. At the same time, the changes in U.S.-Soviet relations and in China's policy to the Soviet Union reduced the perceived U.S. need to sustain and develop close strategic cooperation with China against the Soviet Union. Meanwhile, some specialists judged that the United States did not consider economic interchange with China important enough to compensate for the reduced anti-Soviet strategic cooperation, even though China remained important for Asian security and international arms control. Reflecting this slow shift in U.S.-China relations, long-standing bilateral and other irritants in China-U.S. relations over human rights, treatment of intellectuals, and Tibet appeared to take on more prominence in China-U.S. relations.

Chinese Foreign Policy after the Cold War

The weakening and collapse of the Soviet threat to China improved China's overall security situation. For the first time, the People's Republic of China was not facing an immediate foreign threat to its national security. However, the sharp international reaction to China's harsh crackdown on dissent after the June 1989 Tiananmen incident caught Chinese leaders by surprise. They reportedly had expected industrialized nations to restore stable relations with China after a few months. They had not counted on the rapid collapse of communism in Eastern Europe, the subsequent march toward self-determination and democratization throughout the Soviet republics, and ultimately the end of the Soviet Union in 1991. These unexpected events for several years diverted the industrialized nations from returning to China with advantageous investment, assistance, and economic exchanges; called into question China's strategic importance as a counterweight to the Soviet Union; and posed the most serious challenge to the legitimacy of the Chinese Communist regime since the Cultural Revolution. Taiwan's concurrent moves toward greater democracy and self-determination received greater positive attention in the United States and the West, adding to China's concerns about broad international trends and what to do about them.[42]

The United States was seen as both the greatest threat and most important partner in Chinese foreign policy. In response to U.S.-led sanctions and criticisms in the late 1980s and early 1990s, the Chinese government and party endeavored to use foreign affairs to demonstrate the legitimacy and prestige of its communist leaders. High-level visits to Asian capitals and elsewhere in the non-Western world were used along with trade and security arrangements in order to strengthen China's image before skeptical audiences at home and abroad. To reestablish internal political stability, Chinese leaders also gave high priority to the resource needs of the military and public security forces.[43]

Recognizing that communist ideology was not popular enough to support their continued monopoly of power, leaders in Beijing played up more traditional themes of Chinese nationalism to support their rule. U.S. and other foreign criticisms of the communist system in China were portrayed not as attacks against unjust arbitrary rule but as assaults on the national integrity of China. These attacks were equated with earlier "imperialist" pressures on China in the nineteenth century and the first half of the twentieth century.[44]

Meanwhile, statements and initiatives by Deng Xiaoping spurring economic reform and opening during a tour of southern China in 1992 forced other Chinese senior leaders away from their hesitant approach to economic modernization and reform after the Tiananmen crackdown. Deng called for faster growth and increased economic interchange with the outside world, especially the developed economies of Asia and the West. This call coincided with the start of an economic boom on the mainland that continued for several years of double digit growth and then declined a bit to the still-rapid pace of 7-8 percent annual growth. The consequences of such rapid growth initially included serious inflation as well as broader economic dislocation and many social problems, but the growth also caught the attention of foreign business and government leaders. Many of China's well-to-do neighbors such as Hong Kong and Taiwan already had become well positioned to take advantage of the mainland's rapid growth. They were followed rapidly by West European, Japanese, Southeast Asian, and Korean entrepreneurs. U.S. business interests in the China market grew markedly from 1992, and were credited with playing an important role in convincing the Clinton administration in 1994 to stop linking U.S. most-favored-nation trade treatment to improvements in China's still poor human rights conditions.[45]

Deng Xiaoping and the new Third generation of leaders headed by president and party leader Jiang Zemin continued the post-Mao policies emphasizing fostering a better economic life for the people of China in order to justify their continued monopoly of political power. As the prestige of Mao and Communism had faded rapidly, Chinese leaders found themselves depending heavily on foreign trade, and related foreign investment and assistance, for China's needed economic development. China depended particularly on its Asian neighbors for aid, investment, and trade benefits, and on the United States and other major consumer markets to absorb its exports, which were growing at double the rate of the fast-developing Chinese economy. To ensure their political survival, China's leaders continued to emphasize the maintenance of a peaceful international environment, especially in nearby Asia, which would facilitate the continued trade, investment, and assistance flows so important to Chinese economic well-being.[46]

The leadership followed earlier steps to put aside self-reliance and to broaden international contacts by increasing efforts to meet the requirements of the United States and others regarding market access, intellectual property rights, and other economic issues, and to become a member of the World Trade Organization (WTO). Chinese leaders accepted more commitments and responsibilities stemming from their participation in such international economic organizations as the World Bank, the Asian Development Bank, and the Asia Pacific Economic Cooperation forum.[47]

Chinese leaders remained sensitive on matters of national sovereignty and international security issues close to home. But they adjusted to world pressure when resistance appeared detrimental to broader Chinese concerns. Examples of this adjustment included Chinese cooperation with the international peace settlement in Cambodia in 1991, willingness to join the 1968 Treaty on Non-proliferation of Nuclear Weapons and to halt nuclear tests by the end of 1996 under an international agreement, willingness to abide by terms of the Missile Technology Control Regime (MTCR), and efforts to help the United States reach an agreement with North Korea in October 1994 over the latter's nuclear weapons development program. Beijing also endeavored to meet international expectations on other transnational issues, such as policing drug traffic, curbing international terrorism, and working to avoid further degradation of the global environment.[48]

China's continued hard line against outside criticism of China's political authoritarianism and poor human rights record continued to illustrate limits of China's accommodation to international norms. China continued to transfer sensitive military technology or dual-use equipment to Pakistan, Iran, North Korea, and other potential flash points, despite criticism from Western countries. Furthermore, Chinese political and military leaders were not reluctant to use rhetorical threats or demonstrations of military force to intimidate those they believed were challenging China's traditional territorial or nationalistic claims in sensitive areas such as Taiwan, the South China Sea, and Hong Kong.[49]

As a general rule, Chinese leaders tended to approach each foreign policy issue on a case-by-case basis, each time calculating the costs and benefits of adherence to international norms. This kind of approach applied especially to security and political issues, while Chinese leaders came to view economic norms differently, seeing China generally well served by embracing economic globalization and the norms associated with it. By 1991, Chinese officials saw that maintaining past support for the Khmer Rouge in Cambodia would counter broader Chinese interests in achieving a favorable peace settlement in Cambodia and solidifying closer Chinese relations with ASEAN members, Japan, and the West—all of whom saw continued Chinese aid to the Khmer Rouge as a serious obstacle to peace. Similarly, in 1994, China had to announce its decision to stop nuclear testing by the end of 1996 and to join the comprehensive nuclear test ban, or it would have risked major friction in its relations with the United States, Japan, Western Europe, and Russia.[50]

Influencing the case-by-case approach was a rising sense of nationalism among Chinese leaders and the Chinese people more broadly. Tending to view the world as a highly competitive, state-centered system, Chinese leaders were slow to embrace multilateralism and interdependence, though they came to accept these trends regarding economic issues. In security and political affairs, however, they were inclined to see the world in fairly traditional balance-of-power terms. They stressed that the world was becoming more multipolar (that is, a number of competing nation states), though in the face of undiminished U.S. dominance, they came to play down multipolarity in favor of multilateralism. The later required the United States to sacrifice some freedom of maneuver for the sake of an interdependent international order, thereby constraining U.S. power that could be used against Chinese interests.[51]

Chinese suspicions of the prevailing Asian and international order centered on the dominant role of the United States and its allies and associates. These nations were seen as setting the agenda of many international regimes in order to serve their own particular national interests, in the process giving short shrift to the interests and concerns of newly emerging powers like China. For example, many leaders in China during the 1990s saw foreign efforts to encourage or pressure China to conform to standards on international security, human rights, and economic policies and practices as motivated by the foreign powers' fear of China's rising power, their unwillingness to share power fairly with China, and their desire to "hold down" China—that is, to keep it weak for as long as possible.[52]

Chinese leaders recognized that the United States exerted predominant strategic influence in East Asia and the western Pacific, was a leading economic power in the region, and was one of only two powers (along with Russia) capable of exerting sufficient power around China's periphery to pose a tangible danger to Chinese security and development. As the world's remaining superpower, the United States was seen by Chinese officials in the 1990s exerting strong influence in international financial and political institutions, such as the World Bank and the United Nations, that were particularly important to Beijing. The United States also played a key role in areas of great sensitivity to China's leaders, notably regarding Taiwan and international human rights.[53]

While Chinese leaders tried hard to work constructively with U.S. leaders in areas of mutual interest, more often than not, U.S. policy in Asian affairs was seen as adverse to Chinese interests. Chinese leaders were preoccupied with maneuvering carefully and sometimes forcefully to defend and protect core interests while accommodating American concerns in other areas. The face-off with U.S. forces over Taiwan in 1996 and the trashing of U.S. diplomatic properties in China after the U.S. bombing of the Chinese Embassy in Belgrade in 1999 illustrated how far Chinese leaders were prepared to go in fending off perceived U.S. pressure. Chinese media in these years was full of affirmations of Chinese determination to make necessary sacrifices to defend important interests against U.S. "hegemonism."[54]

In sum, there is a clear pattern of Chinese maneuvering against great power involvement and influence around China's periphery that remains important today. During the Cold War, China faced serious national security threats from U.S. and Soviet forces in Asia and from their Asian allies. The threat of superpower war declined with the end of the Cold War and collapse of the Soviet Union. However, it was replaced by strong Chinese leadership concern that the United States was leading efforts to contain China, to end its Communist rule, and to undermine its territorial integrity in the years after the Tiananmen incident and the end of the Soviet Union. This concern arguably declined as the global war on terrorism diverted

U.S. strategic attention to Southwest Asia, but U.S. military deployments throughout China's periphery and U.S. policies and practices regarding Taiwan and North Korea seen as contrary to Chinese interests headed the list of reasons for Chinese policy makers to continue to seek to reduce great power influence around China's periphery.

Notes

1. Positive assessments of U.S.-China relations in Asia include Wang Jisi, *China's Changing Role in Asia* (Washington, D.C.: The Atlantic Council of the United States, January 2004); Thomas Christensen, "Optimistic Trends and Near-term Challenges: Sino-American Security Relations in Early 2003," *China Leadership Monitor*, Issue 6 (Spring 2003); Bonnie Glaser, "Wen Jiabao's Visit Caps an Outstanding Year," *Comparative Connections*, January 2004; "Beijing to Take an Amiable Approach in U.S.-China Diplomacy This Year, *Wenweipo News*, 28 January 2004; Phar Kim Beng, "China's Strategic Shift to Common Security," *Asia Times*, 26 November 2002 (Internet version); David M. Lampton, "The Stealth Normalization of U.S.-China Relations," *The National Interest* 73 (Fall 2003): 37-48.

2. Robert Suettinger, *Beyond Tiananmen* (Washington, D.C.: Brookings Institution, 2003); David M. Lampton, *Same Bed, Different Dreams* (Berkeley: University of California, 2001).

3. Thomas Christensen, "The Party Transition: Will It Bring a New Maturity in Chinese Security Policy?" *China Leadership Monitor*, www.chinaleadershipmonitor.org/20031/tc.html (Winter 2003, Issue 5) (accessed 29 June 2004); Michael Swaine, *Reverse Course? The Fragile Turnabout in U.S.-China Relations*, Policy Brief 22 (Carnegie Endowment for International Peace, February 2003).

4. International Crisis Group Reports, *Taiwan Strait I, II, III*, www.crisisweb.org/library/documents/report_archive/A400990_06062003.pdf; www.crisisweb.org/library/documents/report_archive/A400991_06062003.pdf; www.crisisweb.org/library/documents/report_archive/A400992_06062003.pdf (accessed 1 September 2003); U.S. Department of Defense, *Annual Report on the Military Power of the People's Republic of China, 2003*, www.defenselink.mil/pubs/20030730chinaex.pdf (accessed 3 September 2003); Bonnie Glaser, "Washington's Hands-on Approach to Managing Cross Strait Tensions," *PACNET* no. 21, www.csis.org/pacfor (accessed 13 May 2004).

5. David Finkelstein, "China Reconsiders Its National Security: The Great Peace and Development Debate of 1999" (Alexandria, Va.: The CNA Corporation, December 2000); Qian Qichen, "The International Situation and Sino-U.S. Relations since the 11 September Incident," Beijing *Waijiao Xueyuan Xuebao* no. 3 (25 September 2002): 1-6; Guo Qiufu, "U.S. Wishful Thinking on Its Military Presence in Central Asia and Its Real Purpose," *Liaowang*, 29 April 2002, 57-59; Jun Niu, "Dongya Anquan de Chulu Hezai" ("Where Is the Exit Solution of East Asian Security?"), www.irchina.org/xueren/china/view.asp?id=644; this article originally appeared in *Huanqiu Shibao* (Global Times), 26 December 2003 (accessed 30 June 2004); Shulong Chu, "*9.11 Wei Gai Shijie Geju*" ("9.11 Did Not Change World Structure") www.irchina.org/xueren/china/view.asp?id=337; this article originally appeared in *Huanqiu Shibao* (Global Times), www.people.com.cn/GB/paper68-/4972/532803.html (accessed 14 December 2001). See also Wang Jisi, "Impact of U.S. Strategic Adjustment on Sino-U.S. Relations," (Beijing) *Xuexi Shibao*, 16 August 2004

(Internet version, translated by FBIS); Tao Wenzhao, "Changes and Drivers in Sino-U.S. Relations," replayed in *China Strategy*, vol. 3, www.csis.org (accessed 20 July 2004).
6. Kerry Dumbaugh, *China-U.S. Relations: Current Issues for the 108th Congress* (Washington, D.C.: Library of Congress), Congressional Research Service, CRS Report RL 31815, 15 September 2003.
7. On Chinese views of multipolarity, see Zhang Yunling, ed., "Huoban haishi duishou I tiaozheng zhong de Zhong Mei Ri E guanxi" (Beijing: Social Sciences Documents Press, 2000); Zhu Feng, "Zai lishi gui yi zhong bawo Zhong Mei guanxi," *Huanqiu Shibao Guoji Luntan*, www.interforum.xilubbs.com (accessed 28 February 2002); Xiong Guankai, "A Review of International Strategic Situation and Its Prospects," *Guoji Zhanlüe yanjiu (International Strategic Studies)* 71, no. 1 (January 2004): 3; Yong Deng, "Hegemon on the Offensive: Chinese Perceptions on U.S. Global Strategy," *Political Science Quarterly* 116, no. 3 (2001): 343-65; David Finkelstein, "Chinese Perspectives of the Costs of Conflict," in Andrew Scobell, ed., *The Costs of Conflict: The Impact on China of a Future War* (Carlisle, Pa.: Strategic Studies Institute, October 2001), 9-27; Denny Roy, *China's Pitch for a Multipolar World*, Honolulu: Asia-Pacific Center for Security Studies 2, no. 1 (May 2003); Mei Zhaorong, "The International Strategic Situation after the Iraq war," Beijing *Foreign Affairs Journal* 70 (December 2003): 50, 52; Shi Yinhong, "Basic Trials and Essential 'Platforms' for China's Peaceful Rise," Hong Kong *Ta Kung Pao*, 14 March 2004 (Internet version); Zhongying Pang, "Building Regional Security System," www.irchina.org/xueren/china/view.asp?id=680; this article originally appeared in the *China Daily*, www.chinadaily.com.cn/english/doc/2004-03/26/content_318149.htm (accessed 26 March 2004).
8. Kerry Dumbaugh, *China-U.S. Relations*, Washington, D.C.: Library of Congress, Congressional Research Service, Issue Brief 98018, updated regularly.
9. David Shambaugh, "China and the Korean Peninsula, *Washington Quarterly* (Spring 2003): 43-56; Bonnie Glaser, "Sustaining Cooperation," *Comparative Connections*, www.csis.org/pacfor (accessed October-December 2002); John Tkacik, "China's Korea Conundrum," *Asian Wall Street Journal,* 2 December 2002 (Internet version); Denny Roy, *China and the Korean Peninsula*, Honolulu: Asia Pacific Center for Security Studies 3, no. 1 (January 2004).
10. Li Heng, "What Is U.S. Vessel up to in Chinese Waters?" *People's Daily*, 30 September 2002 (Internet version); Bill Gertz, "Chinese Jet Fighters Fly Near U.S. Spy Planes," *Washington Times*, 27 June 2002, 1.
11. Suisheng Zhao, "A State-led Nationalism: The Patriotic Education Campaign in Post-Tiananmen China," *Communist and Post Communist Studies* 31, no. 3 (1998): 289; Lampton, *Same Bed-Different Dreams*, 279-312; Robert Suettinger, *Beyond Tiananmen*; Suisheng Zhao, "Chinese Nationalism and Its International Orientations," *Political Science Quarterly* 115, no. 1 (Spring 2000): 5.
12. Lampton, *Same Bed-Different Dreams*, 111-58; Suettinger, *Beyond Tiananmen*; Dumbaugh, *China-U.S. Relations: Current Issues for the 108th Congress.*
13. Lampton, *Same Bed, Different Dreams*, 60.
14. David Shambaugh, *Beautiful Imperialist* (Princeton, N.J.: Princeton University Press, 1991).
15. Phillip Saunders, "China's America Watchers: Changing Attitudes toward the United States," *The China Quarterly* (March 2000): 42-43.
16. Rosalie Chen, "China Perceives America," *Journal of Contemporary China* 12, no. 35 (2003): 286. See also Xiong Guankai, "A Review of International Strategic Situation and Its Prospects," *International Strategic Studies* 71, no. 1 (January 2004): 3.

17. Yong Deng, "Hegemon on the Offensive," 344-46.

18. For supporting data and assessment of negative Chinese views of U.S. policy in the 1990s, see Robert Sutter, *Shaping China's Future in World Affairs* (Boulder, Colo.: Westview Press, 1996), 125-28.

19. Finkelstein, "China Reconsiders Its National Security."

20. Chen, "China Perceives America," 288-92.

21. Chen, "China Perceives America," 288-92.

22. Robert Ross and Jiang Changbin, *Re-examining the Cold War* (Cambridge, Mass.: Harvard, 2001), 19-21.

23. The mix of challenge and opportunity posed by the United States for Chinese interests and policies in Asian and world affairs has prompted differing assessments by Chinese and foreign specialists. Some emphasize positive and cooperative aspects of U.S.-China relations. See Joseph Kahn, "Hands across the Pacific," *New York Times*, 11 November 2002 (Internet version); Elaine Kurtenbach, "China Emerges as a Possible U.S. Partner," *AP*, 21 October 2003 (Internet version); Yoichi Funabashi, "China's 'Peaceful Ascendancy,'" *Yaleglobal*, www.yaleglobal.yale.edu (accessed 19 December 2003); Nailene Chou Wiest, "Beijing Presents a New Face in an Innovative Year for Diplomacy," *South China Morning Post*, 2 January 2004, 1; Ye Zicheng, "Adopting a Diplomatic Strategy That Adapts to Changes in the Environment," (Beijing) *Xiandai Guoji Guanxi* 20, no. 11 (November 2002): 24-25. Others emphasize more negative and competitive aspects. John Pomfert, "In Its Own Neighborhood, China Emerges as a Leader," *Washington Post*, 18 October 2001; Jane Perlez, "China Races to Replace U.S. as Economic Power in Asia," *New York Times*, 28 June 2002; U.S.-China Security Review Commission, *Report to Congress July 2002*, www.uscc.gov/anrp02.htm (accessed 1 September 2002); Eric Eckholm and Joseph Kahn, "Asia Worries about Growth of China's Economic Power," *New York Times*, 24 November 2002; Thomas Woodrow, "The New Great Game," *China Brief* III, no. 3 (11 February 2003); Lu Baosheng, "World Multipolar Trend Develops and Meanders," *Jiefangjunbao* 1 September 2003, 11; Fang Ning, Wang Xiaodong, and Qiao Liang, *Quanqiuhua yinyang xia de Zhongguo zhi lu* (Beijing: Chinese Academy of Social Sciences Press, 1999), 47.

24. Lampton, *Same Bed-Different Dreams*, 249-312.

25. Joseph Fewsmith, *China Since Tiananmen* (Cambridge: Cambridge University Press, 2001), 75-158.

26. Fewsmith, *China Since Tiananmen*. See also Suisheng Zhao, "A State-led Nationalism," 289; Suisheng Zhao, "Chinese Nationalism and Its International Orientations," 5.

27. Joseph Fewsmith and Stanley Rosen, "The Domestic Context of Chinese Foreign Policy: Does 'Public Opinion' Matter?" in David M. Lampton, ed., *The Making of Chinese Foreign and Security Policy Decision-making in the Era of Reform* (Stanford, Calif.: Stanford University Press, 2001), 179-86.

28. Michael Swaine, *Reverse Course?*

29. Lampton, *Chinese Foreign and Security Policy*.

30. Lampton, *Chinese Foreign and Security Policy*, 373.

31. Consultations with Chinese foreign policy specialists, October 2003-May 2004.

32. A. Doak Barnett, *China and the Major Powers in East Asia* (Washington, D.C.: Brookings Institution, 1977), chapters 1 and 3.

33. Robert Sutter, *Chinese Foreign Policy: Developments after Mao* (New York: Praeger, 1986), 5.

34. Tony Saich, *Governance and Politics in China* (New York: Palgrave 2001), 52-59; Merle Goldman, "The Post-Mao Reform Era," in John Fairbank and Merle Goldman, *China: A History* (Cambridge, Mass.: Harvard University Press, 1999), 406-10.

35. Sutter, *Chinese Foreign Policy: Developments after Mao*, 9.

36. John W. Garver, *Foreign Relations of the People's Republic of China* (Englewood Cliffs, N.J.: Prentice Hall, 1993), 70-109.

37. The rest of this section draws on Sutter, *Chinese Foreign Policy: Developments after Mao*, 10-12. For an alternative view, see Garver, *Foreign Relations of the People's Republic of China*, 70-109.

38. See the insightful analysis of China's shifting stance and U.S. policy in Jim Mann, *About Face* (New York: Knopf, 1999), 128-54.

39. This period is treated in Barnett, *China and the Major Powers in East Asia*; Garver, *Foreign Relations of the People's Republic of China*, 70-85; Sutter, *Chinese Foreign Policy: Developments after Mao,* 13-43; Sutter, *Shaping China's Future*, 28-29.

40. This period is treated in Garver, *Foreign Relations of the People's Republic of China*, 98-102; Sutter, *Chinese Foreign Policy: Developments after Mao*, 44-130; Sutter, *Shaping China's Future*, 29-30.

41. This period is treated in Garver, *Foreign Relations of the People's Republic of China*, 98-109; Sutter, *Chinese Foreign Policy: Developments after Mao*, 131-220; Andrew Nathan and Robert Ross, *The Great Wall and Empty Fortress* (New York: Norton, 1997), 46-51, 67-73; Sutter, *Shaping China's Future*, 31-32.

42. Sutter, *Shaping China's Future*, 32-33.

43. Harry Harding, *A Fragile Relationship* (Washington, D.C.: Brookings Institution, 1992), 235-39.

44. Fewsmith, *China Since Tiananmen*, 21-43, 75-158.

45. Robert Sutter and Kerry Dumbaugh, *China-U.S. Relations* (Washington, D.C.: Library of Congress), Congressional Research Service, CRS Issue Brief 94002, 5 November 1994.

46. Sutter, *Shaping China's Future*, 33-34.

47. Nathan and Ross, *The Great Wall*, 158-77.

48. Sutter, *Shaping China's Future*, 33-34.

49. Shirley Kan, *China as a Security Concern in Asia* (Washington, D.C.: Library of Congress), Congressional Research Service, Report 95-465, 22 December 1994.

50. Lampton, *Chinese Foreign and Security Policy*, 34-36.

51. Evan Medieros and Taylor Fravel, "China's New Diplomacy," *Foreign Affairs*, November/December 2003 (Internet version); Zhang Yunling and Tang Shiping, "More Self-confident China Will Be a Responsible Power," *Straits Times*, 2 October 2002, www.Taiwansecurity.org (accessed 4 October 2002); Denny Roy, "Rising China and U.S. Interests: Inevitable vs. Contingent Hazards," *Orbis* 47, no. 1 (2003): 124-43.

52. Sutter, *Shaping China's Future*, 35.

53. *Trends of Future Sino-U.S. Relations and Policy Proposals* (Beijing: Institute for International Studies of the Academy of Social Sciences, September 1994).

54. Lampton, *Same Bed, Different Dreams*, 59-60.

Chapter 2

Recent Chinese Domestic and Foreign Policies and Priorities

Proper context is important in understanding the relative significance and priority for Chinese leaders of China's recent policies and behavior in Asia. In recent years, Chinese initiatives and cooperativeness in the region have greatly improved China's overall image in Asia. This image building has led some specialists and commentators to exaggerate China's power and influence in Asia, neglecting the constraints on Chinese policy and behavior imposed by difficulties, challenges, and realities at home and abroad. Recent Chinese actions in Asia also have caused some observers to see Chinese efforts as a top leadership priority, when in fact domestic issues and other concerns preoccupy Chinese leaders.[1] This chapter presents an overview of recent Chinese leadership policy and priorities in order to show the relative importance for Chinese leaders of Chinese actions around its periphery dealt with in subsequent chapters.

Recent Chinese Policies and Priorities

Party leader and President Jiang Zemin exerted increasing influence in Chinese policy making during the 1990s. Jiang was successful in maneuvers against formidable leadership competition, notably from the likes of former President Yang Shangkun and his nephew Yang Baiping. He initiated a more flexible position that became a central tenet in Chinese stance toward Taiwan, even though it was temporarily upset by Lee Teng-hui's visit to Cornell University and the crisis and military standoff in cross-strait relations. And he worked with Vice Premier Zhu Rongji and other senior government leaders to bring inflation under control while sustaining strong economic growth seen as needed to sustain stability and support for the Communist system of rule in China. Jiang pursued and advanced policies generally consistent with those set forth by Deng Xiaoping, whose health declined in the several years before his death in February 1997.[2]

Deng's passing allowed Jiang to assume the mantle and actual position as China's paramount leader. His overall standing, of course, was much weaker than that of Deng, whose prestige and leadership credentials traced back to the Long March. But Jiang was especially active in foreign affairs, leading Chinese efforts to sustain an effective approach toward the United States, adjusting the mix of incentives and sanctions in Chinese policy toward Taiwan, and creating a more coherent and active Chinese policy toward China's periphery in Asia.[3]

Chinese leaders in 1997 were anxious to minimize problems with the United States and other countries in order to avoid complications in their efforts to appear successful in completing three major tasks for the year.

*   The July 1, 1997, transition of Hong Kong to Chinese rule;
*   The reconfiguration of Chinese leadership and policy at the fifteenth CCP Congress in September 1997, the first major party meeting since the death of senior leader Deng Xiaoping in February 1997;
*   The Sino-U.S. summit of October 1997, which China hoped would show people in China and abroad that its leaders were now fully accepted as respectable world leaders following a period of protracted isolation after the 1989 Tiananmen crackdown.[4]

Generally pleased with the results of these three endeavors, Chinese leaders headed by President Jiang Zemin began implementing policy priorities for 1998. At the top of the list was an ambitious multiyear effort, begun in earnest after the National People's Congress (NPC) meeting in March 1998, to transform tens of thousands of China's money-losing state-owned enterprises (SOEs) into more efficient businesses by reforming them (for example, selling them to private concerns, forming large conglomerates, or other actions).

Beijing embarked on major programs to promote economic and administrative efficiency and protect China's potentially vulnerable financial systems from any negative fallout from the 1997-1998 Asian economic crisis and subsequent uncertainties. Thus, at the NPC meeting in March 1998, it was announced that government rolls would be drastically cut in an effort to reduce inefficient government interference in day-to-day business management. China's new premier, Zhu Rongji, initiated sweeping changes in China's banking and other financial systems designed to reduce or eliminate the vulnerabilities seen elsewhere in Asia.[5]

As a result of the September 1997 party congress and the March 1998 NPC meeting, a new party-government team was in place, managing policy without such powerful leaders of the past as Mao Zedong and Deng Xiaoping. There were problems reaching consensus on the power-holding arrangements made at the party and people's congresses, but on the whole, top-level leaders seemed to be working smoothly together pursuing Chinese policy interests.[6]

Making collective leadership work was an ongoing challenge for China's top leaders. One senior decision maker traditionally dominated the People's Republic of China (PRC). Periods of collective leadership, notably after Mao's death in 1976, were short and unstable. President Jiang Zemin gained in stature and influence in recent years, but his power still did not compare to that exerted by Mao and Deng. Also, in the background lay the scenario that when it came time for Jiang and his senior colleagues to retire, some struggle for power and influential positions by up-and-coming leaders remained a distinct possibility. All were aware that if a major economic, political, or foreign policy crisis were to emerge, leadership conflict over what to do, how to do it, and who should do it could be intense.[7]

There were few signs of disagreement among senior leaders over the broad recent policy emphasis on economic reform, though sectors affected by reform often resisted strenuously. The ambitious plans for economic reform, especially reform of the SOEs, were needed if China's economy was to become sufficiently efficient to sustain the growth rates seen as needed to justify continued communist rule and to develop China's wealth and power. China anticipated joining the World Trade Organization (WTO) in 2001 or 2002, strengthening the need for greater economic efficiency and reform. The reforms also exacerbated social and economic uncertainties, which reinforced the regime's determination to maintain a firm grip on political power and levers of social control. By late 1998, instability caused by economic change and growing political dissent prompted the PRC leadership to initiate significant suppression of political dissidents and related activities. The repression continued through 2004 and possibly would last for the duration of the economic reform efforts.[8]

Against this background, foreign affairs generally remained an area of less urgent policy priority. Broad international trends, notably improved relations with the United States and an upswing in China's relations throughout its periphery, supported the efforts by the Chinese authorities to pursue policies intended to minimize disruptions and to assist their domestic reform endeavors. The government remained wary of the real or potential challenges posed by a possible renewed Asian economic crisis, by Taiwan, by efforts by Japan and the United States to increase their international influence in ways seen as contrary to Beijing's interests, by India's great power aspirations and nuclear capability, and by other concerns. The PRC voiced special concern over the implications for China's interests of U.S. plans to develop and deploy theater ballistic missile defense systems in East Asia, and a national missile defense for the United States. Chinese officials also voiced concern over the downturn in U.S.-China relations at the outset of the George W. Bush administration, but appeared determined to cooperate with the U.S.-led antiterrorism campaign begun in September 2001.[9]

Determinants of Chinese Government Priorities

Chinese government priorities were dependent on key internal domestic and external variables determining the future of the communist regime and its role in Asian and world affairs. A mainstream view among U.S. China specialists held that the regime appeared resilient enough to deal with most anticipated problems internally, at least for a number of years. China was wary of the United States and was steadily building military power. But unless Beijing was challenged by circumstances, China was seen as unlikely to break with the United States or engage in disruptive military buildups or aggressive foreign behavior. Alternative views included those who saw Chinese leaders ready and able to confront the United States, by military means, if necessary, over such key issues as Taiwan. These views were in the minority among U.S. China specialists but they received wide attention in the U.S. media and in congressional and other government deliberations.[10]

Political Leaders and Institutions

China's "third-generation" leadership (Mao's was the first generation and Deng's was the second; Jiang Zemin led the third generation) and its successors were thought likely to continue the process of political regularity and institutionalization that had made China's political behavior much more predictable than it was during the Maoist period (1949-1976). The political leaders lacked charisma but were more technically competent and less ideologically rigid than past leaders; they were aware of the problems they faced and were prepared to deal with at least some of the most important ones.[11]

Some experts noted that fourth-generation leaders (headed by Hu Jintao, who was selected as party leader at the sixteenth Party Congress in November 2002 and president at the tenth National People's Congress in March 2003) did not share the same background; a number also questioned the capabilities of these leaders in comparison with their predecessors. Fourth-generation leaders came of age during the Cultural Revolution but often had diverse political views and lacked the binding solidarity of experiences that the previous generations of leaders gained on the Long March and during the Anti-Japanese War, for example. Collectively, fourth-genera-tion leaders were seen as less dogmatic and confrontational, more compromising, and more highly educated. The level of political skills of the fourth generation also was questioned.[12]

Composed of technocrats, economists, managers, and other professionals, the fourth generation was seen as likely to be more capable and innovative than previous leaders when confronted with economic and social problems; their behavior was seen as likely to be more technically competent and pragmatic when dealing with domestic and foreign policies. Despite being more highly schooled than their predecessors and the beneficiaries of numerous and varied exchanges with the United States and other countries, the forthcoming leaders had a limited understanding of the West.[13]

The institutionalization of China's politics was the result of a proliferation of institutions from the top down. Accompanying this growth in the number of institutions was a distinct break with the Maoist past as evidenced by growing regularization and routinization. Chinese Communist Party (CCP) and National People's Congress (NPC) sessions and plenums were regularly scheduled and held since the late 1970s, and planning and budgetary cycles were adhered to. The principles of class struggle were replaced by budgets geared to a socialist market economy and political constituencies. Socialist laws continued to be promulgated, although enforcement remained problematic. Some experts argued that however important institutionalization was, one of the most significant changes in China's political landscape was occurring outside of the state—the growth of civil society amid the increasing wealth and influence of businesspeople and academics. On July 1, 2001, China's party leader Jiang Zemin made a major speech advocating recruiting such wealthy and influential people into the party's ranks. His injunction was followed at the sixteenth Party Congress in November 2002. A stabilizing factor, increasing institutionalization meant less arbitrary decision making. A disadvantage was that China's current and future leaders might not be as decisive as Mao Zedong or Deng Xiaoping because they were hemmed in by the growing bureaucracy and procedures.[14]

The military had less representation at the top-level CCP Politburo. Some Western specialists approved this development, but others saw a bifurcation between the CCP and the People's Liberation Army (PLA). This trend also occurred in the Soviet Union before its demise and was viewed as a possible precursor to future instability in China. An urban, educated elite, the leadership was civilian based: only two of the twenty-four members of the fifteenth Communist Party Congress Central Committee Politburo and the sixteenth Communist Party Central Committee Politburo had military experience or could be considered "military politicians." The majority of Politburo members had experience in the more modernized, coastal provinces. Experts pondered the meaning of the civilian majority and some wondered if the military would be able to muster sufficient support for its modernization programs, though evidence of China's steady military buildup showed strong leadership support behind military modernization.[15]

Leadership succession, nepotism and favoritism, and increased corruption were serious problems. Though China's politics were becoming more stable and predictable, with battles being fought on the institutional level, personal rivalries and relations remained important and could not be ignored. Jiang Zemin's ability at the sixteenth Party Congress to avoid complete retirement by retaining the chairmanship of the party's Central Military Commission, and his show of power in ensuring that the new Politburo Standing Committee had a majority of members personally loyal to him, illustrated these points.[16]

Economic and Social Trends

Economic growth continued to outpace population growth, continuing the overall rise in the standard of living that characterized Chinese development over the previous two decades. A relatively young, highly trained labor force with modern technical skills increased in numbers. The infrastructure of rail, roads, and electronic communications greatly reduced perceived distance and helped to link the poorly developed interior to the booming coastal regions. Chinese development remained heavily dependent, and would deepen its dependency on foreign trade, investments, and scientific/technical exchange. The regime faced daunting problems—notably ailing SOEs and a weak banking/financial system. Also worrisome were the increasing number of unemployed and laid-off workers, the divestiture of military enterprises, and bad loans and bankruptcies. The leadership took concrete steps to remedy a few but certainly not all of these problems and weaknesses.[17]

One result of China's external outreach was the growing importance of ministries with responsibility in foreign affairs, such as the Ministry of Foreign Affairs (MOFA) and the Ministry of Foreign Trade and Economic Cooperation (MOFTEC). The latter, especially, became more important as Beijing joined the WTO. The ministry changed its name in 2003 to become China's Commerce Ministry. Central regulatory bodies such as the State Economic and Trade Commission (SETC) also became more important. The old bureaucracies and their stakeholders associated with the planning system, such as the State Planning Commission (SPC), became less important and had to reorganize themselves for alternative functions. As China instituted a market economy to be successful, the changes this approach created in society clashed with the very nature of Communist ideology and the authoritarian political system favored by many Chinese officials and other opinion leaders and interests.[18]

Manifestations of social discontent seen in recent years with demonstrating peasants, laid-off workers, and Falungong sect members continued, but these developments seemed to have a long way to go before they posed a major threat to the regime. Notably, they needed to establish communications across broad areas, establish alliances with other disaffected groups, and put forth leaders prepared to challenge the regime and gain popular support with credible moral claims. Success also required a lax or maladroit regime response. The attentiveness of the regime to dissidence and the crackdown on the Falungong strongly suggested that Beijing remained keenly alert to the implications of social discontent and prepared to use its substantial coercive and persuasive powers to keep it from growing to dangerous levels.

A variety of sources of social tension and conflict in China presented opportunities for expressions of discontent. Groups that could have exploited such tensions included those people living in the poorer interior provinces (versus the richer coastal regions), ethnic minorities, farmers, members of the unemployed or underemployed floating population, laid-off state-enterprise workers and other laid-off workers, students and intellectuals, and members of sects such as the Falungong.[19]

Security and Foreign Policies

China remained dependent on its economic connections with the developed countries of the West, Japan, and its Asian neighbors. Nonetheless, Chinese nationalism was in the lead among forces in China that exerted pressure to push policy in directions that resisted U.S. "hegemony," the power of the United States, and U.S. allies in East Asia, notably Japan and Taiwan. Chinese leaders resolved these contrasting pressures by attempting to stay on good terms with its neighbors and by keeping open economic and other channels with the United States, while endeavoring to weaken overall U.S. power and influence in Asia and elsewhere in its long-term attempt to create a more "multipolar" world. Military modernization adopted a more rapid pace, posing some challenge to the already modern and advancing militaries of the United States and its allies and associates in East Asia, especially in such nearby areas as Taiwan, where the Chinese development of ballistic and cruise missiles and acquisition of advanced Russian weaponry posed notable dangers.[20]

China also saw a challenging international security environment and was apprehensive about several international security trends. It was particularly concerned about the perceived U.S. "containment" and military "encirclement" of China, U.S. national and theater missile defense programs, and the potential for Japan to improve its regional force projection capabilities. A drawback for China of the U.S.-led antiterrorism campaign was that it sharply increased U.S. influence and presence along China's western periphery—adding to Beijing's overall sense of being surrounded by U.S. power and influence. Despite some successes in military modernization, the PLA remained limited in its ability to quickly absorb sophisticated weapon systems and to develop the joint operations doctrine necessary to use these weapons effectively.[21]

Taiwan, however, was China's main security focus, and it was the biggest problem, both politically and militarily, in China-U.S. relations. The issues of continuing U.S. arms sales and missile defense deployments in the region remained problematic for the future. China and the United States attempted to find common ground and interest in rebuilding relations in the wake of the 1999 Belgrade embassy bombing, and they did so again following the downturn in relations resulting from the EP-3 incident of 2001. Beijing continued to press for reunification with Taiwan. China's overtures to South Korea and elsewhere in East Asia were a possible counter to Washington's moves vis-à-vis Taiwan.[22]

The Importance of Regime Survival

Regime survival remained the core concern of China's leaders. The balance sheet of challenges facing the regime and strengths of the regime argued for its continuing in power, though there was considerable debate among specialists about the future and directions of China's rulers. The array of political, social, and economic pressures facing China's authoritarian regime seriously challenged the regime's legitimacy and survival. However, the Communist regime's residual power, coercive capabilities, and other strengths still outweighed its weaknesses.[23]

The sweeping structural changes necessitated by the WTO entry and the broader demands of economic globalization and the information revolution generated significantly new levels and types of social and economic disruption that added to an already wide range of domestic and international problems. The cumulative impact of these steep challenges seriously tested the capacity of China's system and the competence and unity of a leadership already stressed by maneuvering for the sixteenth Chinese Communist Party Congress in 2002. Developing succession arrangements and policies that sustained leadership unity, advantageous economic growth, and a modicum of popular support was essential to regime continuity.[24]

The Communist regime retained important strengths that it would exploit to manage this increasingly complex and growing set of challenges:

- Generally pragmatic leaders under Jiang Zemin were in the process of passing power to equally pragmatic and technologically knowledgeable successors headed by Hu Jintao.
- The Communist leadership maintained the command of strong military, police, and other security forces, and used them against dissident political and social movements, the Falungong, ethnic separatists, and other perceived opponents.
- There was no clear alternative to Communist rule, and there remained strong popular and elite aversion to fragmentation or chaos that could accompany regime change. Popular acquiescence to regime authority also came from the positive performance of the economy, which continued to grow amid a mixed revival of Asian economies following the regional downturn during the late 1990s. China's economic management and reforms were sufficiently sound so as to provide the regime the basis for maintaining a degree of legitimacy.[25]

These strengths, however, were arrayed against the party's growing weaknesses and challenges:

- Jiang Zemin's intention to remain in a senior leadership position while seeking the retirement of many of his Politburo Standing Committee colleagues headed the list of potentially fractious succession issues. Leadership tensions over these issues were highest in the period leading to the 2002 Party Congress, but continued thereafter.

- Decisions on economic opening and reform required by the WTO benefited some Chinese groups while disadvantaging others, increasing the risk of leadership divisions. Other economic problems included massive debt, lagging reforms of SOEs, financial sector weaknesses, rising inequalities, large-scale unemployment, and the inadequacy of the national welfare and health system. These problems remained interlocked, with reforms helping development in one area while having negative consequences in others, thus offering no easy solutions.
- Though the Communist Party was able to recruit some talented newcomers, ideological commitment remained very weak despite recent efforts to reinvigorate ideological training and propaganda. Rampant corruption at all levels of party and state authority added to widespread disaffection among elite and popular opinion.
- Economic change went hand in hand with social changes, producing increasing pressure on the regime to adjust its policies. The flexibility of the regime in adapting to new trends continued to be tested, with high potential for further dissonance between citizens and government and greater instability in both urban and rural areas. Aggrieved and disaffected groups present in all parts of society continued demonstrations and work stoppages. The Chinese government's initial handling of the epidemic caused by Severe Acute Respiratory Syndrome (SARS) in 2003 was widely seen as inept and prompted wide-ranging popular protests and other manifestations of concern. Democratic activists, ethnic separatists, and religious believers outside official channels continued to push the limits of the regime's tolerance for their behavior.[26]

Seeking continued economic engagement with the rest of the world, PRC leaders continued to try—with little success—to control entry of perceived adverse outside information and other sources of pressure that came with greater economic openness and information exchange. Taiwan's separate status and democratic example fundamentally challenged regime legitimacy and added to leadership debate, as to a lesser degree did the example of Hong Kong's greater freedoms. U.S. and other international pressure in support of principles championed by ethnic and democratic activists in China combined with the strengthening U.S. strategic posture to appear to Beijing as a challenge to regime goals.[27]

Over time, certain factors appeared posed to cause China to become more stable or less stable. Any one factor by itself probably was insufficient to produce significant regime change, but a combination could.[28]

Leadership

Leadership unity probably was the most important factor determining regime stability. Tests of the leadership were particularly acute in 2002-2003 as many top leaders retired and passed power to the next generation. A failure to accomplish this transition smoothly—or to choose a competent core of new leaders who inspired some level of popular confidence—would have increased greatly the prospects for political crisis.[29]

Civil-military tensions could have risen. Despite Jiang's efforts to win loyalty with appointments over the past decade—through which many in the new PLA hierarchy were beholden to him at least to some degree—his personal lack of military experience limited his own authority. This was true for his successor as president and party chief, Hu Jintao, even as Jiang remained as chairman of the party's Central Military Commission. Potential also existed for growing and serious policy differences, particularly if military leaders believed that the civilian leadership was risking sovereignty over Taiwan by reluctance to turn to military options.[30]

In addition to some anticipated Chinese leadership differences over policy preferences, many Western specialists also anticipated some divergence based on organizational perspective. The membership of the CCP, over sixty million, was larger than the population of France, yet it was a small elite (around 3 percent) when compared with China's total population. The party was responsible for making decisions and for overseeing their implementation. Over the years, the large bureaucracies that administered the party and the government acquired institutional interests and positions that frequently conflicted. The struggles over turf and primacy became reflected in policy debates in the party. Struggles over budgets, for example, led to winners and losers, as did struggles over reform and reorganization. These led to bureaucratic rivalry and leadership dissension.[31]

Beyond policy and organizational differences was that characteristic of single-party authoritarian regimes, the problem of endemic personal factionalism. Personal loyalty networks (*guanxi*) were pervasive in the CCP and often supplanted organizational hierarchy. At the sixteenth Congress in 2002, at least twelve of the twenty-one Politburo members reached the mandatory retirement age of seventy, including five of the seven Standing Committee members. Competition was heated to ensure placement of protégés and continued influence, with Jiang Zemin exerting extraordinary influence to safeguard his continuation in power and the ascendancy of his key protégés.[32] Media reporting in 2002 indicated continuing ferment in the leadership on the future role of Jiang Zemin, who was due to retire at the sixteenth Party Congress. Some reporting indicated Jiang tried to stay on as General Secretary. Other reporting indicated he was grooming Vice President Hu Jintao as his successor. Still other accounts suggested Zeng Qinghong, a close ally of Jiang Zemin and head of the CCP Central Committee General Office, might challenge Hu as Jiang's successor.[33] Personal animosity between Premier Zhu Rongji and National People's Congress Chairman Li Peng (both members of the fifteenth Party Congress Politburo Standing Committee) was strong; it probably intensified as the sixteenth CCP Congress approached and they worked to get people who were loyal to them promoted.

Based on these factors, various questions and forms of divergence continued to challenge China's leadership, including:

- Given Jiang's staying on in power and promoting protégés to the Politburo Standing Committee, the transition in 2002 and 2003 was not seen as accomplished or complete. The potential for stalemate or open airing of differences could grow if leaders were faced with serious policy crises or competition for power.
- To what degree the PLA should be involved in formulating policy and participating in personnel appointments.
- How to manage economic growth and development and their uneven effects, as well as how to adjust internal economic policies to accommodate the WTO.
- To what degree to use force or persuasion in dealing with Taiwan.
- How to deal with the outside world, including pressures from the United States, Japan, Taiwan, North Korea, and others. For example, leaders could have diverged on how to respond to U.S. decisions on the deployment of theater and national missile defenses.

An ability to minimize the destructive effects of factionalism and limit its disruptiveness to policy was evidence of a stronger and more cohesive China. On the other hand, economic decline and external pressures were likely catalysts for unconstrained factionalism, which could lead to violent strife.[34]

Economic Change

A different pace of economic growth had different consequences. Rapid economic growth could have:

- Led to opportunities for the regime to build greater popular support by creating new jobs and achieving a distribution of wealth that reflects well on government policies.
- Enabled new economic elites with control of resources to emerge, which would sharpen class distinctions.
- Shifted the debate between the center and the provinces over the control of budget spending.
- Led to inflation, a catalyst for mass protests in the past. Moreover, if rapid growth were the result of a return to unsound government investment and forced bank lending, existing problems with SOEs and the financial sector would worsen.

Slow economic growth probably would have:

- Increased joblessness and contributed to social tension by heightening the anxieties of "have-nots."
- Limited the ability of the government to reduce poverty levels in urban and rural areas.

- Sharpened conflict among the leadership over priorities for scarcer budgets, including competition between the center and regions for revenues.[35]

Although low economic growth was bad for the regime, better-than-expected growth was not all good, mainly because of the authoritarian nature of the regime. Much depended on how well the growth or decline was managed by the government. For example, good growth could produce structural shifts in the economy and rising expectations that include political liberalization and demands for greater leadership accountability. Such pressure could have negatively affected political stability.

The Impact of the Information Revolution

China continued to experience profoundly the effects of the information revolution. Telecommunication was growing rapidly. According to estimates, China had over one hundred million cell phones in use in 2003 and the number of Internet users probably was around eighty million. Communications analysts believed the rapid growth of wireless access to the Internet would expand dramatically in the next few years. Despite efforts of the Chinese government to control access to the Internet, the amount of information flowing freely in China increased exponentially. Some business publications predicted that online commerce would grow rapidly.[36]

The challenge to the government's ability to control information seemed clear. For example, the China Democracy Party organized some of its activities in 1998-1999 by cell phone, Internet, and fax. News of the SARS epidemic traveled widely over these unofficial channels during the first months of 2003, despite the authorities' efforts to curb coverage of the issue. Government propaganda machinery and controlled media increasingly competed with other sources of information for public attention.[37]

The social and political consequences of the development of the Internet, though not entirely predictable, further weakened authoritarian controls, but the Chinese government encouraged increased communications as the price of economic modernization. As the party recruited technical specialists, they seemed likely to press for changes in the party's policies toward information management. How rapidly the party adjusted to this reality would influence its control of the nation.[38]

The External Environment

Changes in the external environment caused shifts in Chinese domestic policy. Particularly important was how China perceived the threat from abroad. Although they no longer saw a major military threat to China's national security, Chinese leaders saw influence from the outside world as constituting a major threat to China's stability; many of their comments about this threat appeared to be exaggerated rhetoric designed in part to justify a firm party grip. This perception of threat could intensify and have important implications for domestic priorities. China also was concerned about the influence of Islamic countries on ethnic minorities in Xinjiang and other parts of northwest and southwest China, and this in part led China to support the U.S.-led antiterrorist campaign after September 11, 2001.[39]

Growing tensions across the Taiwan Strait and over North Korea, in the territorial disputes with Japan, India, and in the South China Sea, or other areas near China could increase China's perception of threat and result in more coercive security policies at home. Stronger disputes with the United States probably would have a similar effect. The recent record showed Chinese leaders were relatively unconstrained in using force to crack down on internal dissidents or suppressing public discussion of foreign policy issues without regard to foreign reaction. In circumstances of growing tensions with the United States or nearby powers, it seemed likely that the use of nationalistic propaganda would become more evident.[40]

Other external developments also could have had a significant effect on China's internal stability:

- Foreign economic developments often helped or hindered China's economic growth. An increased ability to absorb China's exports fostered growth, but recessions among China's key trading partners or a significant drop-off in foreign direct investment hurt growth and contributed to social problems in China.
- Cultural change abroad spilled over into China. China's opening to outside cultural influence, including television, music, and other media, probably amplified dissent, notably among youth, especially if the regime did not permit greater openness and pluralism.
- Chinese efforts to host international events such as the 2008 Olympics were a source of pride and nationalism but also risked further opening to outside influence. Beijing's failed bid for the 2000 Olympics became a source of political tension with the United States and other Western countries; success in winning the bid to host the 2008 Olympics avoided the wounded vanity seen previously.[41]

Strategic Objectives—China's Role in Recent World Affairs

With regime survival as the leaders' top priority, Chinese government policies and practices reflected certain long-range goals and objectives that existed in China for decades and seemed likely to continue well into the twenty-first century. Chinese leaders appeared to have reached consensus on these objectives although they frequently did not agree on the means to achieve them.[42]

To recap, Chinese leaders continued to share certain overarching objectives:

- They sought to perpetuate their power and avoid the fate of the Soviet Union and other East European Communist regimes.
- They pursued territorial unification and integrity, especially Taiwan and, to a lesser degree, claims in the East and South China Seas.
- They also sought to modernize China's economy, technology, and military capabilities and improve social conditions while maintaining stability.

In addition, China had strategic objectives that reflected its status as a rising power.

- *Regional preeminence.* Although U.S. and other foreign specialists differed fairly widely on China's regional and world goals, a middle-range view saw China's leaders wanting to be in a position of sufficient strength (with both positive and negative incentives—carrots and sticks) so that other countries in the region would routinely take China's interests and equities into account in determining their own policies. Beijing wished to be seen as the leading power in Asia and not as lower in prestige or regional influence than neighbors. It also wished to be able to project power out sufficient to counter hostile naval and air power.
- *Global influence.* Representatives of a permanent member of the United Nations Security Council, China's leaders desired status and prestige among the community of nations. They intended to be a major player in the International Monetary Fund, the World Bank, the WTO, and other key international institutions. They sought to assert influence on issues that were deemed important to China, not only to protect and defend Chinese interests but also to bolster China's standing as a major power. Chinese leaders believed that international power and prestige were an extension of national economic and technological prowess, which they intended to develop.

China's Perceptions of Power Relations in the Post-Cold War World

China's officials approached these broad strategic objectives in an international environment where Chinese leaders tended to view China's influence as growing but far from dominant, and where external and internal factors limited China's assertiveness in world affairs.

Chinese leaders' pursuit of the above-noted goals—especially those dealing with China's role in Asian and world affairs—were heavily influenced by Chinese leaders' perceptions of China in the overall power relations after the Cold War. At the start of the twenty-first century, Chinese perceptions of global trends appeared to be in flux and a matter of considerable internal debate. Chinese leaders and academics, as reflected in official comment, had believed the world was becoming multipolar, with the United States as the single superpower but increasingly less able to exert its will as other countries and regions opposed U.S. initiatives. This view changed sharply in the mid- to late 1990s, owing to the striking disparities between U.S. economic performance and that of other major powers and also to U.S. leadership in the Balkans crisis, U.S. policy on missile defense, the U.S. war on terrorism, and other issues.[43]

The Chinese apparently concluded that the world would be unipolar in the near term, with the United States exerting greater influence than Chinese commentators had originally calculated. Chinese leaders often perceived that this influence might not be benign vis-à-vis China's core interests, notably Taiwan. They were ambivalent about the spread of U.S. influence along China's flank in Central Asia as a result of the U.S.-led antiterrorism campaign of 2001-2002.[44] Chinese commentary expressed concern about the expansion and strengthening of the U.S. alliance structure and the ability of U.S.-led alliances to intervene globally. Chinese officials worried that the Kosovo intervention had implications for China; they particularly were concerned that the United States could use this precedent to justify intervention in Tibet or Taiwan. Chinese officials judged that China therefore had to be on guard to counter actions by the United States or its expanded alliance structure that were detrimental to Chinese interests.[45] Chinese officials also were particularly anxious about what was perceived as a strengthening U.S.-Japanese military relationship and the potential for revived Japanese militarism. The acceleration of either trend was seen as likely to alarm China.[46]

Despite China's turn from traditional Marxist-Leninist-Maoist ideology, there remained components of this tradition that continued to influence the thinking of some leaders. Some Chinese officials saw themselves locked in a struggle of values with the West, and particularly the United States, which they saw as bent on dividing or "Westernizing" China. China, the last major Communist state, was seen by these Chinese officials as on the defensive. More common was the long-standing Chinese tendency to focus on a primary adversary in world affairs, to exaggerate its threat to China, and to seek domestic and foreign power to offset and counter this threat. Patterns of behavior reflecting this tendency were seen repeatedly in Chinese leaders' policies and behavior toward the United States and U.S. interests in Asia in the post-Cold War period.[47]

China's Role in Defining the International Environment. Preoccupied with domestic issues of modernization and stability, Chinese leaders tended to see China primarily as reactive to international developments. Deng Xiaoping stated that China should not get out in front on key issues but should take advantage of opportunities, bide its time, and gradually build Chinese power and influence; his successors generally held to this view. In international forums (the UN, WTO, arms control, and other arenas), however, China increasingly tried to ensure that it was one of the rule-makers for the global environment of the twenty-first century and China became notably more active in multilateral and other world forums.[48] Beijing also perceived that it had to continue to build its military capabilities to be able eventually to back up its diplomacy with the threat of force, especially over the status of Taiwan.[49]

Threats to China's National Security. Chinese statements averred that the overall external military threat to China was significantly less than it was during the Cold War. Chinese commentary and official pronouncements nevertheless perceived, or believed it had to foster the impression, that internal threats to its stability were often encouraged from the outside. China was convinced that the United States, directly or indirectly, interfered with Beijing's ability to recover Taiwan and maintain control in Tibet and even Xinjiang.[50]

The United States as Colleague, Competitor, and Adversary. China's leaders saw elements of each of these roles in its relations with the United States. The two sides spoke of building a "strategic partnership" after 1997, but this ended with the start of the Bush administration. At the same time, China saw the United States as a competitor, partly in reaction to perceived anti-China rhetoric and action by the United States. State-fostered education in nationalism was accompanied by the widespread perception among Chinese that the United States was behind many of China's problems:

- Chinese leaders saw the need to construct a U.S. policy that protected China's economic interests while resisting what they saw as the domination of U.S. security arrangements.
- Nevertheless, the prevailing view of China's leaders was that China should not risk opposing the United States directly.
- Beijing also saw many areas of common ground with U.S. policy, notably regarding the broad-gauge objective of both countries to promote regional and world stability, encourage greater economic development, and combat such common threats as terrorism and narcotics trafficking.[51]

Other Key Players in the International Environment. In commentary and official pronouncements, China perceived that such international organizations as the United Nations, the IMF, World Bank, and the WTO were becoming increasingly important to its interests of economic development and political stature, but remained dominated by the United States and other Western powers. Regional players in Asia and Europe also were seen able to hinder or help China achieve its goals and thus were important to China. Although China wanted to bolster its status in the developing countries, it was clear-eyed about their generally low relevance to its core interests, except when such issues as recognition of Taiwan and the security of Chinese borders were at issue.[52]

General Consensus among the Leadership. Chinese statements regarding foreign and international security policy suggested that Chinese leaders for the most part saw the importance for China's strength and development of trying to reach consensus on international questions and thereafter mute differences, at least in public. When differences did arise, they more likely were over how to solve problems rather than over the nature of the problems themselves. Such differences arose from bureaucratic and institutional interests as well as from personal rivalries and policy preferences of senior leaders. Unlike in the Maoist period, however, such differences did not rise to the level of strong factionalism over strategic priorities. The pressures arising from China's domestic environment, the overarching desire for stability, and the cautious style of decision making pushed toward consensus, or at least acquiescence, rather than factionalism.[53]

The Imperative of Economic Growth and Political and Social Stability. Chinese leaders generally accepted the importance of economic growth and domestic stability and perceived that China continued to face significant economic, political, and social problems. These problems were seen as likely to preoccupy Chinese leaders and incline them to persist with a cautious approach to foreign affairs that avoided initiatives or other actions that would complicate dealing with the daunting agenda of domestic issues.

- Economic reform, particularly of state-owned enterprises and the ailing financial system, was a key challenge. Further progress on reform complemented and benefited from China's WTO membership and participation and foreign direct investment and trade. Interaction with the West was widely seen as necessary for sustaining economic reform in China.
- China would continue to resort to widespread coercive measures when deemed necessary to maintain social stability as was evidenced by the crackdown on Falungong. Chinese leaders, based on China's historical experience, believed foreign interests encouraged domestic opposition to the government. Part of the cost of economic interaction was increased exposure to outside influence, and China had to balance heightened concern about internal social stability with economic benefit. This contradiction heightened Chinese suspicion of and hesitation in various forms of interaction with the West.
- China wanted to manage the effects of economic change by improving the legal system. Progress in this regard was likely as China retained a high priority on engagement with the outside world. Such progress alleviated outside pressure on China to improve business practices.[54]

Military Capabilities. Many key leaders, especially in the military, perceived that China needed to devote more resources to military modernization. Their argument, reinforced by perceptions of the U.S.-led intervention in Kosovo, U.S. increased support for Taiwan, and demonstrations of U.S. military power in Afghanistan and Iraq, was that countries without strong military capabilities would be threatened and intimidated by the countries that have such capabilities. Furthermore, they argued that action was needed now because of the long lead-times required to develop military strength. They were especially sensitive of the need to have a military capable of dealing with Taiwan contingencies and to secure China's other territorial interests.[55]

China's programmed conventional and strategic improvements—aided by substantial Russian and Israeli assistance—provided increased capacity for coercion against Taiwan and for asserting Chinese claims in the South and East China Seas. The tenth Year Plan (2000-2005) resulted in additional resources for these goals.

Strategic Behavior—China's Role in World Affairs

The mix of Chinese goals and Chinese leaders' perceptions regarding Asian and world affairs influenced China's strategic behavior. Chinese actions abroad duly took account of domestic priorities of stability and economic growth. Consensus —following a risk-adverse approach that usually represented the lowest common denominator among senior Chinese leaders—appeared to be the norm in dealing with the outside world. Such an approach emphasized nationalism and took a skeptical view of free interchange with the West.

China's leaders, however, sought to advance growing international interests. China not only reacted to events in the international environment, but also asserted China's influence as opportunities arose. In particular, Chinese leaders appeared to calibrate actions to those of the United States as well as those of Taiwan, Japan, and other countries around China's periphery and in other locales where China had important equities.

Preventing Taiwan's Independence. The PRC's long-term objective remained reunification, but for the next several years Beijing's priority was to prevent further Taiwan steps toward permanent separation. There remained a distinct possibility that China would conduct a major military exercise near Taiwan as it did in March 1996. Also, there was a chance that there would be small-scale incidents between the military forces of the two sides ranging from an accidental air incident to the seizure by Beijing of a lightly manned offshore island. Chances remained low, however, that Beijing would actually follow through with such large-scale combat operations as invading Taiwan or a heavily defended offshore island, conducting missile attacks against targets on Taiwan, or blockading Taiwan with air or naval forces. At bottom, Beijing did not have the military ability to carry out these operations successfully.[56]

Sustain Economic Growth and Manage Its Consequences. Economic growth was equal to stability as a priority, but these goals were sometimes contradictory.

- The reform of state-owned enterprises (SOEs) continued to be gradual because it was difficult to accomplish and because China's leaders feared that increasingly high levels of unemployment would lead to instability.
- China encouraged foreign participation in the economy but tried to limit the effects; bureaucratic measures were used to control what was perceived as foreign ability to manipulate the economy. The leadership also sought to control the social effects of foreign participation.[57]
- As noted previously, Chinese authorities escalated the use of coercion when they believed social stability was at risk.

Enhance Military Capabilities. China's leaders perceived that China needed a long period of peace and stability to improve the economic foundation of its national power. China continued to see that economic growth was the basis of military power but starting in the 1990s increasingly accorded the improvement of military capabilities a higher priority than previously. China's adjustments stemmed from its evaluation of external events such as the results of the Kosovo intervention and because of the perceived implications of Taiwan's separatism. A key component of the military priority was to sustain the credibility of China's strategic nuclear and missile capabilities in the face of advancing American technology.

China was increasing defense expenditures, and this trend continued or even strengthened at the end of the 1990s and the start of the new decade. Although competing priorities arose from economic and social objectives, the government nevertheless was able to devote additional resources to military modernization. China, long disappointed by its underperforming defense industries, continued to rely heavily on Russia and Israel for advanced weapons and production technologies. China also tried to obtain military technology from the United States, Europe, Japan, and elsewhere via purchase, joint ventures, or espionage.

Emphasizing quality over quantity, China's conventional military acquisitions were designed to counter U.S. and Taiwan military capabilities that could be brought to bear in a Taiwan Strait crisis, to advance China's claims in the East and South China Seas, and generally project Chinese regional power. China emphasized missile, naval, and air modernization, because its military specialists identified these as its most immediate needs.[58] China also developed its strategic programs, information warfare, and electronic countermeasures.[59]

Regarding proliferation of WMD and related delivery systems and technologies, China continued to engage in some sales of military equipment and technology not to the liking of the United States. Beijing at times used proliferation behavior in part as a tool to influence U.S. decisions on weapons sales to Taiwan.[60]

Regional Preeminence. China promoted Asian regional stability—that is, stability according to Beijing's definition. Besides preventing Taiwan's steps to independence, China's priorities in Asia were:

- Counter Japan's growing military cooperation with the United States and prevent a rebirth of Japanese "militarism." But at the same time engage Japan to obtain economic benefit.
- Maintain stability on the Korean peninsula while engaging South Korea without further straining ties to North Korea. Curb North Korea's nuclear weapons program without resorting to war or steps that would result in major instability on the Korean peninsula.
- Prevent the development and implementation of theater missile defense in the region.
- Cope with challenges to Chinese claims in the East and South China Seas.
- Support China's economic interests via bilateral and multilateral mechanisms, while building its political influence in and avoiding challenges from a coalition of states via ASEAN, APEC, or the ARF.

The United States remained central to these regional priorities. Consequently, Beijing's actions in the region reflected its assessment of U.S. policies, particularly with respect to U.S. alliance relations including South Korea and Japan. While recognizing the centrality of the United States, China tried to marginalize Washington when opportunities arose. It had tried to keep U.S. influence out of Central Asia and along China's western flank, but felt compelled to reverse course and endorse the upswing in U.S. influence there as part of the antiterrorist campaign after September 11, 2001.[61]

Global Influence. Chinese leaders continued to seek to enhance China's stature as a global power, not only because it wanted the prestige but also because it believed that dealing with the United States and Taiwan, economic development, and other priorities required a position of global strength. Yet China recognized the pitfalls of multilateralism, especially competition with U.S.-led coalitions within the UN and elsewhere. China preferred bilateral diplomacy but also continued to expand its engagement in multilateral institutions because it believed international stature requires such participation and that multilateralism at times served as a check on unbridled power politics, especially by the U.S. superpower.[62]

- China increasingly wanted to influence how international rules were developed and enforced. Beijing wanted to have a voice in the WTO and sought other opportunities to exploit multilateral organizations when the risks and costs appeared to be low.
- China joined the U.S.-led coalition against terrorism in part to steer the campaign in directions that did not jeopardize important Chinese interests.
- China traditionally portrayed itself as a developing country and probably attached some priority to acting under the mantle of the "Third World" when the costs were low. Beijing continued to give high priority to competing with Taiwan for international recognition, even in remote Third World areas, and

it broadened its worldwide search for economic opportunities and efforts to promote China's international influence and stature.

China preferred to avoid concrete diplomatic and military initiatives that confronted important U.S. interests and accepted international norms. For example, Beijing did not see a major advantage in advancing cooperation with Russia to reestablish an alliance. China, however, supported states like Iran and Libya that often were anti-U.S. in order to foster a range of Chinese objectives.

In Europe, the Middle East, and the rest of the developing world, China's commercial and strategic interests expanded. Some of its interests—use of sea-lanes for oil supplies, market access, and discouraging export of Islamic fundamentalism, for example—paralleled those of the United States. But competition with the United States for markets, oil supplies, and influence at other times also led China to work against U.S. policies.

Much of China's effort in the Third World seemed designed to compete diplomatically with Taiwan for recognition and to seek opportunities for trade and arms sales. Until mid-2001, China frequently orchestrated denunciations of "hegemonism," a term Beijing commonly applied to American actions and influence beyond the U.S. alliance structures.

Notes

1. Jane Perlez, "China Is Romping with the Neighbors (U.S. is Distracted)," *New York Times*, 3 December 2003 (Internet version); James Przystup, "A Different China When U.S. Refocuses on Asia," *Straits Times,* 12 December 2003 (Internet version); John Pomfret, "In Its Own Neighborhood, China Emerges as a Leader," *Washington Post*, 18 October 2001 (Internet version); Jane Perlez, "China Races to Replace U.S. as Economic Power in Asia," *New York Times*, June 27, 2002 (Internet version); Elaine Kurtenbach, "China Emerges as Possible U.S. Partner," *AP*, 21 October 2003 (Internet version).

2. Joseph Fewsmith, *China After Tiananmen* (Cambridge: Cambridge University Press, 2001), 159-89.

3. H. Lyman Miller and Liu Xiaohong, "The Foreign Policy Outlook of China's 'Third Generation' Elite," in David M. Lampton, ed., *The Making of Chinese Foreign and Security Policy* (Stanford, Calif.: Stanford University Press, 2001), 143-50.

4. Robert Sutter, *Chinese Policy Priorities and Their Implications for the United States* (Lanham, Md.: Rowman & Littlefield, 2000), 18.

5. See, among others, Barry Naughton, "China's Economy: Buffeted from Within and Without," *Current History* (September 1998): 273-78.

6. Joseph Fewsmith, "China in 1998," *Asian Survey* 39, no. 1(January-February 1999): 99-113.

7. Cheng Li, "Fourth Generation Leadership in the PRC," in *China's Future: Implications for U.S. Interests* (Washington, D.C.: U.S. National Intelligence Council, Conference Report CR99-02), 13-36, www.odci.gov/nic (accessed 15 July 2002).

72   *Chapter 2*

8. Catherin Dalpino and Bates Gill, eds., *Brookings Northeast Asia Survey 2000-2001* (Washington, D.C.: Brookings Institution, 2001), 53-56; Jean-Pierre Cabestan, "The Tenth National People's Congress and After," *China Perspectives* 47 (May-June 2003): 4-20.

9. Thomas Christensen, "China," in Richard Ellings and Aaron Friedberg, eds., *Strategic Asia: Power and Purpose, 2001-2002* (Seattle, Wash.: National Bureau of Asian Research, 2001), 27-70; Christensen, "China," in Richard Ellings and Aaron Friedberg, eds., *Strategic Asia: Power and Purpose, 2002-2003* (Seattle, Wash.: National Bureau of Asian Research, 2002), 51-94.

10. See the differing views in *China's Future*. For background, see Richard Bernstein and Ross Munro, *The Coming Conflict with China* (New York: Knopf, 1996), and Andrew Nathan and Robert Ross, *The Great Wall and Empty Fortress* (New York: Norton, 1997).

11. Cheng Li, "Fourth Generation Leadership," in *China's Future*, 13-36.

12. Robert Sutter, "Introduction and Findings," in *China's Future*, 1-5.

13. Cheng Li, "Fourth Generation Leadership," in *China's Future*, 13-36; Cheng Li, *China's New Leaders* (Lanham, Md.: Rowman & Littlefield, 2001).

14. H. Lyman Miller, "Institutions in Chinese Politics: Trends and Prospects," in *China's Future*, 37-48. See Miller's quarterly assessments of these issues in *China Leadership Monitor*, www.chinaleadershipmonitor.org.

15. Sutter, "Introduction and Findings," *China's Future*, 1-5; Wei-chin Lee, "China's Military after the Sixteenth Party Congress," *Journal of Asian and African Studies* 38, no. 4-5 (December 2003): 416-46.

16. H. Lyman Miller, "Chinese Leadership Transition: The First Stage," *Chinese Leadership Monitor*, Issue 5, www.chinaleadershipmonitor.org (Winter 2003) (accessed 28 June 2004).

17. Fewsmith, "China in 1998," *Asian Survey*, 99-113; Cheng Li, "China in 1999," *Asian Survey* 40, no. 1 (January-February 2000): 112-29; Cheng Li, "China in 2000," *Asian Survey* 41, no. 1 (January-February 2001): 71-90; Peter Chow, "China's Sustainable Development in Global Perspective," *Journal of Asian and African Studies* 38, no. 4-5 (December 2003): 392-415.

18. Miller and Liu Xiaohong, "China's 'Third Generation' Elite," in Lampton, *Chinese Foreign and Security Policy*.

19. Martin King Whyte, "Chinese Social Trends: Stability or Chaos," in *China's Future*, 67-84; Tony Saich, *Governance and Politics of China* (London: Palgrave, 2002), 194-211; *Journal of Democracy* 14, no. 1 (January 2003, entire issue).

20. Mark Stokes, "Weapons of Precise Destruction: PLA Space and Theater Missile Defense," in *China and Weapons of Mass Destruction: Implications for the United States* (Washington, D.C.: U.S. National Intelligence Council, Conference Report CR99-05), 183-236, www.odci.gov/nic (accessed April 2000); U.S. Department of Defense, *Annual Report on the Military Power of the People's Republic of China, 2003*, www.defenselink.mil (accessed 10 September 2003).

21. David Shambaugh, "The Future of China's Foreign Relations and Security Posture, 2000-2005," in *China's Future*, 85-103; Ralph Cossa, "Is China the Odd Man Out?" *Japan Times*, 1 November 2001; Wu Xinbo, "Four Contradictions Constraining China's Foreign Policy Behavior," *Journal of Contemporary China* 10, no. 27 (May 2001): 293-302.

22. Dalpino and Gill, *Brookings Northeast Asia Survey 2000-2001*, 36-47; Xu Shiquan Beijing *Guoji wenti yanjiu*, 13 November 2003, no. 6, 1-6; Denny Roy, "Rising China and U.S. Interests," *Orbis* 47, no. 1 (2003): 124-43.

23. Cheng Li, "China in 2000," 71-90.

24. Dalpino and Gill, *Brookings Northeast Asia Survey 2000-2001*, 53-55.

25. Sutter, "Introduction and Findings," in *China's Future*, 1-5; T. Y. Wang, "Introduction: China after the Sixteenth Party Congress," *Journal of Asian and African Studies* 38, nos. 4-5 (December 2003): 323-28; Jean-Pierre Cabestan, "The Tenth National People's Congress and After," *China Perspectives* 47 (May-June 2003): 4-20.

26. Joseph Fewsmith, "China's Response to SARS," *China Leadership Monitor*, Issue 7, www.chinaleadershipmonitor.org (Summer 2003) (accessed 15 November 2003). For quarterly reviews of salient political, economic, military, and foreign policy issues facing China's leaders, see *China Leadership Monitor*. See also *Journal of Democracy* 14, no. 1 (January 2003) and *Journal of Asian and African Studies* 38, nos. 4-5 (December 2003).

27. David Shambaugh, "Sino-American Strategic Relations: From Partners to Competitors," *Survival* 42, no. 1 (Spring 2000): 97-115; Andrew Nathan and Bruce Gilley, *China's New Rulers: The Secret Files* (New York: New York Review Book, 2002), 207-9; Pei Minxin, "Contradictory Trends and Confusing Signals," *Journal of Democracy* 14, no. 1 (January 2003): 73-81.

28. Sutter, "Introduction and Findings," *China's Future*, 4.

29. Cheng Li, *China's Leaders: The New Generation* (Lanham, Md.: Rowman & Littlefield, 2001).

30. David Shambaugh, "China's Military Views the World," *International Security* 24, no. 3 (Winter 1999-2000): 52-79; Wei-chin Lee, "China's Military after the Sixteenth Party Congress," *Journal of Asian and African Studies* 38, nos. 4-5 (December 2003): 416-46.

31. Cheng Li, "The 'new deal': Politics and Policies of the Hu Administration," *Journal of Asian and African Studies* 38, nos. 4-5 (December 2003): 329-46.

32. Joseph Fewsmith, "The 16th Party Congress: The Implications for Understanding Chinese Politics," *China Leadership Monitor* Issue 5, www.chinaleadershipmonitor.org (Winter 2003) (accessed 2 April 2003).

33. Willy Lam, "Beijing Reportedly Debating Jiang Zemin Political Future," *South China Morning Post*, 16 February 2002; Peter Harmsen, "Analysts Say Jiang Zemin Force to Make Concessions for Party Platform," *AFP*, 27 September 2001 (FBIS Internet version, accessed 1 October 2001).

34. Arthur Waldron "Comments: China's Future—Implications for U.S. Interests," in *China's Future*, 103-9; Bruce Gilley, "The Limits of Authoritarian Resilience," *Journal of Democracy* 14, no. 1 (January 2003): 18-26.

35. Barry Naughton, "The Chinese Economy Through 2005," in *China's Future*, 49-66; Organization for Economic Cooperation and Development (OECD), *China in the World Economy: The Domestic Policy Challenges* (Paris: OECD, 2002); Nicholas Lardy, *Integrating China in the Global Economy* (Washington, D.C.: Brookings Institution, 2002). See also quarterly reviews of contemporary Chinese economic issues written by Barry Naughton in *China Leadership Monitor*.

36. William Overholt, "Keeping the Bad News at Bay," *Newsweek*, 6 August 2001, 15; Dalpino and Gill, *Brookings Northeast Asia Survey 2000-2001*, 67-70.

37. Fewsmith, "China in 1998," *Asian Survey*, 99-113.

38. *Global Trends 2015*, Washington, D.C., U.S. National Intelligence Council, Report NIC 2000-02, 60-64, www.odci.gov/nic (accessed 2 July 2001).

39. Shambaugh, "China's Military Views the World," 52-79; Evan Feigenbaum, "China's Military Posture and the New Economic Geopolitics," *Survival* 41, no. 2 (Summer 1999): 71-88; Christensen, "China," in Ellings and Friedberg, *Strategic Asia: Power and Purpose, 2001-2002*, 27-70; Christensen, "China," in Ellings and Friedberg, *Strategic Asia, 2002-2003*, 53-80.

40. On nationalism and Chinese foreign policy, see Deng Yong, "The Chinese Conception of National Interests in International Relations," *China Quarterly* 154 (June 1998): 316; Suisheng Zhao, "A State-led Nationalism: The Patriotic Education Campaign in Post-Tiananmen China," *Communist and Post-Communist Studies* 31, no. 3 (1998): 289; Yongnian Zhung, *Discovering Chinese Nationalism in China* (Cambridge: Cambridge University Press, 1999); Maria Hsia Chang, *Return of the Dragon* (Boulder, Colo.: Westview, 2000); Jonathan Unger, ed., *Chinese Nationalism* (Armonk, N.Y.: M. E. Sharpe, 1996); Suisheng Zhao, "Chinese Nationalism and Its International Orientations," *Political Science Quarterly* 115, no. 1 (Spring 2000): 5.

41. Peter Gries refers to this kind of sensibility as "face nationalism." Peter Hayes Gries, "A China Threat? Power and Passion in Chinese 'Face Nationalism,'" *World Affairs* 162, no. 2 (Fall 1999): 67.

42. On Chinese leaders' goals, especially as they relate to world affairs, see, among others, Denny Roy, *China's Foreign Relations* (Lanham, Md.: Rowman & Littlefield, 1998); Samuel Kim, ed., *China and the World: Chinese Foreign Relations in the Post-Cold War Era* (Boulder, Colo.: Westview Press, 1998); Lampton, *Chinese Foreign and Security Policy*; Steven Mosher, *Hegemon: China's Plan to Dominate Asia and the World* (New York: Encounter Books, 2000); Michael Pillsbury, ed., *China Debates the Future Security Environment* (Washington, D.C.: National Defense University Press, 2000).

43. Yong Deng, "Hegemon on the Offensive: Chinese Perspectives on U.S. Global Strategy," *Political Science Quarterly* 116, no. 3 (Fall 2001): 343-65; Qian Qichen, "The International Situation and Sino-U.S. Relations Since the 11 September Incident," Beijing *Waijiao Xueyuan Xuebao*, 25 September 2002, no. 3, 1-6; Fang Ning, Wang Xiaodong, and Qiao Liang, *Quanqihua Yinying xia de Zhongguo Zhilu* (Beijing: Chinese Academy of Social Sciences Press, 1999), 47; Zhang Yunliang, ed., *Huoban haishi duishou: Tiao zheng zhong de mei ri e guanxi* (Beijing: Social Science Departments Press, 2000), 24-30; Alastair Iain Johnston, "Is China a Status Quo Power?" *International Security* 27, no. 4 (Spring 2003): 5-56.

44. On Chinese elite views of U.S. power and prospects for a multipolar world, see the quarterly review of U.S.-Chinese relations done by Bonnie Glaser in *Comparative Connections*, Honolulu, CSIS/Pacific Forum, www.csis.org/pacfor.

45. Shambaugh, "China's Military Views the World," 52-79.

46. Thomas Christensen, "China, the U.S.-Japan Alliance, and the Security Dilemma in East Asia," *International Security* 23, no. 4 (Spring 1999): 49-80; Alan Tonelson, *A Necessary Evil? Current Chinese Views of America's Military Role in East Asia* (Washington, D.C.: Henry Stimson Center, May 2003); Wu Xinbo, "Remarks on Future U.S. Military Presence in East Asia," a paper presented to a conference in Washington, D.C., 9 October 2003; Yang Yi, "A Dedicated Strategic Choice for National Interests: Improving U.S.-China Relations in a New Global Context," a paper presented to a conference in Vail, Colorado, 14 November 2003; Shi Yinhong, "The 15 Years of China's Diplomacy and Strategy toward the United States," a paper presented to a conference in Vail, Colorado, 14 November 2003; Jia Qingguo, "Making the World More Secure for the World? Comments on Bush's National Security Strategy," a paper presented to a conference in Vail, Colorado, 14 November 2003.

47. Sutter, *Chinese Policy Priorities*, 46-53.

48. Evan Medieros and M. Taylor Fravel, "China's New Diplomacy," *Foreign Affairs*, November-December 2003 (Internet version).

49. Denny Roy, *China's Foreign Relations*. See also Tang Shiping, *Zai lun Zhongguo de dazhanlue, Zhanlue yu guanli* (Beijing, 2001), vol. 4, 29-37.

50. Sutter, *Chinese Policy Priorities*, 39-58.

51. David Shambaugh, "Sino-American Strategic Relations: From Partners to Competitors," *Survival* 42, no. 1 (Spring 2000): 97-115; Qian Qichen, "The International Situation and Sino-U.S. Relations," 1-6.

52. Elizabeth Economy, "The Impact of International Regimes on Chinese Foreign Policymaking," in Lampton, *Chinese Foreign and Security Policy.*

53. Miller and Liu Xiaohong, "China's 'Third Generation' Elite," in Lampton, *Chinese Foreign and Security Policy.*

54. Christensen, "China," in Ellings and Aaron, *Strategic Asia: Power and Purpose, 2001-2002,* 27-60.

55. U.S. Department of Defense, *Military Power of the People's Republic of China, 2003.*

56. Michael O'Hanlon, "Why China Cannot Conquer Taiwan," *International Security* 25, no. 2 (Fall 2000): 51-86; Denny Roy, "Tensions in the Taiwan Strait," *Survival* 42, no. 1 (Spring 2000): 76-96; U.S. Department of Defense, *Military Power of the People's Republic of China, 2003;* International Crisis Group, Reports *Taiwan Strait I, II, III,* available at www.intl-crisis-group.org/projects/project.cfm?subtypeid=35 (accessed 1 September 2003).

57. Organization for Economic Cooperation and Development (OECD), *China in the World Economy: The Domestic Policy Challenges* (Paris: OECD, 2002).

58. David Shambaugh, *Modernizing China's Military* (Berkeley: University of California, 2002); articles by James Mulvenon in *The China Leadership Monitor,* www.chinaleadershipmonitor.org; U.S. Department of Defense, *Military Power of the People's Republic of China, 2003.*

59. Dalpino and Gill, *Brookings Northeast Asia Survey 2000-2001,* 36-47; Harvey Feldman, "The U.S.-PRC Relationship," in Hung Mao Tien and Tun-jen Cheng, eds., *The Security Environment in the Asia-Pacific* (Armonk, N.Y.: M. E. Sharpe, 2000), 19-35.

60. Bates Gill, "Two Steps Forward, One Step Back: The Dynamics of Chinese Nonproliferation and Arms Control Policy Making," in Lampton, *Chinese Foreign and Security Policy,* 257-88; Evan Medieros, "The Changing Character of China's WMD Proliferation Activities," in *China and Weapons of Mass Destruction,* National Intelligence Council Conference Report CR99-05, 111-47.

61. Douglas Paal, "The Regional Security Implications of China's Economic Expansion, Military Modernization, and the Rise of Nationalism," in Hung Mao Tien and Tun-jen Cheng, eds., *The Security Environment in the Asia-Pacific* (Armonk, N.Y.: M. E. Sharpe, 2000), 79-91; Bonnie Glaser, "Terrorism Strike Gives U.S.-China Ties a Boost," *Comparative Connections,* Honolulu, CSIS/Pacific Forum, www.csis.org/pacfor (July-September 2001) (accessed 1 November 2001); Asia Pacific Center for Security Studies, *Asia's China Debate,* www.apcss.org (December 2003) (accessed 30 January 2004); Roy, "Rising China."

62. See varying treatment of these issues in Samuel Kim, ed., China and the World; Elizabeth Economy and Michael Oksenberg, eds., *China Joins the World* (New York: Council on Foreign Relations, 1999); Lampton, *Chinese Foreign and Security Policy;* Medieros and Fravel, "China's New Diplomacy," *Foreign Affairs;* Dennis Roy, "China's Reaction to American Predominance," *Survival* 45, no. 3 (Autumn 2003): 57-78.

Chapter 3

China's Relations with the United States

Convergence and Divergence in U.S.-China Ties

The goals, perceptions, strategies, and behavior of Chinese leaders reviewed above illustrate the central position of the United States, especially regarding Chinese priorities in Asian and world affairs. Core Chinese development, territorial, and security interests center on the United States. There was growing convergence in China-U.S. economic interests as China developed rapidly and its leaders saw their interests well served by closer adherence to norms of international economic behavior supported by the United States. Chinese leaders also adhered more closely to U.S.-backed standards on sensitive political and security questions, notably WMD proliferation and arms control. At the start of the twenty-first century, official Chinese pronouncements endorsed more fully multilateral mechanisms to deal with regional and international problems, and soft-pedaled China's past angst that such mechanisms could be used by bigger powers to work against Chinese interests in Asian and world affairs.[1]

There was optimism among some specialists in China and abroad who emphasized growing convergence between the United States and China in Asian and world affairs. Indeed, Chinese leaders had put aside much of the rhetoric of the previous decade and earlier criticizing the United States as a global hegemon, and they seemed prepared to accept an international situation where U.S. forces guaranteed order in the international "commons," such as sea lines of communication so important for China's increasingly trade-dependent economy. Chinese officials also were prepared to work more closely with the United States in dealing with terrorist issues, even in areas sensitive to China's security along the periphery of the country, and they were prepared to work more closely with the United States in dealing with North Korea's nuclear weapons program and related provocations.[2]

Nevertheless, a thorough assessment of the Chinese approach toward the United States came up with a more mixed picture that complicates the perceived trend toward China-U.S. convergence in Asian and world affairs. Chinese leaders continued to see the United States as perhaps the most important obstacle in the top priority Chinese leadership efforts to reverse trends toward Taiwan separatism and independence, and to move Taiwan toward reunification with the mainland. Though muting differences with the United States, Chinese leaders still seemed driven by many of the nationalistic goals and foreign policy strategies that characterized Chinese behavior in Asia for decades. Chinese officials in recent years were at pains to emphasize long-standing pledges that China was not expansionist or a threat and did not seek dominance in Asia. But the upsurge of Chinese nationalism, fostered actively by the Chinese leaders after the Tiananmen crisis in 1989, reinforced a firm Chinese position on territorial and other sensitive issues in relations with China's neighbors and the United States. It also underlined a continued wariness in the Chinese leadership's view of great power involvement around China.[3]

As evidenced by the record of Chinese behavior toward the Soviet Union and the United States in the post-Mao period, Chinese actions in Asia were driven at first by a strategic imperative to work against efforts by the dominant hostile power, the USSR, to encircle, intimidate, and constrain China. During much of the 1990s, following the collapse of the USSR, Chinese officials saw the United States endeavoring to use advances in Asia and other means to pressure and contain China, endeavoring to hold back its rise in Asian and world affairs.[4]

The lessons and implications of these experiences seemed clear for Chinese policy in Asia and what it meant for the United States at the start of the twenty-first century. Chinese officials had a long history of tending to think of power and influence in the region in zero sum terms, and did little at the authoritative leadership level to disavow this view, despite more forward-leaning and progressive views occasionally voiced by some officials and intellectuals in China. They also had a long history of tending to see larger powers like the United States, and also Japan, India, and even post-Soviet Russia, as following their own selfish interests that were often not in accord with China's interests. When large powers like the Soviet Union in the past and the United States more recently pursued policies and behavior along China's periphery in ways that were or could be detrimental to China's interests, Chinese officials emphasized a need to find ways to respond that would protect core Chinese interests while gradually building China's greater national wealth and power. This was the logic that undergirded the foreign policy maxims of Deng Xiaoping, which Chinese officials affirm still guide Chinese policy in Asian and world affairs in the twenty-first century.[5]

A key outcome to avoid is a great power seemingly hostile to China's interests consolidating its strategic position along important areas of China's periphery. Such consolidation would give this power or powers greater leverage and leeway in trying to pressure and intimidate China and influence its policies. Chinese officials also felt justified in spreading Chinese influence in Asia based on growing Chinese economic, political, and military power. Chinese nationalism, educational training, and media conditioning underlined the point that China was held down in the past and was deserving of a greater regional role.[6] Having increased confidence because of China's growing power, Chinese officials have maneuvered in regional subgroups (e.g., ASEAN Plus Three, Shanghai Cooperation Organization, China-ASEAN Free Trade Agreement) in competition with the United States, and also with Japan, India, and others, in order to improve China's position relative to the power and influence of others. Prevailing conditions—including Chinese need for cooperation with these and other powers for the sake of Chinese economic development and sustaining regional stability—argued for such Chinese competition with the United States and other powers for influence in Asia to be done without some of the aggressive and assertive Chinese tactics of the past.

As China expanded its influence, there often were clear signs of strong Chinese frustration with the United States. China's behavior toward the United States varied between postures of confrontation and cordiality. Its frustration did not become extreme or result in a fundamental shift in its policy toward the United States. China sought to avoid confrontation with the United States, calculating that it needed the United States for economic and technological progress. Chinese leaders also took note that the U.S. administration of George W. Bush showed a U.S. resolve, not seen in decades, to use the recent unprecedented levels of U.S. power in order to punish enemies.[7] China's senior leaders seemed to view engagement with the United States and the West not as ends in themselves but rather as means to stability and economic prosperity.[8]

China used personal diplomacy to engage the United States. Beijing signaled its displeasure when it calculated Washington was becoming too supportive of Taiwan, or the United States government pursued policies in other sensitive areas (e.g., missile defense) that challenged important Chinese concerns. In those instances, Chinese diplomats made veiled threats of the peril to U.S.-China ties. Throughout the 1990s, the Chinese press harshly criticized U.S. policy on a wide range of Asian and international issues; and military demonstrations were designed not only to intimidate Taiwan but also to place pressure on the United States to curb Taiwan's behavior and to back away from full U.S. support for the island government.

Beyond the Taiwan situation, China used diplomacy and rhetoric to work against closer U.S.-Japan military ties. China portrayed the U.S. military presence in Asia as anachronistic and a reflection of Cold War thinking, though it tried to muffle past calls for a U.S. military drawdown from the region. At the same time, Beijing saw its interests well served by cooperating generally with U.S.-backed efforts to ensure stability on the Korean peninsula, particularly by participating in the Four Party talks of the 1990s and playing a key role in talks with the United States and North Korea in 2003-2004.[9]

As noted in chapter 1, there was debate among U.S. and other specialists about the significance of the more accommodating and moderate Chinese posture toward the United States in Asian and world affairs evident since 2001. Was it evidence of new thinking by Chinese leaders seeking to embrace closer strategic cooperation with the United States in Asia to complement China's growing economic cooperation with the United States; or did it represent tactical adjustments based on cost-benefit assessments of how such adjustments would serve longer-term Chinese interests? The argument in chapter 1 is that it was more the latter than the former. The argument was supported by recent patterns in Chinese policies and behavior in Asia, which continued to try to balance real or potential adverse U.S. power and influence in nonconfrontational ways, often coming in "under the radar" of U.S. decision makers and Asian leaders and thereby avoiding adverse consequences for Chinese interests. The competitive and antagonistic aspects in China's stance toward the United States in Asia showed more in some areas of Asia than others. Key determinants seemed to include the degree of U.S. and Chinese sensitivity, and their respective influence, in particular parts of Asia.

Taiwan, as might be expected, was in a class by itself. Official Chinese complaints, though much muted after 2001, repeatedly laid down public markers against U.S. policy and behavior.[10]

Chinese rhetoric against Japan was more restrained than in the late 1990s, despite Prime Minister Koizumi's repeated visits to the Yakasuni shrine against explicit warnings from top Chinese officials, and the much greater Japanese military activism in Asian and world affairs. Nevertheless there were frequent sharp Chinese media complaints against Japanese military activism which was seen as fostered by U.S. policy as a means to enhance U.S. dominance in Asia.[11]

Chinese leaders were notably restrained in dealing with anti-U.S. themes in Korea.[12] They generally avoided explicit comment on the anti-American sentiment sweeping South Korea since 2002 and the often sharp U.S.-South Korean differences on relations with North Korea. The Chinese ambassador in Seoul voiced oblique opposition to U.S. forces in Korea in August 2002,[13] but such comments were rare. Presumably Chinese officials judge that such Chinese rhetoric, seen at times in the 1990s, would work against immediate Chinese concerns to avoid military conflict and encourage engagement among the powers concerned with the volatile situation on the peninsula. While Chinese officials worked with the United States and other powers in dealing with the North Korean nuclear crisis, Chinese media sided with South Korea in occasionally criticizing U.S. pressure tactics against North Korea.[14] It also took the Korean side in criticizing Japan over its alleged inadequate sensitivity to its colonial past, but presumably on account of the South Korean President Kim Dae Jung's moderation toward Japan in the late 1990s, there was no repetition of Jiang Zemin's joint statement with the previous South Korean president in 1995 explicitly criticizing Japan.[15]

In Southeast Asia—an area that receives relatively lower priority by the United States while China's influence there rose markedly in recent years—Chinese policy and behavior often veiled only thinly competition or opposition to U.S. or other powers.[16] Greater Chinese flexibility on territorial disputes and the management of relations with Southeast Asia was evident by 1997 when Chinese officials inaugurated their "New Security Concept" (NSC) initially in an ASEAN setting. By this time, Chinese leaders were showing more flexibility in dealing with territorial issues with many neighbors, and were more willing to participate in multilateral fora that focused on these and other regional concerns. Chinese leaders from that time forward also were very active in diplomatic, economic, and military contacts to persuade Southeast Asian neighbors and others that the image of the "China threat" was an illusion. Of course, as was the case in other areas of Chinese foreign policy, the shift toward greater moderation in Southeast Asia in 1997 did not include U.S. policy. The moderating effect of China's New Security Concept was offset by the strident Chinese opposition to American power, influence, and policies.

The shift toward moderation in Chinese policy toward the United States during 2001 was evident when China revised and relaunched its New Security Concept (NSC) in meetings in Southeast Asia in 2002—the NSC was no longer sandwiched by strong anti-U.S. rhetoric.[17] Meanwhile, Chinese officials were said to devote less attention to the NSC, preferring to be more flexible in responding constructively to security arrangements proposed by ASEAN and other neighbors, and to avoid calling attention to China as a "leader" in Asia.[18]

Nonetheless, Chinese policy and behavior continued to work, albeit much more subtly, to build Chinese influence at the expense of the United States and other powers in Southeast Asia. This came at the same time Chinese policy in the region stressed the mutual benefit—"win-win"—in Chinas new approaches toward neighboring countries. When a U.S.-backed high-level security forum in Singapore, sponsored by the Institute for International and Strategic Studies, proved popular with regional leaders, China for the first two years sent only low-level functionaries while devoting high-level attention to promoting a new Asian-centered security dialogue that marginalized the United States. China eventually agreed in the third year of the forum to join in the deliberations at a higher level in June 2004, but cancelled participation at the last minute over a Taiwan scholar's presence at the forum. Greater Chinese flexibility and willingness to engage in negotiations with the various claimants to South China Sea territories also saw Chinese officials endeavor to use the discussions with ASEAN members about a code of conduct over the disputed claims in the South China Sea as a means to restrict U.S. naval exercises in the area. The multilateral U.S. "Cobra Gold" military exercise in 2001 saw China conduct its own military exercise in apparent competition. In 2003, lower-level Chinese officials occasionally resorted to sharp anti-U.S. rhetoric regarding the occupation of Iraq that played well in Southeast Asian countries. China also maneuvered in its Free Trade Agreement initiative with ASEAN to shore up China's position relative to the United States, as well as to compete with Japan, South Korea, and India, undergirding China's position in the region. In 2003 China became the first major power to agree to sign ASEAN's 1976 Treaty of Amity and Cooperation, prompting Russia, India, and Japan to pledge to do the same and placing the United States in a less flattering light.[19]

ASEAN also was the main arena for Chinese initiatives in broader regional groups that have excluded or tried to marginalize the United States. While cooperating with Japan, South Korea, and other Asian powers in promoting Asia-only groupings that explicitly exclude the United States, at the same time, China also actively competed with them for leadership in Asian forums.

The ASEAN Plus Three emerged in the late 1990s as the most important of regional groupings designed to promote Asian economic cooperation that excluded the United States and other outside powers, and Chinese leaders took a leading role in the group's various initiatives to promote intraregional cooperation and economic safeguards. China opposed a Japanese government initiative to establish an Asian monetary fund at the height of the Asian economic crisis in 1997, but it came to support a more recent Asian Monetary Fund initiative, sponsored by ASEAN Plus Three, which did not directly redound to Japan's leadership role in regional affairs. With Chinese entry into the WTO seen as key driver of Asian growth, Chinese officials and media since 2000 highlighted China's free trade initiatives with ASEAN, including the "early harvest" concessions dealing with agricultural trade, that served to undercut concurrent Japanese and South Korean trade initiatives toward Southeast Asia that do not include liberalized agricultural trade. Chinese leaders also supported efforts to broaden the ASEAN Plus Three dialogue to include salient political and security as well as economic issues.[20]

Beijing also initiated important regional multilateral mechanisms. The Boao Forum for Asia (BFA), which met April 11-14, 2002, in Hainan Island, was presented by China as the "first annual session" of an Asian version of the Davos World Economic Forum. The Forum's goal was to provide a high-level dialogue platform for Asian countries to review the economic and social challenges and promote economic cooperation in Asia. Working with Chinese sponsors of the Forum, Thailand's Prime Minister proposed that the first Asian Cooperation Dialogue (ACD) of foreign ministers be held in June in Thailand as an official counterpart to the BFA. Its first meeting was held at a resort in Thailand in June 2002. The foreign ministers of most ASEAN Plus Three members attended the session and agreed to further meetings.[21]

Elsewhere around China's periphery, Chinese leaders' tendency to work explicitly against U.S. interest was muted. In Russia, President Putin was less willing in recent years to make common political ground with China against U.S. policy, though occasional references to multipolarity and opposition to hegemonism and unilateralism were seen in Russian-Chinese pronouncements. Russia remained willing to supply China with an increasingly sophisticated and expensive array of advanced weapons for use in a possible Taiwan contingency that could involve the United States, and Russian-Chinese trade was growing from a low base. Energy projects were central to future Russian-Chinese trade, though Russia continued to barter with Japan in seeking a better deal for its limited Far Eastern oil exports.[22]

Chinese commentary in the 1990s envisaged the Shanghai Cooperation Organization (SCO) as excluding the United States from Central Asia.[23] Chinese commentary often viewed negatively the rapid upswing of U.S. military presence and influence in Central and South Asia in 2001 but China adjusted without posing major opposition. China was in the lead in keeping the SCO moving forward, providing funding and participating in small joint and multilateral military exercises with SCO members—unprecedented steps for the PLA. Beijing also stressed recently broadening SCO interests to include economic interchange—steps that may enhance China's leadership role in the SCO based on the overall strength of the Chinese economy. The United States and other interested powers (e.g., India) continued to be kept out of the SCO deliberations. China also sought and received Mongolia's pledge not to allow foreign troops in Mongolia.

In South Asia, Chinese leaders cooperated with the United States even though their leading position in Pakistan was altered as a result of the strong assertion of U.S. leadership there in 2001.[24] Incremental Chinese efforts to improve relations with India in the recent past focused on some Sino-Indian common ground against U.S. foreign policy, but this was largely put aside as New Delhi rapidly improved relations—especially military relations—with the United States even before September 11, 2001. China also saw its interests better served by focusing on improved relations with the United States than by seeking common ground with India against U.S. interests. Improvement in Sino-Indian relations continued, albeit hampered by key differences, notably over Pakistan; the two powers generally eschew anti-U.S. elements in their recent interaction.

The George W. Bush Administration and China's Response— Implications for China's Approach to Asia

Some specialists forecasting great convergence in U.S.-China relations in Asian and world affairs were encouraged by the surprising improvement in U.S.-China relations during the administration of President George W. Bush. They tended to emphasize greater Chinese leadership confidence and maturity as the cause for the turnabout in relations, arguing that such confidence and maturity prompted the Chinese government to deal more moderately and with restraint regarding some of the seeming challenges posed by the new U.S. administration and its policies regarding Taiwan, weapons proliferation, ballistic missile defense, and the overall greater U.S. assertiveness and national security power in Asian and world affairs.[25]

Another group of specialists was less convinced that U.S.-China relations were destined to converge substantially over Asian and world affairs. These specialists emphasized the importance of what they saw as the Bush administration moving fairly rapidly from an initial toughness toward China to a stance of accommodation and compromise. The shift toward a moderate U.S. stance prompted Chinese leaders to pursue greater moderation in turn in their overall approach to Asian and world affairs.[26]

A third view involved specialists, including this writer, who gave more weight to the Bush administration's firm and effective policies toward China, which were seen to have curbed assertive and potential disruptive Chinese tendencies and served to make it in China's interests to avoid confrontation, seek better U.S. ties, and avoid challenge to U.S. interests in Asian and world affairs. This view held that it was more China than the United States that took the lead in seeking better ties in 2001, and that greater U.S.-China cooperation in Asian affairs depended not so much on Chinese confidence and maturity than on effective U.S. use of power and influence to keep assertive and disruptive Chinese tendencies in check and prevail upon China to limit emphasis on differences with the United States.[27]

All three schools of thought judged that the improvement in U.S.-China relations reinforced generally moderate Chinese tendencies in Asian affairs, but their differences over the causes of the U.S.-China thaw had implications for assessing future Chinese policy and behavior toward the Asian region. In the first instance, the key variable seemed to be Chinese confidence and maturity, which presumably would continue to grow along with Chinese development and moderation, suggesting a continued moderate Chinese approach for the next several years if not longer. The latter two views depended heavily on the United States, with the first view arguing that continued U.S. moderation and accommodation of Chinese interest was required, as a more firm U.S. stance presumably could lead to a more assertive and aggressive Chinese stance in the region. The second of the latter two views indicated that much depended on continued U.S. resolve, power, and effectiveness in dealing with China. Weakness or extremism in the U.S. stance could reverse the prevailing trend of Chinese moderation in the region and lead to a more assertive and disruptive approach.

At the outset of 2001, there appeared to be few indications that Chinese leaders planned significant change in China's long-term approach toward China's neighbors. Managing leadership succession, domestic economic development, and social and political stability remained the top Chinese leadership concerns for the time being. Foreign policy issues continued to give pride of place to dealing with the United States and Taiwan. China's fourth-generation leaders were actively involved in the high-level exchanges with China's neighbors and showed no sign of deviating from the prevailing policies. Beijing on balance appeared poised over time to exert ever-greater regional influence.

China's leaders seemed to recognize that direct Chinese competition with the United States and other larger powers for influence in Asia was counterproductive for Chinese interests. Most Asian governments wanted to remain on good terms with a rising China as they sought more advantageous economic interchanges with the United States and other powers, and encouraged a stabilizing U.S. security presence in the region. There was plenty of evidence in Chinese approaches to South Korea, ASEAN Plus Three, the Shanghai Cooperation Organization, and other venues that China remained opposed to U.S. power and influence in Asia over the longer term. China also was not yet heavily constrained by interdependence, and presumably could decide at some point to put aside its current pragmatism for a more assertive and disruptive policy.

Given China's long-standing sensitivity to great power involvement around its periphery, there was the possibility that changes undertaken by the Bush administration in Asian and world affairs could have led to a major shift in China's approach to the region and in China's overall relationship with the United States. In fact, the Bush administration did undertake a number of changes in policy toward China and Asia, but on balance they reinforced PRC perceptions of the utility of a moderate approach to Asia and added to reasons for growing common ground between the United States and China in Asian and world affairs.

The Bush administration entered office without a clear China policy. The administration's vision was based in large measure on a fundamental uncertainty—China was rising and becoming more prominent in Asia and world affairs, but U.S. leaders were unsure if this process would see China emerge as a friend or foe of the United States.[28] The administration dealt with this ambiguous China situation within a broader U.S. international strategy that endeavored to maximize U.S. national power and influence in key situations, including relations with China. This involved strengthening:

- U.S. military and economic power;
- U.S. relations with key allies—Japan, South Korea, and Australia received high priority; and
- U.S. relations with other power centers—the Bush administration was successful in moving quickly, before September 11, 2001, to build closer relations with the two major flanking powers in East Asia, Russia and India.[29]

In 2001, the new U.S. president and his leadership team displayed a notably less solicitous approach to China than the Clinton administration had displayed. During its second term, the Clinton administration adopted an "engagement" policy toward China that received the top priority among U.S. relations with Asia. The administration was anxious to avoid "swings" or serious downturns in U.S.-China relations over Taiwan and other issues, and also repeatedly sought negotiations with Beijing to develop "deliverables"—agreements and other tangible signs of forward movement in U.S.-China relations. Not surprisingly, PRC bargainers used a prevailing atmosphere of strong Chinese criticism of U.S. policies and warnings of Chinese actions against Taiwan to press for concessions in areas of importance to them, notably regarding U.S. relations with Taiwan. The Chinese criticism of U.S. policy had a broad scope involving Taiwan and a wide range of issues in U.S. foreign and security policy including missile defense, NATO expansion, U.S.-Japan security cooperation, U.S. human rights policy, U.S. efforts in the United Nations to sanction Iraq, and U.S. policy toward Cuba, Iran, the Middle East, and other areas in the Third World. Clinton administration concessions fueled the white-hot U.S. domestic debate over the proper direction of U.S. China policy.[30]

By contrast, the Bush administration lowered China's priority for U.S. decision makers, placing the PRC well behind Asian allies and even Russia and India for foreign policy attention.[31] The EP-3 incident of April 1, 2001, led to a sharp downturn in relations. Significantly, the Bush administration did not resort to high-level envoys or other special arrangements often used to resolve difficult U.S.-China issues, insisting on working through normal State Department and Defense Department channels that did not raise China's stature in U.S. foreign policy. Other U.S. officials were instructed to avoid all but the most essential contacts with Chinese officials in Washington and elsewhere.[32]

While receptive to Chinese efforts to broaden common ground in U.S.-China relations, Bush administration interest in seeking negotiations with China in order to create "deliverables" and other agreements remained low. Its reaction to the April 1, 2001, EP-3 episode markedly increased U.S. support for Taiwan, and new U.S. focus on China as a potential threat showed Beijing leaders that the Bush government, while seeking to broaden areas of cooperation where possible, was prepared to see U.S.-China relations worsen if necessary. The firm U.S. stance seemed to have U.S. domestic backing, fitting well with mainstream congressional and U.S. media opinion regarding China.[33]

Chinese leaders by mid-2001 seemed to recognize that if U.S.-China relations were to avoid further deterioration, it was up to China to take steps to improve ties. In a period of overall ascendant U.S. influence and leverage in Asian and world affairs, Beijing saw its interests best served by a stance that muted differences and sought common ground. Chinese officials became more solicitous and less acrimonious in interaction with U.S. officials, toned down Chinese rhetoric against the United States, and gave some tentative signs of public PRC support for the U.S. military presence in East Asia. The U.S. side also signaled an interest to calm the concerns of friends and allies in Asia over the state of U.S.-China relations and to pursue areas of common ground in trade and other areas with the PRC.[34]

The antiterrorism campaign after September 11, 2001, saw an upswing in cooperation, though China was somewhat tentative and reserved in supporting the U.S. war against Afghanistan. President Bush's visits to Shanghai in October 2001 and Beijing in February 2002 underlined differences as well as common ground. The U.S. president repeatedly affirmed his strong support for Taiwan and his firm position regarding human rights issues in China. His aides made clear China's lower priority in the administration's view of U.S. interests as the Bush administration continued to focus higher priority on relations with Japan and other allies in Asia and the Pacific. The Bush administration imposed sanctions on China over issues involving China's reported proliferation of weapons of mass destruction more times than during the eight years of the Clinton administration. The U.S. Defense Department's Quadrennial Defense Review unmistakably saw China as a potential threat in Asia. U.S. ballistic missile defense programs severely challenged China's nuclear deterrent and intimidation strategy against Taiwan; rising U.S. influence and prolonged military deployments were at odds with previous Chinese strategy along China's western flank.[35] The U.S. Defense Department's annual reports on the Chinese military pulled few punches in focusing on China's military threat to Taiwan and to U.S. forces that might come to Taiwan aid in the event of a conflict with the PRC. The Bush administration's September 2002 National Security Strategy Report called for better relations with China but clearly warned against any power seeking to challenge U.S. interests with military force.[36]

U.S. leaders showed an increased willingness to meet Chinese leaders' symbolic needs for summitry, and the U.S. president pleased his Chinese counterpart by repeatedly endorsing a "constructive, cooperative and candid" relationship with China. Amid continued Chinese moderation and concessions in 2002, and reflecting greater U.S. interest in consolidating relations and avoiding tensions with China at a time of growing U.S. preoccupation with the war on terrorism, Iraq, and North Korea, the Bush administration broadened cooperation with China and gave U.S. relations with China a higher priority as the year wore on. The October 2002 Crawford meeting highlighted this trend. Concessions and gestures, mainly from the Chinese side dealing with proliferation, Iraq, release of dissidents, U.S. agricultural imports, Tibet, and Taiwan, facilitated a positive Crawford summit in October 2002.[37] Senior U.S. leaders began to refer to China and Jiang Zemin as a "friend."[38] They adhered to public positions on Taiwan that were acceptable to Beijing. They sanctioned an anti-PRC terrorist group active in China's Xinjiang region. The U.S. Defense Department was slow to resume high-level contacts with China, reflecting continued wariness in the face of China's ongoing military buildup focused on dealing with Taiwan and U.S. forces that may seek to protect Taiwan, but formal relations at various senior levels were resumed by late 2002.[39]

China's carefully calibrated and generally moderate approach to Asia combined with the restraint Beijing showed in the face of new departures in U.S. policy and behavior under the Bush administration argued for a continuation of PRC moderation at least during the next few years. Preoccupied by late 2002 and 2003 with major problems in Iraq and the war on terrorism, the Bush administration valued Chinese cooperation, especially in dealing with the crisis brought about by North Korea's provocative nuclear weapons program beginning in 2002. The U.S. president also pleased Chinese officials by rebuking the Taiwan president in late 2003 when the Taiwan leader pursued changes in Taiwan's constitution that Beijing saw as moves toward independence.[40] At the same time, as noted above, there remained clear limits on Chinese moderation and flexibility, and ample evidence of continued Chinese frustration and wariness regarding U.S. policies and behavior in Asia. They suggested that a major breakthrough toward strategic China-U.S. cooperation in Asia was unlikely, and that an abrupt shift in U.S. policy or behavior, or other changes, could result in a marked shift in China's approach to Asia.[41]

Underlying the latter tendency was Chinese discussion of China's "peaceful rise" in Asia evident in 2003-2004. As explained in this book's conclusion, Chinese leaders saw this new emphasis as seeking greater cooperation with Asian neighbors and the United States. Chinese foreign policy specialists emphasized that this was a strategic change in Chinese policy, but they also emphasized that if the moderate Chinese policy did not elicit reciprocal and constructive reactions from the United States, more "hard-line" Chinese policies would result. In short, the new approach remained contingent, and depended to a considerable degree on the United States continuing an overall cooperative approach toward China and its interests in Asian and world affairs. In particular, Chinese concern over continued active U.S. military and other support for Taiwan at a time of the Taiwan government's movement toward greater separatism and independence was a major challenge to Chinese officials trying to keep China-U.S. relations on a positive footing as China pursued a broadly peaceful approach to Asian and world affairs.[42]

Chinese Perceptions of U.S. Strength and Leadership in Asia

Amid extensive Western and Asian media and other commentary highlighting China's rising image of power and influence in Asia in the twenty-first century was a concurrent tendency on the part of Chinese officials and specialists to play down China's leading role in Asia. At one level, such diffidence played well in the region, more used to assertive Chinese behavior over the decades. It also reflected widespread Chinese government recognition, acknowledged in passing by official Chinese commentary but more fully supported by private consultations with Chinese officials and specialists, that the United States by far was Asia's leading and dominant power and was likely to remain so for the foreseeable future despite U.S. preoccupations in other world areas. In this context, Chinese officials and specialists were at pains to avoid calling undue U.S. attention to China's rising profile in Asia, fearing an adverse U.S. reaction that, given the realities of asymmetrical power in U.S.-China relations in Asian and world affairs, could have severely negative consequences for China's interests.

Consultations with fifty Chinese specialists and officials in 2003-2004 repeatedly saw the Chinese experts emphasize that Chinese leaders were well aware of the negative record of Germany's rise to power before World War I and Japan's rise to power before World War II. The rising power promoted other states and their allies to work against the rising power, and ultimately to defeat them in war. Chinese leaders were said to seek to avoid such a situation as China rises, and they saw the United States, the world's dominant power and the dominant power in Asia, as the chief problem in this regard. Chinese leaders, according to the Chinese experts interviewed by this writer, were trying to avoid adverse U.S. reaction to China's growing power and influence in Asia, recognizing that confrontation with the United States in the region would be very negative for China's interests.[43]

Chinese officials and specialists were well aware of and often contributed to criticism of the Bush administration's record in Asia, including mishandling Korean issues, issuing unilateralist policy declarations adding to tension in the region, and paying little attention to economic, environmental, and multilateral measures seen as important to long-range Asian stability. They followed closely North Korea's provocative actions in late 2002 and 2003, breaking declared nonproliferation commitments and reactivating nuclear facilities frozen under the 1994 U.S.-North Korea Agreed Framework accord, which posed a major challenge for U.S. policy that was not well anticipated by the U.S. government. Bush administration reaction was complicated by deep division within the administration over how to handle North Korea, and by strong differences in U.S.-South Korean policy toward North Korea and broader alliance relations.[44] Tensions in U.S.-South Korean alliance relations and anti-American sentiment in South Korea rose markedly during the Bush administration, and were important factors in the election of South Korea's president in December 2002. Subsequent U.S. and South Korean efforts to ease tensions, bridge differences, and solidify relations remained awkward in 2003-2004 and added to the arguments of those claiming that the U.S.-South Korean alliance was in crisis and poised for a major change in the next few years.[45]

Significant additional problems for U.S. policy in Asia came as Asian elite and public opinion—including those in China—joined the worldwide complaints against U.S. unilateral actions and dominance in international affairs seen at the time of the U.S.-led attack on Iraq and repeated U.S. policy declarations supporting preemptive actions against adversaries.[46] The *Far Eastern Economic Review* cited a June 2003 study by the Pew Research Center for the People and the Press to assert that "the image of the United States plummeted in the wake of the war in Iraq." Only 15 percent of Indonesians polled in spring 2003 had a positive view of the United States, down from 75 percent in 2000. Most Indonesians polled attributed their negative views about the United States to the policies and behavior of President Bush. A major decline also took place among South Koreas and Pakistanis. In all three countries, support for the U.S.-led war on terrorism was under 30 percent.[47]

Chinese popular opinion was against the U.S. action in Iraq and later polls showed that Chinese opinion favored a UN refusal to support the post-war U.S. reconstruction efforts in Iraq, arguing that "when the United States decided to invade Iraq, it held the UN in contempt," and a UN rebuff would teach the United States "a profound lesson." The vast majority of Chinese urban dwellers polled in September 2003 said they admired France and Germany for standing up to the United States over the Iraq war.[48]

In Southeast Asia, government leaders took account of the strongly negative view of the U.S. attack on Iraq on the part of Muslim populations, notably in Indonesia and Malaysia. Indonesian President Megawati Sukarnoputri allowed police and security forces to cooperate with U.S., Australian, and other security forces to solve the 2002 Bali bombing case, but she maintained some distance from the overall U.S. war on terrorism. Megawati faced elections in mid-2004 and needed support from Muslim parties. In Malaysia, Prime Minister Mahatir sharply criticized the United States for inflaming radical movements without addressing root causes of terrorism.[49]

Antipathy to the U.S. assault on Iraq and perceived disregard for UN prerogatives elicited large-scale demonstrations and other actions in Australia, South Korea, Japan, India, and elsewhere, indicating that even U.S. allies and Asian government leaders leaning to support President Bush had to take account of strong elite and popular opinion moving in anti-American directions.[50]

For their part, Chinese authorities did not allow significant public demonstrations against U.S. policy. Chinese officials and specialists appeared to balance the impact of the recent controversies and criticisms of U.S. policies toward Iraq, the United Nations, Korea, and other issues with attention to the many continuing favorable trends in Asia for U.S. policy and interests. On balance, they saw U.S. leadership in Asia as remaining strong, and they sought to avoid controversy and to broaden cooperation with the United States. They specifically hoped that China's rising power and influence in Asia would not be perceived negatively in the United States and lead to U.S. reactions damaging to China's interests.

At a time of U.S. preoccupation with Iraq and other priorities, the Bush administration was seen among Chinese officials and specialists to have adjusted in generally pragmatic ways to unexpected Asian challenges, notably in the Korean peninsula—an area of much more salient concern than Iraq to the Chinese and most Asian governments. While repeatedly justifying the principle of U.S. preemption and unilateral action in other parts of the world, the Bush administration in practice sought to deal with the North Korean crisis and other issues in Asia through broad international consultation and engagement.

In the view of Chinese specialists, the U.S. administration's ability to manage without undue negative consequences the crises it faced in dealing with North Korea's nuclear program, its differences with the South Korean public and government opinion over handling North Korea, and other possible difficulties, and to sustain U.S. leadership and other regional interests, was seen as good for the next few years. In particular, there were several important underlying strengths in the U.S. leadership position in Asia, and the Bush administration also succeeded in markedly improving U.S. relations with each of the great powers in Asia.[51]

Among U.S. strengths, government leaders on both sides of the Pacific continued to put a high value on the U.S. security commitment and military presence in Asia. U.S. resolve to remain actively involved in regional security was strengthened by U.S. government efforts after the September 11, 2001, terrorist attack on America. The strong U.S. military presence was generally welcomed by Asian government leaders, and Chinese leaders notably modified their past criticism of the U.S. security role.[52]

Debate over the size and deployment of U.S. forces in South Korea became a key element in the crises facing U.S. policy on the Korean peninsula. Nevertheless, the South Korean and U.S. governments appeared determined to manage the debate without jeopardizing strong mutual interests supported by a continued U.S. military presence in South Korea.[53] U.S. officials took pains to reassure South Korea and others in Asia that the proposed realignment of U.S. forces on the Korean peninsula, and the broader U.S. realignment of forces abroad, would enhance, not reduce, U.S. ability to deter and defeat foes. These assurances had more weight as they came after the impressive U.S. military campaigns toppling regimes in Afghanistan and Iraq.[54] Meanwhile, the 2003 polls that showed setbacks for the U.S. image in certain countries in Asia also showed that most of those polled retained overall positive views of U.S. leadership and that clear majorities in Asia agreed that their interests would suffer if the United States were no longer the world's dominant power.[55]

The Bush administration had a less activist international economic policy than the Clinton administration, but the United States maintained open markets despite aberrations such as moves in 2002 to protect U.S. farmers and steel manufacturers. U.S. open market policy was welcomed and deeply appreciated by China and other Asian governments that viewed the U.S. economy as more important to Asian economic well being, especially after the Asian economic crisis and Japan's persisting stagnation. Chinese leaders duly acknowledged China's new role as an engine of regional growth, but they remained aware that U.S. economic prospects were much more important for their own and overall Asian development. The United States in recent years absorbed an increasing percentage (about 40 percent, according to U.S. government figures) of the exports from China, the export-manufacturing base for investors from a wide range of advanced Asian economies. The U.S. market continued to absorb one-third of the exports of Japan. The economies of South Korea, Taiwan, and ASEAN relied on the U.S. market to receive around 20 percent of their exports. Meanwhile, U.S. direct foreign investment grew notably in China, but the level there was only about a third of the level of U.S. investment in Australia, Hong Kong, or Singapore, and less than 20 percent of the U.S. investment in Japan.[56]

After the Cold War, strong U.S. domestic pressure pushed democracy, human rights, and other U.S. values in Asia, and met resistance from the Chinese authorities and other authoritarian governments seeking to preserve their ruling prerogatives and Asian democracies fearing regional instability. Despite strong rhetorical emphasis, Bush administration policy was pragmatic in this policy area, especially as the United States sought allies and supporters in the global war on terrorism and other endeavors. This adjustment generally was welcomed in Asia and worked to ease U.S. differences with authoritarian governments in Asia.[57]

In the Chinese view, the United States held the preeminent power position in the region, especially after September 11, 2001. U.S. power appeared to belie predictions in earlier decades of an inevitable U.S. decline, as the United States became more powerful and influential in Asia and the Pacific than at any time since the defeat of Japan in World War II. There was recognition of possible U.S. "overreach"—stretching military and economic commitments beyond U.S. capabilities, but existing commitments in the wake of the toppling of Saddam Hussein allowed for planned realignment and downsizing of U.S. forces in Asia and elsewhere abroad. While some in the Asian region might wish to challenge or confront the United States, most were loath to do so given the dangers they would face in opposition to the world's dominant power, with a leadership seemingly prepared to use that power against its enemies.[58]

Consultations with Chinese specialists and officials showed that they judged the asymmetry of power between the United States and China and other Asian governments probably will not change soon. U.S. realigned military forces in Asia, backed by the unsurpassed U.S. military capabilities demonstrated in recent conflicts in Europe and Asia, seemed well positioned to deal with regional contingencies. The United States leadership was preoccupied with protracted difficulties in Iraq and Southwest Asia, but this situation did not fundamentally affect U.S. strategic leadership in Asia, according to Chinese specialists. The massive size and overall importance of the U.S. economy to Asian economic well being rose in the post-Cold War period in the eyes of the Chinese and other Asian governments seeking international outreach and economic development as a foundation for their conventional nation-building strategies.

The major regional powers, including slowly growing Japan and such rising powers as China and India, were seen by Chinese experts as domestically preoccupied and likely to remain so for some time to come.[59] Focused on internal issues, they sought support from the United States and other powers, and did not seek difficulties in their foreign relations. In theory, there was a danger that the Asian powers might align against the United States and its interests in significant ways. The Asian nations, including leading regional powers Japan, China, and India, were actively maneuvering and hedging, seeking new and more multifaceted arrangements to secure their interests in the uncertain regional environment. They sometimes cooperated together in broader arrangements like Sino-Japanese cooperation in ASEAN Plus Three. ASEAN Plus Three promoted U.S.-backed goals of regional cooperation, though some Americans were wary of such regional arrangements that excluded the United States. At bottom, however, the Asian nations—especially the leading powers—were seen by Chinese experts as divided by deep suspicions, indicating that any meaningful cooperation seriously detrimental to U.S. interests remained unlikely.[60]

U.S. policy makers also were seen by Chinese specialists to have done a better job in managing the often-strong U.S. domestic pressures that in the post-Cold War period tended to drive U.S. policy in extreme directions detrimental to a sound and balanced approach to Asia. President Clinton's engagement policy toward China in his second term was more coherent that the policy in his first term that appeared driven by competing U.S. domestic interests. President Bush's policy was better suited to mainstream U.S. opinion regarding China and had the added advantage of avoiding the need for significant U.S. concessions toward China on sensitive issues like Taiwan that seriously exacerbate the U.S. domestic debate about China policy.[61] President Bush's attention to Japan reduced Japanese concerns caused by the Clinton administration's emphasis on China and its tough public criticism of Japan's economic policies, avoiding U.S. domestic controversy over this policy area.[62]

As seen by Chinese specialists and others, a major U.S. weakness—more important in Asia than the Bush administration's aggressive policy regarding Iraq and other world issues—remained the Bush administration's tough stance toward North Korea, which posed obvious and serious difficulties for U.S. influence in Asia. The difficulty of meshing a tough U.S. stance to North Korea while supporting South Korea's asymmetrical engagement efforts with Pyongyang was not fully addressed. For a time, U.S. policy drifted with leaders in Washington and much of the rest of the world focused on other more immediate problems. North Korean brinksmanship in 2002-2003 brought the issue to a head, forcing the United States to act. There remained a possibility for unilateral, forceful U.S. actions, including military attack on North Korea. However, the danger that Bush administration hard-liners would push policy to an extreme and create a major crisis in U.S.-Asia relations was mitigated to some degree by strong countervailing opinion in the administration and more broadly in the Congress, the media, and among U.S. experts and opinion leaders warning of dire consequences of excessive U.S. pressure on the North Korean regime. The Chinese government worked hard to support a more moderate U.S. stance on the North Korean issue.[63]

Meanwhile, adding to Chinese perceptions of U.S. strength and leadership in Asia was the Bush administration's success in improving U.S. relations with all the great powers in Asia. The United States having good relations with Japan and China at the same time was very rare. The United States being the dominant power in South Asia and having good relations with both India and Pakistan was unprecedented, as was the U.S. maintenance of good U.S. relations with both Beijing and Taipei during the Bush administration.

The administration came to power with plans to markedly enhance political-military partnership with Japan. The Japanese government of Prime Minister Junichiro Koizumi was a responsive partner, though constraints posed by Japanese economic stagnation and political differences in Japan limited cooperation to some degree. Japan provided strong support in the war on terrorism, including an unprecedented Indian Ocean naval deployment in support of allied operations in the war in Afghanistan. Prime Minister Koizumi was outspoken in backing the U.S.-led attack on Saddam Hussein and in sending Japanese troops to Iraq in support for the allied cause. Koizumi may have diverged from U.S. interests in meeting Kim Jong Il in September 2002, but he found common ground with the Bush administration in its subsequent efforts to deal with North Korea's provocative nuclear weapons development, and Koizumi's May 2004 visit to Pyongyang appeared to be well coordinated with the United States.[64]

Compared with traditional U.S. allies, India's government was less critical and more understanding of Bush administration policy regarding sensitive issues in missile defense, arms control, the United Nations, and the war in Iraq. It welcomed the U.S. administration's plans for a greater Indian role in Asian security and world affairs and the steadily expanding U.S. military relationship with India. The terrorist attacks of September 11, 2001, proved to be a catalyst in improving U.S.-Indian relations.[65] The Indian Parliament supported strong popular and elite opposition to U.S. intervention in Iraq, but the Indian administration was more circumspect.

The improvement of U.S. relations with Russia seen in the first Bush-Putin summit in the months before the terrorist attack on America was markedly enhanced by U.S.-Russian cooperation after September 11, 2001. Russia saw its interests served by fostering closer economic and strategic cooperation with the United States and the West, and by playing down past major differences over U.S. missile defense programs and NATO enlargement. Maneuvering in the UN in the months prior to the war in Iraq saw Russia join with France and others in standing against U.S. military actions to topple Saddam Hussein without renewed UN approval. After the U.S.-led coalition succeeded in toppling Saddam and senior Bush administration officials made significant gestures to ease tensions with Moscow, Russia appeared prepared to resume a more cooperative stance toward the United States.[66]

The breakthrough in U.S. relations with China by far was the most important success for Bush administration policy in Asia. The rise of China's power and influence in world affairs, especially around China's periphery in Asia, initially received negative Bush administration attention and prompted a steady stream of U.S. media, congressional, and other commentary warning of PRC efforts to push the United States out of Asia. In contrast, as noted above, actual Chinese behavior in the region and in improving relations with the Bush administration seemed to underscore strong awareness by Chinese leaders of the difficulties involved in China competing directly with the U.S. superpower.[67]

Outlook

Chinese officials and specialists fully recognized that the large-scale deployment of U.S. military forces and other government resources to the U.S.-led war and occupation in Iraq seemed to ensure that U.S. government strategic emphasis will focus on southwest Asia well beyond the rest of the U.S. presidential term. Stabilizing Iraq and avoiding negative trends in the Persian Gulf and the Middle East following the toppling of Saddam Hussein represented large tasks for U.S. leaders. Building and maintaining international coalitions to help with peacekeeping, reconstruction, and establishing good government in Iraq required U.S. officials to engage in attentive diplomacy and other persuasive efforts in the face of widespread international antipathy to the U.S. decision to launch the war against Iraq without the full endorsement of the UN Security Council.[68]

Popular and elite opinion in much of the world opposed the U.S. war and demonstrated broader concerns over U.S. dominance and "hegemony" in world affairs. France, Germany, Russia, and governments in the Middle East and much of the Muslim world strongly criticized the U.S. decision to attack Iraq. In China and much of Asia, however, the governments stood at odds with their publics and nongovernment elites and reacted more pragmatically in dealing with the United States over the Iraq war and broader concerns flowing from U.S. international dominance. Prime Minister Koizumi was outspoken in support of Japan's U.S. ally, quick to lend military support within the confines of Japan's existing constraints on deployments abroad, and prominent in leading the post-war aid effort. South Korea's new president pushed a reluctant parliament to approve the deployment of troops to Iraq, repeatedly stressing the importance for South Korea of preserving a close alliance relationship with the United States in the face of North Korea's provocations. Chinese leaders showed little interest in being associated closely with international resistance to U.S. leadership in Iraq. Similarly, India's government remained restrained in criticizing the U.S. attack on Iraq.[69]

Contingencies could seriously weaken U.S. policy in Asia. They included possible setbacks in the war on terrorism involving large-scale terrorist attacks, possibly including the use of weapons of mass destruction (WMD) against U.S. or allied targets, and regime failure in such frontline states as Afghanistan or Pakistan, where political conditions and governance remained unstable and weak. A major—possibly nuclear—war between India and Pakistan, precipitated by disputes over Kashmir or other issues, would be disastrous for regional peace and stability. World economic trends remained uncertain, with the U.S. economy among those grappling with recovery and large-scale government budget and trade deficits. If past practice was any guide, major setbacks in the pace and scope of the U.S. economic recovery and other perceived failures were likely to prompt heavy partisan attack, as U.S. leaders seeking to unseat President Bush in the 2004 election targeted the costs to the United States of the Bush administration's wide-ranging military deployments abroad.[70]

The crisis with North Korea presented the most immediate problem for U.S. policy in Asia. The Bush administration had some success in the immediate aftermath of the war in Iraq in limiting the damage from the crises in U.S. relations with North Korea and in U.S. alliance relations with South Korea, but few predicted a quick solution to either set of problems. The crises placed U.S. policy on the peninsula in a reactive stance, responding to sometimes unanticipated events and endeavoring to formulate options that limit the damage to U.S. interests, and hold out the possibility of resolution in accord with U.S. interests.

Most likely was a protracted process involving diplomacy, negotiations, and possible sanctions and military moves to seek safeguards regarding North Korea's nuclear program. Recent U.S. policy regarding North Korea bought time and kept South Korea and other powers in an ostensibly common front, but it might not resolve North Korea's nuclear weapons development or deep U.S. differences with South Korea, China, and others at home and abroad on how to deal with North Korea. Negotiations and other aspects of the U.S. and international efforts to deal with North Korea over the next months and possibly years might have episodes of improvement in U.S. relations with concerned powers and episodes of crisis brought on by North Korea's brinksmanship or other factors. The process was likely to be prolonged because of the mix of North Korean rigidity and frequent brinksmanship, Bush administration refusal to be blackmailed, and seemingly insufficient U.S. power/influence to coerce the North. In this context, U.S. alliance management (notably, relations with South Korea) and great power diplomacy (notably, relations with China) over this issue would be complicated and probably difficult. Bush administration ability to manage U.S. domestic critics might also be challenged, especially at times of tension with North Korea. Overall, the process promised to preoccupy and weaken U.S. leadership in Asian affairs.

Less likely was a more assertive U.S. policy, presumably involving U.S. pressure or perhaps military attack. This could follow the military success in Iraq or come in response to a North Korean nuclear test or transfer of nuclear material to terrorists. Such an assertive U.S. stance faced North Korea's military power and strong opposition of key powers—especially South Korea and China. It made more probable a war on the Korean peninsula that would place the United States at odds with China, South Korea, and many others.

Also less likely was the Bush administration offering major concessions to the North, without a clear path to the North's denuclearization, in order to ease the crisis and meet demands of South Korea, China, and U.S. domestic critics. This could smooth U.S. relations with South Korea, China, and others in Asia, but would face strong opposition from within the Bush administration and from U.S. conservatives in Congress and elsewhere.

It is significant to observe Chinese government behavior in this context of U.S. government difficulties over Korean issues, notably in U.S. relations with both North and South. Chinese foreign policy specialists made clear that China was seeking its own interests as it worked closely in parallel with the United States in dealing with the North Korean crisis. When it entered office, the Bush administration had not planned to work closely with China in dealing with the North Korean issue, preferring to rely on its own strength and on U.S. allies, notably Japan and South Korea. The difficulties in U.S.-South Korean relations were among the factors moving U.S. decision makers to work more closely with China, whose officials worked hard to cooperate with the United States while preserving stability and enhancing Chinese influence on the Korean peninsula.

Other potential flashpoints in Asia included the Taiwan Strait. At least for the duration of the Bush administration, Chinese leaders seemed sufficiently constrained by U.S. power. They also seemed pleased with burgeoning mainland-Taiwan economic relations, though they worried about growing political separatism on the island. On balance, these circumstances appeared likely to prompt Chinese leaders to avoid aggressive actions unless provoked by Taiwan or the United States.

When the Taiwan president initiated constitutional reforms during a highly competitive election campaign in 2003-2004, Chinese officials became alarmed at such "pro-independence" moves. They recognized that a harsh Chinese response would further alienate Taiwan from the mainland, and were pleased when President Bush publicly rebuked the Taiwan president during a U.S.-PRC summit meeting with Premier Wen Jiabao. Chinese foreign policy officials and specialists pressed the United States to keep pressure on the Taiwan president to prevent further moves toward greater independence.[71]

Chinese foreign policy specialists indicated there probably will be little letup in the Chinese military buildup opposite Taiwan as PRC leaders remained on a long-term course to achieve military dominance over Taiwan.[72] Taiwan leaders chafed under the carrots and sticks of Chinese policy, and sought to take initiatives in cross-strait or international relations, sometimes even at the risk of disrupting the prevailing modus vivendi in cross-strait ties. However, the Bush administration came down hard against Taiwan leaders who risked such disruption, and the fear of alienating U.S. support probably would help to curb possible Taiwan actions that might provoke a harsh response from China.[73] In 2004, Chinese foreign policy specialists placed great emphasis on the importance of a strong U.S. effort to curb such Taiwan actions.[74]

Southeast Asia was an area of serious concern in the war on terrorism but appeared to hold few major problems for U.S. policy, though managing sometimes-difficult U.S. security ties with countries like Indonesia and the Philippines represented a complication in the broader U.S. war on terrorism. As noted earlier, there remained the distinct possibility of such major failures for U.S. policy in Asia as government collapse in Afghanistan or Pakistan or a war between India and Pakistan; there appeared to be too much at stake for U.S. leaders not to give a high priority to diplomatic and other efforts to prevent such a negative outcomes in Central and South Asia.

In sum, U.S. assertiveness over Iraq and other issues continued to be widely criticized among Chinese and other Asian popular and elite opinion, and damaged the image of the American government in Asia. However, the Chinese and other Asian governments were reacting pragmatically. They remained focused on domestic concerns involving conventional nation building. From their perspective, the crisis posed by North Korea's nuclear weapons development was more important, and the Bush administration was dealing with that issue in a consultative manner acceptable to China and other concerned Asian powers.

Recent U.S. crises in Korea, involving U.S. relations with both North and South Korea, seemed unlikely to be resolved soon or satisfactorily. The process for dealing with the Korean crises likely would preoccupy U.S. policy in Asia, and on balance probably would weaken U.S. leadership in the region. Nevertheless, the crises appeared likely to remain manageable for U.S. policy, particularly given the continued broad strengths in U.S. power and influence in Asia. Those strengths would continue to support U.S. regional leadership, notably in the war on terrorism, and regional stability and development compatible with American interests. Chinese specialists and officials recognized the power and strength of U.S. leadership in Asia and worked to find ways to ensure that China's rise in regional power and influence did not prompt an adverse U.S. reaction contrary to Chinese interests.[75]

Meanwhile, circumstances on the Chinese side also appeared to support a continued smooth course for U.S.-China relations over Asian and world affairs for a few years, and perhaps longer. The preoccupation of Chinese leaders with other policy priorities appeared likely to continue beyond the transition of leadership in 2002-2003. Chinese leaders faced difficult leadership succession issues and protracted economic and social challenges to China's internal stability. Beijing leaders notably sought to preserve advantageous U.S. economic contacts, to do what they could to sustain the health of the U.S. economy, and to avoid the broad and internally wrenching ramifications of any major change in China's U.S. policy. At least for a time, they also were a bit more sanguine about the Taiwan situation, as cross-strait economic ties continued brisk growth. Seeking to consolidate China's rising international stature as a constructive player in Asian and world affairs, Chinese leaders found that their Olympic bid for 2008 and a smooth transition into the WTO added to reasons for moderation in policy in Asian affairs and toward the United States.

Also, during 2001-2002, Jiang Zemin closely identified his legacy with smooth U.S.-China relations and an overall moderate approach in Chinese foreign policy, including policy toward Asia. In this context, newly installed Chinese leaders probably would not seek to carry out a major reevaluation of policy toward the United States or other areas unless pressed by events.[76]

Finally, even though U.S. academic and foreign policy specialists differed on what factors best explained the recent improvement in U.S.-China relations, the different explanations noted earlier in this chapter—each in its own way—reinforced the judgment that China was following a moderate approach toward its periphery that was likely to continue, along with continued U.S.-China cooperation in Asia.

• Those U.S. specialists who emphasized the importance of effective uses of U.S. power in influencing Chinese policy said that Chinese leaders saw little to be gained from an assertive posture with pressure tactics directed against the United States and U.S. interests in Asia. Such an approach risked friction and worsened China-U.S. relations, calling negative attention to China at a time when the U.S. superpower seemed prepared to confront its enemies in strong and concrete ways. A better path for China was to endeavor to try to cooperate with or wait out the United States.

• Those U.S. specialists who claimed it was the Bush administration that first changed its policy in a bid to accommodate China said that the perceived positive Bush administration shift toward China seemed to work to China's advantage. As the U.S. government became more accommodating to Chinese interests, Chinese leaders presumably were in an ever-more influential position in Asian and world affairs. The utility of a more assertive and potentially disruptive Chinese stance toward Asian affairs appeared low in this context.

• And those U.S. specialists who emphasized that Chinese leaders had become more confident and mature in their foreign policy approach said that a Chinese leadership that was more confident of China's power and influence in Asian affairs appeared unlikely to resort to an assertive or aggressive stance that could disrupt the many recent gains in relations. It had taken the Chinese leadership several decades to come up with a seemingly winning strategy toward China's neighbors, and circumstances did not appear to warrant major change in the recent approach.

There remained debate, as noted above, about how lasting the Chinese change would be, how dependent it was on U.S. policy and behavior, what China's longer-term goals were in the region, and how China's approach would be received by the United States over the long term. On the Chinese side, a case can be made that China's leaders are likely to continue along current policy lines unless influenced or challenged by changed circumstances. The fourth generation of leaders headed by Hu Jintao repeatedly emphasize pursuing the foreign policy guidelines laid down by previous leaders. They remain focused on domestic development and sustaining political stability in China. Foreign policy is viewed as a secondary concern that needs to serve these primary domestic goals for the foreseeable future. In this context, it is fair to say that under prevailing circumstances, Chinese leaders generally will not be inclined toward more aggressive, assertive, or disruptive positions in Asia.

On the U.S. side, a case can be made that a key factor in circumstances driving China's recent moderate approach in Asia has been the power and policies of the United States. On this score, the George W. Bush administration has done a better job than the Clinton administration in balancing a firm U.S. posture against possible or real Chinese pressure and assertiveness regarding U.S. interests in Taiwan, Asian stability, and other areas, with U.S. accommodation and gestures regarding such key Chinese concerns as Taiwan, North Korea, and trade relations with the United States. However, the record of U.S. policy and behavior toward China since the end of the Cold War is much more erratic than the record of China's policy and behavior toward the United States in the same period. Thus, prudent forecasts will have to take account of shifts in U.S. policy that might so offend Chinese interests as to provoke strong and assertive Chinese responses; or that might reflect a weakening of U.S. resolve on Taiwan or other sensitive issues, prompting more assertive Chinese probes seeking to improve China's position regarding Taiwan or other questions. While the global war on terrorism has broadened U.S.-China common ground and added to reasons for U.S. cooperation and not confrontation with China, there is no guarantee that future developments in the war on terrorism might not prompt U.S. weakness that China may seek to probe, or U.S. assertiveness that would alarm China, prompting Chinese resistance.

Meanwhile, key variables defining future Chinese policy and behavior in Asia and cooperation with the United States lie in the hands of third parties. Heading the list is the Chen Shui-bian government in Taiwan. If Taiwan moves toward de jure independence, Chinese officials and specialists repeatedly emphasize that Chinese leaders will put aside other interests arguing for moderation and will use force to prevent Taiwan independence. Others prominent on this list include North Korea's Kim Jong Il. Swinging between moderation and aggression, Kim could easily create a heightened crisis on the Korean peninsula that would surely test the fragile U.S.-China cooperation that has marked the two powers' stance on the Korean peninsula over the past two years.

Notes

1. Evan Medieros and Taylor Fravel, "China's New Diplomacy," *Foreign Affairs*, November/December 2003 (Internet version); Nailene Chou Wiest, "Beijing Presents a New Face in an Innovative Year for Diplomacy," *South China Morning Post*, 2 January 2004, 1; Alastair Iain Johnston, "China's International Relations: Political and Security Dimensions," in Samuel Kim, ed., *The International Relations of Northeast Asia* (Lanham, Md.: Rowman & Littlefield, 2004), 65-100; Thomas Moore, "China's International Relations: The Economic Dimension," in Kim, *Northeast Asia*, 101-36.

2. Wang Jisi, *China's Changing Role in Asia* (Washington, D.C.: The Atlantic Council of the United States, January 2004), 1-5, 16-17; Bonnie Glaser, "Sustaining Cooperation: Security Matters Take Center Stage," *Comparative Connections*, www.csis.org/pacfor (January 2003) (accessed 1 March 2003); Bonnie Glaser, "Wen Jiabao's Visit Caps an Outstanding Year," *Comparative Connections*, January 2004; Qian Qichen, "Adjustment of the United States National Security Strategy and International Relations in the Early New Century," Beijing *Foreign Affairs Journal* 71 (March 2004): 1-7; Wang Jisi, "Xinxingshi de zhuyao tedian he zhongguo waijiao, *Xiabdai guoji guanxi* 4 (April 2003): 1-3; Liu Jianfei, "Zhanlue jiyuqi yu zhongmei guanxi, *Liaowang* 20 January 2003, 56-57; Yuan Peng "9.11 shijian yu zhongmei guanxi," *Xiandai guoji guanxi*, 11 November 2001, 19-23, 63. See also Tao Wenzhao, "Changes and Drivers in Sino-U.S. Relations," replayed in *China Strategy*, vol. 3, www.csis.org (accessed 20 July 2004). See also Wang Jisi, "Impact of U.S. Strategic Adjustment on Sino-U.S. Relations," (Beijing) *Xuexi Shibao*,16 August 2004 (Internet version, translated by FBIS); Peng Guangqian, "The Reorientation of China's Taiwan Policy," replayed in *China Strategy*, vol. 3, www.csis.org (accessed 20 July 2004).

3. Suisheng Zhao, "A State-led Nationalism: The Patriotic Education Campaign in Post-Tiananmen China," *Communist and Post Communist Studies* 31, no. 3 (1998): 289; Suisheng Zhao, "Chinese Nationalism and its International Orientations," *Political Science Quarterly* 115, no. 1 (Spring 2000): 5; Denny Roy, "Rising China and U.S. Interests: Inevitable vs. Contingent Hazards," *Orbis* 47, 1 (2003): 124-43; Robert Sutter, "China Remains Wary of U.S.-led World Order," *YaleGlobal online*, www.yaleglobal.yale.edu (accessed 8 June 2003); Bates Gill, *Contrasting Visions: United States, China, and World Order* (Washington, D.C.: Brookings Institution, 2004); Zhu Qiangguo, "Meiguo heweishe zhanlue de tiaozheng—hetaishi shenyi baogao pingxi, *Xiandai guoji guanxi* 14 (8 February 2002): 28-31; Zhu Qiangguo, "U.S. Seeks Absolute Military Superiority, *China Daily,* 13 March 2002; Zhou Jiangguo, "Nuclear Strategy of Bush Administration Moving Gradually From Deterrence to Actual Combat," *Liberation Army Daily*, 18 March 2002, 12; Zhu Feng, "Meiguo zhunbei fadong hegongji?" *Zhongguo ribao wangzhan*, 11 March 2002 (Internet version).

4. See discussion in chapter 2, above.

5. Consultations with Chinese foreign policy specialists, Beijing and Shanghai, May 2004.

6. Suisheng Zhao, "A State-led Nationalism," 289; Suisheng Zhao, "Chinese Nationalism and Its International Orientations," 5.

7. See, among others, David M. Lampton, *Same Bed, Different Dreams* (Berkeley: University of California Press, 2001); David Shambaugh, "Sino-American Strategic Relations: From Partners to Competitors," *Survival* 42, no. 1 (Spring 2000): 97-115; Catherin Dalpino and Bates Gill, eds., *Brookings Northeast Asia Survey 2000-2001* (Washington, D.C.: Brookings Institution, 2001), 36-47.

8. Chinese foreign policy specialists also reflected this approach when assessing the implications of China's new strategy of "peaceful rise," and its implications for the United States. Consultations, Beijing and Shanghai, May 2004.

9. To track the convergent and divergent elements in recent U.S.-China relations, see the quarterly reviews by Bonnie Glaser in *Comparative Connections*. See also the yearly treatment of China development by Thomas Christensen in Richard Ellings and Aaron Friedberg, eds., *Strategic Asia, Power and Purpose* (Seattle, Wash.: National Bureau of Asian Research), 2001, 2002, and 2003.

10. See quarterly reviews by David Brown and Bonnie Glaser in *Comparative Connections*, www.csis.org/pacfor.

11. "Japan Building Up Its Arsenal," *China Daily*, 5 July 2003, 4; Li Heng, "Is Japan Advancing toward a 'Normal Country,'" *People's Daily*, 3 July 2003; Chen Zhijiang, "Japan Accelerates Construction of Missile Defense System," Beijing *Guangming Ribao*, 24 June 2003; "Japan Has an Ax to Grind," *People's Daily online*, 7 August 2003; Zhang Baiyu. "Analysis of Japan's New Defense White Paper," 14 August 2003; Zhi Qiu, "Martime Interception Exercise Conducted by Member States of the 'Proliferation Security Initiative,'" Beijing *Zhongguo Guofang Bao*, 23 September 2003, 2.

12. See Scott Snyder's quarterly reviews of China-Korea relations in *Comparative Connections*; David Shambaugh, "China and the Korean Peninsula"; You Ji, "China and North Korea," *Journal of Contemporary China* 10, no. 28 (August 2001): 387-98; and Victor Cha, "Engaging China: The View from Korea," in Alistair Iain Johnston and Robert Ross, eds., *Engaging China* (London: Routledge, 1999), 32-56.

13. Kim Ji-ho, "Chinese Envoy: DPRK Needs to Execute Independent Model of Economic Reform," *Korea Times*, 21 August 2002 (Internet version).

14. Zhi Qiu, "Maritime Interception Exercise Conducted by Member States of the 'Proliferation Security Initiative,'" Beijing *Zhongguo Guofang Bao*, 23 September 2003, 2.

15. "The New Korea," *Asiaweek*, www.asiaweek.com/asiaweek/95/1201/ed.html (accessed 1 February 1996).

16. For quarterly reviews of developments in China-Southeast Asian relations, see *Comparative Connections*, Honolulu: CSIS, Pacific Forum, www.csis.org/pacfor. Other sources include Rosemary Foot, "China and the ASEAN Regional Forum," *Asian Survey* 38, no. 5 (1998): 425-40; Ho Khai Leong, "Rituals, Risks and Rivalries: China and ASEAN in the Coming Decades," *Journal of Contemporary China* 10, no. 29 (November 2001): 683-94; John Pomfret, "In Its Own Neighborhood, China Emerges as a Leader" *Washington Post*, October 18, 2001; Kenneth Allen, "China's Foreign Military Relations with Asia-Pacific," *Journal of Contemporary China* 10, no. 29 (November 2001): 645-62; Michael Richardson, "Seeking Allies in Terror War, U.S. Woos Southeast Asia," *International Herald Tribune*, 29 November 2001; Lee Lai, "To the Lion and the Dragon," *Journal of Contemporary China* 10, no. 28 (August 2001): 415-26; articles by Michael Leifer, Yuen Foong Khong, and Amitav Acharga in Johnston and Ross, *Engaging China*, 87-151.

17. Lyall Breckon, "Beijing Pushes 'Asia for Asians,'" *Comparative Connections*, October 2002.

18. Consultations with Chinese foreign policy specialists, December 2003.

19. These events are noted in the quarterly reviews of Lyall Breckon in *Comparative Connections* at www.csis.org/pacfor. See also Denny Roy, "Rising China and U.S. Interests: Inevitable vs. Contingent Hazards," *Orbis* 47, 1 (2003): 124-43; *Asia's China Debate* (Honolulu: Asia Pacific Center for Security Studies, December 2003), chapters 7, 14, 16.

20. See coverage of Chinese activities during various ASEAN related meetings in October 2003 replayed at www.aseansec.org.

21. Lyall Breckon, "Former Tigers Under Dragon's Spell," *Comparative Connections*, July 2002.

22. Sources for this topic include *Asia's China Debate*, chapter 11; Sherman Garnett, ed., *Rapprochement or Rivalry? Russia-China Relations in a Changing Asia* (Washington, D.C.: Carnegie Endowment for International Peace, 2000); Alexander Lukin, "Russian Perceptions of the China Threat," in Herbert Yee and Ian Storey, *The China Threat: Perceptions, Myths, and Realities* (London: Routledge, 2002), 86-114; Gang Lin, *Sino-Russian Strategic Partnership: A Threat to American Interests?* (Washington, D.C.: Woodrow Wilson International Center for Scholars, Asia Program special report, September 2001); Rajan Menon, "Russia," in Ellings and Friedberg, *Strategic Asia: 2001-2002*, 200-6; Lowell Dittmer, "The

Sino-Russian Partnership," *Journal of Contemporary China* 10, no. 28 (August 2001): 399-414. See also Yu Bin's quarterly reviews of Russia-China relations in *Comparative Connections.*

23. *China's New Journey to the West* (Washington, D.C.: Center for Strategic and International Studies, August 2003). See also Yu Bin's quarterly reviews of Russia-China relations with reference to Central Asia in *Comparative Connections.*

24. *Asia's China Debate,* chapters 6, 10; C. V. Ranganathan, "The Chinese Threat: A View from India" and Perviaz Iqbal Cheema, "The China Threat: A View from Pakistan," in Yee and Storey, *The China Threat,* 288-301, 302-11; John W. Garver, *Protracted Contest: Sino-Indian Rivalry in the 20th Century* (Seattle, Wash.: University of Washington, 2002); Mohan Malik, "High Hopes: India's Response to U.S. Security Policies," in *Asia-Pacific Responses to U.S. Security Policies* (Honolulu: Asia Pacific Center for Security Studies, 2003), Internet version.

25. Medieros and Fravel, "China's New Diplomacy"; Chou Wiest, "Beijing Presents a New Face," 1; Michael Yahuda, "China's Win-Win Globalization," *Yaleglobal,* 19 February 2003; Liang Xing-guang, "China's New Peace Strategy," *Japan Times,* 17 November 2002 (Internet version).

26. Michael Swaine, *"Reverse Course? The Fragile Turnabout in U.S.-China Relations,"* Carnegie Endowment for International Peace, Policy Brief no. 22, February 2003.

27. Robert Sutter, "Bush Policy toward Beijing and Taipei," *Journal of Contemporary China* 12, no. 36 (August 2003): 477-92.

28. Murray Hiebert, *The Bush Presidency: Implications for Asia* (New York: The Asia Society), Asian Update January 2001, and 5-9.

29. Robert Sutter, *Grading Bush's China Policy,* Honolulu: CSIS Pacific Forum, PACNET 10, 8 March 2002.

30. Bonnie Glaser, "Bilateral Relations on Reasonably Sound Footing" *Comparative Connections,* Honolulu: CSIS Pacific Forum, www.csis.org/pacfor (accessed 1 February 2001).

31. Glaser, "First Contact: Qian Qichen Engages in Wide-ranging, Constructive Talks," *Comparative Connections,* Honolulu: CSIS Pacific Forum, www.csis.org/pacfor (1st quarter 2001).

32. John Keefe, *Anatomy of the EP-3 Incident* (Alexandria, Va.: Center for Naval Analysis, January 2002).

33. Sutter, *Bush's China Policy.*

34. Nick Cummings-Bruce, "Powell Will Explain Bush's Asia Policy," *Wall Street Journal,* 23 July 2001, A11. See also the review of this period by Bonnie Glaser in *Comparative Connections.* There are alternative explanations for improved China-U.S. relations. For example, some specialists attribute the improvement in relations in 2001 largely to a change in Bush administration attitudes rather than a change in China's approach. These specialists argued that most U.S. governments enter office promising a harder-line policy toward China, only to adjust and moderate their policy in the face of realities involving China's importance for vital U.S. interests in Asian and world affairs. They averred that the September 11, 2001, attack on America added significantly to the Bush administration's imperative to work constructively with Chinese leaders in the global war against terrorism. (Michael Swaine, *"Reverse Course? The Fragile Turnabout in U.S.-China Relations,"* Carnegie Endowment for International Peace, Policy Brief no. 22, February 2003.) Other specialists agreed that Chinese moderation and accommodation in the face of Bush administration firmness played a key role in encouraging the upswing of relations in 2001, but they averred that Chinese leaders came to the judgment largely on the basis of greater confidence in China's regional

tional situation. Their concern over Bush administration firmness and maneuvers was low while their moderation and accommodation came from a judgment that amid strong economic growth and unchallenged political dominance, the Communist Party-led Chinese government was making significant gains in its global standing, notably around its periphery in Asia. Relations with Southeast Asia and South Korea were particular bright spots, while relations with Russia, Central Asian governments, and South Asia remained on a positive footing. Other sources of Chinese leadership satisfaction and confidence resulted from acceptance of Beijing as the site of the 2008 Olympics, China's relatively smooth entry into the World Trade Organization, and its concurrent status as the largest recipient of foreign direct investment in 2002. (Joseph Kahn, "Hands across the Pacific," *New York Times*, 11 November 2002 (Internet version); Michael Yahuda, "China's Win-Win Globalization," *Yaleglobal*, www.yaleglobal.yale.edu (accessed 19 February 2003); also reviewed in Swaine, *"Reverse Course."*)

35. "Concern Over U.S. Plans for War on Terror Dominate Jiang Tour," *Reuters*, 7 April 2002; Willy Wo-Lap Lam, "U.S., Taiwan Catch Jiang Off-guard," CNN, www.cnn.com (accessed 19 March 2002).

36. Bonnie Glaser, "Playing up the Positive on the Eve of the Crawford Summit," *Comparative Connections*, www.csis.org/pacfor (accessed 30 October 2002).

37. "U.S. Says China Regulations Should Free Up Soybean Exports" Office of the U.S. Trade Representative, usinfo.state.gov (accessed 18 October 2002); "Mainland Offers Taiwan Goodwill Gesture," *China Daily*, 18 October 2002 (Internet version); "China Tightens Rules on Military Exports," *Reuters*, 21 October 2002 (Internet version); Ashcroft to Open China FBI Office," *Reuters*, 22 October 2002 (Internet version); "U.S. and China Seal Billion Dollar Deals," *BBC*, 22 October 2002; "U.S. and China Set New Rights Talks," *Washington Post*, 24 October 2002 (Internet version).

38. "Transcript of Hong Kong Phoenix TV interview with Secretary of State Colin Powell," Hong Kong *Feng Huang Wei Shih Chung Wen Tai* in Mandarin, 18 October 2002. Lu Zhenya, "Jiang Zemin, Bush Agree to Maintain High-level Strategic Dialogue," Beijing *Zhongguo Xinwen She*, 26 October 2002 (Internet version).

39. Nathan Hodge, "U.S., China to Resume High-level Military Talks," *Defense Week Daily Update*, 28 October 2002. Glaser, "Sustaining Cooperation," *Comparative Connections*.

40. See quarterly reviews of U.S.-China-Taiwan relations during this period by Bonnie Glaser and David Brown in *Comparative Connections*.

41. Robert Sutter, "China's Rise in Asia," *PACNET 11A*, www.csis.org/pacfor (accessed 7 March 2003).

42. Consultations with Chinese foreign policy specialists, Beijing and Shanghai, May 2004.

43. Consultations with fifty Chinese specialists and officials, 2003-2004. This section is based heavily on the findings of those consultations.

44. Nicholas Eberstadt and Joseph Ferguson, "North Korea: The Korean Nuclear Crisis" in Ellings and Friedberg, *Strategic Asia: 2003-2004*, 131-64.

45. Ralph Cossa, "Diplomacy Fails with Iraq; Is North Korea Next?" and Donald Gross, "Tensions Escalate in Korea as the U.S. Targets Iraq," in *Comparative Connections*, www.csis.org/pacfor (accessed 1 June 2003); Larry Niksch, *Korea: Korea-U.S. Relations: Issues for Congress* (Washington, D.C.: Library of Congress), Congressional Research Service, Issue Brief 98045, 5 May 2003.

46. *What the World Thinks in 2002*, The Pew Research Center, www.people-press.org/reports/display.php3?ReportID=165 (accessed 1 February 2003); Raymond Copson, coordinator, *Iraq War: Background and Issues Overview* (Washington, D.C.: Library of Congress), Congressional Research Service, Report RL31715, updated 22 April 2003.

47. "American out of Favor in Asia," *Far Eastern Economic Review*, www.feer.com (accessed 24 July 2003).

48. David Hsieh, "Chinese Feel UN Should Teach U.S. a Lesson," *Straits Times*, www.taiwansecurity.org (accessed 19 September 2003).

49. Jay Solomon, "Asian Muslim Nations Join China to Denounce U.S. Attack on Iraq," *Wall Street Journal/WSJ online*, 20 March 2003.

50. David Sanger, "On His High-speed Trip, Bush Glimpses a Perception Gap," *New York Times*, 24 October 2003, A1.

51. These are reviewed in more detail in Robert Sutter, "United States: U.S. Leadership—Prevailing Strengths Amid Challenges," in Ellings and Friedberg, *Strategic Asia: 2003-2004*, 36-41; *What the World Thinks in 2002*, December 2002, T-45, T-50.

52. Michael Swaine, *Reverse Course*, 1-3; Bonnie Glaser, "China and U.S. Disagree, but with Smiles," *Comparative Connections*, April 2003; Sutter, "Bush's China Policy," *PACNET* 10, no. 8, www.csis.org/pacfor (accessed 15 March 2002).

53. Ralph Cossa, "Bush-Roh: Closing the Gap," *PACNET* 20, www.csis.org/pacfor (accessed 20 May 2003).

54. Greg Jaffe, "Pentagon Prepares to Scatter Soldiers to Remote Corners," *Wall Street Journal*, 27 May 2003, 1; Paul Wolfowitz, "Sustaining the U.S. Commitment in Asia," *PACNET* 22A, 5 June 2003; Ralph Cossa, "Force Restructuring Anxiety," *PACNET* 22, 3 June 2003, both available at www.csis.org/pacfor.

55. *What the World Thinks in 2002*, T-45, T-50.

56. Figures from U.S. Department of Commerce, 2002. Chinese government figures show Chinese exports to the United States as much less than seen in U.S. government figures.

57. The United States did not seek to bring China's human rights conditions before the UN Human Rights Commission in 2003. George Gedda, "U.S. Won't Propose Resolution on China," *Associated Press*, 11 April 2003 (Internet version)

58. "The Acceptability of American Power," *Economist* 29, June 2002 (Internet version).

59. See the chapters on China, Japan, India, and Russia in Ellings and Friedberg, *Strategic Asia:2003-2004*. See also Wang Jisi, *China's Changing Role*, 1-5, 16-17; Alan Tonelson, *A Necessary Evil? Current Chinese Views of America's Military Role in East Asia* (Washington, D.C.: Henry Stimson Center, May 2003); Wu Xinbo, "Future U.S. Military Presence in Asia," a paper presented to a conference in Washington, D.C.,October 2003; Shi Yinhong, "The 15 Years of Chinese Diplomacy and Strategy toward the United States," a paper presented to a conference paper in Vail, Colo., November 2003; Yang Yi, "Improving U.S.-China Relations in the New Global Context," a paper presented at a conference in Vail, Colo., November 2003.

60. Benjamin Self, "China and Japan: A Façade of Friendship," *Washington Quarterly* 26, no. 1(Winter 2002-2003): 77-88; Robert Sutter, *The United States and East Asia* (Lanham Md.: Rowman & Littlefield, 2003), 199-200, 222-23.

61. Hugo Restall, "Tough Love for China," *The Wall Street Journal*, 21 October 2002 (Internet version).

62. Richard Cronin, coordinator, *Japan-U.S. Relations: Issue for Congress* (Washington, D.C.: Library of Congress), Congressional Research Service, Issue Brief 97004, updated 25 April 2003.

63. Ralph Cossa, "Diplomacy Fails with Iraq, Is North Korea Next?" *Comparative Connections* Honolulu: CSIS Pacific Forum, www.csis.org/pacfor (accessed 15 May 2003).

64. Brad Glosserman, "U.S.-Japan Relations: How High is Up?" *Comparative Connections*, April 2003; John Miller, "The Glacier Moves: Japan's Response to U.S. Security Policies," in *Asia-Pacific Responses to U.S. Security Policies*; consultations with U.S. officials, Seoul, June 2004.

65. Mohan Malik, "High Hopes," in *Asia-Pacific Responses to U.S. Security Policies.*

66. Joseph Ferguson, "U.S.-Russian Partnership: A Casualty of War?" *Comparative Connections*, April 2003; Rajan Menon, "Why Russia Says 'Nyet' to the U.S.," *Chicago Tribune* 12 March 2003 (Internet version); William Wohlforth, "Russia," in Ellings and Friedberg, *Strategic Asia: 2002-2003*, 183-222; William Wohlforth, "Russia: Russia's Soft Balancing Act," in Ellings and Friedberg, *Strategic Asia:2003-2004*, 165-80.

67. Andrew Nathan and Bruce Gilley, *China's New Rulers: The Secret Files* (New York: New York Review Book, 2002), 207-9; Thomas Christensen, "China," in Ellings and Friedberg, *Strategic Asia:2002-2003*, 51-94; Thomas Christensen and Michael Glonsny, "China: Sources of Stability in U.S.-China Security Relations," in Ellings and Friedberg, *Strategic Asia:2003-2004*, 53-80.

68. Thomas Donnelly, "Lessons of a Three Week War," *Weekly Standard*, 22 April 2003; Thomas Donnelly, "Brave New World: An Enduring Pax Americana," *AEI National Security Outlook*, www.aei.org (accessed 15 May 2003).

69. *Asia-Pacific Responses to U.S. Security Policies.* See articles reviewing U.S. relations with Asian governments in *Comparative Connections*, www.csis.org/pacfor (April, July, October 2003).

70. For a review of post-Iraq war issues for the United States, see Raymond Copson, coordinator, *Iraq War: Background and Issues Overview* (Washington, D.C.: Library of Congress),Congressional Research Service, Report RL31715 (accessed 22 April 2003).

71. Consultations, Beijing and Shanghai, May 2004. See full discussion in chapter 9.

72. U.S. Department of Defense, *Annual Report on the Military Power of the People's Republic of China, 2002*, www.defenselink.mil/news/Jul2002/p07122002_p133-02.html (accessed 2 December 2002); Wang Jisi, "Meiguo baquan de luoji" ("The Logic of American Hegemony"), *Zhongguo Ribao* (China Daily) www.chinadaily.com.cn/gb/doc/2003-08/21/content_257020.htm (accessed 15 January 2004); Honghua Men, *Yingdui Guojia Shibai de Bujiu Cuoshi* ("Assistance Toward State Failure—In Line with Discussion of Strategic Points in the China-America Security Cooperation"), *Zhongguo Guoguan Zaixian*, www.irchina.org/xueren/china/view.asp?id=741 (accessed 30 June 2004); Wang Jisi, "ZhongMei keyi bimian xinlengzhan" ("China and America can Avoid New Cold War"), *Huanqiu Shibao* (Global Times).

73. David Brown, "Chen Adopts a More Cautious Approach," *Comparative Connections*, April 2003; David Brown, "Strains Over Cross Strait Relations," *Comparative Connections*, January 2004.

74. Consultations, Beijing and Shanghai, May 2004

75. Wang Jisi, *China's Changing Role*, 1-5, 16-17; Wu Xinbo, "Future U.S. Military Presence in Asia," Washington, D.C., October 2003; Jia Qingguo, "Comments on Bush's National Security Strategy," a paper presented to a conference in Vail, Colo., November 2003; Wang Jisi, "Impact of U.S. Strategic Adjustment on Sino-U.S. Relations"; Tao Wenzhao, "Changes and Drivers in Sino-U.S. Relations."

76. Andrew Nathan and Bruce Gilley, "China's New Rulers: What They Want," *New York Review of Books*, 10 October 2002.

Chapter 4

China's Relations with Russia

In the wake of the end of the Cold War and the collapse of the Soviet Union, China's relations with Russia developed in positive and constructive ways that minimized differences and at times allowed Beijing and Moscow to use the image of closer cooperation to boost their respective international leverage, especially against the United States. For Beijing, the "strategic partnership" with Moscow provided a model for Chinese efforts to ensure stable relations with neighbors and major world powers. It facilitated China's more active interaction with the former Soviet republics in Central Asia, notably through the Shanghai Cooperation Organization that included Russia and four Central Asian states. The Chinese defense modernization and military buildup directed against Taiwan and possible U.S. involvement in a Taiwan contingency drove Chinese defense leaders to make large-scale purchases of advanced Russian military equipment, amounting to $2 billion annually by the late 1990s. Western military suppliers maintained an embargo on sales to China following the Tiananmen crackdown of 1989.

Wary of China's rising power along Russia's sparsely populated and weakly controlled Asian periphery, Russian leaders nonetheless found the advantages of arms sales and defense cooperation with China irresistible. Bilateral economic relations also grew, but from a low base; bilateral trade with Russia represented a very small percentage of China's overall foreign trade, though it was a higher percentage of Russia's more limited foreign trade.

Chinese leaders showed keen awareness of the limits of Russian economic strength and political stability. The Russian leadership under Vladimir Putin established a clearer priority where relations with China generally ran second to Russia's relations with the United States and the West. Chinese and Russian leaders rarely allowed rhetorical and political gestures in support of Russian-Chinese assertiveness and independence against the West to get in the way of their respective strong interests in maintaining close working relations with the United States and its allies and close associates.[1]

Background to Improved Relations

China and Russia have had a long and often troubled history. Czarist Russia's expansion into the Far East came largely at the expense of the declining Chinese Empire. Nineteenth-century treaties saw vast stretches of territory formerly under China's rule become part of the Russian Empire. China's internal weakness and political dislocation during the first half of the twentieth century provided opportunities for Vladimir Lenin and Joseph Stalin to seek allies and foster revolutionary movements favorable to the USSR. Soviet involvement was often ham-handed and, on occasion, worked against the immediate interests of the communist guerilla movement in China led by Mao Zedong.[2]

Seeking economic support and strategic backing in the face of an indifferent or hostile West, Mao Zedong's newly formed People's Republic of China sought an alliance with Stalin's USSR in 1949. After many weeks of hard bargaining, the alliance was signed on February 14, 1950. The alliance relationship was essential to China's security and its military, economic, and social development in the 1950s. Soviet aid, advisers, and guidelines were key features fostering the changes under way in China. But steadily escalating differences arose over strategy toward the United States and international affairs, the proper ideological path to development, and the appropriate leadership roles of Mao and Soviet leader Nikita Khrushchev in the world communist movement. Soviet aid was cut off in 1960. Polemics over strategy and ideology led to more substantive disputes over competing claims to border territories. Armed border clashes reached a point in 1969 at which the Soviet Union threatened to attack Chinese nuclear installations, and Chinese leaders countered with a nationwide war preparations campaign against the "war maniacs" in the Kremlin. Party relations were broken, trade fell to minimal levels, and each side depicted the other in official media as a dangerous international predator.

The start of Sino-Soviet talks on border issues in October 1969 eased the war crisis, but each side continued preparations for the long-term struggle against its neighboring adversary. As the weaker party in the dispute, China attempted to break out of its international isolation and gain diplomatic leverage against perceived Soviet efforts at intimidation and threat. Beijing's opening to the Nixon administration was an important element in this policy. The Soviet Union continued its previous efforts to build up military forces along the Sino-Soviet and Sino-Mongolian borders in order to offset any perceived threat from China. It also pursued this course to provide a counterweight against any Chinese effort to exert pressure on countries around China's periphery that were interested in developing closer relations with the USSR (for example, India, Vietnam).

The death of Mao Zedong in 1976 and the gradual emergence of a more pragmatic leadership in China reduced the importance of ideological and leadership issues in the Sino-Soviet dispute, but the competition in Asia again reached a crisis in 1979. China countered Soviet-backed Vietnam's invasion of Cambodia by launching a limited military incursion into Vietnam. The Soviet Union responded with warnings and large-scale military exercises along China's northern border. China also denounced the Soviet invasion of Afghanistan in 1979 and sided with the U.S.-backed anticommunist guerillas in Afghanistan. Chinese leaders spent much of the two decades from the late 1960s building military defenses and conducting diplomatic and other international maneuvers to deal with the perceived dangers of the prime strategic threat to China posed by the USSR. Particularly important were the buildup of Soviet military forces along the Sino-Soviet and Sino-Mongolian borders and Soviet military and political presence and influence in key areas along China's periphery, notably Vietnam, Laos, Cambodia, India, Afghanistan, North Korea, and the Western Pacific and Indian Oceans.[3]

Over time, both countries attempted to moderate the tensions. Soviet leader Leonid Brezhnev made several public gestures calling for improved economic, government, and party relations with China before he died in 1982. This prompted the start of a series of political, economic, technical, and cultural contacts and exchanges.

By 1982, the Soviet leadership concluded that their post-1969 strategy toward China (including the massing of forces along the eastern sector of the border and media campaigns of denunciation against China's domestic and international policies) had backfired. The post-1972 normalization of China's relations with the United States and Japan and the signing of the 1978 China-Japan friendship treaty showed a strategic convergence among the United States, China, and Japan, which added to the Soviet defense burden and worsened the security environment on its long, remote, and thinly populated eastern flank. To undo this problem, Brezhnev and later leaders held out an olive branch to the Chinese leadership.

Political contacts and trade increased and polemics subsided, but real progress came only after Mikhail Gorbachev consolidated his power in the mid-1980s and made rapprochement with China an urgent priority. Gorbachev was prepared to make major changes in what China referred to as the "three obstacles" to improved Sino-Soviet relations: Soviet troops in Afghanistan, the buildup of Soviet forces along the border (including the deployment in Mongolia), and the Soviet-backed Vietnamese military occupation of Cambodia.[4] Motivated by a desire to repair relations with China, to ease the defense burden on the Soviet economy, and to reciprocate China's reduction of its 4 million troops to 2.95 million from 1982 to 1986, the Soviet government announced in 1987 that a phased reduction of its troops (roughly sixty-five thousand in total number) from Mongolia would be initiated with the aim of eliminating the deployment by 1992.[5] The Soviet formations in Mongolia had been kept at a higher level of readiness than others along the border, and the Chinese had long viewed them as a first-echelon strike force aimed at Beijing. In December 1988, Gorbachev announced at the United Nations that Soviet conventional forces would unilaterally be reduced by five hundred thousand. Soviet spokesmen later clarified that, of the total, one hundred and twenty thousand would come from the troops arrayed against China, and that remaining Far Eastern units would progressively be configured in a defensive mode. In late 1989, following Gorbachev's visit to Beijing in May, Chinese and Soviet officials began negotiations on reducing forces along the border, and during Chinese Prime Minister Li Peng's visit to Moscow in April 1990, an agreement was reached on governing principles regarding force reductions. By the time the Soviet Union collapsed in 1991, five rounds of talks on force reductions had been conducted.

The reduction of the conventional threat to China was complemented by the 1987 U.S.-Soviet Intermediate Nuclear Forces (INF) treaty under which Moscow dismantled all its medium- and intermediate-range nuclear missiles, including 180 mobile SS-20 missiles that were based in the Asian regions of the USSR. Meanwhile, the USSR agreed under the April 1988 Geneva Accords to withdraw its combat forces from Afghanistan by May 1989, and encouraged Vietnam to evacuate its troops from Cambodia by the end of 1989.

High-level political contacts helped to alter the adversarial character of Sino-Soviet relations, the most important being the visits of Foreign Minister Eduard Shevardnadze and Gorbachev to Beijing in 1989, and of Li Peng and Chinese Communist Party General Secretary Jiang Zemin in Moscow in 1990 and 1991, respectively. Talks on resolving the border dispute, which had been derailed by the Soviet invasion of Afghanistan, resumed in 1987. A treaty delimiting the eastern sector of the border was signed in May 1991. These military and political transformations in Sino-Soviet relations were supplemented by a significant growth in trade—especially along the border—and agreements providing for thousands of Chinese workers to be employed in construction projects in Siberia and the Soviet Far East.[6]

Chinese leaders welcomed Gorbachev's military withdrawals from around China's periphery, and the collapse of the USSR in 1991 removed the Soviet military threat that had been the central focus of Beijing's strategic planning since the 1960s. The changes came at a time when Chinese leaders were beleaguered in the face of national and international resentment over their handling of the Tiananmen Square demonstrations of 1989. Representing one of the few surviving communist regimes in the post-Cold War world, Chinese officials were especially suspicious of Boris Yeltsin and his proposed democratic reforms, which were anathema to Chinese leaders determined to maintain the Communist Party's monopoly of political power. Nevertheless, more pragmatic consideration of the national interests of China and Russia saw Yeltsin and Chinese leaders continue the process of gradually improving relations begun in the 1980s.

Regarding political issues, the ideological grounds for polemics between Moscow and Beijing were basically removed in the Gorbachev years—party-to-party ties were reestablished during the 1989 Deng Xiaoping-Gorbachev summit. The end of Communist Party rule in Russia coming against the background of the reforms that China had embarked upon since 1978 rendered the old schismatic disputes about "revisionism," "social imperialism," and "hegemonism" irrelevant. Beijing's poor human rights record and its use of force to suppress the Tiananmen demonstrations were criticized by Russians but did not become major problems in government-to-government relations. Also, Russia did not allow its expanded economic ties with Taiwan to offend Beijing. Meanwhile, progress on resolving Russo-Chinese border disputes continued. The May 1991 eastern sector border agreement was followed by the signing of an agreement in September 1994 on the western sector of the border. As a result, except for some small areas, the entire Russo-Chinese border was delimited.[7]

Both countries maintained the momentum of political contacts at the highest levels. The presidents and premiers of each country visited the other an average of once every two years. In addition, there were numerous meetings between foreign ministers, defense ministers, and economic officials of both countries.

Concerning military issues, Yeltsin's government completed in 1992 the withdrawal of troops from Mongolia initiated by Gorbachev in 1987. By May 1996, Russia reportedly had cut a hundred and fifty thousand troops from its Far Eastern deployment, and the Pacific Fleet had been reduced by 50 percent from its 1985 level. At the eighth round of negotiations on force reductions along the border in December 1992, both sides agreed that their formations would be pulled back one hundred kilometers from the border. Offensive weapons (tanks, strike aircraft, artillery, and tactical nuclear weapons) were to be reduced in the two hundred-kilometer zone that resulted.[8]

Efforts to reduce forces and institute confidence-building measures (CBMs) along the border became multilateral with the addition of the Soviet successor states, Kazakhstan, Kyrgyzstan, and Tajikistan—all of which share borders with China—to a joint Commonwealth of Independent States (CIS) delegation. Guidelines, including force reductions, warnings preceding military exercises, and the attendance at exercises of observers from the signatories, were incorporated in an agreement signed by the leaders of the four CIS states and China in Shanghai during Yeltsin's April 1996 visit. This initiated the "Shanghai Five," a precursor to the Shanghai Cooperation Organization (SCO) that added Uzbekistan, the first multilateral organization involving Sino-Russian cooperation in Central Asia in the modern period.[9]

A joint declaration signed at the end of Yeltsin's visit to China in December 1992 called for reducing troops along the border to "a minimal level" and for increased contact between Chinese and Russian military personnel. Each party also pledged to eschew the use of force against the other, including the use of force in the domain of third countries, and to refuse to enter any "military and political alliances" directed against the other party, or sign with third countries any treaties or agreements detrimental to the state sovereignty and security interests of the other party.[10]

In July 1994, the Russian and Chinese defense ministers agreed on measures (such as preventing accidental missile launches, ending the electronic jamming of communications, and establishing signals to warn aircraft and ships in danger of violating the other side's border) to reduce the danger of inadvertent military escalation. In September 1994, the two sides agreed to the principle of no-first-use for nuclear weapons and to retarget nuclear missiles away from each other's territory. In May 1994, Chinese warships from the North China Fleet visited Vladivostok. Units of the Russian Pacific Fleet called at Qingtao that August. Local Chinese commanders also visited Russian military districts.[11]

China became the largest customer for Russian arms. Major purchases in the Yeltsin era included two hundred Su-27 fighter-ground attack aircraft, fifty T-72 tanks, one hundred S-300 surface-to-air missiles, ten Il-76 transport aircraft, several *Kilo*-class (diesel electric) submarines, and two Sovremenny-class destroyers. Moscow was also providing China with technology to improve the accuracy of surface-to-surface and air-to-air missiles, and training in Russia for personnel who would operate the weapons purchased. Several of the sales agreements were difficult to reach. The Su-27 transaction was in the works since 1992; the first twenty-four aircraft were delivered in 1992. Additional deliveries were held up by a dispute over China's desire to pay for two-thirds of the cost through barter. Although precise details of how the dispute was settled were unavailable, after the visit to Russia in December 1995 by Chinese military leader Liu Huaqing, the way was finally cleared for the delivery of the forty-eight Su-27s, and an agreement was reached (reportedly worth $2 billion) allowing China to manufacture this high-capability aircraft under license.[12]

These sales reflected a pragmatic marriage of important bilateral needs. For Russia, arms sales to China supplied much-needed hard currency and consumer goods from China, provided orders for severely distressed Russian defense industries, and reduced the tendency of the United States, Japan, and others to take Russia for granted in the post-Cold War Far East. Russia's political disarray also facilitated these arms sales, as reduced central control from Moscow gave defense industries more independence to make such deals. For China, the Russian equipment was relatively cheap, compatible with the existing Chinese inventory, and came without political or other preconditions. Both Russian and Chinese leaders were sensitive to concerns in the United States and Japan, and among Asian governments along China's periphery, that the Russian transfers could have substantially added to China's power projection and altered the prevailing military balance in East Asia. In general, Russian and Chinese officials said that China had a long way to go before it could use the recently acquired Russian weapons effectively or project the augmented power in ways that would have seriously upset the military balance in the region. There was debate in the West over when and if such weapons would alter the regional balance.[13]

Regarding economic and social interchange, trade between the two countries grew substantially from a low base. In 1985, Sino-Soviet trade was $300 million. Russian-Chinese trade reached $7 billion in 1995, and cross-border trade, which resumed in 1982 and was conducted largely in barter, accounted for a third of the volume, although its proportion began to decline in the mid-1990s in accordance with the desire of both governments to exert better control over cross-border interchange. China became Russia's second-largest trade partner after Germany.[14]

Along the economically more important eastern section of the Russo-Chinese border, roads and rail connections linked nineteen working border checkpoints between the two sides, with two more planned in the latter 1990s. In addition, direct postal and telephonic links were created between northeastern China and the Russian Far East. Russia also signed contracts to build nuclear and hydroelectric power plants in China. Both countries planned extensive pipeline and other projects to carry Russian oil and natural gas to Chinese consumers.[15]

Problems caused by an influx of Chinese into the Russian Far East, particularly those who remained in violation of visa regulations, led Russia and China to work out a more stringent visa regime in 1994. But the problem of Chinese migration into the Russian Far East persisted. Both countries faced the unprecedented challenge of managing the movement of what could be millions of people across a long border. Russia, in particular, could not afford to pump large sums of money into securing that border more effectively. There was a structural supply-and-demand dynamic at work: the high population density and unemployment that prevailed on the Chinese side stimulating people to cross into the Russian Far East, which traditionally suffered from severe labor shortages. The entire eastern third of Russia (east of Lake Baikal, a territory almost the size of the United States) had fewer than twenty million inhabitants—and its population was shrinking as people emigrated toward Russia's European heartland. This was exacerbated by economic distress in the Russian Far East that was worse than in most other regions, including severe food and energy shortages and wage arrears.[16]

Yeltsin-Jiang Summits

The extent of Sino-Russian cooperation—and its clear limits—were well illustrated during the frequent formal and informal summit meetings between the two leaders. Chinese media coverage of Russian President Boris Yeltsin's November 9-11, 1997, visit to China suggested that Beijing continued to seek a broader and firmer foundation for its post-Soviet relationship with Russia but that the conditions for doing so were limited. As in their treatment of past China-Russia summits, the media this time signaled Beijing's intention to use its relations with Russia as a counterweight to U.S.-global influence.[17]

Reflecting China's interest in moving Sino-Russian relations forward, despite continuing obstacles, Yeltsin's visit followed the pattern of previous Sino-Russian summits in the post-Soviet era, the meeting portrayed as the latest step in a continuous process of improving relations. Echoing Beijing's assessment of PRC President Jiang Zemin's visit to Russia in April 1997—which PRC media described at the time as "remarkably successful" and occurring in a "sincere and friendly" atmosphere—the joint statement issued at the end of Yeltsin's visit said that the meeting with Jiang on November 10 was a "complete success." *Xinhua* also cited the two leaders as praising their "strategic cooperative partnership" and quoted Jiang as asserting that bilateral relations were based on a "solid political foundation" whose "system of regular meetings" between two leaders constituted an improvement in relations.

Similarly, the joint statement itself played up the "active development" of bilateral relations and stressed the "important role" played by the four previous Sino-Russian joint statements in "implementing" the partnership. The statement went on to "reconfirm" what it called the "especially significant" principles contained in the previous statements, namely (1) strengthening "trust and mutual respect" for sovereignty and "noninterference in each other's internal affairs"; (2) regularizing high-level visits and setting up "consultation mechanisms"; and (3) "strengthening mutual coordination on major international issues."

While the agenda of Yeltsin's visit was less weighty than that of Jiang's visit in April—which included a joint pronouncement on the "multipolarization of the world," the signing of a five-nation agreement on border forces reduction, and the formal establishment of a Sino-Russian committee for friendship, peace, and development—it nevertheless included the additional step of resolving remaining border issues and attempted to expand the scope of bilateral economic cooperation. Reflecting these goals, the joint statement asserted that the two sides had "settled" most outstanding border issues and reached agreements on cooperation in a number of areas, including "large-scale" cooperation in energy extraction and production, financial and investment relations, science and technology, transportation and communications, and "military technology."[18]

Viewing border issues, PRC media portrayed the signing of agreements on Sino-Russian border issues as the major accomplishment of the summit, claiming that border conflicts were a thing of the past and playing down remaining disputes. For example, the joint statement asserted that "all issues" concerning demarcation of the "eastern sector" of the Sino-Russian border had been "settled" and that the demarcation of the eastern border had for the first time been "marked on the ground."[19] Although the statement said nothing about remaining differences over disputed frontier islets on the Amur and Ussuri rivers, the French News Agency, *AFP*, quoted a Chinese Foreign Ministry spokesman as saying it was "entirely possible" to find a "settlement" of this issue.[20] In addition, a November 10 *Xinhua* report on the visit also stated that Chinese and Russian officials had signed an agreement on "guiding principles" for joint economic utilization of "individual islets" in "border rivers and surrounding waters," although it did not specify the islets or rivers concerned.[21] The joint statement was more cautious in commenting on the "western sector" of the border. Describing this sector as being "about fifty-five km" in length, it said that the two sides "declared their readiness" to implement demarcation work "within an agreed time frame" and to continue talks aimed at a "fair and rational" solution of "certain outstanding issues."

The strongest indication that Beijing did not intend to allow differences over borders to sour future Sino-Russian relations came in remarks by Jiang at his meeting with Yeltsin. According to *Xinhua*, Jiang glossed over any remaining border disputes, saying that the signing of the Sino-Russian agreements, including agreements on the demarcation of borders, was a "successful example" of "settling questions left over by history through equal consultation, mutual understanding, and accommodation."

Regarding economic relations, the two sides appeared to have made little progress beyond rhetorical affirmations of their goals. *Xinhua* cited Jiang as telling Yeltsin that the two sides should make "even greater efforts" to "fully tap their respective vast potentials" and as calling for "breakthroughs" in cooperation on "large and medium-sized projects." He also urged enterprises from the two countries to "expand contacts" in order to "find partners for cooperative ventures." Similarly, the joint statement noted the "huge potential" for strengthening bilateral cooperation in nine areas that covered a broad and diverse spectrum of economic activity.

Although *Xinhua* reported that in addition to the joint statement a number of "other documents" were signed on "economic and technological cooperation," the media were not observed to report the contents of most of these agreements, suggesting that little was accomplished in the way of concrete business deals. Reinforcing this impression, the two "memorandums of understanding" (MOU) for which some detail was provided did not go beyond general statements of purpose. According to the *Xinhua* report, Chinese Vice Premier Li Lanqing and Russian First Deputy Prime Minister Boris Nemtsov signed one MOU on the "basic principles" for laying gas pipelines and developing gas fields and another on the "basic orientation" of economic, scientific, and technological cooperation.[22]

Finally, media coverage of Jiang's talks with Yeltsin during both summits in 1997 implied that the two sides were skeptical that their bilateral trade target of $20 billion in total volume by the turn of the century would be met. For example, Jiang reportedly told Russian Prime Minister Viktor Chernomyrdin during Jiang's April 1997 visit to Moscow that he and Yeltsin had agreed on the need for both sides to "make efforts to raise" trade levels and "stand on higher ground" on the bilateral trade issue and that he hoped Russia would make a "positive study" of proposals for cooperative projects. Similarly, *Xinhua* cited both leaders as stating during the November summit that it was "entirely possible" to reach their bilateral trade targets as long as both sides made "unremitting efforts." At least one report, carried by the PRC-owned Hong Kong news service *Zhongguo Tongxun She* prior to Yeltsin's visit, implied that the trade target was unrealistic.[23]

Rhetoric directed against U.S. leadership in Asian and world affairs was well in evidence throughout the summit. Building on the joint statement signed by Jiang and Yeltsin during the April summit—which pledged to "promote the multipolarization of the world and establishment of a new international order"—PRC media commentary on Yeltsin's visit underscored China's intention to continue using its warming relationship with Russia to counter what it viewed as U.S. efforts to dominate the post-Cold War world. Both the joint statement and Jiang's remarks to Yeltsin reiterated Beijing's line that its newly established "partnerships" with major powers, including Russia, were necessary to ensure a global balance of power in a "new, improved international political and economic order."

For example, in discussing the Sino-Russian relationship of "friendship and cooperation," the joint statement cited recent summit meetings between China, Russia, the United States, and Japan as evidence that "state-to-state alliances" or "strategic unions" directed against a "third country" were a "thing of the past" and that "larger nations" should back the trend toward a "multipolar" world. The statement also intimated that China and Russia were seeking these goals for altruistic motives, since it said neither state was pursuing "expansionist" or "hegemonistic" aims—an allusion to the United States.

Similarly, in his talks with Yeltsin at which both presidents endorsed their two countries' "strategic cooperative partnership," Jiang made another pitch for the concept of a "new world order," noting Beijing's belief that world affairs should be decided upon by "all countries." Jiang appeared to indirectly criticize the United States, telling Yeltsin that "great powers" should abandon a "Cold War mentality," respect the "reality of a diversified world," and conform to the "trend" of "world multipolarization."

An editorial in the PRC-owned Hong Kong newspaper *Wen Wei Po* on November 10, 1997, played up the importance of the Sino-Russian "strategic cooperative partnership" and the two countries' partnerships with other countries in "preventing superpowers from manipulating and guiding international security." It asserted that the "new international order" promoted by China and Russia, which opposed "hegemony and the world's centralization," served the interests of "all countries that refuse to be controlled by others."[24]

Convergence and Divergence in the Late 1990s

The improvement of Russian-Chinese relations continued, with frequent high-level visits laced with anti-U.S. rhetoric. The development of closer relations caused concern among some observers in the West and in Asia. Both Russia and China faced the prospect of continued difficulties with the U.S. superpower's intention of maintaining and developing its international strategic advantage through such means as NATO enlargement, the strengthening of U.S.-Japanese military alliance, and ballistic missile defense. Some Western experts and commentators warned of an ever closer Russo-Chinese strategic alignment. They saw the beginnings of this structure in joint Russo-Chinese statements supporting a multipolar world, in increasing military cooperation, and in efforts by Russia and China to work together politically and diplomatically to thwart U.S. efforts at the UN Security Council and elsewhere to pressure countries like Serbia, Iraq, Iran, Libya, and others to conform to international norms supported by the United States.[25]

Others argued that there were serious limitations to Russian-Chinese cooperation and major obstacles to a strategic alliance between them.[26] The condition that would be most conducive to the emergence of a Sino-Russian strategic alliance was seen to be a crisis or rupture in Russia's or China's relations with one of the other major powers, such as the United States or Japan. The hypothesis here was that if Russia or China—and particularly both of them—were to become locked in a protracted geostrategic confrontation and hostility with the United States and/or a resurgent Japan, this could push Moscow and Beijing to forge a strategic alliance to counter their powerful enemy. One such scenario might have arisen if China and Russia, for whatever reasons, simultaneously became embroiled in conflicts with Taiwan and with some of the Soviet successor states, provoking conflict or confrontation with the United States and its allies; this could lead to a Moscow-Beijing alliance. Absent such developments, or a mounting strategic confrontation, the limits to Russian-Chinese cooperation seemed substantial and the obstacles to a strategic alliance formidable.[27]

During this period, China and Russia both found that their relations with the advanced industrial democracies, particularly the United States, remained difficult. China faced problems over human rights abuses, trade and weapons proliferation questions, the status of Tibet, and especially the Taiwan question. For Russia there were problems concerning its relations with other Soviet successor states, Russian military operations in Chechnya, tension over NATO enlargement, and nuclear proliferation. Internationally, Russia supported China's position on Taiwan, and China backed Russia's opposition to NATO enlargement. Each opposed international interference in what the other views as its internal affairs. Some Chinese and Russians viewed themselves as outsiders vis-à-vis the Group of Seven (G7), which they saw as the "rich countries' club." As still-developing economies, they tended to resist certain G7-supported economic and trade policies in areas such as protectionism, dumping, intellectual property rights, transparency, and government regulations.

Russia badly needed the China market to export arms and industrial products for which, for various reasons, it had relatively few other buyers who could afford to pay. Food and inexpensive consumer goods from China played a vital role in helping sustain the Russian Far East. These factors helped propel China into the position of Russia's second-largest trade partner. Economically, China was far less dependent on Russia. But Russia could provide China with relatively cheap advanced weapons, nuclear reactor technology, and other industrial products that might have otherwise been much more costly for Beijing or unavailable for political reasons.

Both Russia and China found it helpful, to some extent, to use their improving bilateral relations for leverage vis-à-vis the West, particularly the United States. This struck some international affairs specialists as reminiscent of Nixon/Kissinger's famous playing of the "China card" against the Soviet Union. Moscow tended to be more explicit about this than Beijing. Many Russian officials, for example, warned that NATO enlargement could have driven Russia into a much closer cooperation, even a strategic alliance, with China.[28]

China and Russia shared some other common interests that strengthened the basis of their cooperation. For example, both saw the possible spread of radical Islam in Central Asia as a threat to their own domestic stability and national security. Both countries desired regional stability in Asia, wanted to avoid crisis on the Korean peninsula, and wished to forestall the reemergence of Japan as a major military power.[29]

Despite the broad basis for Russian-Chinese cooperation, there were serious limits to that cooperation—and even more to the creation of a strategic alliance between them. In the aftermath of the collapse of the Soviet Union and the loss of its peripheral territory and population, Russia's relative economic weakness and political instability vis-à-vis China made many Russians nervous. Russia's population (roughly 150 million) was about half that of the former Soviet Union's—and the sparsely populated Russian Far East was losing people. Russia's economy had contracted significantly during the still far from complete transition to a market economy. Industrial production appeared in the late 1990s to be as low as 50 percent of 1991 level.[30]

With President Yeltsin's ailments and other problems, the political situation remained unstable. One aspect of that instability was the difficulty Moscow had in controlling distant regions, such as Eastern Siberia and the Far East. Leaders in those resource-rich regions sought greater autonomy from Moscow and some flirted with the idea of separatism. Finally, many Russians were keenly aware of the deterioration of their country's military strength. The Russian Army's remarkably poor performance in cracking down against armed insurgents in Chechnya was one indication of this.

In contrast, from Moscow's perspective, China—with its dynamic economy, huge and growing population, apparent national self-confidence and assertiveness, stable, authoritarian political system, and large and modernizing army—seemed strong. Some among the Russian policy elite found Beijing's example admirable and saw in China both a model to emulate and a natural ally. Others—mindful of Russia's declining power vis-à-vis China and of the history of Russia's seizure of vast territories in Eastern Siberia and the Russian Far East from China in "unequal treaties" in the later part of the nineteenth century—saw China's renaissance and burgeoning power as a challenge and potential threat. A Russian nightmare scenario from this perspective was that a resurgent China might try to retake vast, thinly populated territories from a weakened Russia.[31]

Although Russia's sale of advanced weaponry to China was widely believed to be motivated in large part by economic necessity on Russia's part and was strongly supported by the Russian defense industrial sector, there were serious reservations in the Russian security community. Some Russian commentators questioned the wisdom of helping to modernize the military of a country that might become a threat to Russian security in the future. These reservations reportedly extended to the Russian military's general staff.[32]

On the Chinese side, too, there were significant limitations and constraints on cooperation with Russia.[33] The radical swings in Soviet and Russian domestic politics and foreign policy since the mid-1980s inevitably made Russia appear somewhat unreliable in Chinese eyes. Russia's economic, political, and military weakness was duly noted by Chinese strategic planners, who nonetheless remained vigilant for any signs of a revival of Russian strength that could have affected Chinese interests in Asia.

Also, Russia was much less important economically to China than vice versa. Russia accounted for less than 2 percent of China's $300 billion in annual foreign trade in the late 1990s. China's trade with and credits and investments from the G7 countries weighed far more heavily in Beijing than did Russo-Chinese trade. China presumably would have been loath to jeopardize its vital economic relations with the advanced industrial democracies on Russia's behalf. The markets, financing, and technology of the West and the developed countries of East Asia represented a key link in China's ongoing program of economic modernization. And economic modernization and the concrete benefits it gave to the broad masses of Chinese people were the key sources of political legitimacy for the post-Mao leaders. It was difficult to imagine circumstances in which Chinese leaders would have allowed closer military, political, or other ties with an economically anemic Russia to jeopardize China's vital links with the world's most important economies—unless China faced a major crisis or geostrategic confrontation with the United States or Japan.

Thus, the pattern of China's relationship with Yelstin's Russia showed Beijing giving priority to keeping relations with the often unstable Russia as calm as possible. It also sought military equipment and some advanced technology. When Chinese relations with the United States, Japan, and NATO were strained, Chinese officials fell back on relations with Moscow as a possible source of political leverage against the Western-aligned states. But when Beijing's higher-priority relations with the United States and the developed powers were in reasonably good shape, Beijing tended to keep at some distance the Russians and their desire to gain Chinese support for a strong, public, anti-U.S., anti-Western stance on sensitive issues. (In general terms, Russian leaders tended to use their relationship with China in a similar way, with the state of Russian relations with the United States as the more important determinant.) Even though Beijing—like Moscow—said it wanted to see a multipolar world order develop, with the U.S. superpower as only one power among many, it saw only limited benefits from tilting strongly toward Russia as it opposed U.S. and Western policies. It saw more to be gained from a positive and constructive engagement with the United States and Western-aligned states—a higher priority in Chinese foreign policy.

Relations under Vladimir Putin-Hu Jintao

The course of Russian-Chinese relations in the early twenty-first century under new leaders Vladimir Putin (2001) and Hu Jintao (2002) followed the same mixed pattern seen in the 1990s. Both sides placed priority on promoting an evolving "strategic partnership." Economic cooperation improved from a low base. A growing arms sales and defense technology sharing relationship provided critically important support for China's military buildup focused on a Taiwan contingency involving the United States. Political cooperation against U.S. interests varied, with Russia's Putin and then Chinese leaders moving to moderate anti-U.S. invective in the face of U.S. resolve and power, especially in the George W. Bush administration.

Putin showed a notably positive response to the United States during his first meeting with George W. Bush in spring 2001. He played down heretofore strong differences over missile defense and NATO expansion in the interest of fostering closer cooperation with the United States and the West. U.S.-Russian cooperation was intensified following the September 11, 2001, terrorist attack on America. Russian support was essential in facilitating U.S.-led military operations in Central Asia directed against the Taliban regime in Afghanistan. Russia saw its interests served by fostering closer economic and strategic cooperation with the United States and the West, and by playing down past major differences.[34]

Maneuvering in the UN in the months prior to the war in Iraq in 2003 saw Russia join with France and others (including China to some degree) in standing against U.S. military actions to topple Saddam Hussein without renewed UN approval. It was unclear if this reversal in Russian-U.S. cooperation was an episode prompted by key Russian concerns involving economic and other interests in Iraq and broader concerns regarding anticipated hostile Islamic reaction in the region and among the sizeable Russian Muslim population; or if it was part of a broader Russian decision to reverse course and seek to join with other world powers to resist and weaken the U.S. superpower. After the U.S.-led coalition toppled Saddam and senior Bush administration officials made significant gestures to ease tensions with Moscow, Russia appeared prepared to resume a more cooperative stance toward the United States.[35]

Seeing Russia trim its opposition to the United States in 2001 took some of the steam out of the then-strong Chinese anti-U.S. rhetoric critical of the American posture on missile defense and NATO expansion. It added to Chinese imperatives to moderate their stance toward the United States by mid-2001, setting the stage for the most important improvement in China-U.S. relations since the end of the Cold War.[36]

In this context, the improved Russian-Chinese relationship continued to grow close but appeared to have less negative implications for U.S. interests in sustaining a leadership position and promoting stability in Asia. Russian arms sales to and military cooperation with China continued the pattern of the past decade and increased somewhat as China's stepped up the pace of military modernization focused on Taiwan. Economic relations also picked up, with prospects of greater trade centered on sales of Russian energy resources to China. Political cooperation against U.S. interests subsided from the intensified level of the late 1990s and early 2000s that at least partly had resulted from various U.S. actions (intervention in Kosovo, posturing over Chechnya and Taiwan, U.S. missile defense plans, NATO expansion), which Moscow and Beijing perceived as contrary to their mutual interests.[37]

The relationship proved to be mixed and somewhat volatile regarding political cooperation, despite the signing of a Russian-Chinese friendship treaty in 2001 and numerous bilateral agreements.[38]

- Arms sales and technology transfers kept growing primarily because Russian economic difficulties and Putin's emphasis on defense industries complemented China's need for advanced military equipment and technology to prepare for regional contingencies, notably a possible confrontation with Taiwan that might risk U.S. military involvement. China had difficulty integrating some of the new arms and technology, but on balance many foresaw improvements in Chinese capabilities to engage hostile forces at increasing distances from its shores.
- Economic relations continued to move forward slowly. For a time, Putin tried to link arms sales to an expansion of commercial trade, but this did not succeed, especially given Moscow's need for the arms sales and Beijing's limited interest in other Russian exports. Ongoing negotiations on large-scale energy and infrastructure projects nonetheless offered potential for some long-term expansion in trade relations, though Russia remained open to possibly better offers from Japan for Russian Far Eastern energy resources.
- Russia and China continued to pursue good neighborly relations and bilateral confidence building measures. Though they both moderated their respective public criticism of U.S. leadership in Asian and world affairs, in principle they remained opposed the regional and global domination of a single power, and occasionally jointly criticized evidence of U.S. "unilateralism" or "interventionism."

Both Moscow and Beijing maintained a grudging respect for U.S. power and influence and a calculation that constructive bilateral relations with the United States were essential to their respective development and reform programs. Accordingly, they were anticipated to continue to try to avoid confronting Washington in ways that would jeopardize the advantages they derived from engagement with the United States. Russian-Chinese political cooperation also was limited by historical mutual suspicions, their respective concerns about each other's long-term threat potential, and the preoccupation of both leaderships with domestic priorities. The Chinese ambassador told a press conference in Moscow in March 2004 that China's development was not a threat or challenge to Russia, but an important opportunity for Russians.[39]

Russian and Chinese leaders endeavored to develop mutual opportunities in businesslike meetings in 2004 focused on cooperation within the SCO and in bilateral economic and military relations. There was a Putin-Hu meeting during the SCO summit in Tashkent, Uzbekistan, in June 2004, the head of China's parliament visited Russia in May, and the Russian Defense Minister visited China in April. The progress in relations failed to disguise a clear awareness in both Moscow and Beijing that past emphasis on Sino-Russian strategic partnership failed to bridge continued mutual awareness that the Russian and Chinese leaderships were prepared to enhance narrow national interests by maneuvering in relations with the United States and others in ways that would come at the expense of declared Sino-Russian solidarity.[40]

Demonstrating how U.S. policy and behavior could affect future Russia-China relations, there were circumstances where Chinese-Russian cooperation could markedly improve. In the event of a harder U.S. policy approach toward the powers, Russia and China might see that their common ground in opposing U.S. policies had grown, or that greater cooperation would not endanger whatever benefits they respectively still derived from relations with Washington. Under such circumstances, Moscow might be more inclined to further relax restrictions on arms and technology transfers to China, and Beijing probably would be similarly inclined to accommodate Russian demands for greater commercial imports from Russia.

There are also prospects for a decline in relations. The two sides could diverge seriously over key U.S. policies (as they did to some degree in 2001 over U.S. missile defense plans), or they could find themselves in competition in courting the United States. Differences could also worsen over lagging economic relations and competition for influence in Korea or elsewhere in Asia. Even in a scenario of divergence, however, the two powers probably would work to limit bilateral friction, continue mutually advantageous arms sales and military cooperation, and persist in common efforts to promote multipolarity against perceived U.S. unilateralism.

In any scenario, the chances of Moscow and Beijing reestablishing a formal alliance—especially one with a mutual defense component—appear low. Bitter memories of their failed alliance in the 1950s, deep-seated mutual suspicions, and the specter of potentially serious political and economic repercussions remain powerful deterrents to the formation of an anti-Western military pact.

Notes

1. For background and recent assessments, see Rouben Azizian, "Russia's China Debate," in *Asia's China Debate* (Asia Pacific Center for Security Studies, December 2003), Chapter 11; Rajan Menon, "Sick Man of Asia," *National Interest* 73 (Fall 2003); Elizabeth Wishnick, "Russia and China: Brothers Again?" *Asian Survey* 41, no. 5 (Sept.-Oct. 2001): 797-821; Sherman Garnett, ed., *Rapprochement or Rivalry? Russia-China Relations in a Changing Asia* (Washington, D.C.: Carnegie, 2000); Gilbert Rozman, "Russia's Foreign Policy in Northeast Asia," in Samuel Kim, ed., *The International Relations of Northeast Asia* (Lanham, Md.: Rowman & Littlefield, 2004); Alexander Nemets, "War Does Not Curtail

the Growing Russia-China Alliance," *China Brief* (Jamestown Foundation) 2 issue 1, www.jamestown.org (accessed 1 March 2003). To track recent developments in Russia-China relations, see the quarterly reviews done by Yu Bin in *Comparative Connections*, www.csis.org/pacfor.

2. John Garver, *The Foreign Relations of the People's Republic of China* (Englewood Cliff, N.J.: Prentice Hall, 1993), 310-13; Lowell Dittmer, *Sino-Soviet Normalization and Its International Implications, 1945-1990* (Seattle, Wash.: University of Washington Press, 1992).

3. Robert Ross, ed., *China, the United States and the Soviet Union: Tripolarity and Policy Making in the Cold War* (Armonk, N.Y.: M. E. Sharpe, 1993).

4. This analysis draws from Rajan Menon, "The Strategic Convergence Between Russia and China," *Survival* 39, no. 2 (Summer 1997): 101-25.

5. James Clay Moltz, "Regional Tension in the Russo-Chinese Rapprochement," *Asian Survey* 35, no. 6 (June 1995): 511-27.

6. Robert Sutter, *Chinese Policy Priorities* (Lanham, Md.: Rowman & Littlefield, 2000), 65.

7. Sutter, *Chinese Policy Priorities*, 65.

8. See the discussions in Menon, "Strategic Convergence," and Stephen Blank, *Dynamics of Russian Weapons Sales to China* (Carlisle, Pa.: U.S. Army War College, Strategic Studies Institute, 4 March 1997).

9. Bates Gill and Matthew Oresman, *China's New Journey West* (Washington, D.C.: Center for Strategic and International Studies, August 2003), 5-6.

10. Moltz, "Regional Tension," 518.

11. Sutter, *Chinese Policy Priorities*, 66.

12. See Blank, *Dynamics of Russian Weapons Sales to China.* See also *China's Rising Military Power* (Washington, D.C.: Library of Congress), Congressional Research Service, Report 96-647F, 31 July 1998.

13. Sutter, *Chinese Policy Priorities*, 67.

14. Reviewed in Menon, "Strategic Convergence."

15. Sutter, *Chinese Policy Priorities*, 67.

16. Sutter, *Chinese Policy Priorities*, 68.

17. This analysis is taken from "Yeltsin's China Visit," Foreign Broadcast Information Service *Trends*, 2 December 1997 (Internet version).

18. Cited in "Yeltsin's China Visit," FBIS *Trends.*

19. The joint statement was carried by Russian and Chinese media on 10 November 1997 and by FBIS.

20. Cited in FBIS *Trends*, 2 December 1997.

21. *Xinhua*, 10 November 1997.

22. Cited in FBIS *Trends*, 2 December 1997.

23. FBIS *Trends*, 2 December 1997.

24. FBIS *Trends*, 2 December 1997.

25. Peter Rodman, "A New Russian-Chinese Alliance?" *Los Angeles Times*, 25 March 1996; Alexander Nemets and Thomas Torda, *The Russian Chinese Alliance* (West Palm Beach, Fla.: Newsmax.com, 2002).

26. Peggy Falkenheim Meyer, "From Cold War to Cold Peace? U.S.-Russian Security Relations in the Far East," in Stephen Blank, ed., *Russian Security Policy in the Asia-Pacific Region: Two Views* (Carlisle, Pa.: U.S. Army War College, Strategic Studies Institute, May 1996).

27. Stuart Goldman, *Russian-Chinese Cooperation: Prospects and Implications* (Washington, D.C.: Library of Congress), Congressional Research Service, Report 97-185F, 27 January 1997, 8-13.

28. Sutter, *Chinese Policy Priorities*, 68.

29. Rozman, "Russia's Foreign Policy," *The International Relations of Northeast Asia*, 201-11.

30. Goldman, *Russian-Chinese Cooperation*, 13.

31. Azizian, "Russia's China Debate," *Asia's China Debate,* chapter 11, 1; Rozman, "Russia's Foreign Policy," *The International Relations of Northeast Asia*, 201-11.

32. Azizian, "Russia's China Debate," *Asia's China Debate,* chapter 11, 6-7.

33. Sutter, *Chinese Policy Priorities*, 74-75.

34. William Wohlforth, "Russia," in Richard Ellings and Aaron Friedberg, eds., *Strategic Asia 2002-2003* (Seattle, Wash.: National Bureau of Asian Research, 2002), 183-222.

35. Wohlforth, "Russia," in Richard Ellings and Aaron Friedberg, eds., *Strategic Asia 2003-2004* (Seattle, Wash.: National Bureau of Asian Research, 2003), 165-80; Joseph Ferguson, "Energizing the Relationship," *Comparative Connections*, October 2003.

36. Ching Cheong, "U.S.-Russia Summit Worries China," *Straits Times,* 31 May 2002; Willy Wo-Lap Lam, "Moscow Tilts West, Beijing Worries," (Jamestown Foundation) *China Brief* no. 12, issue 12, 12 June 2002; Yu Bin, "A 'Nice' Treaty in a Precarious World," *Comparative Connections*, October 2001.

37. Robert Sutter, *The United States and East Asia* (Lanham, Md.: Rowman & Littlefield, 2003), 114.

38. Azizian, "Russia's China Debate," *Asia's China Debate,* chapter 11; Rozman, "Russia's Foreign Policy," *The International Relations of Northeast Asia*, 201-11.

39. Sutter, *The United States and East Asia*, 115; Azizian, "Russia's China Debate," *Asia's China Debate,* chapter 11; Rozman, "Russia's Foreign Policy in Northeast Asia," *The International Relations of Northeast Asia*, 201-11. See also Shao Da, "PRC Ambassador Denies 'Population Expansion' in Russia," Beijing *Zhongguo Wang* in English, 1 April 2004 (Internet version).

40. See also Alexandre Mansourov, "China-Russia Relations" in *Asia's Bilateral Relations* (Honolulu: Asia-Pacific Center for Security Studies, 2004), www.apcss.org (accessed 1 November 2004); Jeanne L. Wilson, *Strategic Partners (*Armonk, N.Y.: M. E. Sharpe, 2004); Alexander Lukin, *The Bear Watches the Dragon* (Armonk, N.Y.: M. E. Sharpe, 2003); Zheng Yu, "Strategic Cooperation Between China and Russia," replayed in *China Strategy*, vol. 3, www.csis.org (accessed 20 July 2004).

Chapter 5

Relations with Japan

Trouble Ahead?

The future stability of East Asia will depend heavily on the relationship between the main regional powers, China and Japan. Relations between the two swung markedly in the post-Cold War period. At first, both powers adjusted their bilateral relations amicably following the demise of the USSR and its strategic influence in East Asia. The rise of China's power and influence in Asian affairs in the 1990s combined with Chinese military assertiveness over Taiwan and the South China Sea in the mid-1990s coincided with a protracted period of lackluster Japanese economic performance and weak political leadership. This called into question the past disparity of the economic relationship between the two powers, added to ongoing differences over territorial, strategic, historical, and economic issues, and strengthened the wariness and occasional antipathy between the two countries.[1]

There was an active debate among specialists about the direction and outlook for Sino-Japanese relations. Some experts predicted an increasingly intense competition, including likely confrontation and possible conflict in future China-Japan relations.[2] They highlighted changes in attitudes of Japanese and Chinese decision makers, opinion leaders, and popular opinion about the status and outlook of their mutual relations. They tended to see initiatives, like Prime Minister Junichiro Koizumi's January 2002 visit to Southeast Asia, as reflecting strong Sino-Japanese friction and rivalry.[3]

Other signs of greater Sino-Japanese competition and rivalry in Asia were said to include:[4]

- Separate and seemingly competing proposals by China and Japan in 2001-2002 to establish free trade arrangements with the ten Southeast Asian nations in ASEAN (the Association of Southeast Asian Nations).
- Japanese support for Taiwan and for stronger U.S. backing of Taiwan during the Bush administration, including strategic dialogue by senior Japanese defense and foreign policy officials with their U.S. counterparts over China-related issues, including Taiwan.[5]
- The first significant cutbacks in Japanese aid to China since the normalization of relations in the 1970s.
- Increased Japanese willingness to deploy military forces in Asia in support of U.S. and UN initiatives.
- Stepped-up Japanese efforts to improve security, aid, and other relations with India, and other nations on China's southern and western flanks, including strong Japanese aid efforts for Pakistan and Afghanistan.
- In the face of China's steadily increasing economic ties and political influence in South Korea, Japanese efforts to improve ties with Seoul, attempting to ease differences over historical, trade, and other issues.[6]

Underlying changes in Japan said to foreshadow greater Japanese-Chinese rivalry involved:

- With the collapse of the Soviet Union and the end of the Cold War, strategic thinkers in the Japanese government and elsewhere in Japan focused more on China's rising power as the major long-term regional security concern for Japan.
- China's continued remarkable economic growth, along with its rising political and military standing, prompted more Japanese to view China as a rival for regional influence.
- Previous Japanese sensitivity and responsiveness to Chinese demands for special consideration on account of Japan's negative war record in China over fifty years ago lessened with the passage of time, the change in Japanese leadership generations, and Beijing's loss of moral standing in Japan on account of its crackdown after the Tiananmen incident, its nuclear testing, and its intimidating military actions against Taiwan and in the South China Sea.[7]
- Undergirding Japan's more critical approach to China was a strong sense of national pride and determination among Japanese leaders and public opinion to preserve Japanese interests in the face of perceived efforts by PRC officials to use charges from the past and recent economic, political, and strategic issues to prompt Tokyo to give way to Chinese interests.

Meanwhile, changes in China said to be leading to greater friction with Japan included:

- Chinese strategists' long-standing concerns about Japan's impressive military capabilities increased as a result of U.S.-Japanese agreements from 1996 onward, which to Chinese observers appeared to broaden Japan's strategic role in East Asia and to provide U.S. strategic support for Japanese politicians wishing to strike a military posture in the region less deferential to China than in the past.[8] U.S. support for Prime Minister Koizumi's strong military actions and deployments to the Indian Ocean in support of the U.S. war against terrorism in Afghanistan during 2001-2002 and the Japanese leader's strong stance in support of the U.S.-led attack on Iraq in 2003 and deployment of Japanese forces to Iraq in 2004 represented new developments in this perceived trend.

- Chinese government specialists acknowledged changes in Japanese attitudes toward China and judged that Beijing appeared likely to meet even more opposition and gain less support from Japan as it sought to expand China's influence in Asian and world affairs. The Japanese decisions to cut aid to China seemed consistent with this trend.

- Chinese nationalism was a focal point of government-sponsored media and other publicity in recent years, especially following the Tiananmen incident and the collapse of communism in Europe and the Soviet Union at the end of the Cold War. Appealing to the sense of China as having been victimized by foreign aggressors in the past, the publicity focused heavily on Japan, by far the most important foreign aggressor in modern Chinese history. The government-sponsored publicity elicited widespread positive response in China and soured the overall atmosphere of China's relations with Japan.[9]

A contrasting perspective gave greater weight to the common interests and forces that continued to bind Sino-Japanese relations and to limit the chances of serious confrontation or conflict. This perspective was more in line with the overall moderate approach China adopted toward its neighbors under the leadership of Jiang Zemin, and especially the improvement in China's relations with the United States and its allies and associates, including Japan, at the beginning of the twenty-first century. Mutual interests centered on strong, growing economic and strategic interdependence between Japan and China, and the influence of the United States and other third parties, including other national powers in Asia—all of whom favored and could be expected to work to preserve Sino-Japanese stability. Specific elements of the argument against the development of serious Sino-Japanese rivalry involved:

- Both the Japanese and Chinese governments remained domestically focused, and continued to give top priority to the economic development of their countries, which they believed require a prolonged, peaceful, and cooperative relationship with their Asian neighbors, notably one another.

- China depended heavily on Japan for economic assistance, for technology and investment, and as a market for Chinese goods; Japan was increasingly dependent on China as a market, source of imports, and offshore manufacturing base.
- Personnel exchanges between Japan and China had grown markedly. Tens of thousands of Japanese students visited or studied in China each year. Government-sponsored exchange programs abounded, and even if they did not always promote positive feelings, they probably did promote more realistic mutual perceptions.
- No other government in Asian affairs would have benefited from or sought to promote greater Sino-Japanese friction. This included the Bush administration, which was careful to balance its strong pro-Japanese slant with reaffirmation of continued interest in closer mutually beneficial relations with China designed in part to sustain regional peace and stability. Such cooperation was especially important to the United States, and to China and Japan, in regard to efforts to deal diplomatically with the North Korean nuclear issue and related provocations coming from Pyongyang in 2002-2004.
- Because the United States remained such a dominant military and economic power in the region, the U.S.-Japan alliance resulted in a marked asymmetry in Japanese and Chinese perceptions of competition and rivalry. While Japanese elite and popular opinion was more focused on China as a future concern, Chinese elite and popular opinion was much more preoccupied with the United States as a possible concern; Japan's role was seen as secondary, the junior partner in one of the U.S. alliances and security arrangements that affect Chinese interests. Given the Chinese focus on dealing with the primary concern posed by the United States, one result that worked against Sino-Japanese rivalry was that Chinese officials had at times sought to avoid disputes with Japan and rather had tried to woo Japan away from close alignment with the United States and toward positions more favorable to China.[10]

The Asian economic crisis of 1997-1998 added to the already strong preoccupations of leaders in Tokyo and Beijing with their respective domestic problems, especially economic problems. At least for the time being, neither government sought to exacerbate tensions over the array of issues that continued to divide them. Thus, they went ahead with senior leaders' meetings in Tokyo and Beijing, capped by President Jiang Zemin's November 1998 visit to Japan. That visit saw Japanese officials stand firm in the face of Chinese pressure on issues related to Taiwan and the history of China-Japan relations. Chinese leaders adjusted their approach, as leaders in both capitals endeavored to emphasize the positive and give less public attention to important and often deeply rooted differences. Lower-level commentary in China and Japan made clear such differences over history, the U.S.-Japan alliance, Taiwan, theater missile defense, and competing visions of regional leadership had not been forgotten.[11]

While emphasizing Sino-Japanese economic and other compatible interests, Japanese Prime Minister Koizumi tested Chinese tolerance on the sensitive history issue with his repeated visits to the Yakasuni Shrine—a Japanese war memorial that included commemoration of the Japanese leaders during the Pacific War who were later convicted as war criminals. After his third visit despite Chinese admonitions, Chinese officials made it known in 2003 that the Japanese prime minister would not be welcome in Beijing; but they were flexible in arranging a meeting between the Japanese prime minister and China's recent installed president at the sidelines of an international summit in Europe in mid-2003. At that time, the burgeoning crisis over North Korea's nuclear weapons program and the danger that tensions on the Korean peninsula might escalate and result in military confrontation and war saw Chinese leaders take unprecedented measures to work cooperatively and pragmatically with the United States and others in order to deal with the crisis through diplomatic means. For their part, Japanese officials were anxious to work closely with South Korea, China, and Russia, while Japan relied strongly on close collaboration with the Bush administration in seeking a political solution to the crisis. At bottom, dealing with the North Korean nuclear challenge posed an added preoccupation for Chinese and Japanese leaders that at least over the short term reduced the likelihood that they would adopt more assertive and potentially disruptive policies. They presumably would be loath to appear to worsen an already delicate situation in ways that could adversely affect their interests in stability, development, and security.[12]

The broad pattern of Sino-Japanese relations after the Cold War saw relations most troubled in the middle and later years of the 1990s. The difficulties involved territorial, strategic, and economic issues, including the following:

- Exchanges of diplomatic complaints backed by strongly worded media and other rhetoric over competing claims to islets in the East China Sea;
- Increasingly evident signs of mutual suspicions over East Asian security issues. Chinese officials and commentators took a jaundiced view of Japan's reaffirmation of its alliance relationship with the United States; particularly after the provocative Chinese military exercises directed at Taiwan in 1995 and 1996, Japanese strategists publicly expressed concern over China's rising power and military capabilities in the region; and the two sides differed sharply over U.S.-Japanese plans to develop a theater missile defense in East Asia. China saw the move as directed at countering Chinese as well as North Korean ballistic missiles.
- Concerns among Japanese government decision makers and other opinion leaders that China's rising economic power, fostered by Japanese aid, trade, investment, and technology, might lead to the expansion of Chinese political, economic, and military influence in regional and world affairs in ways contrary to Japanese interests.[13]

The tensions in Japanese-Chinese relations in the mid- to late 1990s contrasted with a period of several years after the Tiananmen incident that was widely acknowledged as the most positive and cooperative period in bilateral relations since the Pacific War. Japan's initial response to the incident was muted. Tokyo went along with group of Seven (G7) sanctions against China. In July 1990, however, Tokyo diverged from the rest of the G7 to announce a resumption of lending to China. The Chinese government strongly supported the Japanese move, which ushered in a three-year period of cooperation and cordiality.[14]

A visit to China by Prime Minister Kaifu in 1991 confirmed that Tiananmen was no longer an obstacle to a cordial relationship. The change in Japanese policy coincided with a surge in Japanese investment in China; many Japanese business leaders judged that Chinese authorities had shown themselves to be capable of maintaining stability, and this and later rapid Chinese economic growth encouraged Japanese investment. In a notable departure from past Japanese practice emphasizing the primacy of relations with the United States and the U.S.-Japan alliance, Japanese Prime Minister Hosokawa declared in late 1991 that Japan's relationship with China was as important as its relationship with the United States. A successful visit to China by the Japanese emperor in 1992 indicated just how far the two sides were willing to go in order to put the past behind them, at least for the time being. More forthright expressions of regret by Japanese leaders, including Hosokawa in 1993 for past Japanese aggression against China, also were appreciated by the Chinese. Economic relations developed rapidly, with China becoming Japan's second-largest destination for direct foreign investment after the United States. Official dialogues and intergovernmental cooperation expanded, including cooperation in military and security matters.[15]

In 1995, several difficult political and security issues surfaced in the bilateral relationship. China's nuclear testing program drew strong protests from Japan, followed by the freezing of a small part of Japan's large aid program in China. Beijing responded angrily, reminding Japan again of its record of aggression in China. The fiftieth anniversary of the end of the Pacific War also was used in China as an opportunity for extensive media examination of Japan's military past.[16]

In November 1995, Japan's alleged failure to address adequately its history of aggression was criticized in a joint press conference in Seoul by the presidents of China and South Korea. Although China and South Korea often had released statements critical of Japan in the past, such high level joint statements had not occurred before as China-South Korean relations had only been normalized for a few years. Japanese politicians and various community leaders reacted very negatively, perceiving this move as political manipulation of the history issue. Some commentators interpreted Japanese actions in 1995 as evidence of increased willingness to toughen Japan's policy toward China.[17]

Relations with Taiwan also became a more difficult issue in PRC-Japan relations in 1995, largely as a result of China's heightened concerns about Taiwan's stepped-up efforts to improve its international standing. The Chinese military exercises designed to intimidate Taiwan in 1995 and 1996 alarmed many officials and opinion leaders in Japan, increasing Japan's wariness of PRC ambitions in the region.[18]

The mixed picture of Sino-Japanese relations after the Cold War—three "good years" followed by several years of "troubled" relations in the mid- to late 1990s, in turn followed by pragmatic and more moderate efforts to shore up bilateral ties—was not unusual in the modern history of Japan-China relations.[19] There were similar ups and downs during previous decades. What the pattern showed was a bilateral relationship with deeply rooted differences that prevent full and lasting cooperation, but a relationship that was being managed without major confrontation or conflict in order to meet the needs of the two sides.[20]

In the early 1960s, for instance, Beijing was stridently opposed to both the United States and the Soviet Union and sharply criticized Japan's government as a "running dog" of "U.S. imperialism" in Asia. However, China faced a major economic crisis as a result of the withdrawal of Soviet economic and technical support in 1960, as well as the disastrous collapse of the Great Leap Forward by 1961-1962. In this context, Chinese leaders proved sufficiently pragmatic to reach a five-year economic agreement with a wide-ranging group of Japanese industries—in effect making Japan the major developed country involved in the support of China's economy.

While continuing to trade with Japan even during the most disruptive and violent years of the Cultural Revolution in the late 1960s, Beijing strove to use its nascent opening—the Nixon administration and growing pro-PRC sentiment in Japan—in order to isolate Japanese Prime Minister Sato and his conservative Liberal Democratic party (LDP) government over their refusal to break ties with Taiwan and establish ties with Beijing. The surprise announcement by President Nixon in July 1971 that he would visit Beijing came as a shock to Sato and undermined his policy toward China. Beijing kept up the political pressure on Japan until a new LDP prime minister was selected and quickly normalized relations on terms agreeable to the PRC in 1972, ushering in a period of Sino-Japanese cooperation.

As post-Mao China developed an "open door" foreign economic policy in the late 1970s, Japan loomed large in China's development calculus. Japan was China's largest trading partner. Aid relations grew rapidly, and by 1982 China was the largest recipient of official Japanese development assistance. Nonetheless, Chinese discontent grew in the 1980s over what China's officials and opinion leaders perceived as asymmetrical aspects of the economic relationship. For example, China sold Japan coal, oil, and raw materials; Japan sold China higher-value-added machinery, autos, and other equipment. Uncertain about the overall business climate in China, Japanese business and government representatives eschewed large-scale direct investment in China; Japan also shared less technology with China than with some other developing countries. Combined with Chinese irritation over the refusal of Japanese officials to take what Beijing saw as an appropriately contrite posture regarding Japan's negative war record in China, the seeming imbalance in economic benefits led to sharp criticisms and demonstrations against Japan by students, other opinion leaders, and some officials. Both governments moved to minimize the disputes, with Japan notably stepping up its aid efforts in China and curbing official references to the war record that were likely to elicit a sharp Chinese response.

China-Japan Differences

Strategic Issues

Many of the important differences that emerged in post-Cold War Sino-Japanese relations related to strategic issues, and particularly to changed views of strategic and security concerns by officials, other elites, and popular opinion in Japan. During the Cold War, Japan and China were preoccupied with the military dangers posed by the Soviet Union. This common threat helped to reduce the salience of security and other strategic differences between the two powers. Thus, though Chinese elite and popular opinion often showed angst over alleged Japanese militarism, Chinese leaders generally supported Japan's military efforts to offset Soviet power in East Asia. Beijing also generally supported a strong U.S.-Japan security relationship aimed at countering the USSR in what China sometimes characterized as an international "anti-hegemony front" directed at Moscow. Japanese leaders for their part soft-pedaled reservations they had over China's missile developments, nuclear weapons programs, and other defense preparations that were targeted against the USSR but had implications for Japan's security.[21]

The collapse of the Soviet Union lowered the tide of Sino-Japanese strategic cooperation, exposing the rocks of security and strategic differences. The end of the Cold War and collapse of the Soviet Union altered Japan's threat environment; dismantled the Cold War strategic framework for East Asia; removed Japan's number-one security threat, against which Japan's force structure was configured; and took away the initial rationale for Japan's post-World War II geostrategic bargain with the United States.

Japanese leaders came to view the strategic situation in East Asia as more unsettled than during the Cold War, with a number of near-term flash points and longer-term uncertainties shaping Japan's security calculus:[22]

- North Korea became the most pressing security issue. Pyongyang's Taepo Dong missile overflight of Japan in August 1998 galvanized a national sense of vulnerability that was strengthened by North Korea's provocative nuclear weapons declarations of 2002-2004. Japan previously had viewed North Korea as posing an indirect threat in terms of regional instability and refugee flows, as well as a potential problem for the alliance should rifts emerge with the United States over expected Japanese involvement in a Korean contingency. The missile launch elevated North Korea to a direct, military threat to Japan.

- The prospect of a unified Korea also bore on Japan's efforts to prepare for future uncertainty. History made Korea an important security concern for Japan. Despite efforts to improve bilateral ties with South Korea, Japan continued to be suspicious of Korea. The external orientation of a future unified Korea—how it would relate to Beijing, the type of military capability it would possess, and the posture it would assume toward Japan—were seen in Japan as a major factor in the future security equation in Northeast Asia.

- Taiwan was a serious near-term concern. Japanese leaders feared that an outbreak of hostilities in the Taiwan Strait involving U.S. forces would draw in Japan under the U.S.-Japan Defense Guidelines. The extent and role of Japanese involvement in a China-Taiwan-U.S. military conflict would require difficult decisions of Japan as it weighed the need to support its ally against the costs such actions would entail for its future relationship with China. Japan faced the probability that it would emerge from a Taiwan crisis with either its U.S. or China relationship—or perhaps both—seriously damaged.

- Other concerns included regional instability in Southeast Asia—a threat to Japanese political, economic, and security interests. Instability in this area could jeopardize sea lines of communication, threaten Japanese nationals, and disrupt regional security dynamics. Japan's security interests were largely compatible with those of Southeast Asia—preventing regional hegemony, maintaining a regional U.S. presence as a stabilizing force, and carefully managing China's regional role as it grew in power. Russia was low on the list of Japan's security worries, but one Japanese concern was Russian weapons proliferation and the problems this posed in Asia, particularly Russia-China arms deals. The Taepo Dong missile launch and the September 11, 2001, terrorist attack on America highlighted the emergence of new, less geographically confined threats that were not only undeterred by the U.S. military presence, but which could make Japan a target partly because of the U.S. military presence. Long-term energy and economic concerns drove much of Japan's diplomatic and economic activity in the Middle East. Japan saw its interests well served by strong support for the U.S.-led antiterrorism operations in Central and Southwest Asia in 2001-2004.[23]

U.S. security policy remained a key question for Japan. Until the 1990s, Japanese policy makers were confident that the United States needed Japan, and that the alliance was just as critical for Washington's security strategy as it was for Tokyo's. After the Cold War, this confidence became more questioned, with Japan unsure of its value to the United States. This uncertainty stemmed from several factors:

- The updated U.S.-Japan Defense Guidelines notwithstanding, Japanese observers envisioned a crisis in the alliance erupting not only from Japan's failing to provide expected assistance to the United States in a contingency, but from the U.S. decision not to engage on a security issue important to Japan. Prime Minister Koizumi endeavored to avoid an image of Japan failing to provide expected assistance by adopting a high profile in support of the U.S. anti-terrorism campaign of 2001-2002 and the U.S.-led war in and military occupation of Iraq in 2003-2004.[24]
- Japanese leaders assessed that Japan's economic stagnation made it less important to the United States, particularly as China rose in economic prominence in the region.[25]
- Japanese were particularly ambivalent about the U.S.-China relationship. They feared a zero-sum dynamic in which the United States could conclude that its long-term national interest depended most importantly on a strategic understanding with China, and could therefore pull back from Japan if it were an obstacle to this agenda. At the same time, however, Japan feared that poor U.S. management of its China relationship could lead Washington to use Japan explicitly to counter growing Chinese power, a role Japan did not want.[26]

In this environment, China loomed as a strategic concern for Japan. Officials and strategists for several years gave primacy to worries about possible social instability and political paralysis in China in the immediate aftermath of the collapse of the Soviet empire. Like the USSR, China had lost its ideological commitment, while the Tiananmen demonstration revealed major political and social cleavages. Beijing's subsequent rapid economic growth, continued political stability, and more assertive military and foreign policies shifted Japanese concerns more toward dealing with the multifaceted consequences of the rise of a power of China's size. In particular, Japanese officials and other strategists became more concerned with Beijing's increased air and naval power abilities; the assertive stance, backed by military force, used by Beijing to deal with disputes with Taiwan and in the South China Sea in the mid-1990s; and China's nuclear testing and practices involving the proliferation of weapons of mass destruction, delivery systems, and related technology.[27]

In China, concern focused on Japan's cooperation with the United States in "revitalizing" the U.S.-Japan alliance. Chinese planners were especially attentive to the U.S.-backed efforts to encourage Japanese forces to play a bigger role in dealing with military contingencies in the East Asian region. Those Chinese commentators and officials who in recent years had seen the United States as determined to hold back or contain China's rising influence in East Asia suggested that the United States was using the alliance with Japan toward this end. They charged that Japan was a willing accomplice because Tokyo feared that China's rising influence would come at its expense. They were especially critical of recently stepped-up U.S.-Japan cooperation to develop a theater ballistic defense in East Asia. They saw this as directed at China as well as against North Korea's ballistic missiles.[28]

The closer U.S.-Japan security cooperation during the George W. Bush-Koizumi administrations saw a number of developments of particular concern to Chinese officials. One was a more active U.S.-Japanese dialogue over the situation in the Taiwan Strait—developments that came in the midst of quiet but clear U.S. military contingency planning to deal with the Chinese military buildup opposite Taiwan and closer U.S.-Japan collaboration on missile defense programs designed to defend Japan and U.S. forces in Japan, including those engaged in activities elsewhere in nearby Asia. Second was the emergence of a formal U.S.-Japan-Australian strategic dialogue—establishing a broader web of U.S.-led alliance relationships in Asia that excluded China and could be seen as adverse to Chinese interests regarding Taiwan and other issues. Third were the impressive Japanese military deployments in the Indian Ocean and other military measures to support the U.S.-led wars in Afghanistan and Iraq. The moves were encouraged by the U.S. government but raised concerns in some quarters in China about the implications of strengthened U.S.-Japanese military cooperation in areas around China's periphery.[29]

History Issues

Japan's aggression against China in the seventy years prior to Japan's defeat in World War II was a potent issue in mainland China.[30] The concerns of Chinese strategists and opinion leaders, as well as broader Chinese public opinion, about a possible revival of Japanese military expansion or more general Japanese untrustworthiness remained strong. This was partly due to the fact that Japanese aggression against China was far more severe than that of any other power; and to the fact that Chinese government-supported media and other outlets repeatedly used accusations of Japanese militarism as a way to build nationalistic feeling in China, to put the Japanese government on the defensive, and to elicit concessions from the Japanese government in the form of aid, trading terms, or other benefits. As China loomed larger and more influential in Asian and world affairs, at the start of the twenty-first century, Chinese officials and opinion leaders tended to see the military threat from Japan posed less by Japan taking independent action and more by Japan's ever closer defense cooperation with the United States and possibly closer ties with Taiwan.

For their part, Japanese officials sometimes exacerbated bilateral difficulties by denying the facts of history or equivocating on Japan's aggression against China up to the end of World War II. While many in Japan felt genuine regret about the war, repeated reminders from China seemed particularly self-serving and undermined positive feelings toward the PRC regime, which had already lost considerable support in Japan on account of its human rights, weapons proliferation, and assertive nationalistic policies in the post-Cold War period. Meanwhile, some Japanese commentators reflected much broader suspicions of elite and public opinion when they speculated that Beijing strove to use its rising economic, political, and military influence to exert a dominant influence in East Asia, placing Japan in a similar kind of subservient position to the one that it held in the historical order in East Asia throughout most of the two thousand-year history of the Chinese Empire.

Territorial Issues

Sino-Japanese tensions over territorial disputes involving the islets in the East China Sea were relatively quiet at the start of the new century, but they had erupted several times in the recent past and remained a focal point of the strong nationalistic sentiment in both Asian states. In February 1992, for example, Beijing passed a law reaffirming China's territorial claims to the eight islets known as the Diaoyu Islands in Chinese and the Senkaku Islands in Japanese. The islets were uninhabited but they occupied an important strategic location, and the region around them was considered highly prospective for oil resources. The Japanese government strongly and promptly protested Beijing's sovereignty law while Taiwan also subsequently reasserted its claim to the islets.[31]

The roots of the dispute went back to the nineteenth century. Japan defeated China in a war and took control of Taiwan in 1895. Following Japan's defeat in World War II, Taiwan was returned to China. But the islets remained under U.S. control. Japan's claim to the islets appeared strengthened when the United States returned them to Tokyo's control along with nearby Okinawa in 1971. Subsequently, the U.S. government at times endeavored to keep from taking sides in the dispute.

In the 1970s, Tokyo and Beijing agreed to put the disputed islets issue aside as they normalized diplomatic relations and signed a peace treaty addressing issues stemming from World War II. Japanese rightists built a makeshift lighthouse on one of the islets in 1978. The Japanese coast guard patrolled near the islets and fended off efforts by fishermen and others from Taiwan, Hong Kong, and elsewhere to assert claims to the islets. Renewed activities by Japanese rightists on the islets in mid-1996 precipitated a period of Sino-Japanese tension over competing territorial claims, and such tension continued in more recent years. Meanwhile, Japan and China also had some differences over how to resolve competing claims to sovereign rights and offshore resources in the East China Sea, and Japanese officials claimed in mid-2004 that China also challenged the scope of the Japanese exclusive economic zone east of the main islands of Japan.[32]

Economic Issues

Economic relations were troubled on several occasions despite Japan's status as China's main trading partner, main source of economic assistance, and a leading source of direct foreign investment. China's economic vibrancy after the Cold War also meant that Japanese manufacturers and other businesses highly valued close interaction with China as a platform for production destined for Japanese and foreign markets, and as an economic market of large potential for Japanese goods and services. China sometimes resisted perceived inequities in the bilateral economic relationship. Alleged efforts by Japanese government-backed companies to dominate key sectors of China's market were an important focal point for anti-Japanese demonstrations in Chinese cities in the mid-1980s.[33]

More recently, analysts sometimes saw a shift in the bilateral economic relationship, as China prospectively became a more important partner for Japan than Japan was for China, and as China continued rapid growth while Japan had little growth. In this context, Japan altered the level and scope of its aid program in China to focus on areas less challenging to Japanese industry and more compatible with other Japanese interests (for example, the environment). Also, Tokyo did not budge in the face of Chinese complaints in the 1990s that the combination of the requirement that they repay Japanese loans in yen and the large rise in the value of the yen in relation to the U.S. dollar and China's currency over the previous decade put a heavy additional burden on China's economic development. Meanwhile, Japanese companies remained reluctant to share their most advanced technology with countries like China, fearing the technology would be absorbed by illegal or legal means, and would be used to compete with Japanese producers.[34]

Highly publicized trade disputes involving the challenge that goods produced in China (often by Japanese companies) for Japanese consumers posed for the producers of similar products in Japan put China at the center of the major economic debate in Japan in the latter 1990s that persisted into the new century. Beset by over a decade of economic stagnation, Japanese opinion leaders and popular opinion were alarmed by the "hollowing out" of Japanese industries, farms, and enterprises no longer able to compete with Chinese-based producers. Some favored protectionist trade measures against China that won some level of political support in Japan and led to some government actions that added to economic friction in relations with China. However, such measures were inconsistent with the international trade regimes supported by the Japanese government. They were generally unsustainable given the broad forces of globalization that Japanese business and other opinion leaders recognized impelled Japanese enterprises to work more closely with China in order to achieve advantages of economic scale needed to keep Japanese firms competitive in the international economy.[35]

Domestic Politics

Political conditions in both Japan and China remained dynamic and leaders needed to assuage important domestic interests in order to stay in power. China and Japan manifested the growing trend of national assertiveness and pride that spread throughout East Asia in the post-Cold War period.[36] In the case of China, the government went out of its way for many years to stoke the fires of nationalism, in part as a way to fill the ideological void created by the failure of communism. National pride in Japan was more understated but emerged as a strong force prompting Japanese leaders to be more assertive in pressing Japan's case over issues dealing with trade disputes with the United States, territorial disputes with China, and the acquisition of a permanent seat in the UN Security Council. As a result, compromise on sensitive issues in China-Japan relations became more difficult.

Mutual Interests in Japan-China Relations

Both the Japanese and the Chinese governments continued to give top priority to the economic development of their countries, which they believed required a peaceful and cooperative relationship with their neighbors, notably one another. China depended heavily on Japan for economic assistance, for technology and investment, and as a market for Chinese goods. Japan was increasingly dependent on China as a market, source of imports, and offshore manufacturing base. Projections suggested that trade links would be increasingly important for both sides. Regarding foreign investment in China, Japan was in the top ranks along with the United States and Taiwan. (Hong Kong was way ahead and likely to remain in first place in this category.)[37]

Personal exchanges between Japan and China grew. Since the inauguration of the post-Mao reforms, over one hundred thousand Chinese students studied in Japan. Japanese students visiting or studying in China numbered twenty thousand in the mid-1990s. Numerous exchange programs—many fostered by the governments—worked to build mutual understanding and improved relations. Such contacts did not always result in more positive feelings toward one another. But they did promote more realistic mutual assessments that could be effective in avoiding alarmist or otherwise excessive reactions concerning the other's capabilities or intentions.[38]

No other government involved in East Asian affairs appeared likely to benefit from or be inclined to promote greater Sino-Japanese friction. The United States was determined to maintain regional stability and to solidify U.S. relations with Japan while seeking U.S. improved relations with China. Russia improved its relations with China markedly in recent years; its relations with Japan remained complicated by territorial disputes and economic incompatibilities, but both sides sought regional stability and mutual development as was evidenced in Russian-Japanese cooperation in the development of important and relatively easy to access energy sources, notably on Russia's Sakhalin Island.

In Southeast Asia, the Association of Southeast Asian Nations (ASEAN) sought to reduce tensions and build mutual trust in the region through political dialogue between ASEAN and Chinese, Japanese, and other leaders, or through Asian-Pacific nations meeting in groups such as the ASEAN Regional Forum, which dealt with regional security questions. ASEAN welcomed different paths in dealing with the two powers to the north. It cooperated closely with various economic and other initiatives in the ASEAN Plus Three (Japan, China, South Korea) framework that featured annual summits involving leaders of the thirteen states; and it also worked to develop separate free trade arrangements offered by China and Japan, as well as the United States and other economic partners, that appeared to some to be competitive as various powers maneuvered for greater influence in Southeast Asia.[39]

Some observers suggested that Taiwan would benefit in its competition with the PRC by a growing split between Japan and China. Presumably, Taipei would seek to side with Tokyo against Beijing. Indeed, Taiwan's leaders repeatedly emphasized the utility of Taiwan linking its security more closely with the U.S.-Japan alliance and enhanced security cooperation with Japan. However, this line of reasoning ignored Taiwan's wariness regarding regional tensions and conflict, which have important negative consequences for the trade-dependent island. Taiwan leaders calling for greater security cooperation with Japan and the United States generally eschewed attention to a possible rise in military tensions with the mainland that might result.[40]

At times, South Korea was not averse to lining up with Beijing to criticize Japan's war record or to work in parallel with China in criticizing Japan's expanded military role in Asian affairs. Privately, South Korea officials also showed some interest in using improved relations with China to balance South Korea's strong dependence on the United States and Japan for security and economic-technological support, respectively. Such manipulation was seen to work well in a peaceful atmosphere; but increased PRC-Japan tensions also were seen to complicate the regional military and economic stability that was so important to South Korea's development. Moreover, South Korea's President Kim Dae Jung and his successor Roh Moo Hyun appeared to put such manipulation aside as they and Japanese leaders reached some rapport during summit meetings in the late 1990s and early 2000s.[41]

North Korea generally was less concerned with development and was preoccupied with survival. It was hard to see what benefit Pyongyang would derive from exacerbated Sino-Japanese tensions. There was perhaps some benefit in keeping Beijing and Tokyo from cooperating with the United States to pressure North Korea in 2002-2004 to agree to verifiable nuclear safeguards. Pyongyang's options to do so appeared limited as its actions were closely scrutinized by all concerned regional powers for signs of North Korean efforts to provoke instability or alternatively signs that North Korea was more prepared to come to terms with its neighbors. It appeared under prevailing circumstances that North Korea's ability to exacerbate China-Japan tensions without having a major effect on overall regional stability was weak.[42]

Recent Exchanges and Issues

The ambiguous state of Sino-Japanese relations in recent years—a potentially volatile balance of conflicting impulses and incentives toward conflict and controversy, and those toward cooperation and accommodation—was manifest at various times during high-level Sino-Japanese meetings in the post-Cold War period. Clear signs that the relationship had begun moving from the strong differences and frictions seen in the mid-1990s to the more calm and cooperative status resulting in part from China's more cooperative and flexible approach in Asia since 1997 were seen in visits by top-level leaders to Beijing and Tokyo in 1997 and 1998. Those visits on the whole accentuated the positive and at least outwardly tried to play down the disputes in Sino-Japanese relations.

Beijing was satisfied with Japanese Prime Minister Hashimoto's fence-mending efforts during his September 4-7, 1997, "successful" state visit, judging from official Chinese press reports.[43] Agreement on annual high-level exchanges—including visits by Premier Li Peng later in 1997 and by President Jiang Zemin in 1998, the twentieth anniversary of the peace and friendship treaty, pointed toward further improvement.

Hashimoto publicly expanded previous Japanese statements of understanding of the PRC position on the Taiwan issue and the expectation of a peaceful resolution; Tokyo pledged no support for "two Chinas" or for Taiwan's independence and declared that Taiwan, as a part of China, was not qualified to enter the UN. Beijing doubtless hoped this would prod Washington to make similar high-level statements during Jiang's visit to the United States and President Clinton's subsequent visit to China in 1997 and 1998.

Beijing was mollified, if not wholly satisfied, with Hashimoto's finessing of the sensitive issue of whether the revised U.S.-Japan defense guidelines covered the Taiwan Strait. He reiterated that the "areas surrounding Japan" did not represent a geographic concept but would be defined according to the nature of a given situation; he also promised that Japan would "act cautiously" on the basis of the Japan-China treaty and the joint statement on normalization of relations.

In his talks with Hashimoto, President Jiang Zemin departed from China's rhetoric of the past decade on Sino-Japanese relations, stressing that relations should be viewed from a "strategic" perspective. Li Peng reemphasized this theme during his visit to Japan on November 11-17, 1997.[44] An authoritative *Renmin Ribao* editorial capping the visit credited him with proposing a new set of "basic principles" for Sino-Japanese relations and asserted that these were formulated by Beijing "from a long-term strategic perspective." Although heralded by *Xinhua* at the time as a new approach, Li's five principles were similar to the guidelines China espoused for relations with other powers and with Japan in the past. The five principles are: (1) noninterference in each other's internal affairs and toleration of ideological differences; (2) "correct" handling of differences to avoid "obstacles" to improving ties; (3) expanding dialogue and exchanges to enhance trust and understanding; (4) expanding economic cooperation; and (5) developing cross-generation friendship.

As the first head of government to visit Japan since before China's crackdown on prodemocracy protestors in 1989, Li's visit carried particular symbolic importance. The *Renmin Ribao* editorial heralded Li's visit as "completely successful," stating that he had received a "warm welcome and lavish hospitality" and had "reached the expected goal" of "deepening understanding, increasing friendship, and strengthening cooperation." It also said that Li had "achieved a broad consensus" with Hashimoto on key issues and predicted that the visit would have a far-reaching impact on the "stabilization and development" of bilateral relations.

As in the authoritative media treatment of high-level bilateral visits in the past, PRC media coverage of the Hashimoto-Li exchange made it clear that economic interest remained the core component of Beijing's diplomacy toward Japan. Underscoring this theme, a *Xinhua* "roundup" on December 28, 1997, praised Japan's official development assistance to China over the past twenty years as having "contributed to China's development" and promoted Sino-Japanese "friendship." Li's trip, in particular, seemed intended as an effort to push Japanese investment and technology exchange to new levels to meet the demands of China's burgeoning economy.

During the visit, Li was portrayed as making an unusually strong bid for investment and technology transfer in a series of speeches to Japanese business and industrial circles. His strongest pitch, in a speech to Japan's federation of economic organizations, the Keidanren, touted China's economic growth and stability, including its ability to withstand the Asian financial crisis, and went on to promise to "gradually open" China's "financial, trade, and other service sectors to foreign investors." Praising the "relentless efforts" of Japanese businesspeople to facilitate the expansion of Japanese investment into new fields, he declared that "the fields for cooperation are broad and the formats flexible." He also asserted that Chinese markets had undergone "profound changes" and that Japanese businesspeople were able to "change their concepts, seize opportunities, and suggest conditions for competing."

During the Li Peng visit, the two sides reached formal agreements on several key issues of importance to China that had been negotiated during Hashimoto's visit to China, including an agreement on bilateral environmental cooperation, a long-awaited fishery accord, and a joint declaration on China's accession to the WTO that implied further Japanese support.

Despite Beijing's efforts to smooth over troubled waters, authoritative media made it clear that past irritants continued to fester and could easily throw relations off track again. For example, during the state visits of both Hashimoto and Li, PRC media described the atmosphere of bilateral talks as "frank and sincere"—a formulation that was used by Beijing to indicate important differences and that was used to characterize high-level visits since the Tiananmen crackdown. In addition, while Chinese leaders toned down their rhetoric on issues in dispute, they pressed Japan to go further in making amends for wartime aggression in China and to clear up the ambiguity over whether the Japan-U.S. security guidelines included Taiwan. Apparently, Beijing chose not to raise the territorial dispute over the Diaoyu (Senkaku) Islands during the visits, even though on the eve of Li's trip to Japan a Foreign Ministry spokesman was quoted by the PRC-owned Hong Kong paper *Wen Wei Po* as stating that this issue, "in particular," remained a problem, claiming that the islands had been China's territory "since ancient times."[45]

Although Hashimoto was quoted during his trip to China as reaffirming Japan's one-China stance, Li Peng nevertheless warned him that Beijing would not accept any effort, "direct or indirect," to include Taiwan in Japan-U.S. "security cooperation." Jiang Zemin told him that "any more" moves by Japan on the Taiwan issue would affect the "political foundation" of bilateral ties. Similarly, both Jiang and Li reiterated to Hashimoto China's views on Japan's wartime aggression, even though they adopted a softer tone than they had used in past public statements to Japanese leaders.

As for Li's visit to Japan, authoritative PRC media portrayed him as glossing over both the Taiwan and the history issues in his talks with Hashimoto but as making more pointed comments in his remarks to other groups. In his talks with Hashimoto, he was quoted as saying that the two countries should "deal in a timely manner with whatever problems arise" and "prevent the overall development of bilateral relations from being interrupted." He went on to say that China had "taken note" of the "promises" made by Hashimoto while in China and "hopes the Japanese side will honor and carry out its promises." Although he said Hashimoto had affirmed Japan's rejection of "two Chinas" or of Taiwanese independence, he did not specifically mention China's concern over the scope of the Japan-U.S. security guidelines; and while he said that Hashimoto had made promises on "historical issues," he did not spell them out.

The visit of Defense Minister Chi Haotian to Tokyo on February 3-8, 1998—the first such high-level substantive military exchange since diplomatic relations were established in 1972—marked more forward movement, while noting continuing differences.[46] Suggesting that China viewed Chi's visit as successful in maintaining the momentum of improving ties, PRC media coverage of Chi's talks with Prime Minister Hashimoto, Foreign Minister Keizo Obuchi, and JDA Director-General Fumio Kyuma continued the generally positive spin that Beijing media had put on Sino-Japanese relations over the previous year and portrayed the establishment of military-to-military relations as a further step toward consolidating bilateral ties. Media coverage of Chi's meeting with Hashimoto, for example, was markedly upbeat and contained no reference to such thorny issues as Taiwan or Japan's wartime actions in China. A *Xinhua* report on February 5 stressed the positive nature of the relationship, quoting Chi as saying his visit was a "good beginning of the new year for bilateral ties" and showed that exchanges between the two nations have "expanded to all spheres."

Media coverage of Chi's talks with Kyuma was more explicit in linking military ties to the improvement of bilateral relations. A February 4, 1998, *Xinhua* report on their talks that day cited Chi and Kyuma as agreeing that defense cooperation was "conducive" to maintaining bilateral relations as well as regional peace and stability. The two officials also agreed on military exchanges between the People's Liberation Army and the Japanese armed forces, and Kyuma reportedly accepted "with pleasure" Chi's invitation to pay a reciprocal visit to China within the year.

Reflecting Beijing's intention to remind Tokyo of areas in which it was closely monitoring Japan's behavior, the *Xinhua* report on Chi's meeting with Kyuma also cited Chi as bringing up Taiwan and historical issues, but as referring to these issues only briefly. Suggesting that the Taiwan issue continued to worry Beijing more than other irritations in the relationship, Chi called on Japan to adopt a "more definite stance" on Taiwan in regard to the U.S.-Japan "Defense Cooperation Treaty." He adopted a softer tone on the history issue, calling on Tokyo to adopt a "responsible attitude toward history" so as to imbue Japanese youth with a "correct historical perspective."

Further progress in Chinese-Japanese relations came during Chinese Vice President Hu Jintao's extensive goodwill visit to Japan in April 1998—an important benchmark in the future Chinese president's grooming for leadership in Chinese foreign policy. Beijing subsequently broadened its contacts in the more fluid and notably less pro-China political arena in Japan by normalizing relations with the Japanese Communist Party after a hiatus of thirty years; and by establishing—after a similarly lengthy wait—normal relations with the conservative Japanese newspaper *Sankei Shimbun*; the only major Japanese daily that refused to close its bureau in Taiwan in return for the opportunity to open a bureau in Beijing. China reacted calmly to the fall of the Hashimoto government in August 1998 and muted its criticism of Japan in the lead-up to President Jiang's first visit to Japan in September 1998. Privately, and sometimes publicly, Chinese officials were critical of Japan's economic policies during the Asian economic crisis, and Jiang Zemin reportedly postponed his September visit in order to put pressure on Japan to adhere more closely to PRC views on Taiwan. Nonetheless, the visit was rescheduled for November 1998 and both governments worked to ensure a positive atmosphere for the trip.[47]

Jiang's visit took place in late November. Gains for China included substantial added economic aid from Japan. Notably, Prime Minister Obuchi went no further than previous Japanese leaders in meeting Chinese demands on Taiwan; he eschewed a formal declaration similar to the so-called three no's—no support for "one China, one Taiwan," Taiwanese independence, or Taiwanese membership in international organizations requiring statehood—voiced by U.S. President Clinton in Shanghai on June 30, 1998. Obuchi's remarks on Japan's past aggression in China and the U.S.-Japan defense treaty were consistent with past practice. Jiang lectured Japanese audiences about historical issues, prompting considerable negative Japanese media coverage.[48]

Jiang's failure to elicit greater Japanese government support for China's position on Taiwan and regarding historical and other sensitive issues did not derail Chinese efforts to keep Sino-Japanese relations on an even keel despite disputes and differences. In 2000, Premier Zhu Rongji endeavored to ease recent tensions over the activities of Chinese research ships in Japan's Exclusive Economic Zone (EEZ), pending cuts in Japan's overseas development assistance (ODA) budget, and Japanese government dissatisfaction with Beijing's level of expressed appreciation for Japan's ODA efforts.[49]

Just prior to the Zhu visit, Beijing hosted a special commemorative reception to celebrate the twentieth anniversary of economic cooperation between China and Japan. Japan was represented by a senior delegation led by Liberal Democratic Party (LDP) Secretary-General Nonaka Hiromu. The Japanese Foreign Ministry viewed the dispatch of this special envoy as extremely important for bilateral relations. Meeting Nonaka in Beijing, Zhu Rongji warmly praised Japanese aid to China.

In Tokyo during October 2000, Zhu met with Japan's political leadership and courted Japanese public opinion. He once again praised Japanese aid efforts in China. His delegation worked out an arrangement for mutual prior notification of maritime research activities in EEZs, and the opening of a bilateral hotline was confirmed. Zhu was notably softer on the history issue than Jiang had been in 1998. In response to a media query in Tokyo, he noted that while former Prime Minister Murayama Tomoichi had in 1995 issued a general apology to the people of Asia, Japan "had never once apologized, in any official documents, to China for its aggression." Nonetheless, Zhu also made clear that China was not intent on asking ceaselessly for an apology. Whether or not to apologize was a decision to be left to the Japanese people; Zhu only asked for Japanese reflection on the matter.

As a result of understandings during Zhu's visit, a Japan-China Security Dialogue resumed in November 2002. Following up on the agreement reached during the Zhu visit for mutual ship visits, it was announced that a Chinese ship would come to Japan in 2001. Progress on defense issues was difficult given the depth of suspicions. China's Defense White Paper, released in October 2000, dealt significantly with Taiwan and Taiwan-related security issues, potentially involving Japan. Beginning with missile defenses, the White Paper underscored China's opposition to any introduction of theater missile defense (TMD) to Taiwan. It also set out Chinese concerns with Japan-U.S. cooperation on TMD research, warning that TMD far exceeds Japan's defense requirements and will set off a regional arms race. The document also expressed concerns with the lack of transparency in the revised Japan-U.S. Defense Guidelines with respect to Taiwan, (i.e., whether or not Taiwan is included as a "regional contingency" for Japan-U.S. defense cooperation). For the first time, the White Paper expressed concern over the extent to which the strengthening of the U.S.-Japan alliance might encourage Taiwan separatism and prevent a resolution of the Taiwan issue. It went on to criticize Japanese legislation to extend rear area support to the United States in the event of a regional contingency as contrary to the trend of the time.

Differences over defense issues, history, Taiwan, trade, and U.S.-Japan security cooperation festered during ensuing years. In 2001, leaders in Tokyo and Beijing were more concerned with adjusting to the shift in policy approach to the region by the new U.S. administration. Japan tried to stay on the sidelines during the U.S.-China impasse over the EP-3 incident and was relieved as the crisis passed without major incident. Prime Minister Koizumi followed through on political promises and visited the Yakasuni Shrine, prompting outrage from Chinese media but little substantive reaction.[50]

China's image in Japan suffered a black eye as a result of the May 2002 incident in Shenyang where Chinese police entered the Japanese consulate and forcibly removed North Korean asylum-seekers. Both governments nonetheless worked to keep relations on track. Agreement was reached on the raising of the mystery (later determined to be North Korean) ship sunk by the Japanese coast guard in China's EEZ. After holding firmly to its position that the actions of the Chinese police at the Shenyang consulate did not violate the Vienna Convention, Beijing offered Japan face-saving talks aimed at developing guidelines to prevent a similar recurrence. At the same time, Japan's growing trade with and investments on the mainland served to cushion relations during the rough patches at this time.[51]

By late 2002, Koizumi's meetings with Chinese leaders at international forums were dominated by the North Korean nuclear crisis. The Japanese prime minister received no invitations to visit Beijing on account of his visits to the Yakasuni shrine, which he did in both 2003 and 2004. The two governments worked through problems posed by North Korean refugees in China (some were Japanese nationals) seeking asylum in Japan. More important, economic relations continued to broaden and deepen. In 2002, Japan imported more from China than from the United States, while Japanese exports to China increased 32 percent that year.[52]

The SARS crisis of 2003 ironically led to a modest improvement in relations. Japanese economists tried to assess the impact of the SARS epidemic, with early projections quite negative but forecasts brightened by early summer. Japan repeatedly extended emergency medical assistance and personnel to help China cope with the epidemic. The Japanese government announced on April 25 that it was sending masks and protective clothing to China and Prime Minister Koizumi added that Japan wanted to do what it could to cooperate in meeting Chinese requests for assistance. On May 7, Koizumi announced that Japan would extend additional assistance to China which included face masks, preventive clothing and equipment, and medical instruments, amounting to approximately ¥18 million. On May 9, it was announced that Japan would send a four-man disaster relief team to China to help deal with the epidemic, and later in the month it was made known that Japan would send an additional ¥1.5 billion of assistance. The Japanese assistance received warm words of thanks from Chinese government officials. Whatever economic damage was done by the epidemic seemed offset by the continued rapid growth of China's economy in 2003.[53]

Outlook

The past cyclical pattern of Sino-Japanese relations and an assessment of their recent status suggest a generally mixed picture of difficulties and cooperation for the future. As in the past, the relationship could be unstable for a time, with periods of warming relations followed by periods of dispute caused by competing international interests or festering domestic resentments in which economic and other mutual interests are damaged to some degree. But the swings in policy are likely to be less wide than during the Maoist period, if only because present-day Chinese leaders are in general agreement that Beijing's interests are best served by working generally with the world as it is, rather than attempting to foster major change in the East Asian region or the world as a whole. For their part, Japanese leaders seem determined to adhere to the general outlines of a policy that fosters Japanese economic growth in an international environment of peace and stability.

Among the many recent areas of controversy and differences between Japan and China is North Korea. The two powers easily could diverge over the North Korean nuclear issue, with Japan likely to side with the United States if it decided a more forceful stance is needed against Pyongyang—a step opposed by China. Unsteady domestic politics in Beijing and Tokyo, rising assertiveness backed by stronger nationalistic feelings, and mutual wariness as the two powers adjust to China's rising power and influence in Asian and world affairs will head the list of other factors complicating smooth China-Japan relations. But until such time as one side or the other feels strong and confident enough to risk a serious break with the other, the forces promoting economic interdependence and mutual accommodation are likely to overrule the forces of assertiveness and confrontation.

Consultations with several Chinese foreign policy specialists in May 2004 and especially consultations and interviews with fifteen Japanese government officials in mid-2004 underlined the mixed prospects for Japan-China relations. The officials were well aware of both positive trends and negative developments affecting China's approach to Japan. The Japanese officials tended to welcome the positive initiatives from Beijing, but continued Chinese criticism of Japan, China's military buildup, and other practices made them wary of China's actual policies and objectives. Their mixed and often wary reaction contrasted sharply with neighboring South Korea. Japanese officials tended to see South Korean officials, businesses, and popular opinion regarding China as reflecting a type of "China fever." They advised that Japan had been dealing with the People's Republic of China for a much longer time than had South Korea; Japan had experienced such China fevers in the past, and Japan had "gotten over" its China fevers.[54]

Japanese officials concerned with Sino-Japanese economic relations advised that Japanese business interests on the whole were positive about Japan's burgeoning trade and investment in China. A few years earlier, they recalled, many in Japan had viewed China's economic rise at a time of protracted Japanese stagnation as a threat to Japan's economic well being. The upswing in Japan's economy in 2003-2004, and clearer Japanese recognition of the need to integrate the Japanese economy more closely to rising Asian economies, changed this perspective. Many in Japan still worried about the "hollowing out" of Japanese manufacturing industries as many Japanese firms invested more in China, and some in Japan also were concerned about Japan losing technological advantage to China as high-technology Japanese firms invest more in China. Concerns over less than firm Chinese support for intellectual property rights and the losses incurred by many Japanese firms investing in China also were cited by some Japanese officials.

On the positive side, Japanese trade and investment to China became so important that Japanese government planners said they tended to see China as one of the three primary drivers of Japanese economic growth—the Japanese domestic market, the U.S. and Western market, and the China market. Japanese firms and Chinese businesses were seen to grow together in mutually beneficial economic relationships, according to Japanese officials. The Japanese officials claimed that the scope of Japanese investments in China grew in anticipation of China's entry into the WTO, prompting Japanese officials to see the current Japanese investment pattern as the "third wave" of Japanese investment since the normalization of Sino-Japanese relations and the onset of economic reform in China; the previous investment waves were said to have taken place in the 1980s and the early to mid-1990s.

Japanese officials were clear-eyed about many areas of economic competition with China and also admitted that Japan and China seemed to be competing for political and economic leadership with their respective approaches to free trade agreements with the developing countries of Southeast Asia. Japan had a range of planned bilateral free trade agreements with Asian states, though it was not yet ready to propose one with China. For the time being, Tokyo expected to work with WTO processes and regulations in dealing with trade and other issues with China, according to Japanese officials.

In the view of Japanese officials, another significant bright spot in China's approach toward Japan was in the area of control of transfers of technologies and materials that might assist in the development of weapons of mass destruction (WMD), their delivery systems, or their components. The Chinese government's approach to such export controls and other trade controls was said to have changed very much for the better in the previous two years. Japanese officials gave high marks to China's enacting in fall 2002 a legal framework to govern such exports by China, and they saw China's joining the Nuclear Suppliers' Group in May 2004 as a similarly positive step. Such Chinese government actions were seen as a marked contrast to the Chinese government's previous suspicious view of such controls. The Tokyo officials emphasized that Japan worked very closely with the United States in international regimes governing sensitive transfers and that China's more positive and constructive stance was well received by U.S. as well as Japanese officials.

The Japanese officials highlighted a few areas of continuing concern regarding China and proliferation issues. One area was the transfer of sensitive goods through China to other destinations. Japanese officials were most concerned with WMD materials reaching North Korea in this way. They said they had worked with China on some cases in this area and they advised that the Chinese dealt with the cases in suitable and correct ways. Another area of Japanese concern was the incomplete transparency of Chinese businesses, which meant that ostensibly private Chinese firms seeking dual-use or sensitive technologies or equipment sometimes turned out to be fronts for Chinese military enterprises. As Chinese state-owned enterprises continued to be reformed and the business environment in China improved and became more transparent, this problem became somewhat less serious than in the past, according to Japanese officials.

Japanese officials concerned with Japan's overall foreign and security policy saw China's approach to Japan, Asia, and world affairs—especially China's emphasis in 2003-2004 on the Chinese "peaceful approach" in Asian and world affairs[55]— as holding considerable benefit for Japan. They were well aware that Japan continued to be singled out for more Chinese criticism than the United States or other countries, but they also noted that the scope, frequency, and intensity of the Chinese criticism were considerably less than in the 1990s.

These Japanese officials tended to assess a balance sheet of pros and cons for Japan regarding China's recent approach to Japan. The advantages for Japan included less criticism by China of Japanese policies and behavior, Chinese willingness to work constructively with Japanese business people and investors in promoting economic development of mutual benefit, and Chinese acquiescence to U.S. leadership in Asian and world affairs. As a key U.S. ally in Asia, Japan welcomed China's stance toward U.S. leadership as it eased difficulties for Japan as it pursued close alliance relations with the United States in such sensitive areas as supporting the U.S.-led military operations in Afghanistan and Iraq. Some of the Japanese officials were cautiously optimistic that China's recent emphasis on its peaceful rise foreshadowed even more Chinese accommodation of the United States and of Japanese interests as Tokyo aligned closely with the United States.

Some Japanese officials also were enthusiastic about Japan-China-South Korea cooperation. Flowing from interactions the three Asian powers continued to have in the ASEAN and ASEAN Plus Three frameworks, such trilateral cooperation in economic, political, and security areas was developing constructively, according to Japanese officials. Reinforcing this trend was cooperation among the three powers and the other concerned governments in the six-party talks dealing with the crisis prompted by North Korea's nuclear weapons development.

Balancing these positive points were many negative features of China's approach to Japan that clearly irritated and worried Japanese officials. In general, the reactions of Japanese officials to these negative features showed that Japanese officials were unlikely to take China's pronounced intentions of peace at face value, but would await concrete Chinese actions in areas of concern to Japan before embracing China's "peaceful intent."

Japanese officials followed Chinese declarations of peaceful intent with great interest, but they found them confusing and unclear. At one level, they believed that the Chinese emphasis on peace and accommodation would usefully calm strong anti-Japanese sentiment in China and reduce what Japanese officials judged were unhelpful Chinese popular beliefs in the alleged dominant power and strength of China and in the need for China to take tough stands in the face of perceived affronts by Japan, the United States, and others.

Japanese officials saw considerable uncertainty and debate in China over the scope and purpose of China's peaceful approach. They believed the peaceful approach might be significantly altered or reversed if circumstances were to change or for other reasons.

On specific issues, Japanese officials emphasized that unless the peaceful Chinese approach dealt clearly with China's military doctrine, military force structure and force planning, Japan would continue to view China's rising capabilities with some concern. They noted that the five hundred Chinese ballistic missiles targeted at Taiwan also can hit Japan. Thus, the PLA buildup threatening Taiwan also was a clear threat to Japan, and without some concrete modifications in China's military approach, Japan could not but view China's emphasis on peace as little more than a public relations exercise. As one Japanese official said, China's peaceful pronouncements are a "shell" and Japan wants to know what is inside the shell. Japanese officials claimed they had asked Chinese counterparts to clarify China's military intentions but received no satisfactory response.

Japanese officials agreed with the judgment of Chinese foreign policy specialists who advised that Chinese domestic politics were an important reason for China to continue sharp criticism of Japan at a time when China muted criticism of the United States and others. They noted that some Chinese intellectuals two years earlier called on Chinese authorities to mute criticism of Japan, but this call failed to gain wide support and prompted a number of sharply negative commentaries from other Chinese intellectuals and commentators. In the end, the anti-Japanese bias of China's approach to world affairs continued, in the judgment of Japanese officials. It even led Chinese officials to allow Chinese people to make strong anti-Japanese charges on the Internet, when Chinese authorities restricted Internet access for such invective against other popular targets, like the United States.

The Japanese officials also saw a hardening of China's approach to Japan on territorial issues. They said that Chinese officials were less discreet than in the past in commenting in support of Chinese activists who sailed to the Diayou/Senkaku Islands to challenge Japan's control of the territory. They claimed that Chinese naval survey ships repeatedly conducted surveys around Japan without providing the prior notification that had been agreed to by Chinese and Japanese officials a few years earlier. They also were concerned by China's private assertion to Japan earlier in 2004 that China no longer recognized the scope of Japan's exclusive economic zone east of Japan that was based on Japan's claim to a small island some distance from the Japanese home islands. China also began gas drilling so close to the line of division established between Japan and China that the drilling was certain to take resources in the Japanese zone, according to Japanese officials.

Other complaints by Japanese officials included China's allegedly heavy-handed warnings to the Japanese government to prevent Japanese legislators from attending Taiwan President Chen Shui-bian's inauguration in May 2004. The Japanese officials also said that China was very strong in reaction to Japan's support for U.S. efforts in 2004 to obtain some form of Taiwan representation in the World Health Organization and Tokyo's support for the U.S. resolution regarding China's human rights practices at the annual UN Human Rights Commission meeting in April 2004. Japanese officials continued to resent China's opposition to Japan gaining a permanent seat in the UN Security Council.

Drawing general implications of trends in China-Japan relations for Japan-U.S. relations, some Japanese officials advised that when Japan-China relations are wary and suspicious, Japan was anxious to keep close ties with the United States. If China were to succeed in markedly improving relations with Japan, they averred, Japan might have somewhat less interest in close alliance relations with the United States.

In sum, the record of alternating "good" and "bad" periods in recent Sino-Japanese relations reveals the difficulty the generally preoccupied and pragmatic PRC leaders have in dealing with a major neighboring power that is allied to a superpower with mixed intentions toward the Chinese government and that has proved of enormous material benefit for the Chinese economy. At the bottom, Chinese leaders are in no position to confront Japan over differences in their relationship unless Japan impinges seriously on a vital PRC concern like Taiwan. There is little positive sentiment between the two governments, but both sets of leaders place a higher priority on development and stability than they do on allowing bilateral differences to drive their relationship. The outlook seems mixed, with suspicion and wariness remaining behind active cooperation in economic and other areas.

Notes

1. See, among others, Greg Austin and Stuart Harris, *Japan and Greater China* (Honolulu: University of Hawaii, 2001); Christopher Howe, *China and Japan: History, Trends, Prospects* (Oxford: Oxford University Press, 1996); Ming Zhang and Ronald A. Montaperto, *A Triad of a Different Kind: The United States, China, and Japan* (London: Macmillan Press, 1999); *Asia's Global Powers: China-Japan* (Canberra: East Asian Analytical Unit, Government of Australia, 1996).

2. Michael Green, "Managing Chinese Power: The View from Japan," in Alastair Iain Johnston and Robert Ross, eds., *Engaging China* (London: Routledge, 1999); Michael Green and Benjamin Self, "Japan's Changing China Policy: From Commercial Liberalism to Reluctant Realism," *Survival* 38, no. 2 (Summer 1996); Benjamin Self, "China and Japan: A Façade of Friendship," *Washington Quarterly* 26, no. 1 (Winter 2002-2003): 77-88; Komori Yoshihisa, *Nit-chi yuko no maboroshi* (Tokyo: Shogakkan, 2002).

3. Yoichi Funabashi, "New Geopolitics Rages over Various Parts of Asia," *Asahi Shimbun,* 15 January 2002.

4. See, among others, Hisane Masaki, "Fresh Irritants May Still Derail Sino-Japan Ties," *The Japan Times* (Internet version), 29 March 2002.

5. "Tokyo-Taipei Links 'Good' Despite Damning Reports," *Asia Times* (Internet version) 29 March 2002. In reporting on the active U.S.-Japanese dialogue regarding China during a background briefing in March 2002, a Bush administration official with responsibility for relations with Japan was particularly struck by the outburst of warm applause that greeted President Bush's reference to strong U.S. support for Taiwan during the president's speech to the Japanese diet during his trip to Asia in February 2002.

6. For a review and chronology of developments in China-Japan relations over the past five years, see the quarterly Japan-China assessments by James Przystup in *Comparative Connections* (Honolulu: CSIS, Pacific Forum), www.csis.org/pacfor.

7. For a particularly articulate example of this line of thinking, see Yoshihisa Komori, "Rethinking Japan-China Relations: Beyond the History Issue," a paper presented at the Sigur Center for Asian Affairs, The George Washington University, Washington, D.C., 5 December 2001.

8. For example, see Tian Peiliang, "Nationalism: China and Japan," *Foreign Affairs Journal* no. 63 (Beijing, Chinese People's Institute of Foreign Affairs, March 2002): 63-83.

9. Benjamin Self and Michael Green are among the specialists associated with the view seeing hardening, especially in Japanese policy and behavior, toward China. See also David Fouse, "Japan's China Debate," in *Asia's China Debate* (Honolulu: Asia Pacific Center for Security Studies, December 2003); Yong Deng, "Chinese Relations with Japan," *Pacific Affairs* 70, no. 3 (Autumn 1997): 379; Michael Armacost and Kenneth Pyle, "Japan and the Engagement of China," *NBR Analysis* 12, no. 5 (Seattle, Wash.: National Bureau of Asian Research, 2001); Joseph Y. S. Cheng, "Sino-Japanese Relations in the 21st Century," *Journal of Contemporary Asia* 33, no. 2 (2003): 268; Wu Xinbo, "The Security Dimension of Sino-Japanese Relations," *Asian Survey* 40, no. 2 (March-April 2000): 301; Denny Roy, *Stirring Samurai, Disapproving Dragon* (Honolulu: Asia Pacific Center for Security Studies, 2003); "Noted Scholar Discusses 'New Thinking' in Sino-Japanese Relations," (Beijing) *Renmin Wang*, 1 January 2004 (Internet version); Liu Xiaobiao, "Where Are Sino-Japanese Relations Heading?" (Beijing) *Renmin Wang*, 13 August 2003 (Internet version). For background on these issues, see Robert Sutter, *Chinese Policy Priorities and Their Implications for the United States* (Lanham, Md.: Rowman & Littlefield, 2000), 79-98. See also "China, Japan Divided Over Bilateral Talks," www.Japantoday.com (accessed 10 March 2004); Wu Jinan, "China-Japan Relations: Politically Cold, Economically Warm," replayed in *China Strategy*, vol. 3, www.csis.org (accessed 20 July 2004).

10. David Pilling, "China and Japan Look to Restore Relations," *Financial Times* (Internet version), 3 April 2002; Kwan Weng Kim, "China-Japan Ties Lack Spontaneity," *Straits Times* (Internet version), 5 April 2002; Robert Sutter, "China-Japan: Trouble Ahead? *The Washington Quarterly* 25, no. 4 (Autumn 2002): 37-49; Mike Mochizuki, "Terms of Engagement: The U.S.-Japan Alliance and the Rise of China," in Ellis Krauss and T. J. Pempel, eds., *Beyond Bilateralism: U.S.-Japan Relations in the New Asia-Pacific* (Stanford, Calif.: Stanford University Press, 2004), 96-100; Ma Licheng, "New Thoughts for China-Japan relations," (Beijing) *Zhanlue yu guanli*, 1 December 2002, 41-47. See also Feng Zhaokui, "Zai lun dui ri guanxi xinsi wei," *Zhanlue yu guanli*, vol. 3 (2003): 78-84; Shi Yinhong, "ZhongRi jiejjin yu 'waijiao geming,' " *Zhanlue yu guanli*, vol. 2 (2003): 71-75; Denny Roy, "China-Japan Relations," in *Asia's Bilateral Relations* (Honolulu: Asia-Pacific Center for Security Studies, 2004); Brian Bremmer and Hiroko Tashiro, "Japan's Joyride on China's Coattails," *Businessweek* (Internet version), 1 March 2004.

11. James Przystup, "Progressing but Still Facing History," *Comparative Connections*, www.csis.org/pacfor (accessed 6 April 2000).

12. Przystup, "Political Breakthrough and the SARs Outbreak," *Comparative Connections* (July 2003); "Cross Currents," *Comparative Connections* (April 2003); "Congratulations, Concern, Competition, and Cooperation," *Comparative Connections* (January 2003).

13. Green, "Managing Chinese Power," *Engaging China*; Green and Self, "Japan's Changing China Policy," *Survival*; Self, "China and Japan," *Washington Quarterly*, 77-88; Komori Yoshihisa, *Nit-chi yuko no maboroshi* (Tokyo: Shogakkan, 2002).

14. Donald Klein, "Japan and Europe in Chinese Foreign Relations," in Samuel Kim, ed., *China and the World* (Boulder, Colo.: Westview Press, 1998), 137-46.

15. Sutter, *Chinese Policy Priorities*, 82.

16. *Japan-China Relations: Status, Outlook and Implications for the United States* (Washington, D.C.: Library of Congress), Congressional Research Service, Report 96-864F, 30 October 1996.

17. "The New Korea," *Asiaweek*, www.asia.com/asiaweek/95/1201/ed.html (accessed 1 December 1995).

18. Sutter, *Chinese Policy Priorities*, 83.

19. Allen Whiting, *China Faces Japan* (Berkeley: University of California Press, 1989); Klein, "Japan and Europe," *China and the World* (Boulder, Colo.: Westview Press, 1998), 137-46; Austin and Harris, *Japan and Greater China: Asia's Global Powers: China-Japan* (Canberra, 1996); Howe, *China and Japan*.

20. Reviewed in Sutter, *Chinese Policy Priorities*, 83.

21. Sutter, *Chinese Policy Priorities*, 86-87; Klein, "Japan and Europe," *China and the World*, 137-46.

22. Michael Green, *Japan's Reluctant Realism* (New York: Palgrave, 2003); *Japan-U.S. Relations* (Washington, D.C.: Library of Congress), Congressional Research Service, Issue Brief 98004, 15 January 2004.

23. See the assessment of these factors in Robert Sutter, *The United States and East Asia* (Lanham, Md.: Rowman & Littlefield, 2003), 131-32.

24. Brad Glosserman, "How High is Up?" *Comparative Connections* (April 2003); "Still on a Roll" *Comparative Connections* (July 2003).

25. Sutter, "Japan and China," *Washington Quarterly*, 39.

26. David M. Lampton and Gregory May, *A Big Power Agenda for East Asia: America, China and Japan* (Washington, D.C.: The Nixon Center, 2001), 19-26.

27. Robert Marquand, "China Gains on Japan in Age-old Rivalry for Asia Influence," *Christian Science Monitor*, 29 October 2003, 1.

28. Chen Zhijiang, "Japan Accelerates Construction of Missile Defense System," (Beijing) *Guangming Ribao*, 24 June 2003 (Internet version). See also Han Jiang, "Shadow of 'Aegis' Clouds Over Sea of Japan," (Beijing) *Zhongguo Guofang Bao* (Internet version, translated by FBIS), 6 April 2004; Han Jiang, "Is Japan Allowing U.S. Nuclear-powered Aircraft Carrier to Enter Its Ports?" (Beijing) *Zhongguo Guofang Bao* (Internet version, translated by FBIS), 13 April 2004; Tang Shiping and Cao Xiaoyang, "Xunqiu Zhaong Mei Ri xianghu anquan de jidian," *Zhanlue yu quanli*, vol. 1 (2002): 49,105.

29. "Japan Building Up Its Arsenal," *China Daily*, 5 July 2003, 4; Li Heng "Is Japan Advancing Toward a 'Normal Country,'" *People's Daily,* 3 July 2003; Chen Zhijiang, "Japan Accelerates Construction," *Guangming Ribao*; "Japan Has an Ax to Grind," *People's Daily online,* 7 August 2003; Zhang Baiyu, "Analysis of Japan's New Defense White Paper," 14 August 2003; Zhi Qiu, "Maritime Interception Exercise Conducted by Member States of the 'Proliferation Security Initiative,'" Beijing *Zhongguo Guofang Bao* (23 September 2003), 2.

30. *Asia's Global Powers*, 11-13; Denny Roy, *China's Foreign Relations* (Lanham, Md.: Rowman & Littlefield, 1998), 163-65; Fouse, "Japan's China Debate," *Asia's China Debate*, 7-8; Roy, *Stirring Samurai*, 7.

31. *Senkaku (Diaoyu) Islands Dispute* (Washington, D.C.: Library of Congress), Congressional Research Service, Report 96-798F, 30 September 1996; *East Asia: Disputed Island and Offshore Claims* (Washington, D.C.: Library of Congress), Congressional Research Service, Report 92-614S, 28 July 1992; Roy, *Stirring Samurai*, 3; "Determined to Defend Diaoyu Islands," *China Daily*, 10 October 2003 (Internet version).

32. Interview, Tokyo, 4 June 2004.

33. Roy, *China's Foreign Relations*, 160-62.

34. Sutter, *Chinese Policy Priorities*, 85-86.

35. Kenneth Pyle and Eric Heginbotham, "Japan," in Richard Ellings and Aaron Friedberg, eds., *Strategic Asia 2001-2002* (Seattle, Wash.: National Bureau of Asian Research, 2001), 76-82.

36. *"Asian Values" and Asian Assertiveness* (Washington, D.C.: Library of Congress), Congressional Research Service, Report 96-610F, 9 July 1996.

37. Roy, *Stirring Samurai*, 5-6.

38. Sutter, *Chinese Policy Priorities*, 87-88.

39. Marquand, "China Gains on Japan," *Christian Science Monitor*, 1.

40. Roy, *Stirring Samurai*, 10.

41. Sutter, *Chinese Policy Priorities*, 88.

42. Victor Cha, "What a Difference a Year Makes," *Comparative Connections*, October 2003.

43. This section is taken from *Sino-Japanese Relations in 1997* (Washington, D.C.: Foreign Broadcast Information Service memorandum, 26 January 1998).

44. See *Sino-Japanese Relations in 1997* detailing media play-by-play during Li's visit.

45. Sutter, *Chinese Policy Priorities*, 91.

46. "Defense Minister Visit Highlights Latest Move Toward Further Normalization of Relations," Foreign Broadcast Information Service *Trends* 5, March 1998 (Internet version).

47. Sutter, *Chinese Policy Priorities*, 92.

48. James Przystup, "Slowed but Not Soured," *Comparative Connections* (July 1999).

49. Przystup, "The Zhu Visit and After . . . Events to Steady the Course," *Comparative Connections* (January 2001). The next three paragraphs are based heavily on this article.

50. Przystup, "Trouble Starts with 'T'," *Comparative Connections* (July 2001).

51. Przystup, "The Good, the Bad and . . . Japan-China Relations," *Comparative Connections* (July 2002).

52. Mariko Sanchanta and Alan Beattie, "China Outstrips U.S. as Top Exporter in Japan," *Financial Times,* 27 January 2003 (Internet version); Roy, *Stirring Samurai*, 7-8.

53. James Przystup, "Japan-China," *Comparative Connections* (July 2003).

54. Consultations with Chinese foreign policy specialists and officials, Beijing and Shanghai, May 2004. Consultations with Japanese officials in Tokyo, June 3-4, 2004. China's approach to South Korea and South Korean reaction is treated in chapter 6.

55. China's "peaceful rise" is discussed at length in the conclusion.

Chapter 6

Relations with the Korean Peninsula

With the collapse of the Soviet Union and the demise of East-West and Sino-Soviet competition for influence in the Korean peninsula after the Cold War, Beijing adjusted Chinese relations to take advantage of economic and other opportunities with South Korea, while sustaining its position as North Korea's most important foreign ally. The international confrontation caused by North Korea's nuclear weapons program and related ballistic missile programs, and the sharp decline in economic conditions and the rise of political uncertainty there following the sudden death of Kim Il Sung in 1994, raised uncertainties in China about the future stability of the peninsula. In general, Chinese officials used economic aid and continued military and political exchanges to help stabilize and preserve Chinese relations with the North, while working closely with South Korea and at times the United States in seeking a peaceful resolution to tensions on the peninsula. In response to the crisis created by North Korea's provocative nuclear proliferation activities during 2002-2004, China was even more active, taking the lead in international efforts to seek a diplomatic solution that would preserve China's influence and interests on the peninsula.[1]

South Korean officials along with U.S. and other outside observers often judged that China has a longer-term interest in seeing a growth of Chinese influence and a reduction of U.S. and Japanese influence on the peninsula.[2] However, Beijing was careful not to be seen directly challenging U.S. leadership in Korean affairs. It apparently judged that Chinese interests were best met with a broadly accommodating posture that allowed for concurrent improvements in China's relations with South Korea and effective management of China's sometimes difficult relations with North Korea. The net result was a marked increase in China's relations with South Korea and continued Chinese relations with North Korea closer than any other power, without negatively affecting Beijing's relations with the United States. During the 2002-2004 crisis over North Korea's nuclear program, China's cooperation with the United States, South Korea, and other concerned powers in seeking a negotiated solution to the problem enhanced overall positive development in China's relations with these countries, while managing tensions over the North Korean program in ways that avoided conflict or instability on the peninsula.

Relations with South Korea

Economic and Other Exchanges

In the post-Cold War period, China's active interest in beneficial economic relations with South Korea continued to grow, and Chinese and South Korean leaders took a variety of initiatives to markedly improve their overall bilateral relations. Top leaders on both sides repeatedly exchanged visits in a warm and cordial atmosphere. Both sides demonstrated similar motives in seeking increased bilateral contacts for economic reasons, to enhance their interests on the Korean peninsula, and to broaden foreign policy options. The positions of Chinese and South Korean leaders remained close in reaction to the North Korean nuclear crisis beginning in 2002. The improved relations kept in check differences that emerged over how to deal with North Korea migrants seeking refuge in China, and some trade and territorial issues.

It was hard to overemphasize the importance of trade and investment to the bilateral relationship. A $5 billion trade at the time of normalization of diplomatic relations in 1992 grew to $41.2 billion in 2002, and to $57 billion in 2003. Including Hong Kong, China was South Korea's largest export target, surpassing the United States for the first time in 2002. China including Hong Kong was South Korea's third-largest source of imports in 2002. Joining the wave of advanced Asian and world entrepreneurs moving manufacturing centers to China, South Korea businesspeople in 2002 invested $1.72 billion in China, reinforcing China's position as the largest recipient of South Korean investment. Ten thousand South Korean enterprises were operating in China in 2003. The two governments' support increased economic coordination and they signed a currency swap agreement in 2002 worth $2 billion that was designed to help forestall a repeat of the Asian financial crisis.[3]

The Asian economic crisis of the late 1990s had a devastating effect on economic conditions in South Korea. Anxious to appear supportive of an important neighbor, trading partner, and investor, China backed International Monetary Fund (IMF) rescue efforts for South Korea. China's commitment not to devalue its currency to better compete with exports from South Korea and other Asian states with devalued currencies scored public relations points in Seoul. It stood in notable contrast to Japanese reluctance to take steps to hold the decline in the value of the Japanese yen—a reluctance that allowed Japanese exporters to cut into South Korean export markets.[4]

The burgeoning Chinese-South Korean economic relationship saw trade grow by as much as 20 percent annually in recent years. In the 1990s, China's demand grew rapidly for electronics, computers, semiconductors, and telecommunication products provided by South Korea. The Sino-South Korean economic relationship was compared with the mainland-Taiwan cross-strait economic relationship. As South Korea's exports to China surpassed those to the United States, it was projected by some that China-South Korean trade would grow much more rapidly than U.S.-South Korean trade, reaching an overall level of $100 billion in 2008, boosted by Beijing's holding the Olympics that year.[5]

South Korean investment in China reflected broad involvement by South Korean enterprises. Small and medium-sized companies as well as the large South Korean conglomerates were deeply involved with Chinese-based investments. Sectors in China benefiting from South Korean investment included automobiles, textiles, information technology, telecommunications, machinery components and other manufacturing, and chemicals and petroleum. The many small and medium-sized South Korean investors continued to focus on nearby areas of northeastern China, including Shandong, Liaoning, and Jiangsu provinces, and Tianjin and Shanghai municipalities. The Export-Import Bank of Korea reported in 2002 that contracted South Korean investment in China reached $8.72 billion and actual investment reached $5.1 billion.[6]

The SARS epidemic of 2003 only briefly cut the pace of growth of the important Chinese economic relationship with South Korea. South Korean exports to China reached $12.4 billion in the first five months of the year. South Korean tourism and service industries suffered more. South Korean businesses imposed restrictions on travel to China but by early summer most travel restrictions to China were lifted and business and leisure travel rates returned to previous levels. Korea had by some estimates 40,000 students and 60,000 (mainly businesspeople) long-term residents in China during the course of the epidemic. Relatively few caught the disease.[7]

Meanwhile, popular cultural exchanges and South Korean empathy with China grew in many areas. Scott Snyder pointed out that South Korea businesspeople tended to find economic conditions in China similar to what prevailed in South Korea in the recent past. Seemingly very familiar and attractive to South Korean businesspeople were the facts that the Chinese economy was bustling and following a late-developing path; the state played an important role in ordering and channeling economic opportunities; there was a lack of regulatory infrastructure; and there were risks and opportunities associated with the mix of political restrictions and economic opportunities that were familiar to experienced South Korean entrepreneurs.[8]

Among other significant China-South Korean exchanges, each year well over one million South Koreans traveled as tourists to China while somewhat less than half that number of Chinese tourists visited South Korea annually. Overall South Korean visits to China in 2002 amounted to 1.7 million. Of South Koreans who traveled abroad, one-quarter went to China by 2003. In 2001, South Korea for the first time received more Chinese visitors (440,000) than visitors from the United States. Chinese tourists to South Korea grew to over one half million in 2002. By 2001, over 16,000 South Koreans were studying in China. An estimated 24,000 South Koreans studied in China in 2002, and numbers as high as 40,000 were seen for 2003-2004. Also, by 2001, the number of flights between South Korea and China exceeded the number of flights between South Korea and Japan. In 2004, the number of South Korea-China flights was roughly 200 a week. The trend gained momentum as more flights leaving Seoul's new international airport went to China than to Japan.[9]

Economic contacts continued to go hand in hand with political contacts. Seoul played a key role in negotiating the participation of China, along with Hong Kong and Taiwan, as full members in the third meeting of the APEC forum in Seoul in November 1991. Such exchanges paved the way to China's decision to normalize diplomatic relations with South Korea despite North Korea's objections in August 1992. South Korea's President Kim Dae Jung played an important role in developing the ASEAN Plus Three multilateral forum and encouraging China's active participation in the group since the late 1990s.

At the official level, with the October 2000 visit of Premier Zhu Rongji to Seoul, all seven members of the Chinese Communist Party's ruling Standing Committee had visited South Korea. Military exchanges and cooperation grew more slowly, presumably on account of China's reluctance to antagonize North Korea. However, the South Korean defense minister visited China in August 1999 for the first ROK-PRC defense ministerial talks, the Chinese defense minister visited Seoul in January 2000, and exchanges grew in ensuing years.[10]

These remarkable developments resulted in a continuing shift of South Korean perceptions of China to one of being a benign and pragmatic economic partner.[11] A 1996 poll conducted by the ROK government found 47 percent of South Koreans chose China as Korea's "closest partner for the year 2006" while 24 percent chose the United States. A media sponsored survey in 2000 found 52 percent of South Koreans respondents predicted China would be the most influential Asian power in ten years; few chose the United States.[12]

Nonetheless, there were plenty of issues to remind South Koreans of difficulties and differences. Dramatic attempts by North Koreans in China to enter diplomatic properties in seeking asylum in South Korea were a major problem in China-South Korean relations. Estimates of the number of North Korean refugees illegally staying in China, primarily in provinces near the North Korean border with China, ranged from official estimates of 10-30,000 to unofficial estimates ten times that size.[13]

Following the entry and eventual transfer to South Korea of twenty-five North Korean who sought refuge in the Spanish Embassy in Beijing in March 2002 came two dramatic and televised cases involving the entry of Chinese public security forces into the Japanese consulate in Shenyang in May 2002 and the South Korean compound in Beijing in June 2002 to deal with North Koreans seeking refuge. The episodes led to difficult Chinese negotiations with both Tokyo and Seoul, and hardened public attitudes in both countries against the Chinese government, but they were resolved with compromise solutions that seemed acceptable to the powers concerned. The consequences included comprehensive Chinese efforts to improve border security along the North Korean border, enforce regulations that punish Chinese citizens for assisting North Korean refuges, deny entry visas to known activists who publicize the fate of North Koreans in China, and increase the level of security around diplomatic compounds in China. A different kind of migrant issue is posed by the estimated 135,000 Chinese-Korean illegal migrant workers from China in South Korea in 2003.[14]

With burgeoning bilateral trade came trade disputes that resulted in a South Korean view of China as a neighbor that also may challenge basic South Korean economic interests. Nonetheless, the underlying force in the relationship remained a widespread perception of China as an irresistible business opportunity and of South Korea as an economic model and significant investor in China's economic growth. As a result, the South Korean government focused on making South Korea a regional transportation hub and international business center. Capitalizing on Korea's location as a supplier of high-value-added goods and services to China and the rest of Northeast Asia, the strategy was designed to turn Korea into a central transit point. The strategy appeared suited to deal with both the economic opportunity associated with Korea's proximity to rising China and the economic threat posed by China's increasing economic competitiveness.[15]

An array of environmental issues in South Korea where China was involved included the so-called yellow dust—windblown soil from eroding fields in northern China. A political issue emerged in 2004 that involved disputes between Chinese and Korean historians and commentators as to whether the achievements of a state on the Korean peninsula centuries ago should be credited to China or Korea.[16] This dispute received broad attention in South Korean media in 2004, becoming the most serious bilateral dispute in relations with China. Chinese officials' efforts to ease the dispute failed to mute South Korean criticism.

Korean Peninsula Issues

In the 1990s, closer relations with China helped to ease South Korean concerns about Beijing's possible support for North Korean aggression against the South.

They also provided Seoul, via Beijing, with an indirect channel of information on and communication with North Korean leaders, who at that time generally refused to interact directly with their South Korean counterparts. Such channels of communication with and information about North Korea helped to reassure South Koreans about trends on the Korean peninsula, including North Korea's repeated efforts to seek progress in relations with the United States at the expense of South Korea. Meanwhile, South Korean enterprises anxious to enter the North Korean market were able to sidestep restrictions on bilateral trade and investments by working with North Korea through South Korean enterprises based in China.[17]

Chinese officials viewed improved relations with South Korea as broadening China's influence on the peninsula. In the 1990s, some Chinese officials asserted that Beijing's improvement of relations set "a good example," which should be reciprocated by the United States and Japan in moving ahead with their respective relations with North Korea. Beijing officials judged that such "cross recognition" would markedly ease North Korea's isolation and fears, and thereby open the way to eased tensions on the peninsula. South Korea officials for many years emphasized that they opposed such U.S. and Japanese relations with South Korea. President Kim Dae Jung, who took power in February 1998, adopted a different position on this issue in mid-1998, urging the United States and others to move forward and improve relations with North Korea. This stance continued under President Roh Moo Hyun in 2003. The more moderate South Korean stance added to common ground with China over Korean peninsula issues.[18]

Although Chinese officials denied it, some South Korean specialists and U.S. experts asserted that one of Beijing's longer-term motives in improving ties with the South was to preclude an increase in the U.S. prominence on the peninsula. According to this view, Chinese officials in the 1990s were particularly concerned by North Korea's apparent focus at that time on relations with the United States as the central element of Pyongyang's foreign policy. The Chinese were determined to avoid a situation in which the United States would become the dominant outside influence in both South and North Korea, and they viewed improved Chinese relations with Seoul as a useful hedge against such an outcome.[19]

Whatever China's long-term objectives, both Beijing and Seoul stressed efforts in recent years to seek closer cooperation to deal with possible contingencies stemming from the increasingly uncertain situation in North Korea. And in this endeavor, both China and South Korea sought close cooperation with the United States and other involved powers.

Chinese specialists strongly affirmed their common ground with South Korea and the United States in trying to preserve peace and stability on the Korean peninsula. Chinese officials were often more optimistic than their American counterparts about the recent situation and the future outlook for the regime in North Korea. Thus, in the latter 1990s, a time when U.S. officials tended to see North Korea in real danger of collapse, Chinese officials claimed that North Korea's regime remained under Kim Jong Il's rule, was able to weather current shortages of food, energy, and foreign exchange without collapse, and was making some small headway in developing relations with and getting assistance from foreign countries. Nevertheless, Chinese specialists were clearly more concerned than in the past about the viability of the North Korean regime unless the Kim Jong Il leadership implemented some economic reforms and opened the country to more international contact. At the same time, they believed that too-rapid North Korea reform and opening could seriously destabilize the Pyongyang regime. China continued to supply food assistance and oil to North Korea. Estimates in 2003 of China's aid were in the range of 1 million tons of food grain and 500,000 tons of heavy fuel oil annually, amounting to 79 percent of North Korea's fuel imports and one-third of total food imports.[20] And China continued leadership contacts, especially by the military, with North Korea.

In the years following the death of Kim Il Sung and the concurrent collapse of the North Korean economy in the 1990s, China supported U.S., South Korean, and other efforts to get North and South Korea to resume an effective dialogue, and to encourage the North to reform itself domestically and open itself up internationally. China backed the U.S.-South Korean-initiated four-party talks (involving North and South Korea, the United States, and China) as a way to ease North-South differences and to bring about a more lasting peace settlement on the peninsula. China continued to oppose direct pressure on North Korea, judging that it could lead to a negative reaction.

Chinese specialists expected that North Korea would raise obstacles, preconditions, or other difficulties in the four-party talks and other interactions with South Korea. At bottom, the North Koreans were said by Chinese experts to want first to build ties with United States, Japan, and others in order to strengthen their hand prior to direct negotiations with the South. Also, North Korean leaders were said to be resentful of past actions of the South Korean government of President Kim Young Sam and to have viewed the Kim Young Sam government as weak on account of corruption scandals and other issues in 1997. Chinese specialists did not expect North Korea to make significant progress in relations with the South until after the election of a new South Korean president in December 1997. Beijing generally welcomed the moderate and positive tone toward North Korea adopted by President Kim Dae Jung following his inauguration in February 1998. President Jiang Zemin highlighted this theme in welcoming Kim Dae Jung during a five-day visit to China in November 1998.[21]

Chinese officials also took pains to emphasize that the improvement in China's relations with South Korea in the 1990s was not directed in any way at the United States or the U.S.-South Korean alliance relationship. Chinese officials acknowledged that while Sino-South Korean relations, especially economic relations, would continue to grow, the U.S.-South Korean relationship remained very broad and multifaceted and had a critical security dimension involving a defense treaty and U.S. troop presence in South Korea. As one Chinese official put it in mid-1997, "for South Korea, the United States is much more important than China." South Korean officials echoed this sentiment. They noted that Seoul needed China's "understanding" and "constructive role" in seeking reunification, but that relations with China could not in any way substitute for South Korea's relations with the United States.[22]

Beijing's stated intention to supplement rather than substitute for U.S.-South Korean relations affected China's attitude toward the U.S. role in South Korea after reunification. Despite the fact that the Chinese government in the 1990s officially encouraged the eventual U.S. military withdrawal from East Asia and strongly criticized the strengthening of the U.S.-Japan alliance relationship, Beijing officials were moderate in response to calls in the United States and South Korea for a continued U.S. military presence in Korea even after Korean reunification. Chinese officials adopted a wait-and-see attitude. They advised that Korean unification could be a long way off. They noted that some in South Korea wanted a continued U.S. military presence, but added that the situation could change in the future.[23]

China strongly supported international efforts to improve relations with Pyong-yang at the time of the North-South Korean summit of 2000 and in line with South Korean President Kim Dae Jung's sunshine policy toward the North. Strong Chinese political support for inter-Korean reconciliation was welcomed by the Kim Dae Jung government at a time of difficulty in U.S.-South Korean relations stemming from of the George W. Bush administration's harder line than the previous Clinton administration toward the North Korean regime.[24]

China's stature with the North increased in 2000-2001 notably as a result of Kim Jong Il's two visits to China and Jiang Zemin's visit to North Korea. Encouraging economic reform and increased international outreach by the North, Beijing urged the United States and others to support the asymmetrical accommodation seen in Kim Dae Jung's engagement policy and avoid confrontation and increased tensions. It did not make major issues of its differences with the United States over the Bush administration's tougher posture toward the North, though it was critical of U.S. strengthening of alliances in Asia (mainly with Japan) and U.S. missile defense plans focused on the North Korean threat.[25]

The North Korean nuclear crisis of 2002-2004 saw Chinese officials initially adopt a passive approach, calling on the United States to engage in bilateral talks as demanded by North Korea in order to solve the problem. Rising tensions prompt-ed by the combination of North Korea's provocative nuclear weapons development, shrill warnings, and assertive military actions and the firm U.S. determination not to be "blackmailed" by Pyongyang saw Chinese officials respond to U.S. requests to take a more active role in seeking a solution to the crisis. The Chinese government adopted a more active stance, hosted the three-party (North Korea, the United States, and China) talks in Beijing in April 2003, and six-party talks (adding South Korea, Japan, and Russia) in Beijing in 2003 and 2004, and engaged in several rounds of shuttle diplomacy with the United States, North Korea, and other concerned powers. Though unhappy to be excluded from the three-party talks in April 2003, South Korea supported China's efforts to seek a negotiated solution. It was pleased to join in the six-party meeting, pushed by the United States, in 2003 and 2004.[26]

The international crisis of 2002-2004 caused by North Korea's provocative actions in breaking past commitments and pursuing development of nuclear weapons saw China follow a course closer to South Korea than the United States. The Bush administration's refusal to be blackmailed by North Korea seemed to preclude significant U.S. compromises on security and aid issues important to North Korea until a verifiable dismantling of North Korea's nuclear program was assured. The South Korean government seemed inclined to favor more U.S. flexibility, and South Korea continued to pursue a flexible approach to North Korea under the leadership of President Roh Moo Hyun elected in December 2002; it continued various economic and other exchanges with North Korea under the rubric of the asymmetrical normalization program set forth in Kim Dae Jung's sunshine policy. Both China and South Korea also seemed to agree that escalating diplomatic, economic, or military pressure against North Korea would be counterproductive as it would increase the risk of war on the peninsula.[27]

Chinese officials adopted a low posture on the concurrent crisis in U.S.-South Korean alliance relations beginning in 2002. Widespread popular resentment in South Korea against the Bush administration's hard line against North Korea, asymmetrical features of the U.S.-South Korean alliance relationship, and strongly negative popular reaction to the accidental deaths of two South Korean youths during exercises by U.S. troops in South Korea fed election-year politics and assisted the December 2002 election of Roh Moo Hyun on an anti-U.S. platform. Although President Roh upon taking power in February 2003 backed away from many of his previous positions critical of U.S. policy, strongly felt resentment against U.S. government policies remained among many in South Korea. Commentators and strategists of this persuasion often urged that South Korea would be better off reducing strong dependency on the United States and relying more strongly on Seoul's ever closer relationship with China. By adopting a low posture on the South Korea-U.S. controversy, Chinese officials and official commentary were careful not to be seen as seeking to take advantage of the anti-American upsurge in South Korea as a means of driving a wedge between Washington and Seoul.[28]

Foreign Policy Concerns

South Korean motives for good relations with China often included foreign policy concerns. At times in the 1990s and later, South Korean officials viewed better relations with China as a useful way to preclude possible Chinese expansion or pressure against South Korea as China grew in wealth and power during the twenty-first century. They also saw good relations with China as providing protection against possible pressure from Japan against South Korea in the future. (Such continued South Korean suspicion of Japan notably complicated U.S. policy in the region, which relied on U.S. alliance relations with both Japan and South Korea. The suspicion of Japan continued, although President Kim Dae Jung helped to ease this suspicion with a landmark visit to Tokyo in late 1998 that involved notable steps toward South Korean-Japanese accommodation.)[29]

Officials in Seoul were careful to add that relations with China also broadened South Korean foreign policy options, allowing South Korea to appear to break out of the constraints imposed by what they saw as a U.S.-centered foreign policy since the 1950s. South Korean opinion leaders judged that with better relations with China, Seoul could afford to be more assertive and less accommodating in relations with the United States, although South Korean officials and knowledgeable scholars also often asserted that relations with China or other foreign policy options provided no substitute for the essential South Korean alliance relationship with the United States.[30]

Meanwhile, given continued difficulties in U.S.-China relations in the 1990s, South Korean officials sometimes expressed an interest in boosting South Korea's international stature as a "mediator" between these two powers, both of which had friendly ties with Seoul. South Korean officials also asserted that South Korea wanted to avoid a situation where it might have to choose between Washington and Beijing if U.S.-Chinese tensions in Asia were to rise sharply. They said that they urged Beijing as well as Washington to try harder to maintain good relations with one another, and claimed that PRC officials "appreciated" what the Republic of Korea (ROK) has to say.

According to South Korean experts, China also viewed good relations with Seoul as a possible hedge against Japanese power, although Chinese officials emphasized that their interests focused on regional peace and stability and on setting a good example in relations with a smaller neighbor, South Korea, in order to reassure China's other neighbors about Beijing's foreign policy intentions. More broadly, Chinese intentions were said by some South Korean experts to reflect a desire to use better relations with South Korea against perceived U.S. efforts to "contain" or hold back China's growing power and influence in Asian and world affairs. In particular, Chinese specialists and officials voiced concern from time to time that the United States might use its alliance relationships with Japan and South Korea in order to check or build a barrier against the allegedly expanding "China threat" in northeast Asia. Closer China-South Korean relations would complicate any such U.S. strategic scheme.[31]

In this context, South Korea and China markedly increased cooperation in Asian regional groups.[32] China's greater willingness in the 1990s and 2000s to cooperate more closely with and play a more active role in Asian multilateral organizations assisted this trend. Previously, Chinese officials had viewed Asian multilateral groups with more wariness and skepticism. Thus, China's greater willingness to cooperate with South Korea and others in the economic deliberations of APEC and in the security related interchanges in the ARF enhanced China-South Korean relations.

The two powers also participated actively in regional forums that excluded the United States. The biannual Asia-Europe (ASEM) meetings initiated in 1996 saw both South Korea and China play significant roles in this body that encouraged greater cooperation between East Asia and the developed countries of Europe, in part as a counterweight to the U.S.-led APEC. The Asian economic crisis of 1997 prompted stronger regional cooperation efforts led by South Korea and China under the ASEAN Plus Three rubric. This group, including the ten ASEAN states plus

Japan along with China and South Korea, became the paramount regional grouping in East Asia, with frequent meetings of senior ministers and state leaders that occasioned major economic and some political and security initiatives, notably proposals by China, South Korea, Japan, and others for free trade agreements in the region and security plans dealing with East Asia.

These actions reflected strong interest in China and South Korea in deepening intraregional cooperation, first in economic areas but then in political and security areas, in order to ease long-standing mutual suspicions among East Asian states and enhance prospects for peace and development in the region. China's public stance focused on its New Security Concept announced in 1997, based on the Five Principles of Peaceful Coexistence that were the mainstay of moderate and accommodating phases in Chinese foreign policy for fifty years. The NSC was well received in South Korea and along with other Chinese policies and behavior provided vague but sufficient basis for many in South Korea and elsewhere in Asia to deal with China's rising power and influence in constructive ways.

As noted in chapter 1, when the NSC was initially proposed, Chinese foreign policy strongly competed with the United States and Chinese officials repeatedly used the NSC to counter to the U.S.-favored alliance structure in Asian and world affairs. Following the moderate turn in China's public posture toward the United States in 2001, Chinese officials and commentary generally avoided calling on South Korean or other Asians to choose between China's NSC and the previously emphasized "Cold War thinking" and "power politics" exemplified by the U.S. insistence on maintaining and strengthening U.S.-led alliance structures in Asia and elsewhere. This more positive Chinese approach, which Chinese officials said will lead to a "win-win" situation in Asia for all concerned powers including the United States as well as South Korea and China, was well received in South Korea and helped to strengthen Sino-South Korean relations.

Consultations in South Korea during May and June 2004 with South Korean government officials concerned with China, and South Korean academic and other specialists who dealt with Chinese affairs, underlined the increasingly positive assessment in South Korea of China's approach toward the Korean peninsula.[33] Beijing's recent emphasis on China's "peaceful" approach in Asia was warmly welcomed. South Korean government officials pointed to the discussion of South Korean-Chinese relations in the May 2004 National Security Strategy of the Republic of Korea entitled *Peace, Prosperity, and National Security*.[34] The section of the document dealing with South Korean-Chinese relations was full of positive statements. It highlighted the July 2003 summit between President Roh Moo Hyun and Hu Jintao, which upgraded the bilateral relationship to a "comprehensive cooperative partnership." South Korean officials welcomed consolidated relations with China as providing a "firm foundation" for regional cooperation and peace and prosperity in Northeast Asia.

Assessing the very positive trends in bilateral political, economic, military, and other kinds of relations, the summit's joint statement on July 8, 2003, pledged to increase the already very active exchanges of personnel and political party leaders, to see South Korea play an important role in China's efforts to develop western China, and to seek a bilateral trade volume of $100 billion by 2008. Both sides also pledged to expand military exchanges and enhance transparency in military policies.[35]

In the view of South Korean officials in mid-2004, South Korea and China also seemed to have a common general interest in multilateral cooperation in Northeast Asia and elsewhere. South Korean government officials noted that they would work hard to promote cooperation with China and others in the United Nations and ASEAN Plus Three, and that South Korea would seek to work with China to develop multilateral security dialogue in Northeast Asia and Asia more broadly.

South Korean officials judged that China continued to play a critically important role in promoting dialogue for the peaceful resolution of the North Korean nuclear issue, and they pledged to work closely with China to speed up the process seen in the six-party talks. China's role in other aspects of inter-Korean cooperation also was seen as centrally important, from the vantage point of South Korean officials.

South Korean government officials and nongovernment specialists believed that China's emphasis in 2003-2004 on China's peaceful rise reflected a long-term trend of moderate Chinese behavior in Asian and world affairs. In their view, Chinese leaders were too preoccupied with internal issues and difficulties to consider a more assertive or disruptive posture in Asia. China was seen as in no position to confront the United States, and Chinese leaders were seen by the South Korean officials and specialists as anxious to avoid confrontation with American power. This overall situation was seen as likely to persist for many years.

South Korean government officials privately were concerned in mid-2004 about what they saw as a "China fever" among large portions of the South Korean people and among many of the recently elected legislators in South Korea's National Assembly. China was becoming more popular among these important groups at a time when tensions in the U.S.-South Korean alliance relationship continued as a result of a variety of bilateral and other issues. The salient issues in U.S.-South Korean alliance relations in mid-2004 had to do with reaching agreement on deployment and reduction of U.S. forces in South Korea in line with an altered U.S. global military strategy that allowed for stationing fewer U.S. soldiers overseas, and using those soldiers flexibly, in response to a variety of possible contingencies. The United States notably made a decision to remove a combat brigade from South Korea and send it to Iraq in mid-2004, and was said to be unlikely to replace the brigade in South Korea.[36]

South Korean government officials privately said they continued to believe that the United States was far more important for South Korea than was China, and they were concerned about preserving a healthy alliance relationship with the United States despite repeated crises and differences in recent years. Nonetheless, they said they faced a difficult challenge in achieving these tasks in the face of widespread South Korean public opinion, and the opinion of recently elected legislators, that gave China the top priority in South Korean foreign policy and took a dim view of the United States and the U.S.-South Korean alliance. In this context, some officials cited recent polls that showed that among the members of the National Assembly elected in April 2004, 63 percent saw China as most important for South Korean interests and only 26 percent saw the United States as most important. The officials said this was similar to other polling dealing with popular South Korean views of the United States and China.[37]

South Korean government officials and some nongovernment South Korean specialists emphasized in 2004 that South Korea more than ever did not want to be in a position of having to choose between the United States and China. On the one hand, they wanted to preserve and enhance the alliance with the United States. Some averred that the alliance was an important reason China treated South Korea in a very friendly manner. Without the alliance, they judged, China would have less incentive to be so accommodating of South Korean interests and concerns. There was a good deal of publicity in South Korea about the cultural and historical affinities that prompted many in South Korea to see closer alignment with China as a natural and comfortable stance for South Korea. South Korean government officials nonetheless said that they were less sanguine that such an alignment or position within China's "sphere of influence" would be good for South Korea, especially without the counterweight of the South Korean alliance with the United States. On the other hand, South Korean officials also acknowledged that there were some South Korean officials who sought to use improved South Korean relations with China as a means to prompt the United States to be more accommodating and forthcoming regarding South Korean issues and concerns.

Reflecting angst by South Korea government officials to preserve the alliance with the United States while improving relations with China, the officials emphasized that the U.S.-Republic of Korea alliance should allow for positive U.S. and South Korean relations with China and should avoid friction with China. Against this background, South Korean officials noted Seoul's unwillingness to follow the United States in pursuing policies that China opposes, including U.S. efforts to criticize China's human rights practices, U.S. development of ballistic missile defenses, and most importantly, U.S. support for Taiwan. It was broadly held among South Korean and U.S. observers in Seoul that one of the main reasons South Korea was reluctant to agree to allow U.S. forces in South Korea to be deployed to other areas was that those forces might be deployed to the Taiwan area in the event of a U.S.-China military confrontation in the Taiwan Strait. Some officials said such a deployment would meet very strong South Korean opposition and would prompt a major crisis in the U.S.-South Korean alliance.[38]

Some South Korean officials tried to put the upsurge in positive South Korean attention to China in 2004 in a more balanced context. They judged that the burgeoning economic ties, China's central role in dealing with North Korea, and the very attentive and accommodating Chinese political approach toward South Korea were major reasons why the recent positive trend would continue. China "respects" South Korean pride, they said, noting how important this was for China's good public image in South Korea. At the same time, the officials saw serious issues in China-South Korean relations and advised that South Korean opinion was volatile and could turn against China if a sensitive issue were to emerge. They cited Chinese-Korean differences over the historical range of China and Korean states—a recently prominent dispute among Chinese and Korean historians that had some possible bearing on current territorial claims of the respective governments. South Korean media and other complaints made this issue the most important dispute in China-South Korea relations in 2004. Trade issues emerged along with rising trade and prompted anger by some in South Korea. Some South Korean officials claimed that China's handling of the six-party talks belittled the South Korean role; were this to become widely known, they said, Chinese-South Korean tensions would rise. The Chinese position on North Korea also was seen as at odds with South Korea, especially in the sense that China was seen wanting to preserve the North Korean state as a buffer while Seoul sought reunification.[39]

In sum, the broad upswing in China-South Korean relations seemed likely to continue. Chinese officials continued to adopt a low profile on issues in U.S.-South Korean alliance relations except where they involved North Korea or possibly Taiwan. Thus, China complained about U.S. efforts seen as applying pressure on North Korea through joint military exercises with South Korea, and they also complained about the U.S.-backed Proliferation Security Initiative that was seen to target North Korea. They were said by South Korean and U.S. officials to have made inquiries about how the possible deployment of U.S. forces from South Korea might affect Chinese interests, notably concerning a possible Taiwan contingency.

China's discretion was consistent with its overall positive posture toward South Korea that was attentive to South Korean sensibilities and pride. China's approach did not confront the United States interests in South Korea directly, but clearly provided a counterpoint for South Korean elite and popular opinion at times of difficulties in U.S.-South Korean alliance relations. Some observers in Seoul in mid-2004 judged that the United States was not in a good position to improve relations with South Korea and that China as a result would loom even more important in South Korea's future. They noted that while President Roh had moved away from anti-U.S. positions since his election in December 2002, the new legislature and the president's administration were seen as looking with disfavor at U.S. efforts to downsize U.S. forces in South Korea and to use those forces in other areas. Goodwill on both the South Korean and U.S. sides had become frayed as a result of many crises and tensions especially since 2002. Several officials on the U.S. side seemed tired of changing and seemingly unreasonable South Korean demands, and a similar "fatigue factor" was also seen by some as taking hold on the part of South Korean officials. If the recent trends were to continue, China's influence in South Korea could rise to a level where it was indeed the leading partner of South Korea, with the United States relegated to a lower overall position in South Korean thinking. The key variable determining this outcome was more U.S. and South Korean policies and behavior than Chinese policies and behavior.

Relations with North Korea

The smooth progress and rapid development of China's relations with South Korea contrasted sharply with more difficult Chinese relations with North Korea after the Cold War. Chinese interests in North Korea remained strong. The newly founded Chinese Communist-led People's Republic of China fought a major war resulting in many hundreds of thousands of Chinese casualties in order to preserve an independent North Korea state free from U.S. domination. Chinese leaders competed actively with the Soviet Union for the favor of Kim Il Sung and his government in order to assure that China would not face a Soviet proxy along China's northeastern periphery.[40]

The cutoff of Soviet aid to North Korea and the normalization of Soviet-South Korean relations in the late 1980s, and the demise of the Soviet Union in the early 1990s, reduced Chinese concern over Moscow's influence in North Korea. However, post-Cold War conditions saw North Korea pursue nuclear weapons development leading to a major crisis with the United States and its allies. The death of Kim Il Sung in 1994 added political uncertainty to the already unstable conditions on account of the collapse of the North Korean economy and widespread famine in the country.[41]

Chinese officials provided a large share of North Korea's outside food and energy supplies, but not in amounts that satisfied North Korean officials.[42] Chinese leaders repeatedly encouraged North Korean counterparts to follow some of the guidelines of Chinese economic reforms and to open more to international economic contact. North Korean officials seemed reluctant to open the country significantly, presumably fearing that outside contact would undermine the regime's tight political control based on keeping North Koreans unaware of actual conditions abroad. North Korea did endeavor to carry out some domestic economic reforms and to open some restricted zones for foreign trade, tourism, and gambling. A proposed zone planned for an area next to the Chinese border in northwestern North Korea did not meet with China's approval and the Chinese government in 2002 arrested on corruption charges the China-born entrepreneur who was selected by North Korean leaders to direct the foreign economic zone.[43]

Chinese diplomacy in North Korea-South Korea-U.S. relations and particularly regarding the crises prompted by North Korea's nuclear weapons program emphasized preserving stability on the Korean peninsula. Chinese frustration with North Korea's nuclear weapons program and other provocations was deep and serious, particularly as the North Korean actions could provoke U.S. attack and the spread of nuclear weapons to Japan, Taiwan, and elsewhere. At the same time, Chinese leaders showed keen awareness that major instability in or collapse of the North Korean regime would have potentially major adverse consequences for China. These included a danger of full-scale war on the Korean peninsula, large-scale refugee flows to China (there already were an estimated 200,000-300,000 North Korea refugees in China in 2003), and the possible establishment of a unified Korean state under the leadership of a South Korean government that maintained a close military alliance with the United States.[44]

For many years after the Cold War, Chinese officials adopted a stance that assumed North Korean nuclear weapons development was unlikely or remote. They stressed the need to avoid international and other pressures that would further destabilize the North Korean regime and overall conditions on the peninsula. Beginning in late 2002, Chinese officials appeared more convinced by U.S. and other evidence that North Korea indeed had developed nuclear weapons and was determined to build more. The tense crisis provoked by North Korea's nuclear program prompted many Chinese commentators to argue for greater Chinese pressure on the North Korean regime, with a few commentators considering regime change in North Korea as an option for Chinese policy. However, prevailing Chinese government actions in 2003-2004 still seemed to strike a balance of support and accommodation of the North Korean regime that sought to avoid the many dangers for key Chinese interests that would follow from major instability or collapse of the North Korean regime. Chinese food aid of about 1 million tons a year and energy supplies of about 500,000 tons of heavy fuel oil annually continued with Chinese President Hu Jintao offering increased aid to Korean leader Kim Jong Il in order to entice North Korea to participate in the six-party talks in Beijing in October 2003.[45]

Symptomatic of the prevailing balance in Chinese relations with North and South Korea were Chinese efforts, largely thwarted, to improve relations with North Korea once Kim Jong Il assumed the post of general secretary of the Korean Workers' Party in October 1997, and the cordial Chinese relationship established expeditiously with the newly installed Kim Dae Jung administration in South Korea in 1998. Chinese party chief Jiang Zemin on October 1997 sent Kim Jong Il a friendly personal message of congratulations on his accession to the position of general secretary of the Korean Workers' Party, and the Chinese Foreign Ministry spokesman also "heartily congratulated" Kim. But despite repeated speculation about a Chinese-North Korean summit, Jiang Zemin told Japanese visitors in February 1998 that no high-level contacts were in the offing. Jiang said that before former North Korean President Kim Il Sung died in 1994, Beijing and Pyongyang had regular state visits, but since Kim's son, Kim Jong Il, has taken the reins of the country, such exchanges have not resumed. "After Kim Il Sung passed away, Kim Jong Il [observed] the three-year custom . . . of mourning . . . now that the three years have passed he has therefore become general secretary of the Workers' Party, but it appears he has not made any plans to visit," he said. Jiang said that as China and North Korea maintained good-neighborly ties of friendship, mutual visits were normal, but "at present we have not had the opportunity."[46]

In contrast with his oblique references to Chinese frustration with North Korea's leadership, Jiang in the same interview extended a warm welcome to South Korea's new president. "We were very happy to see that Kim Dae Jung won the South Korean elections and will be the next president. We welcome him to China for a visit after assuming his presidential duties."[47]

Beijing significantly made high-level approaches to the new South Korean leadership. Chinese Vice President Hu Jintao, selected by the Ninth National People's Congress in March 1998, made his first trip abroad to Japan and South Korea in April 1998. In meetings with South Korea President Kim Dae Jung, acting Prime Minister Kim Jong Il, and Foreign and Trade Minister Park Chung Soo, Hu highlighted the progress in Sino-South Korean ties since relations were normalized in 1992 and emphasized the importance of a stable Korean peninsula for the entire Asia-Pacific region. The PRC vice president also assured his hosts that China's currency would not succumb to the financial pressures buffeting those of other East Asian countries. Opportunities for closer cooperation were discussed in the areas of fisheries, visa-free tourism, and nuclear energy projects. Hu also sought reaffirmation of Seoul's commitment to a one-China policy, though Taiwan-South Korea business contacts continued to thrive. Further solidifying relations, South Korean President Kim Dae Jung was warmly received by President Jiang Zemin and other senior leaders during an official visit to Beijing in November 1998.[48]

Military ties between Seoul and Beijing grew more slowly than political and economic relations, presumably because China wanted to maintain ties to the North Korea armed forces and was wary of the effect of closer China-South Korean security ties on China's military relationship with the North. In the 1990s, Seoul continued pushing for strengthened military exchanges, but Beijing sought to limit the scope and pace of their military relationship. Military ties grew concurrently with political and economic relations, but at a slower pace. The South Korean vice defense minister visited China for the first time in November 1997, the highest-level military exchange to date. Higher-level contacts gradually developed and Beijing slowly responded to repeated South Korean overtures to establish regular exchanges between their defense ministers and other senior military officials.[49]

Meanwhile, presumably in deference to North Korean sensitivities, Beijing delayed in the face of repeated South Korea efforts establishing a consulate in Shenyang, in northeastern China, closer than Beijing to the North Korean border. There were millions of ethnic Koreans in this part of China and many thousands of North Korea refugees, many of whom have knowledge about developments in North Korea. The South Korean consulate opened in 1999.[50]

In sum, China's policy in the late 1990s continued to balance often conflicting imperatives regarding North and South Korea as it dealt with the delicate and potentially volatile situation on the peninsula. Beijing did not appear to seek big changes in the political or military status quo; it appeared intent on promoting as much stability as possible, while benefiting economically and in other ways by improving its relations with South Korea. As economic conditions in North Korea deteriorated, and as the North Korean regime persisted with provocative military and other actions, Beijing officials privately worried about possible adverse consequences for China. Nonetheless, Chinese officials still saw their basic interests as well served with a policy of continued, albeit guarded, support for the North, along with improved relations with the South and close consultations with the United States over Korean peninsula issues.

The situation for China's relations with North Korea improved for a time with the unexpected breakthrough in North-South Korean relations leading to the Pyongyang summit in June 2000. This event raised hopes in China of eased tensions and peaceful accommodation on the Korean peninsula. China figured importantly in the North-South summit preparation as the site of secret North-South negotiations. Moreover, Kim Jong Il seemed to be seeking Chinese advice and support in the new approach to South Korea as he made two visits to China and Jiang Zemin visited North Korea. The overall trend in North Korean actions suggested more openness to Chinese advice and greater willingness to adopt policies of detente and reform that would reduce the danger of North-South military confrontation, promote economic revival in North Korea, and lower the chances of economic collapse and social instability, including the need for massive Chinese assistance and the large-scale flow of North Korean refugees to China.[51]

This hopeful period ended with the impasse in North Korean-U.S. relations following the Bush administration policy review on North Korea in 2001, the sharp rise in tensions on the peninsula posed by North Korea's provocative nuclear weapons development in 2002-2003, and signs of strong differences between North Korean-Chinese leaders over reform in North Korea's economy. China was instrumental in persuading North Korea to participate in the three-party and six-party talks in Beijing in 2003-2004 dealing with the nuclear crisis and related issues. Chinese diplomats were careful not to take sides in the discussions, endeavoring to find common ground between the positions of North Korea on one side and the United States on the other. In this regard, Chinese positions were close to those of South Korean officials who also sought common ground and stressed the need to reduce confrontation, avoid pressure, and preserve peace. China showed its support for North Korea in welcoming Kim Jong Il who again visited China in 2004.

Well aware that dealing with North Korea involved unpredictable twists and turns perpetrated mainly by the idiosyncratic dominant leader of this isolated state, Chinese leaders by 2004 appeared resigned to a protracted effort to deal with the North Korean nuclear crisis through diplomatic means. They made known China's continued opposition to strong pressure on North Korea, reportedly warning of North Korea using military means to lash out in response to pressure. Continued but less than sufficient Chinese food and energy assistance were among key Chinese sources of leverage with North Korean leaders, but Beijing remained hesitant to use these levers for fear of provoking a sharp North Korean response contrary to Chinese interests of promoting stability on the peninsula. Chinese officials also worried about U.S. actions, fearing that as the United States became impatient in the face of North Korea's continued development of nuclear weapons, it might resort to strong political, economic, or military pressures. Chinese officials realized that the massive U.S. military preoccupation trying to stabilize post-war Iraq, along with U.S. preoccupations with the war on terrorism and other issues, made it unlikely in the short term that the United States would risk confrontation or war on the Korean peninsula by substantially increasing U.S. pressure on North Korea. The situation remained volatile, however, with concern focused especially on the U.S. reaction or other international fallout from such possible North Korean steps as a nuclear weapons test, a ballistic missile test seemingly targeted against Japan or U.S. forces in Japan, or North Korean nuclear weapons cooperation with international terrorists.[52]

Notes

1. Samuel Kim, "The Making of China's Korea Policy in the Era of Reform," in David M. Lampton, ed., *The Making of Chinese Foreign and Security Policy* (Stanford, Calif.: Stanford University Press, 2001), 371-408; David Shambaugh, "China and the Korean Peninsula," *Washington Quarterly* 26, no. 2 (Spring 2003): 43-56; Denny Roy, *China and the Korean Peninsula*, Honolulu: Asia Pacific Center for Security Studies, 3, no. 1 (January 2004); Jae Ho Chung, "From a Special Relationship to a Normal Partnership?" *Pacific Affairs* 76, no. 3 (Winter 2003-2004): 549-68; You Ji, "Understanding China's North Korea Policy," Jamestown Foundation, *China Brief*, 3 March 2004; Ming Liu, "China and the North Korean Crisis," *Pacific Affairs* 76, no. 3 (Fall 2003): 347-73; Samuel Kim, "Chinese-North Korean Relations at a Cross-roads," *International Journal of Korean Studies* 7, no. 1 (Spring-Summer 2003): 39-56; Andrew Scobell, "China and North Korea," *Current History* (September 2002): 278-79; Eric McVadon, "China's Goal and Strategies for the Korean Peninsula," in Henry Sokolski, ed., *Planning for a Peaceful Korea* (Carlisle, Pa.: U.S. Army War College, Strategic Studies Institute), 134-35; See also, Denny Roy, *China-South Korean Relations in Asia's Bilateral Relations* (Honolulu: Asia-Pacific Center for Security Studies, 2004); Zhu Feng, "China's Policy on the North Korean Nuclear Issue," replayed in *China Strategy*, vol. 3, www.csis.org (accessed 20 July 2004); Guo Feixiong, "China's Role and Objectives in the North Korean Nuclear Crisis," replayed in *China Strategy*, vol. 3, www.csis.org (accessed 20 July 2004).

2. Taeho Kim, "China's Evolving Bilateral Ties in Northeast Asia," in Jaushieh Joseph Wu, ed., *Rising China* (Taipei: Institute of International Relations, National Chengchi University, 2001), 205-6; Roy, *China and the Korean Peninsula*; Fei-ling Wang, *Tacit Acceptance and Watchful Eyes: Beijing's Views about the U.S.-ROK Alliance* (Carlisle, Pa.: U.S. Army War College, 1997).

3. Scott Snyder, "Clash, Crash, and Cash," *Comparative Connections,* April-July 2002.

4. *Korea: Improved South Korean-Chinese Relations* (Washington, D.C.: Library of Congress), Congressional Research Service, Report 97-681F, July 1997; "ROK Exports to PRC Decline," Seoul *Yonhap* in English, 2 March 1998 (Internet version); Caroline Cooper, "China and Korea: Partners or Competitors?" *Korean Insight*, Korean Economic Institute 4, no. 9 (September 2002): 2-3.

5. James Brooke, "China Looming Large in South Korea as Biggest Player, Replacing U.S.," *New York Times*, 4 January 2003 (Internet version).

6. Snyder, "Clash, Crash, and Cash," *Comparative Connections.*

7. Snyder, "Turning Point for China?" *Comparative Connections,* July 2003; consultations, Washington, D.C., March 2004.

8. Snyder, "Economic Interests Uber Alles," *Comparative Connections*, July 2001.

9. Snyder, "Transit, Traffic Control and Telecoms," *Comparative Connections,* April 2002; consultations, Washington D.C., March 2004.

10. Snyder, "Consummating 'Full-scale Cooperative Partnership,'" *Comparative Connections*, January 2001; Scott Snyder, "Upgrading Communication Channels, Messages Are Getting Clearer," *Comparative Connections*, April 2000.

11. Kim, "China's Evolving Bilateral Ties," *Rising China*, 205-6.

12. Kim, "Chinese-North Korean Relations," *International Journal of Korean Studies*, 39.

13. Snyder, "Telecoms," *Comparative Connections*, April 2002.

14. Kim, "Chinese-North Korean Relations," *International Journal of Korean Studies*, 45.

15. Snyder, "Clash, Crash, and Cash," *Comparative Connections*.

16. Anthony Faiola, "Kicking Up the Dust of History," *Washington Post*, 22 January 2004, A15.

17. *Korea*, Report 97-681F, July 1997, 2.

18. *Korea: U.S.-South Korean Relations* (Washington, D.C.: Library of Congress), Congressional Research Service, Issue Brief 98045, 15 December 2003; Robert Sutter, *Chinese Policy Priorities and Their Implications for the United States* (Lanham, Md.: Rowman & Littlefield, 2000), 99.

19. *Korea: Improved South Korean-Chinese Relations*; Bonnie Glaser and Ronald Montaperto, "Northeast Asia Interviews With Chinese Defense Officials," in Han Binnendijk and Ronald Montaperto, eds., *Strategic Trends in China* (Washington, D.C.: National Defense University, 1998), 111-12.

20. Kim, "Chinese-North Korean Relations," *International Journal of Korean Studies*, 44.

21. Sutter, *Chinese Policy Priorities*, 100.

22. *Korea*, Report 97-681F, July 1997, 4.

23. Sutter, *Chinese Policy Priorities*, 101; Glaser and Montaperto, "Northeast Asia Interviews," *Strategic Trends in China*, 111-12.

24. Scott Snyder, "Beijing at Center Stage or Upstaged by the Two Kims?" *Comparative Connections*, July 2000; Snyder, "Economic Interests," *Comparative Connections*.

25. Snyder, "Economic Interests," *Comparative Connections*.

26. Roy, *China and the Korean Peninsula*; You Ji, "Understanding China's North Korea Policy"; Ming Liu, "China and the North Korean Crisis," 347-73; Kim, "Chinese-North Korean Relations," *International Journal of Korean Studies*, 39-56.

27. Scott Snyder, "Middle Kingdom Diplomacy and the North Korean Crisis," *Comparative Connections*, October 2003.

28. Snyder, "Sino-Korean Relations and the Future of the U.S.-ROK Alliance," *NBR Analysis* 14, no. 1 (Seattle, Wash.: National Bureau of Asian Research, June 2003): 51-72.

29. Sutter, *Chinese Policy Priorities*, 101.

30. *Korea*, Report 97-681F, July 1997, 4.

31. See, among others, Roy, *China and the Korean Peninsula*; Fei-ling Wang, *Tacit Acceptance*, 1997.

32. Snyder, "Sino-Korean Relations," *NBR Analysis*, 55-59.

33. Consultations with fifteen South Korean officials and nongovernment China specialists, Seoul and Busan, South Korea, May-June 2004. The following assessment of South Korean perspectives is based heavily on these consultations.

34. *Peace, Prosperity, and National Security* (Seoul: National Security Council, Republic of Korea, 1 May 2004), 61-63.

35. *Peace, Prosperity*, Republic of Korea, 62.

36. Consultations with U.S. and South Korean officials, May 31, June 1, 2004.

36. Consultations with U.S. and South Korean officials, May 31, June 1, 2004.

37. Consultations with South Korean officials, May-June 2004.

38. Consultations, Seoul, May 31, 2004.

39. Consultations, Seoul, May 31, 2004. See also Zhu Qiu, "'Maritime Interception' Exercise Conducted by Members of the 'Proliferation Security Initiative,'" (Beijing) *Zhongguo Guofang Bao*, 23 September 2003, 2; "Korea, China Work Out Verbal Compromise on Koguryo History," *Chosan Ilbo*, 24 August 2004 (Internet version).

40. Roy, *China and the Korean Peninsula*.

41. Kim, "The Making of China's Korea Policy," *Chinese Foreign and Security Policy*, 374-84.

42. Kim, "Chinese-North Korean Relations," *International Journal of Korean Studies*, 44.

43. Ming Liu, "China and the North Korean Crisis," 370-72.

44. Roy, *China and the Korean Peninsula*.

45. Kim, "Chinese-North Korean Relations," *International Journal of Korean Studies*, 45-49; Wang Jisi, *China's Changing Role in Asia* (Washington, D.C.: Atlantic Council of the United States, Asia Program, January 2004), 9-12.

46. "Jiang Invites Kim Dae Jung to Visit PRC," *Kyodo*, 24 February 1998 (Internet version).

47. "Jiang Invites Kim," *Kyodo*.

48. Sutter, *Chinese Policy Priorities*, 103.

49. Sutter, *Chinese Policy Priorities*, 103.

50. *The Korean Herald*, 18 January 1999 (Internet version).

51. Snyder, "Beijing at Center Stage," *Comparative Connections*; Snyder, "Economic Interests," *Comparative Connections*.

52. Roy, *China and the Korean Peninsula*; You Ji, "Understanding China's North Korea Policy"; Kim, "Chinese-North Korean Relations," *International Journal of Korean Studies*, 51-53.

Chapter 7

China-Southeast Asia Relations

Evolution and Overview

The rise of China as an economic and regional power is an important development affecting Southeast Asia after the Cold War. China's rapidly growing economic, political, and military interaction with the members of ASEAN (the Association of Southeast Asian Nations, which includes Brunei, Cambodia, Indonesia, Laos, Malaysia, Myanmar [Burma], the Philippines, Singapore, Thailand, and Vietnam) presents important opportunities and challenges for these countries, which make up the bulk of Southeast Asian states. China's past assertive policies toward Southeast Asia, and its rising military power and occasional resort to forceful rhetoric or military action concerning regional territorial disputes during the 1990s, have produced continued wariness about China's intentions among many Southeast Asian leaders. At the same time, Chinese officials have been effective in recent years in using attentive and accommodating diplomacy along with the attraction of China's growing economy to assuage Southeast Asian concerns and win greater influence in the area.[1]

Chinese trade with and investment in Southeast Asian countries grew in the 1990s at an annual rate double the impressive rate of growth of the ASEAN and Chinese economies. This was accompanied by an ever-widening array of high-level official contacts. In 1997, ASEAN and China set up an umbrella organization, the ASEAN-China Joint Cooperation Committee, to oversee already established ASEAN-Chinese political, economic, security, and science-technology exchanges. Chinese President Jiang Zemin led a delegation to ASEAN's thirtieth anniversary

celebration and informal summit, and signed the first Chinese-ASEAN joint statement in December 1997.[2]

At the time, both China and ASEAN were preoccupied with efforts to deal with
the consequences of the Asian economic crisis. Beijing's careful responses to the
crisis, including its pledges to maintain economic growth, eschew devaluation of the
Chinese currency, support IMF rescue efforts, and provide supplementary support
of $1 billion to Thailand and a reported several billion dollars to Indonesia, were
well received in the region. Of course, it was widely known that the first two Chinese
measures were mainly for Chinese domestic purposes, that Chinese support for IMF
funding actually cost Beijing little, and that extra funding and support for Thailand
and Indonesia were slow in coming as Beijing became more concerned with its own
financial health and was particularly wary of deep involvement in Indonesia without
significant economic and political reform there.[3]

Beijing was generally discreet in reaction to anti-Chinese violence that swept
Indonesia in the late 1990s. It was sharply critical of Taiwan's efforts to use offers
of economic aid in the wake of the economic crisis to foster high-level government
contacts in the region, but the Chinese authorities stopped well short of taking
significant retaliatory measures against the Southeast Asian governments involved.[4]

The underlying issues in Chinese relations with Southeast Asia in the post-Cold
War period remained focused on economic competition for markets and foreign
investment, territorial disputes in the South China Sea, and concerns over regional
security, especially the implications of China's military modernization. Many
government officials in ASEAN cooperated with China in the 1990s in promoting
"Asian values" as a counterpoint to U.S.-backed efforts to foster greater support for
international human rights; but they also privately were concerned about China's
support for and widespread interaction with the repressive regime in Burma and also
occasionally voiced concerns about the extensive Chinese involvement with the
authoritarian Hun Sen regime in Cambodia. ASEAN leaders also continued to
support the U.S.-Japan alliance and the U.S. military presence in Asia, despite strong
China's criticism of these during the 1990s until mid-2001.[5]

The pattern of Chinese involvement in Southeast Asia was consistent with the
broad goals and practices of Chinese leaders' post-Cold War policies throughout
China's periphery. Seeking to secure China's periphery and expand advantageous
economic, political, and military contacts, Chinese leaders made substantial gains
in Southeast Asia. Isolated by the West and Japan after the Tiananmen incident of
1989, China redoubled efforts to sustain and improve ties with developing neighboring states and others in the Third World.[6]

It accommodated international pressure leading to a peace settlement in Cambodia in 1991, and in the process shifted Chinese support from the reviled and discredited Khmer Rouge to its former adversary, Cambodian strongman Hun Sen, who had
been sharply criticized by China in the past. Later in the decade, the Sino-Cambodia
relationship had evolved to the point that Hun Sen's regime had closer ties with
China than any other Southeast Asian state, as Chinese military, economic, and
political support appeared both generous and without major conditions. Beijing

leaders also solidified China's position as the main international backer of the military regime that grabbed power in Burma after aborted elections in 1988. China provided military equipment, training, and economic and political assistance to the internationally isolated regime.[7]

Though they remained suspicious of Chinese intentions in Cambodia, Burma, and elsewhere in the region, Southeast Asian governments generally welcomed markedly increased relations with China, as Chinese economic, political, and military power and influence grew in the 1990s. Southeast Asian leaders were positively impressed by Chinese leaders' more active and accommodating stance to Southeast Asia evident in the late 1990s and the early years of the next decade. Southeast Asian leaders remained pragmatic in seeking an appropriate balance with other powers in the region.[8]

U.S. influence in Southeast Asia declined following the withdrawal of U.S. forces from the Philippines in 1992, and episodic and inconsistent U.S. attention to the region followed for several years. The September 11, 2001, terrorist attack on America saw U.S. leaders focus renewed attention on Southeast Asia as a second front in the war on terrorism. Japan had been the dominant outside economic power in Southeast Asia but its position declined in the post-Cold War period as economic weakness sapped Japanese influence in Southeast Asia. The European Union (EU) remained interested in the region largely for economic reasons, but this interest fell in tandem with the economic downturn in Southeast Asia caused by the Asian economic crisis of 1997-1998. Russia exerted little influence, though Russian arms were relatively cheap and capable, and therefore attractive to some Southeast Asian buyers. As a power with rising capabilities and ambitions, India grew in power and took initiatives regarding Burma, Vietnam, and ASEAN more broadly, and in securing sea lines of communications in Southeast Asia.[9]

Chinese officials tended to be accommodating and diplomatic in most interactions with Southeast Asia during the post-Cold War period, but they showed a hard edge over territorial disputes with Southeast Asian countries in the early 1990s that worked against improving China-ASEAN relations. Chinese officials at this time also appeared very wary of multilateral discussions on these and related issues, presumably suspicious that these fora would put China at a disadvantage on territorial and other sensitive questions. Chinese military-backed expansion of territorial control in disputed islets in the South China Sea came in tandem with the aggressive Chinese military reaction to the Taiwan president's visit to the United States in 1995, prompting U.S. military countermeasures that were welcomed by many leaders in Southeast Asia. In 1995, ASEAN showed unusual unity in confronting China diplomatically over its military-backed expansion in disputed areas of the South China Sea, and some in ASEAN, notably Singapore and the Philippines, took steps to solidify security ties with the United States in the perceived uncertain environment caused by China's expansion.[10]

Greater Chinese flexibility on territorial disputes and the management of relations with Southeast Asia was evident by 1997 when Chinese officials inaugurated their "New Security Concept" (NSC) initially in an ASEAN setting. By this time, Chinese leaders were showing more flexibility in dealing with territorial issues with many neighbors, and were more willing to participate in multilateral fora that focused on these and other regional concerns. Chinese leaders from that time forward also were very active in diplomatic, economic, and military contacts to reassure Southeast Asian neighbors and others that the image of the "China Threat" was an illusion. The image had been prominent in Southeast Asia as a result of Chinese assertiveness in the South China Sea and Taiwan up to the mid-1990s, and China's overall military and economic expansion.[11]

The shift toward greater moderation in 1997 did not include U.S. policy, however. Chinese moves in Southeast Asia for many years explicitly targeted the United States and U.S. interests. Official Chinese media and comment by Chinese leaders portrayed Chinese initiatives as part of a broader international struggle against the "hegemonism," "power politics," and "Cold War thinking" of the United States, whose leaders were consistently portrayed as taking initiatives in Southeast Asia and elsewhere along China's periphery with a design to "contain" and "hold back" the rise of China's power and influence in this and other world areas. Thus, in Southeast Asia, the moderating effect of China's new security concept was offset by the strident Chinese opposition to American power, influence, and policies. The NSC was often juxtaposed to the U.S. efforts to revitalize the alliance relationship with NATO and Japan, seen by Chinese leaders as evidence of "Cold War thinking" adverse to Southeast Asian interests and global peace and development. To leaders in Southeast Asia, Chinese rhetoric seemed to be calling on them to make a choice between Chinese and U.S. approaches—a choice they were loath to make. The net effect of the Chinese anti-U.S. rhetoric was to complicate and hold back Chinese influence in the area.[12]

Taiwan's efforts to expand diplomatic and economic influence in the region also ran up against repeated and strenuous Chinese complaints and pressure on Southeast Asian governments, though in the 1990s the pressure was not as intense as that applied to the United States or Japan over Taiwan. For a decade after Lee Teng-hui initiated his "informal diplomacy" with a visit to Singapore in 1989, Taiwan's president and other senior leaders traveled informally many times to the region to visit with Southeast Asian counterparts, and some senior Southeast Asian leaders even ventured to Taiwan. As China became more influential in Southeast Asia, it used that influence to restrict ever more tightly Southeast Asian interactions with Taiwan officials, as well as to curb Southeast Asian interaction with the Dalai Lama and activities in Southeast Asia by the Chinese-outlawed Falungong movement.[13]

Other targets of Chinese pressure in Southeast Asia in the post-Cold War period included Japan. Chinese officials and comment were especially critical of Japanese security cooperation with the United States and its alleged negative impact on Southeast Asia.[14]

The sharp shift toward moderation in Chinese policy the United States during the George W. Bush administration beginning by mid-2001 was clearly evident in China's approach toward Southeast Asia, as in other areas of China's foreign policy, once again demonstrating the strong influence China's relations with the U.S.

superpower continued to have on China's regional policies. The previous strident Chinese rhetoric and strong diplomatic and other pressure regarding the United States were greatly reduced, much to the satisfaction of Southeast Asian governments that generally did not wish to choose between the United States and China and sought to moderate great power contention seen to work against regional interests.[15] There was also a falloff in Chinese criticism of Japan and its security cooperation with the United States dealing with Southeast Asia.

Nonetheless, Chinese policy and behavior continued to work, albeit much more subtly, to build Chinese influence at the expense of the United States and other powers in Southeast Asia. This was seen in active Chinese efforts to foster an ever-growing variety of Asia-only economic, political, and security fora that took pains to exclude the United States. When a U.S.-backed high-level security forum, inaugurated in Singapore in 2002 and sponsored by the Institute for International and Strategic Studies, proved popular with regional leaders, China sent only low-level functionaries while devoting high-level attention to promoting a new Asia-only security dialogue that excluded the United States. Greater Chinese flexibility and willingness to engage in negotiations with the various claimants to South China Sea territories also saw Chinese officials endeavor to use the discussions with ASEAN members about a code of conduct over the disputed claims in the South China Sea as a means to restrict U.S. naval exercises in the area. The multilateral U.S. "Cobra Gold" military exercise saw China conduct its own military exercise in apparent competition. China also maneuvered in its Free Trade Agreement initiative with ASEAN not only to shore up China's position relative to the United States, but also to place in a negative light trade initiatives from Japan, South Korea, and India, undergirding China's leading position in the region in this area.[16]

Moreover, as Chinese influence in the region grew, Chinese officials were prepared to use their increased leverage firmly and forcefully regarding certain issues. Heading the list was Taiwan. By the start of the new century, Chinese officials were in a position to block all visits by Taiwan's president to Southeast Asia and no head of state or government in Southeast Asia visited Taiwan—a sharp turnabout from the high point of Taiwan's informal diplomacy in the 1990s. It was increasingly difficult for lower-ranking Taiwan leaders to travel in the region and meet with Southeast Asian counterparts. Chinese influence also kept the Dalai Lama in general isolation from regional leaders and Chinese leaders went all out to press Southeast Asian governments to work with Chinese authorities against the Falungong movement banned in China in 1999.[17]

Chinese-Southeast Asian Cooperation

The rapid growth of trade and other economic interchanges was the most important indication of Chinese-Southeast Asian cooperation in the post-Cold War period. By 1992, Sino-ASEAN trade was fifteen times the volume in 1975. In 1993,

Sino-ASEAN trade amounted to 5.4 percent of China's foreign trade, making ASEAN China's fifth-largest trading partner after Japan, Hong Kong, the United States, and the EU. Trade increased by about 30 percent in 1994, and by 40 percent in 1995, reaching a level of $20 billion annually that was sustained in 1996 and 1997. ASEAN in the mid-1990s accounted for about 7 percent of China's foreign trade, and China accounted for just under 5 percent of total ASEAN trade. In general, imports and exports in China-ASEAN trade were in balance.[18]

The trade volume increased as ASEAN states emerged with mixed success from the negative fallout of the Asian economic crisis on 1997-1998, while China continued its strong, outward-oriented economic growth. The value of China-ASEAN trade was over $41 billion in 2001. Singapore was the largest trading partner, followed by Malaysia, Thailand, and Indonesia, with the Philippines lagging further behind. In 2001, ASEAN was China's fifth-largest trading partner, following Japan, the United States, the EU, and Hong Kong. The share of ASEAN's trade in China's total trade continued to rise, reaching 8.2 percent in 2001. China was the sixth-largest trading partner for the predominantly export oriented economies of ASEAN. China-ASEAN trade was valued at $55 billion in 2002.[19] It was valued at $78 billion in 2003.[20] Trade relations improved as ASEAN in 2004 recognized officially China's market status.

John Wong and Sarah Chan along with other observers were struck by the changing composition of China-ASEAN trade. In the early 1990s, ASEAN exports to China tended to be natural resources and primary goods and materials. By 2001, Chinese imports and overall ASEAN-China trade items were predominantly manufactured goods, notably machinery and electric equipment. Chinese exports to ASEAN long had been diversified, including agricultural commodities, metals, and mineral products along with manufactured goods. By 2001, manufactured goods including machinery and electrical equipment and apparel and footwear amounted to over 60 percent of Chinese exports to ASEAN.[21]

It is difficult to achieve such a large growth in trade and economic relations without encountering difficulties. For China and ASEAN these included competition for world markets and the potential impact of an ASEAN-China Free Trade Agreement (ACFTA) proposed by China's premier at the ASEAN-China summit in November 2000. ACFTA developed rapidly in following years. The formal agreement was signed during the ASEAN-China summit held in Phnom Penh in November 2002. This "Framework Agreement on Comprehensive Economic Cooperation between the ASEAN Nations and the People's Republic of China" set goals for establishing a China-ASEAN FTA, and offered specific early benefits for ASEAN agricultural exports to China. Negotiations on a FTA were to be completed by 2004, establishing the FTA for trade in goods for the original six ASEAN countries by 2010 and by 2015 for newer ASEAN members. Tariffs on some agricultural imports and food items were to be reduced earlier, as an "early harvest," before other tariff reductions. In addition to the Framework Agreement, Chinese Minister of Trade Shi Guangsheng signed a separate document establishing a zero tariff in January 2004 on certain imports from ASEAN's poorest members, Cambodia, Laos, and Burma.[22]

Striving to foster positive economic trends in ASEAN-China relations, China worked with Thailand to demonstrate the mutually beneficial effects of China opening its agricultural markets to ASEAN exporters under terms of the "early harvest" provisions of the proposed China-ASEAN FTA. China and Thailand signed an agreement in mid-2003 to eliminate tariffs on some 200 varieties of fruits and vegetables beginning on October 1, 2003. The Philippines also agreed on May 8, 2003, with some reservations, to sign an "early harvest" agreement with China for eighty-two items, including agricultural products. The agreements not only reduced some of the dissatisfaction in ASEAN over the negative effects for Southeast Asian exporters of China's rising economic competitiveness, but they stood in positive contrast to Japan's reluctance to open its agricultural markets to ASEAN exporters despite Tokyo's efforts to forge free trade agreements and related accords in order to solidify Japanese-ASEAN economic ties.[23]

An ASEAN group of experts concluded that ACFTA when fully implemented would increase ASEAN exports to China by 48 percent and China's exports to ASEAN by 55 percent; and it would increase ASEAN's GDP by .9 percent and China's by .3 percent. Nevertheless, Wong and Chan argued that ACFTA and other probable economic conditions affecting China and ASEAN were unlikely to reduce soon the strong competitive factors in China-ASEAN economic relations. Though ASEAN-China trade would grow, the two economies had a relatively low level of trade interdependence. Rather, both sides were economically oriented toward the industrialized countries of the West and Japan for their export markets, as well as sources of capital and technology. In 2000, for instance, 56 percent of China's total exports and 57 percent of the top four ASEAN producers went to U.S., Japanese, or EU markets.[24]

Chinese-ASEAN competition continued in the export of both traditional and nontraditional manufactured goods. Wong and Chan reinforced other assessments to predict that as China rapidly industrializes and integrates into the world trading system, its trade expansion would intensify competition with and displace the ASEAN economic exports in developed country markets. Most Chinese light manufactured goods were targeted at the U.S., Japanese, and EU markets that also were the targets of the export-oriented manufacturers in ASEAN. In areas of traditional labor-intensive industries like textiles, clothing, and footwear, Chinese gains since the 1990s in Western and Japanese markets came at the expense of ASEAN exports, among others.[25] The phasing out of quotas on textiles and clothing exports due under WTO guidelines in 2005 could enable China to accelerate its share of global apparel goods, severely impacting ASEAN and other producers for the world market. In more sophisticated products including computers, printers, and electronic goods, the fast rise in Chinese exports foreshadowed seemingly unbeatable competition for many export-oriented industries in ASEAN, Latin America, and elsewhere. Machinery and electronics grew rapidly and came to dominate China's export structure. Chinese manufacturers in these areas were beating out ASEAN competitors in the U.S. market in the 2000s. China was becoming a major outsourcing center for the global electronics industry, notably as Taiwan companies—major players in this industry—increasingly invested in the Chinese mainland.[26]

On the investment front, ASEAN-China investment also grew rapidly in the post-Cold War period. By the end of 1991, the ASEAN states had committed $1.41 billion in 1,042 projects approved by Beijing. Singapore led the ASEAN states in trade and investment in China. By mid-1994, Singapore became China's fifth-largest overseas investor after Hong Kong, Taiwan, the United States, and Japan. By that time, Singapore had invested in 3,834 projects in China with a promised investment of $6.8 billion. Most notable was the agreement to jointly develop a multibillion-dollar industrial park in China's Jiangsu Province. By early 1996, the Chinese government had approved 10,926 ASEAN country-invested projects with agreed investments of $26.4 billion, of which $6.2 billion was already paid. By the end of that year, there were 12,342 approved investment projects valued at $34 billion, of which $9.4 billion was already paid. Five hundred ninety-six were added in the first half of 1997. In 2001, ASEAN-utilized investment in China was valued at $26.2 billion and contracted investment was valued at $53.5 billion.[27] By the end of 2002, ASEAN had invested $45.8 billion in 20,000 projects in China.[28]

Chinese investment in ASEAN was much smaller in scale (less than $1 billion in the 1990s and valued at $1.4 billion in 822 projects in late 2002). It was valued at about $2 billion in 2004.[29] Beijing was closely collaborating with ASEAN and the ASEAN countries most closely concerned in the development of the Mekong River region. A large number of Chinese companies set up operations in ASEAN countries, notably in Singapore, as a base from which to penetrate global markets, and Chinese companies won labor contracts (that is, deals involving large groups of Chinese laborers working under contract in foreign countries) in the ASEAN region (in 1993 Beijing completed 609 labor contracts valued at $250 million).[30] Mutual investment patterns continued in more recent years with Singapore accounting for three-quarters of FDI flows from ASEAN to China in 2001.[31]

Investment patterns also showed that China and ASEAN directly competing for investment funds from Western and advanced Asian countries. In 2002, China became the world's largest recipient of FDI, gaining about half of FDI going to Asia, excluding Japan. In the early 1990s, China had received less than 20 percent of FDI to developing Asia, while ASEAN countries received over 60 percent. This shifted sharply during the 1990s and by the end of the decade, the figures were reversed, with China receiving over 60 percent and ASEAN under 20 percent. Predictably, the increase in FDI added to China's overall competitiveness in such manufactured products as electronics and consumer goods that were a mainstay in ASEAN exports to advanced economies.[32]

Given the broad similarities in trade structures and the competitive nature of China-ASEAN economic relations, there appeared to be plenty of opportunities for China and ASEAN to compete as well as to complement one another. Chinese and ASEAN leaders seemed aware of these determinants as they endeavored to develop mutual interests and to manage tensions through the ACFTA and other arrangements. Other ASEAN-China economic accords included the Joint Committee on Economic and Trade Cooperation, agreed to in 1994. There also were agreements between China and some of the individual ASEAN states on investment protection and avoidance of some double taxation, helping to facilitate Sino-ASEAN economic cooperation.[33]

Meanwhile, some ASEAN states were interested in promoting Chinese scientific and technological cooperation with an eye toward furthering each side's competitiveness. China had a relatively strong scientific and production process. For their part, some of the ASEAN states were experienced in commercialization of science and technology, application of scientific and advanced technological findings to the production process, and marketing. As a result, some of the ASEAN states signed agreements on joint scientific and technological cooperation with China, and ASEAN as a whole signed an agreement with China to set up a Joint Committee on Science and Technology in 1994.[34]

High-level political interaction and cooperation reinforced economic convergence of interests, as Chinese and ASEAN leaders undertook a wide range of senior-level political contacts and exchanges. In the 1990s, top-level Chinese leaders like Jiang Zemin, Li Peng, Zhu Rongji, and the Chinese foreign and defense ministers traveled to the ASEAN region and reciprocated with warm welcomes for their visiting counterparts from ASEAN countries. This pattern was followed closely by the new generation of Chinese leaders headed by Hu Jintao and Wen Jiabao who took top leadership positions in late 2002 and early 2003. Notably, China set a new pattern in its close relations with Thailand by releasing, on February 5, 1999, an elaborate joint statement to guide the two countries' close cooperation in the twenty-first century. Over the next few years, China's signed similar agreements with each of the ten ASEAN states.[35]

China and the ASEAN countries established various bilateral mechanisms for regular high-level political dialogue, and such dialogue between China and ASEAN developed markedly. Since 1991, the Chinese foreign minister has attended, by invitation, the annual ASEAN foreign ministers' conference. In 1995, China asked to become a "full dialogue partner" of ASEAN at the annual ASEAN foreign ministers' meeting, and this was accepted. In December 1997, President Jiang Zemin attended the informal ASEAN summit in Kuala Lumpur, and China and ASEAN issued their first joint statement. Earlier in 1997, ASEAN and China set up an umbrella panel, called the ASEAN-China Joint Cooperation Committee (JCC), to oversee ASEAN-China relations. The JCC was to identify projects to be undertaken by ASEAN and China and to coordinate four other parallel mechanisms, namely:

- The ASEAN-China senior officials' political consultations;
- The ASEAN-Chinese Joint Committee on Economic and Trade Cooperation;
- The ASEAN-China Joint Committee on Science and Technology;
- The ASEAN Committee in Beijing

Top-level Chinese leaders' active participation in ASEAN functions and interaction with ASEAN states far surpassed such contacts by other powers with a strong interest in Southeast Asia including Japan, South Korea, India, the United States, Australia, Russia, and the EU.[36]

On security issues, China was invited by ASEAN in 1994 to become a consultative partner in the regional security dialogue carried on by the ASEAN Regional Forum (ARF). China became more actively involved in the ARF, notably hosting, along with the Philippines, an ARF meeting on regional confidence-building measures in March 1997.[37]

At the ASEAN-China summit in Phnom Penh in November 2002, China and ASEAN finally made some progress in efforts over several years to manage more effectively tensions arising from competing territorial claims in the South China Sea. China's rising military power and its occasional assertive stance over disputed territorial claims in the South China Sea had continued to complicate ASEAN-Chinese relations. The two sides used a variety of consultative mechanisms to deal with these questions. China preferred to deal with the issues bilaterally, as was evidenced in the Sino-Philippines agreements reached in 1996 on a military code of conduct, military exchanges, and the establishment of some communications between military detachments in disputed areas in the South China Sea. China and the Philippines also agreed on joint maritime scientific research, fishing, control of piracy, and other endeavors. This convergence did not prevent continued friction, however. In 1999, the Philippines were particularly upset with Chinese military-backed construction on Mischief Reef—a set of islets close to the Philippines and claimed by them. Media speculation said Chinese forces were taking advantage of ASEAN's preoccupation with the Asian economic crisis to assert Chinese territorial claims in disputed parts of the South China Sea. ASEAN often favored a multilateral approach in dealing with security issues involving China. Thus, Indonesia succeeded in gaining China's participation in an annual multilateral workshop on "managing potential conflicts in the South China Sea," where participants exchanged ideas on dealing with the disputed territories. ASEAN officials also discussed the territorial issues in ASEAN-PRC meetings of senior working-level officials.[38]

China's increased willingness in recent years to engage in multilateral dialogue on regional security issues complemented continued use of bilateral channels to deal with territorial issues. Years of discussion among Chinese officials and those representing other claimants led to the agreement in November 2002 on managing disputes over territorial claims in the South China Sea. The disputes remained far from settled and Chinese leaders continued to use high-level interchange with the Philippines, Vietnam, Malaysia, and others to discuss territorial problems. Indeed, in early 2004, China publicly registered objections to unspecified foreign encroachment on Chinese claims in the South China Sea.[39]

Under terms of the November 2002 agreement, China and the ASEAN claimants agreed on restraint and confidence building in the disputed areas of the South China Sea, with some limitations. The compromise document did not include reference to the Paracel Islands that had been pushed by Vietnam and ASEAN; China has held all these islands since the 1970s, but Vietnam claims them as well. There was no commitment in the declaration that the parties would not build new structures on islets and reefs, as ASEAN wanted. Also, there was evidence of efforts by China aimed at U.S. interests; Chinese officials tried to use the declaration to limit military exercises and other activities in the area. This effort failed, though ASEAN did agree to a provision on voluntary prior notification of "joint/combined" military exercises in the South China Sea. Meanwhile, the two sides agreed to strengthen cooperation on counternarcotics, human trafficking, piracy at sea, counterterrorism, arms trafficking, economic crimes, and cyber-crime; few concrete new measures were proposed in these areas, however.[40]

At the annual ASEAN Regional Forum (ARF) meeting in Phnom Penh on June 18, 2003, Chinese officials pledged to seek legislative approval to sign ASEAN's 1976 Treaty of Amity and Cooperation. The treaty is a generalized set of commitments to respect the independence, sovereignty, and territorial integrity of the parties, not to interfere in their internal affairs, to settle disputes peacefully, and to renounce the threat or use of force. ASEAN members opened the treaty to outside accession in the late 1990s. China's pledge helped induce India, Russia, and Japan to join as well.[41]

Chinese officials also proposed in 2003 that the ARF establish a new "Security Policy Conference," whose participants would be primarily military personnel, to draft a new concept or pact among ASEAN nations and their ARF partners on promoting peace, stability, and prosperity in Southeast Asia. The proposal was consistent with the principles emphasized in China's "New Security Concept," aimed at giving equal attention to the security concerns of each country, and guaranteeing security for all through united action. China's move was interpreted as running counter to the annual meeting of Asian defense officials sponsored by the International Institute of Strategic Studies with the strong support of the United States Defense Department leaders. China had viewed that U.S.-backed forum with suspicion and had participated in its deliberations in 2002 and 2003 only with relatively low-level representation.[42]

Chinese Attentiveness and Support for Southeast Asian States

China was consistent in seeking common ground with all ASEAN states, including the more politically authoritarian ASEAN states that often met with U.S. and Western criticisms of human rights and other conditions in those countries. Following the May 30, 2003, violent attack in Burma on a motorcade of Nobel Laureate Aung San Suu Kyi and her followers, and Ms. Suu Kyi's arrest and detention, a PRC Foreign Ministry spokesperson declared that China is a friendly neighbor, "believes that the Burmese people have the capability of properly handling their own affairs," and would not be interfering in a matter that is between the Burmese government and the opposition parties.[43]

Earlier, Senior Gen. Than Shwe, chairman of Burma's ruling State Peace and Development Council (SPDC), visited China January 6-11, 2003, and Hu Jintao pledged to maintain and strengthen close relations. China also announced a $200 million preferential loan for development assistance, and signed agreements with Burma on economic and technology cooperation, public health, and sports. Jiang Zemin told the Burmese visitors that every nation has the right to choose its own path without any outside interference. Chinese Vice Premier Li Lanqing subsequently visited Rangoon, bringing proposals for further assistance to Burma and partial relief of earlier maturing Chinese loans to Burma.[44]

Chinese leaders were steadfast in support of the authoritarian Cambodian government, which dragged its feet before strong U.S.-backed international pressure via the United Nations and other channels to bring Khmer Rouge leaders expeditiously to trial consistent with Western legal norms. China's interest in avoiding high-profile scrutiny of its close support for the Khmer Rouge seemed to be an important incentive for China-Cambodian cooperation on this issue. Beijing also eschewed criticism of the Phnom Penh government's often heavy-handed treatment of political opponents, maintained generous aid programs, and lavished high-level attention on the small southeast Asian state. Chinese leaders were also discreet in dealing with Vietnam, Laos, and other authoritarian Asian governments subjected to criticism from the West for human rights violations and limits on political freedom.[45]

Jiang Zemin took a strong personal interest in nurturing relations with small authoritarian regimes in ASEAN despite their poor international reputations. President Jiang visited Laos November 11-13, 2000, the first visit by a Chinese head of state. Jiang reached "complete consensus" on all issues discussed with President Khamtai Siphandon. A Joint Declaration on Establishing a Framework for Bilateral Cooperation was signed. Both sides agreed to further cooperation in high-level political exchanges, foreign policy, economic matters, cross-border trade, and environmental protection; to enhance cooperation between their respective governments, armed forces, and nongovernment organizations, and to intensify cooperation between their police and judiciary in an effort to crack down on transnational crimes (smuggling, drug trafficking, and illegal immigration).[46]

Jiang followed with a visit to Cambodia on November 13-14, 2000. A joint statement reinforced bilateral cooperation, making Cambodia the tenth and last ASEAN member to reach such an accord with China. The joint statement outlined a number of areas for future cooperation, including increased political and economic exchanges and continuing efforts to fight against transnational crimes. Seven other cooperation accords were signed, including an extension on preferential loans already granted, a new loan package valued at $12 million for road building and agriculture, an extradition treaty, disaster relief, welfare assistance, and technology.[47]

Visiting Myanmar during December, 12-15, 2001, President Jiang observed that the two countries have a deep brotherly relationship. He avoided any critical reference to the junta's suppression of Nobel Prize winner Aung San Suu Kyi and her party. Agreements signed during the visit dealt with border control, suppressing the flow of narcotics from Myanmar into China, economic and technical cooperation, plant and animal quarantine, fisheries, and oil and gas exploration. Jiang promised to encourage greater Chinese investment in Myanmar, and he reportedly offered a total package of aid and investment of $100 million.[48]

President Jiang made his second visit as president to Vietnam during February 27-March 1, 2002. Vietnamese leaders said they saw China as an economic model and the two powers signed economic agreements on science and technology cooperation and on preferential credits amounting to $12 million. Trade between the two countries rose from $37.7 million in 1991 to over $3 billion in 2001 with a target of $5 billion in 2005. Agreements on demarcation of the land border were reached in 1999 and on maritime zones in the Tonkin Gulf in 2000. Neither was fully implemented by the time of Jiang's visit, and the two sides said they would continue to work on disputes related to competing territorial claims. Meanwhile, Chinese media in the weeks before the visit commented negatively on U.S. military intentions toward Vietnam, criticizing alleged U.S. efforts to return militarily to the country through access to Vietnamese naval bases.[49]

The transition toward democracy in Indonesia was accompanied by widespread violence against ethnic Chinese Indonesian citizens that seriously complicated China's approach to the country. However, high-level Chinese leadership exchanges showed that relations were gradually improving amid repeated Chinese gestures and supporting actions toward the Southeast Asian state. In a major speech during a visit to Indonesia marking the fiftieth anniversary of Sino-Indonesian relations on July 24, 2000, Vice President Hu Jintao called for concerted efforts in four areas: economic development, regional economic cooperation, fostering a "new security concept," and the establishment of a new equitable international political and economic order. Hu highlighted ASEAN Plus Three as a model of regional economic cooperation, and railed against the "Cold War mentality and hegemonism and power politics" of the United States and others portrayed as dangerous and out of step with new Asian norms.[50]

Premier Zhu Rongji visited Indonesia November 7-11, 2001. He endorsed Indonesian efforts to deal with separatist movements in Aceh and Irian Jaya, widespread religious and ethnic strife, and economic stagnation. China and Indonesia signed six agreements, involving small amounts of Chinese aid, banking, tourism, and other subjects.[51] More substantial progress was noted when President Megawati visited China in March 2002. Chinese leaders offered strong political support for the Indonesian leader and announced a $400 million loan to Indonesia. Bilateral trade, amounting to $6.7 billion in 2001, seemed poised to increase with increased energy cooperation. In January 2002, China's national offshore oil company invested in energy assets in Indonesia that reportedly made it the largest foreign offshore oil producer in that country. Indonesia was competing with Australia and others on a $10 billion liquefied natural gas (LNG) deal to supply China's first LNG reception terminal, in Guangdong Province. Australia ultimately was selected but Indonesia was compensated with a smaller LNG deal in another part of China.[52]

Such Chinese attentiveness to ASEAN and ASEAN member states came in the context of greater Chinese flexibility and interest regarding regional economic and other multilateral organizations important to ASEAN and its members. Chinese leaders strongly embraced economic globalization by the late 1990s, seeing their interests best served by close integration in the world economy through the World Trade Organization and other means. In Asia, China on the one hand worked closely with Asia-only groups like ASEAN Plus Three, while on the other hand it continued interaction with groups like the Asian Pacific Economic Cooperation (APEC) forum and the Asia-European forum (ASEM) that facilitated Asian interaction with non-Asian economic powers.[53]

Continued opposition to U.S. international dominance was among reasons prompting Chinese leaders to join with others in the region in fostering Asia-only economic, political, and security groups that excluded or marginalized U.S. leadership. The Chinese government was a strong supporter of the Malaysian prime minister's call in the 1990s for the establishment of an East Asian Economic Caucus (EAEC). The proposed EAEC was viewed warily by the United States, which was to be excluded, along with Australia, Canada, and other Pacific-rim countries, from membership in the group. The United States strongly supported the more inclusive APEC forum, which was actively dealing with regional economic issues for several years.[54]

The Asian economic crisis of 1997-1998 led to an array of regional initiatives designed to broaden Asian cooperation separate from the United States, the IMF, and international economic institutions supported by the West. Thailand, South Korea, Indonesia, and others were subjected to strong IMF requirements, backed by the United States, that were deeply resented. This prompted them and others to seek regional means and mechanisms to deal with economic issues. Chinese leaders joined this regional movement which coincided with a concurrent increased Chinese emphasis on multilateralism in dealing with world problems.[55]

Chinese leaders initiated some regional multilateral mechanisms and participated actively in others, establishing China as a leader in groups that explicitly excluded the United States and its Western allies. Japan remained an important potential or actual competitor with China for regional leadership in these groups and elsewhere. Chinese officials placed a premium on sustaining generally cordial ties with Japanese counterparts in the various regional groupings that emphasized amity and consensus. At the same time, Chinese officials also maneuvered in ways to reduce Japan's regional stature and highlight China as the dynamic new leader in Asian economic political and security cooperation. For instance, Chinese officials joined with the United States in 1997 in order to block the Japanese government's efforts at the time of the Asian economic crisis to create an Asian monetary fund. A few years later, China supported such a fund that no longer had a "made in Japan" trademark.[56] Chinese officials in the 2000s also were in competition with Japanese counterparts in pushing free trade arrangements in Asia. China's willingness to open agricultural markets put the Japanese at a distinct disadvantage with ASEAN's many exporters of agricultural products. Meanwhile, the rapid growth of China's economy and Japan's continued stagnation also influenced ASEAN opinion to look more to China for leadership on regional economic cooperation.[57]

The ASEAN Plus Three emerged in the late 1990s as the most important of regional groupings designed to promote Asian economic cooperation that excluded powers outside of East Asia, and Chinese leaders took a leading role in the group's various initiatives to promote intraregional cooperation and economic safeguards. When the ASEAN Plus Three endorsed an Asian Monetary Fund initiative, China was an active supporter, even though China had opposed a similar Japanese initiative for such a fund in 1997. Chinese officials and media highlighted China's free trade initiatives with ASEAN, including the early harvest concessions dealing with agricultural trade, as well as China's entry into the WTO, as key drivers in regional economic growth.[58]

More confident in China's leading position dealing with Southeast Asian and other regional and global affairs, Chinese leaders supported efforts to broaden the ASEAN Plus Three dialogue to include salient political and security as well as economic issues. Beijing also initiated important regional multilateral mechanisms. The Boao Forum for Asia (BFA) met April 11-14, 2002, in Hainan Island. It was presented by China as the "first annual session" of an Asian version of the Davos World Economic Forum. The forum's goal was to provide a high-level dialogue and platform for Asian countries to review the economic and social challenges and promote economic cooperation in Asia.[59]

Working with Chinese sponsors of the Boao Forum, Thailand's prime minister proposed that the first Asian Cooperation Dialogue (ACD) of foreign ministers be held in Thailand as an official counterpart to the BFA. Its first meeting was held at a resort in Thailand in June 2002. The foreign ministers of most ASEAN Plus Three members attended the session and agreed to further meetings. Meanwhile in April 2002, China hosted the third annual meeting of the Association of Asian Parliaments for Peace.[60]

Outlook and Issues in Chinese-ASEAN Relations

There was no question in 2004 that China was exerting growing influence in Southeast Asia. Attentive, flexible, and accommodating Chinese diplomacy and growing economic interchange headed the list of reasons why Chinese influence was growing and was likely to continue to advance in the years ahead. However, China's approach to Southeast Asia also faced issues and obstacles that would not be overcome easily or soon. This suggested that Chinese relations with Southeast Asia would continue to present a mixed picture of substantial gains for Chinese influence but continued signs of regional differences and wariness of the growing Chinese power. Beijing seemed intent on pursuing a generally pragmatic and moderate approach to regional developments, though it continued to look for opportunities to expand its control of contested territory in the South China Sea and its bilateral and regional influence relative to other powers in Southeast Asia.[61]

Lessons of History

The PRC's relations with most of the countries of Southeast Asia were volatile, contentious, and often violent until recent years. China saw many of these states as aligned at one time or another with its major adversaries (the United States in the 1950s and 1960s, the USSR in the 1970s and the 1980s) and pursuing policies designed to pressure China or "contain" the expansion of Chinese influence. Beijing often adopted truculent and confrontational policies, short of an all-out war directly involving China, in order to intimidate the Southeast Asian states and fend off their great-power backers. Examples included strong support for the Viet Minh's all-out assault against the French forces in Indochina in the 1950s, support of Hanoi's militant stance against the United States in the 1960s, and widespread support for antigovernment guerrilla movements in most noncommunist Southeast Asian countries in the 1960s and 1970s.[62]

Relations between China and the noncommunist Southeast Asian countries gradually normalized beginning in the mid-1970s. Malaysia, Thailand, and the Philippines improved their official relations with China following the end of the Vietnam War and the decline of the U.S.-backed military presence in the region. Indeed, these and other states in the region saw common ground with China, along with the United States, in resisting the danger in the late 1970s of a militarily strong Vietnam, backed by the Soviet Union, occupying Cambodia by military force. To persuade Vietnam to pull out of Cambodia and no longer serve as a base for Soviet military operations, China launched a monthlong border war against Vietnam in 1979. It kept up military pressure along the border for ten years and remained the main supporter of Cambodian resistance to the Vietnamese military occupation.[63]

The Cambodian quagmire, declining Soviet support, and deteriorating internal conditions made Vietnam change course and seek reconciliation with China in the early 1990s. By that time, the ASEAN states most wary of China's intentions, notably Indonesia, had normalized their diplomatic relations with China. Beijing had cut its ties with indigenous guerrilla groups in Southeast Asia, which no longer posed a substantial security problem to the governments there. China also endeavored to clarify its policies toward overseas Chinese, notably passing a nationality law in 1989 that appeared to end Chinese government claims to authority over ethnic Chinese who had taken citizenship in foreign countries and advised Chinese citizens residing abroad to adhere to local laws.[64]

By the 1990s, the importance of largely negative historical record in China-Southeast Asian relations was gradually declining. Nevertheless, mutual suspicions based on the past rose up from time to time as China occasionally strongly asserted its claim to disputed territories in the South China Sea, continued to modernize its naval and air power capabilities, and took strong military action in nearby areas, notably near Taiwan in 1995-1996. Against this backdrop, many in ASEAN welcomed, either publicly or privately, U.S., Japanese, Australian, and other statements and actions showing concern over Chinese assertiveness. This in turn aroused

Chinese suspicions that at least some in the region may be interested in reviving previous practice, which it perceived as working with outside powers in order to hold back China's rising power and influence in the region.[65]

Chinese officials and commentaries for years focused on the danger of U.S. power and policies in the region. China's sharp shift toward a moderate approach toward the United States in 2001 meant that Chinese opposition to U.S. leadership in the region was reflected only infrequently, despite the uptick in U.S. military and other activities in Southeast Asia related to the war on terrorism begun in September 2001. Targets of Chinese concern included increased U.S. military deployments and closer security cooperation with the Philippines, Japan, Australia, India, and others in Southeast Asia, U.S. policy in the lead-up to the military attack on Iraq in 2003, U.S. economic leadership in the region, and U.S. political pressure over human rights and other issues against authoritarian Asian governments. Chinese economic, political, and security initiatives also had the effect of increasing Chinese influence in Southeast Asia relative to that of the United States, Japan, India, and other powers.[66]

Recent Issues

Economic Competition. Officials and entrepreneurs in Southeast Asia saw the rapidly rising Chinese economy as a major competitive challenge as well as an economic opportunity. For example, of the $100 billion in direct foreign investment flowing into developing countries in 1994, about 40 percent went to China. By contrast, the total going to ASEAN was about 15 percent.[67] This trend continued and arguably worsened for ASEAN in following years as China became the world's largest recipient of FDI in 2002 while ASEAN economies grew with poor or mixed results and attracted much less foreign investment.[68]

As the rapidly developing Chinese economy attracted the attention of Japanese, Korean, Taiwanese, U.S., and Western investors, who might otherwise have been inclined to invest in Southeast Asia, ASEAN leaders felt pressured to take steps to liberalize their economies. They also discussed further liberalizing the investment opportunities in ASEAN and endeavored to establish special economic zones along the lines of those in China. The Asian economic crisis led to redoubled ASEAN efforts to attract outside investment.[69]

At least some ASEAN officials were concerned about the net imbalance in ASEAN-Chinese investment, with ASEAN investment in China being many times greater than Chinese investment in ASEAN. In late 2002, the ratio was $58 billion to $1.4 billion.[70] Most ASEAN investment in China was carried out by overseas Chinese businesspeople. Some nonethnic Chinese observers in countries like Indonesia and Malaysia argued that such investment was made at the expense of domestic development and reflected PRC efforts to work with overseas Chinese communities for China's benefit. Periodic discussion of the concept of a possible "greater China economic circle" involving ethnic Chinese businesspeople on the China mainland, Hong Kong, Taiwan, Singapore, and elsewhere in Southeast Asia concerned some Southeast Asian officials. Thus, the Malaysian deputy finance minister said in 1996 that it was Malaysia's view that "overzealousness on the part of Malaysian businessmen of Chinese origin could have adverse repercussions racially in their own country." Malaysian Prime Minister Mahatir balanced a positive assessment of China with warnings of China posing "a threat to the economies of Southeast Asian countries" in a major address in August 2003.[71]

Also, as noted above, ASEAN and Chinese exporters were often at similar levels of economic development. They competed for market shares in light manufactured products such as textiles, shoes, leather wares, electric appliances, toys, and electronics. This competition was expected to intensify.[72]

Territorial Claims. Conflicting claims in the South China Sea represent the most salient security issue in the Sino-ASEAN relations. ASEAN followed an approach emphasizing establishing confidence-building measures first, through a series of technical and scientific cooperation efforts, and solving problems of sovereignty later. ASEAN sought to promote a peaceful atmosphere and maintain the territorial status quo. China was in general agreement with this approach. But China and other disputants occasionally took military actions, or actions involving oil exploration or fisheries, that seemed to challenge the status quo.[73]

China was wary about discussing military matters involving the disputed territories at the Indonesian-sponsored workshops on the South China Sea in the 1990s; it preferred to deal with claimants bilaterally rather than multilaterally; and it bristled in response to statements by outside parties, notably the United States, about their concern that conflicting territorial claims should not disrupt sea lines of communication and broader regional stability.[74] China gradually moderated its stance, leading notably to the November 2002 China-ASEAN agreement on managing conflicts in the South China Sea.[75]

Some ASEAN officials were cautiously optimistic that they were making headway in persuading China that its broader interests in the region were best served by an approach that works closely with ASEAN's incremental effort to reduce tensions, develop common ground, and preserve the territorial status quo. Others pointed to periodic Chinese assertiveness over the territorial disputes, the increased capability of Chinese air and naval forces in the region, and the strong sense of nationalism among Chinese elites and common people to warn of an alleged Chinese dual-track approach. That is, while Chinese diplomats conciliated their ASEAN counterparts in various fora about the South China Sea, the Chinese military was preparing to expand its hold in the region whenever the benefits of such a move would outweigh the costs.[76]

China's Military Policies. ASEAN and Chinese observers alike recognized that China's growing defense capabilities and possible intentions to use these forces represented a serious problem in ASEAN-Chinese relations. In general, the immediate problem was the lack of transparency in China's military policies and practices. ASEAN observers know China's economic growth meant that China was more and more capable of building up its military power and that China was increasing its defense expenditures; but they had little sound idea as to what this meant for regional stability. As a result, they urged China to participate more actively in regional security forums, notably the ARF, and to take unilateral steps in order to make Chinese defense policies and practices more transparent. Some in the ASEAN were optimistic that China's recently more active stance in ARF forums would lead to a convergence of ASEAN-Chinese approaches to regional stability. They also took solace in the increased Chinese military diplomacy with ASEAN, often involving high-level military exchanges and discussions that helped to clarify mutual intentions. Others judged that China's purchase of advanced Russian jet fighters, surface naval combat vessels, and submarines presaged a PRC-military-backed effort to intimidate Southeast Asian countries and become the dominant power in the region.[77]

Other Issues

Burma. Many in ASEAN remained concerned by instability in Burma since the uprising of 1988 and the ascendancy of the repressive military regime that was in power since that time. Part of the concern involved China. Despite deteriorating economic conditions in the country, the Burmese regime maintained a half million-person armed force backed by a stockpile of weapons—over $1 billion, primarily from China. China reportedly supplied helicopters, armored vehicles, field guns, assault rifles, and patrol boats. There were recurrent though unsubstantiated reports of China establishing listening posts or disguised bases of operation along the Burmese coast.[78]

Meanwhile, Chinese-made manufactured goods were pervasive in Burma. China also developed a strong interest in opening its isolated southern provinces via the Irawaddy corridor in Burma and other river/overland routes. Rich entrepreneurs from China's southern rim bought real estate in traditional residential areas of prominent Burmese cities. Some people worried about a replay of the vicious anti-Chinese bloodletting that occurred in Burma in the mid-1960s, due largely to perceived economic disparities. Meanwhile, Beijing was particularly wary of cross-border drug trafficking affecting stability in China.[79]

For these and other reasons, ASEAN leaders moved to integrate Burma into ASEAN. China did not oppose the move. Chinese involvement in Burma was openly criticized by some U.S. and other Western officials who objected strongly to the Burma regime's human rights violations. Unlike the leaders of ASEAN, these Westerners have often opposed ASEAN's moves to welcome the Burmese regime into ASEAN. India, meanwhile, moved to improve its relations and influence in Burma partly in order to offset China's rising influence in the country.[80]

Cambodia. Following the 1991 Paris peace accords, Beijing ended support for its former ally, the Khmer Rouge, and began efforts to normalize relations with the Phnom Penh leadership. Cambodia's stormy internal politics—in particular the incessant sparring between Hun Sen's Cambodian People's Party (CPP) and Prince Ranariddh's royalist National United Front for an Independent, Neutral, Peaceful, and Cooperative Cambodia (FUNCINPEC) party—presented Beijing with a dilemma. China wanted to work with ASEAN in finding a resolution to the turmoil but also saw Hun Sen as the strongest force in Phnom Penh. Fostering good relations with Hun Sen served broader PRC interests in securing a stable southeastern perimeter and balancing the influence of other major countries, including United States and Japan, in the region. China also exploited the relationship to cramp Taiwan's efforts to establish strong ties with Cambodia.[81]

As Beijing sensed that Hun Sen was gaining the upper hand in his rivalry with Ranariddh, it consented to meetings in 1996 with Jiang Zemin and Li Peng without FUNCINPEC participation. The Hun Sen visit signaled increased trade, investment, and PRC-CPP relations. China was, notably, the first foreign power to provide substantial military equipment—heavy trucks—to Hun Sen's regime following the violent July 1997 conflict between Hun Sen and Ranariddh forces. It welcomed Hun Sen's decision in 1997 to break existing relations with Taiwan. The close China-Hun Sen relationship strengthened during the Cambodian leader's February 1999 trip to China where he signed five new agreements with the PRC. The two sides also worked together to fend off international calls for trials of Khmer Rouge leaders for crimes against humanity. As of 2004 those trials have yet to take place.[82]

Despite its obvious tilt to Hun Sen, Beijing maintained an ostensibly hands-off policy toward Cambodia and urged other powers to do the same. China accepted ASEAN's mediating role in the Cambodia dispute, viewing the organization as an increasingly important counterbalance to U.S. and Japanese influence in Southeast Asia. Beijing was reluctant to support the U.S.-backed "Friends of Cambodia" initiative in part because it perceived the group as aligned with Western interest in intervening in Cambodia. Beijing's stance eased anxieties among most in ASEAN over China's ultimate objectives in Cambodia, though Vietnam continued to look warily at any close China-Cambodia relations.[83]

Taiwan. Taiwan President Lee Teng-hui first practiced his controversial "pragmatic diplomacy," making visits to states that recognize the PRC, by going to ASEAN states in the late 1980s and early 1990s. Beijing reacted fairly mildly to the trips. Following Lee's successful private visit to the United States in 1995, however, Beijing reacted with force, launching repeated military exercises in the Taiwan Strait. Eventually, the PRC actions prompted a strong U.S. show of force in the region.[84]

ASEAN officials derived mixed lessons from the developments. On the one hand, they were reluctant to provoke PRC ire by again allowing Lee or other senior leaders to make similar visits to the region. On the other hand, some were concerned that the forceful PRC treatment of Taiwan could presage PRC action against ASEAN if the issues were seen as of sufficient importance to the PRC. Territorial disputes over the South China Sea were viewed to represent a possible cause for forceful PRC action.[85]

Taipei was quick to exploit the diplomatic opportunities flowing from the Asian economic crisis. Possible aid from Taiwan entrepreneurs, including the businesses owned by the ruling Nationalist Party, was likely to come to Southeast Asia a lot faster than government programs promised by interested countries and international organizations. Thus, senior-level leaders in Indonesia, Malaysia, Singapore, and the Philippines met with their Taiwan counterparts to discuss the crisis. Unwilling to match Taiwan's aid offers, and recognizing that a harsh response to the Southeast Asians could be counterproductive, Beijing focused its invective against Taiwan and took little substantive action against the ASEAN states.[86]

As the crisis passed and Chinese influence in ASEAN grew, Chinese officials were more effective in establishing a virtual embargo on top-level Taiwan-ASEAN exchanges, and in prompting ASEAN governments to sharply restrict lower-level exchanges. In a clear demonstration of Beijing's strong efforts to restrict access to Southeast Asia by prominent officials from Taiwan and to tighten the diplomatic isolation of the Taiwan government, a proposed trip to Thailand by a group of Taiwan lawmakers led by the Legislative Yuan Vice President was aborted in early 2003 as Thailand refused to issue visas. Taiwan complained bitterly as it had over a similar visa issue the previous year.[87] More graphic illustrations of Chinese pressure leading Southeast Asian governments to restrict access to Taiwan officials included Indonesia's refusal of a visit by the Taiwan president and its very circumspect treatment of Taiwan's vice president during a visit in 2002.[88]

Tibet, Falungong. Chinese officials also applied heavy pressure in Southeast Asia to sharply limit the activities of the Dalai Lama and so-called Tibetan splitists and to curb the Falungong movement that was banned in China in 1999. As in the case of Chinese pressure against Taiwan, there appeared to be little letup in this pressure even though Chinese officials endeavored to show flexibility and accommodation toward Southeast Asia, and also moderated their approach toward the United States, Japan, and some others after mid-2001.

In the face of strong Chinese pressure, few Southeast Asia leaders even considered meeting with the Dalai Lama, who still managed to get prominent meetings with leaders in world capitals less dependent on goodwill with China. The harsh Chinese approach to the Falungong was illustrated by the Chinese government's successful pressure on the newly installed Thai government of Prime Minister Thaksin to halt a world gathering of Falungong adherents planned for Bangkok in April 2001. According to Thai media reports, the Chinese government and its embassy in Bangkok went to great lengths to exert pressure on the Thaksin government. Local Chinese business groups were mobilized to reinforce the Chinese official line that Falungong was an "evil cult." The Chinese government protested to the Thai embassy in Beijing, while the Chinese embassy in Bangkok called on the Thai government to ban the sect.[89]

Indonesia. Beijing's cautious approach to the Asian economic crisis in Southeast Asia was graphically illustrated in China's relations with Indonesia—the most seriously affected and most unstable of the ASEAN states impacted by the crisis. China waited until April 11, 1998, before sending a senior official to Indonesia to discuss the situation. Newly appointed Foreign Minister Tang Jiaxuan, a regional expert, met with President Suharto and explicitly endorsed his "leadership," pledged $3 million in Chinese medicine, $200 million in export credits, and greater use of barter in Sino-Indonesian trade, and recognized without complaint that then rampant anti-Chinese violence in Indonesia was an Indonesian "internal affair."[90]

The timing and scope of the visit did not appear to be accidental. China was reluctant to commit aid to Indonesia until Jakarta worked out relief arrangements with the IMF. And Chinese aid was largely tied to exchanges that would have little or no net cost to the Chinese economy.

The subsequent collapse of the Suharto regime amid widespread anti-Chinese violence tested China's policy of noninterference and prompted acute Chinese concern that China's one-party regime could follow the Indonesian example if it did not manage the Chinese economy more effectively. While eschewing any change in its policy stance against meddling in other countries' "internal affairs," Chinese officials in August 1998 began publicly to strongly urge Indonesian authorities to protect ethnic Chinese in Indonesia. This came in the wake of a groundswell of pressure for public condemnation of widely reported rapes of ethnic Chinese in Indonesia. The pressure came from Chinese communities throughout the world and also prompted the Taiwan and Hong Kong authorities to publicly condemn the rapes and demand protection for ethnic Chinese. The Chinese media also drew lessons from the Suharto regime's collapse, seeing the cause primarily as economic misman-agement, not the absence of political democracy and government accountability as seen by a number of Western officials and media commentators.[91]

Gradual improvement in China's relations with Indonesia was evident during high-level official visits. As noted earlier, Vice President Hu Jintao visited in July 2000, marking the fiftieth anniversary of establishment of diplomatic relations. And Premier Zhu Rongji visited Indonesia November 7-11, 2001, achieving positive results, as did Indonesian President Megawati when she visited China in 2002.

Mekong Development, China-ASEAN Transport Integration. Chinese economic interaction with nearby ASEAN states has been accompanied by a variety of initia-tives designed to integrate southern China with neighboring states through river, rail, road, and other connections. These have seen Chinese officials work closely with Burmese counterparts to provide road and river connections from Burmese ports to inland Chinese cities; similar plans are under way involving the Mekong River and bordering countries. A Mekong River project backed by the Asian Development Bank and involving China and other countries that border on the river deals with dams, electric power, and other resources as well as transportation issues. China participates actively in deliberations. Issues of controversy include Chinese dams that have the potential to limit water flows in ways disadvantageous to down-river fishing and other interests. Strategists in India and elsewhere sometimes see the Chinese-backed development of commercial links between Burmese ports and inland Chinese cities as foreshadowing a strategic expansion of Chinese influence into the Indian Ocean.[92]

U.S. Leadership, Military Presence. The ASEAN countries, including the two U.S. military allies, Thailand and the Philippines, generally supported a continued U.S. military presence in Asia and a continued U.S.-Japan alliance. The U.S. military relationship with both strengthened in important ways since the United States began focusing on Southeast Asia as a second front in the global war on terrorism. Bangkok and Manila were like other ASEAN states in avoiding taking sides in disputes between China on the one hand and the United States and Japan on the other about the strategic framework for post-Cold War East Asia. Chinese officials placed this issue at the forefront of Chinese policy toward Southeast Asia in the late 1990s; the sharp shift toward moderation in Chinese commentary regarding the United States in mid-2001 saw much less frequent reference to the dispute.

Nevertheless, demonstrating continued sensitivity regarding U.S. military deployments and leadership in Southeast Asia, Chinese officials, as noted above,

- tried in vain to use an arrangements with ASEAN over the South China Sea to regulate U.S. exercises in the area;
- voiced sharp criticism of U.S. policy in Iraq;
- competed with U.S., Japanese, and other free trade arrangements in the region;
- voiced concern over reported U.S. interest in military access to Vietnam;
- cast a critical eye on U.S. military deployments in the Philippines and U.S.-backed efforts to encourage greater Japanese military actions in Southeast Asia.

Regarding the U.S.-Japan alliance and broader security cooperation in Asia, the United States and Japan said that strengthening their alliance was in accordance with their own and broader regional interests. By contrast, China continued to argue, albeit much more discreetly after 2001, that such Cold War alliances should not govern the future order of the region. China's public approach until mid-2001 had been that U.S. forces should be withdrawn, allowing Asian countries to manage their own security. Since 2001 and the moderate PRC approach to the United States, Chinese comment was largely silent on this issue.

Consultations in China, Southeast Asia, May-June 2004

Discussions with officials and specialists in China, Singapore, and elsewhere in Asia in May-June 2004 clarified the state of play in China's increasing influence and role in Southeast Asia.[93] The positive elements of China's recent approach to the region, backed by the attraction and challenge of China's rapidly growing economy, overshadowed past and present issues and concerns. Experienced observers in government, academic, media, and other organizations foresaw growing convergence in Chinese-Southeast Asian policies and behavior. However, unlike in the case of South Korea where a widespread positive sentiment toward China, a "China fever," seemed to prevail in both popular and elite opinion, opinion in ASEAN and among its member states was somewhat more guarded and calculating. Government officials and nongovernment specialists clearly saw Southeast Asian interests well served by growing cooperation with China, but they reserved judgment about the possible future directions and other consequences of Chinese policies and behavior and their potentially negative implications for Southeast Asia.

Officials and nongovernment specialists in Southeast Asia had a long list of positive accomplishments, benefits, and other features of China's recent approach to Southeast Asia. Many stressed how far China's image had changed from the 1960s when China was the source of a "communist threat" in supporting insurgencies in Southeast Asia, and the 1970s when China posed a "war threat" to Southeast Asia given China's military offensive against Vietnam. China now had a much more benign image that it had developed among ASEAN members in recent years.

China's growing economy was providing significant trade surpluses for most ASEAN members. China-ASEAN trade of $78 billion in 2003 saw ASEAN register a trade surplus of $16 billion; Malaysia, Thailand, and the Philippines saw their respective exports to China in 2003 to be more than double the value of their imports from China. This beneficial trade relationship reduced at least for a time concerns in ASEAN economies about the ability of Southeast Asian producers to compete with increasingly competitive Chinese producers for Asian and world markets.

Southeast Asian officials and nongovernment specialists repeatedly emphasized the dramatic change in Chinese diplomacy in the region. China's flexible, moderate, and accommodating approach was most welcomed by Southeast Asia. It showed, in the view of Southeast Asian observers, that China "had learned to play the game" of carefully nuanced and attentive diplomacy in order to win favor in the region. Specific examples of such diplomacy included Chinese officials avoiding the placing of conditions regarding good Chinese relations with Southeast Asian states—a perceived contrast to the United States and others in the West stressing human rights and democracy as influencing Western diplomacy and policy toward Southeast Asia. China, of course, did insist on Southeast Asian governments strictly adhering to the "one China" principle and shunning all official ties with Taiwan.

Meanwhile, Chinese officials were said to make few demands of Southeast Asian counterparts as they endeavored to develop common ground and put aside differences in a Chinese strategy emphasizing common geoeconomic interests with the ASEAN states. Asian governments were said to be especially welcoming international relationships that enhanced their nation's development and nation-building efforts. In contrast, the United States was seen pursuing a geostrategic approach that forced ASEAN states to take actions that they were not necessarily inclined to do, notably in the war on terrorism.

An effect of such benign and attentive Chinese diplomacy was that Chinese "soft power" was seen as on the rise in Southeast Asia. This happened in contrast to a perceived decline in U.S. "soft power" in the region on account of perceived heavy-handed U.S. actions in the war on terrorism and the conflict in Iraq, and U.S. continued strong support for Israel against Palestinian interests. The rise of China's soft power also was said to have resulted in and been reflected by the rising prominence of ethnic Chinese communities in several Southeast Asian states, including Malaysia and Thailand. Even in Indonesia, where ethnic Chinese were subjected to great prejudice and repeated violence, the Chinese community was achieving greater prominence and in the process was asserting itself as a more pro-China force in the country. Meanwhile, there was an upsurge in the travel and migration of Chinese nationals to Southeast Asia as tourists, students, and businesspeople that was said to be welcomed by many in Southeast Asia, a further indication of the attractiveness of China and China's "soft power" to the people and officials of Southeast Asia.

The Chinese government was seen by Southeast Asian officials and nongovernment specialists as increasingly supportive of regional stability. Several officials and specialists pointed in particular to the more moderate Chinese approach toward the United States in Asian and world affairs, evident in Chinese commentary since 2001 and underlined by China's recent emphasis on "peaceful rise." Such flexibility and moderation served to reassure Southeast Asian officials and commentators that ASEAN states would not be forced to choose or take sides between the United States and China—a choice the Southeast Asian governments were loath to make. It also improved the likelihood of U.S.-China cooperation in Asian affairs—a key goal of ASEAN members.

Other factors influencing positive trends in Southeast Asia's more positive view of China included geography. China's size and location meant that it would always be a reality Southeast Asia would have to deal with. The recent positive trends in Chinese policies and behavior encouraged ASEAN officials, who saw a big opportunity to deepen engagement of China in regional and international relationships that would incrementally see China conform to international norms that would secure ASEAN interests. The ASEAN officials advised that China was now a central player in all salient Asian issues. The long-term ASEAN effort to engage China required careful handling by Southeast Asian leaders, among others. ASEAN was in no position to confront or resist rising Chinese power and influence, and hoped to turn China's greater cooperation into arrangements and assurances that would preserve ASEAN interests in a stable and peaceful regional order.

Southeast Asian officials vividly remembered the tension and confrontations with China in the past. To avoid this situation being repeated, they tried to persuade the United States and Japan to work cooperatively with rising China. Several in Southeast Asia were optimistic that China would continue along its recent moderate path so long as China was not provoked or confronted with outside pressures. The imperatives of China's moderate approach were said to lie within China, in the many problems and issues in Chinese development. To sustain stability and strong economic growth required China to modify its foreign posture and avoid outside conflicts and entanglements.

Among the few issues that could derail this course of moderation in Chinese policy was Taiwan. Southeast Asian officials and nongovernment specialists took strong exception with Taiwan's greater assertiveness against the Chinese mainland. They foresaw that Taiwan's actions would precipitate a crisis and military confrontation in the Taiwan Strait that would involve the United States as well as China and Taiwan. They argued this would be a disaster for ASEAN and Southeast Asian interests. They pressured Taiwan to halt its perceived provocations, while seemingly siding with Beijing in strongly reaffirming adherence to a one-China policy.

The closer ASEAN/Southeast relationship with China also served ASEAN/Southeast Asian interests by encouraging other powers to pay more attention to the region and its governments. China's growing role elicited a kind of rivalry among other powers, including Japan, the United States, and India; ASEAN welcomed these states' increased interest in ASEAN and Southeast Asia prompted by Chinese activism in Southeast Asia. Thus, the Chinese-ASEAN Free Trade Agreement prompted a variety of free trade arrangements from Japan, the United States, and other powers. China signing the ASEAN security treaty prompted India and Japan, among others, to sign the treaty.

While tending to highlight the positives in China-Southeast Asian relations, Southeast Asian and also Chinese officials and nongovernment specialists also were attentive to differences, potential problems, and/or other real or possible negative implications and features of China's rising influence in Southeast Asia. As noted above, these received much less overt attention than in the past, but they were raised regularly, even in discussions that tended to focus on the positive aspects of China-ASEAN relations. The comments made clear that the two sides were approaching each other in calculated ways, less influenced by sentiment and more influenced by perceptions of interests.

Southeast Asian officials and nongovernment specialists saw differences in their reaction to China's recent forthcoming approach to Asia to that of South Korea. The extent of the China fever in Southeast Asia was more limited, while the need of ASEAN and the respective Southeast Asian governments to maneuver and hedge in order to deal with rising China was strongly seen. The Southeast Asian governments and ASEAN sought balance among the larger powers involved in Southeast Asia. They endeavored to encourage close ties with the United States, Japan, India, Russia, and Australia. They recognized that the United States represented the largest outside counterweight to China, but sought a more diversified range of contacts in order to avoid a situation of having to choose between the United States and China.

According to Southeast Asian officials and nongovernment specialists, Southeast Asian governments varied in their approach to China, with the Philippines and Indonesia being more reserved, and Thailand, Malaysia, and Singapore in the lead of those seeking close ties with China. A recent manifestation was Singapore's agreement to recognize China as a market economy, a step seen as likely to prompt others in ASEAN to do the same in order to keep pace in relations with China. Of course, Singapore at the same time concluded recent free trade agreements with the United States and Japan. According to some nongovernment specialists, there also was a long-standing distinction between the way continental Southeast Asian states dealt with China, versus the approach of maritime states of Southeast Asia. The former had to be more sensitive and generally deferential to Chinese concerns given China's proximity and easy access, while the latter were more free to follow policies either favorable or not to China.

In the burgeoning economic relationship, Chinese specialists were seen to echo the concerns of many Southeast Asian counterparts about the competitive as well as collaborative aspects of the China economic relationship with Southeast Asian countries. They admitted that China and ASEAN sought to export the same kinds of goods to the same international markets; and both sides competed intensely for investments from the same sources of foreign direct investment.

Some Southeast Asian officials and specialists also judged that measuring the growth of Chinese influence in and importance for Southeast Asia was inexact. They agreed that Chinese influence was hard to gauge when Chinese officials generally did not ask ASEAN governments to do things they did not want to do. In effect, they judged, China had focused on doing "easy things," emphasizing common ground and working especially with and within the ASEAN organizations where decisions become less sensitive in long processes of consultations that lead to often vapid final outcomes. Some Southeast Asian officials and nongovernment specialists made rough comparison with the rise of Chinese influence in Southeast Asia in recent years and the rise of Japan's influence in Southeast Asia in the 1980s. They judged that Japan's influence relative to other powers (e.g., the United States, Soviet Union, China) in Southeast Asia in the 1980s was greater than China's influence relative to other powers in Southeast Asia today.

These Southeast Asian observers also felt that the importance of Chinese trade with ASEAN was of growing significance, but still amounted to considerably less than ASEAN trade with the United States and Japan. The latter two powers also were the source of many times more investment and assistance to Southeast Asia than provided by China, according to these observers. Now that the U.S. and Japanese economies were on the rebound, it was judged that their importance for ASEAN would grow accordingly.

The most pervasive concern voiced by Southeast Asian officials and nongovernment specialists had to do with the future role of China in Asia. The recent trajectory of Chinese policies and behavior was seen as broadly positive. Given uncertainties about developments in China, past Chinese assertiveness in Southeast Asia, and the record of other states flexing their muscles seeking narrow national interests as they became stronger, officials and observers in Southeast Asia were cautious in predicting that China's recent peaceful and moderate approach would last. Many foresaw the possibility of China adopting a more interventionist stance, a "big brother" approach, toward relatively weak neighbors to the South. Some saw a glimpse of this kind of behavior in China's intervention in a Thai-Cambodia dispute the previous year, an intervention that was said to have raised concerns among many in

Southeast Asia about how China would behave in dealing with ASEAN states and their issues in the future.

Notes

1. Brantly Womack, "China and Southeast Asia: Asymmetry, Leadership and Normalcy," *Pacific Affairs* 76, no. 3 (Winter 2003-2004): 529-48; Joseph Y. S. Cheung, "Sino-ASEAN Relations in the Early 21st Century," *Contemporary Southeast Asia* 23, no. 3 (December 2001): 420-52; Alice Ba, "China and ASEAN: Renavigating Relations for the 21st Century," *Asian Survey* 43, no. 4 (July-August 2003): 622-47; Carlyle Thayer, "China's 'New Security Concept' and Southeast Asia," in David Lovell, ed., *Asia-Pacific Security: Policy Challenges* (Singapore: Institute of Southeast Asian Studies, 2003), 89-107; John Wong and Sarah Chan, "China-ASEAN Free Trade Agreement," *Asian Survey* 43, no. 3 (May-June 2003): 507-26; Catherin Dalpino and Juo-yu Lin, "China and Southeast Asia," in Richard Bush and Catherin Dalpino, eds., *Brookings Northeast Asia Survey 2002-2003* (Washington, D.C.: Brookings Institution, 2003), 77-90; *China and Southeast Asia*, Stanley Foundation Policy Bulletin, October 16-18, 2003; Denny Roy, *China and Southeast Asia*, Honolulu: Asia-Pacific Center for Security Studies, 1, no. 4 (November 2002): 1-4; Richard Sokolsky, Angel Rabasa, C. R. Neu, *The Role of Southeast Asia in U.S. Strategy toward China* (Santa Monica, Calif.: Rand Corporation, 2000); Rosemary Foot, "China and the ASEAN Regional Forum," *Asian Survey* 38, no. 5 (1998): 425-40; Ho Khai Leong, "Rituals, Risks and Rivalries: China and ASEAN in the Coming Decades," *Journal of Contemporary China* 10, no. 29 (November 2001): 683-94; John Pomfret, "In Its Own Neighborhood, China Emerges as a Leader," *Washington Post,* 18 October 2001; Kenneth Allen, "China's Foreign Military Relations With Asia-Pacific," *Journal of Contemporary China* 10, no. 29 (November 2001): 645-62; Michael Richardson, "Seeking Allies in Terror War, U.S. Woos Southeast Asia," *International Herald Tribune*, 29 November 2001; Lee Lai To, "The Lion and the Dragon," *Journal of Contemporary China* 10, no. 28 (August 2001): 415-26; articles by Michael Leifer, Yuen Foong Khong, and Amitav Acharga in Alastair Iain Johnston and Robert Ross, eds., *Engaging China* (London: Routledge, 1999), 87-151; Ian James Storey, "Living with the Colossus: How Southeast Asian Countries Cope with China," *Parameters* (Winter 1999-2000): 111-25; Koong Pai Ching, *Southeast Asian Countries Perceptions of China's Military Modernization* (Washington, D.C.: George Washington University Sigur Center for Asian Studies, 1999); "China's Policy in the South China Sea," *Liaowang Dongfang Weekly*, 12 January 2004, www.newsxinhuanet.com/mil/2004-01/12/content_1270457.htm (accessed 20 January 2004); Chung Chien-peng, "China's Engagement with Southeast Asia After the Leadership Transition: A Counter-hedging Strategy?" *EAI Working Paper* 86 (Singapore: National University of Singapore, 9 May 2002); Wang Gungwu, "China and Southeast Asia: Myths, Threat, and Culture," *EAI Occasional Paper* 13 (Singapore: National University of Singapore, 1999); John Wong, "The Rise of China: Challenges for the ASEAN Economies," in John Wong and Zheng Yongnian, eds., *China's Post-Jiang Leadership Succession* (Singapore: Singapore University Press, 2003), chapter 14; Carl Baker, "China-Philippine Relations," in *Asia's Bilateral Relations* (Honolulu: Asia-Pacific Center for Security Studies, 2004).

2. Jiang Zemin, "Speech at East Asian Summit," *Xinhua*, 15 December 1997, carried by Foreign Broadcast Information Service (FBIS) (Internet version).

3. "China Says Actively Funding IMF Indonesia Plan," *Reuters,* 17 March 1998 (Internet version); "News Analysis Views ASEAN Challenges," *Xinhua,* 21 July 1998, carried by FBIS (Internet version); "Kyodo Reports on PRC Media Coverage of Indonesia Crisis," Kyodo, 22 May 1998, carried by FBIS (Internet version).

4. *China-Southeast Asia Relations: Trends, Issues, and Implications for the United States* (Washington, D.C.: Library of Congress), Congressional Research Service (CRS), Report 97-553F, 20 May 1997.

5. Robert Sutter, *Chinese Policy Priorities and Their Implications for the United States* (Lanham, Md.: Rowman & Littlefield, 2000), 114; *China-Southeast Asia Relations*, CRS Report 97-553F, 20 May 1997; Joseph Y. S. Cheung, "Sino-ASEAN Relations in the 1990s," *Contemporary Southeast Asia* 21, no. 2 (August 1999): 176-202.

6. Ba, "China and ASEAN," *Asian Survey*, 632.

7. Nayan Chanda, "China and Cambodia," *Asia-Pacific Review* 9, no. 2 (2002): 1-11; Sophie Richardson "Sino-Cambodian Relations: Trends and Prospects," a paper presented to a conference, Washington, D.C., 1 June 2001; Sutter, *Chinese Policy Priorities*, 114-15; Wayne Bert, *The United States, China, and Southeast Asian Security* (London: Palgrave, 2003), chapter on Burma.

8. On Southeast Asian maneuvers among powers in the region, see the chapters on Southeast Asia in *Asia's China Debate* (Honolulu: Asia-Pacific Center for Security Studies, December 2003); chapters on Southeast Asia in Herbert Yee and Ian James Storey, *The China Threat: Perceptions, Myths, and Reality* (London: Routledge 2002); Roy, *China and Southeast Asia.*

9. Roy, *China and Southeast Asia*, 4.

10. Ba, "China and ASEAN," *Asian Survey*, 633; Roy, *China and Southeast Asia.*

11. Ba, "China and ASEAN," *Asian Survey*, 634, 638; Robert Sutter, "China's Recent Approach to Asia: Seeking Long-term Gains," *NBR Analysis* 13, no. 1 (March 2002): 22-23.

12. David Finkelstein, *China's New Security Concept* (Alexandria, Va.: The CNA Corporation, April 1999); Roy, *China and Southeast Asia.*

13. Carlyle Thayer, "Regional Rivalries and Bilateral Irritants," *Comparative Connections*, www.csis.org/pacfor (accessed 1 June 2001); Lyall Breckon, "Focus Is Elsewhere but Bonds Continue to Grow," *Comparative Connections*, April 2003.

14. Yoichi Funabashi, "New Geopolitics Rages Over Various Parts of Asia," *Asahi Shimbun*, 15 January 2002; Tian Peiliang, "Nationalism: China and Japan," *Foreign Affairs Journal*, Beijing: Chinese People's Institute of Foreign Affairs, no. 63 (March 2002): 63-83; David Fouse, "Japan's China Debate," in *Asia's China Debate* (Honolulu: Asia Pacific Center for Security Studies), December 2003; Yong Deng, "Chinese Relations with Japan," *Pacific Affairs* 70, no. 3 (Autumn 1997): 379; Michael Armacost and Kenneth Pyle, "Japan and the Engagement of China"(Seattle, Wash.: National Bureau of Asian Research), *NBR Analysis* 12, no. 5 (2001); Joseph Y. S. Cheng, "Sino-Japanese Relations in the 21st Century," *Journal of Contemporary Asia* 33, no. 2 (2003): 268; Wu Xinbo, "The Security Dimension of Sino-Japanese Relations," *Asian Survey* 40, no. 2 (March-April 2000): 301; Denny Roy, *Stirring Samurai, Disapproving Dragon* (Honolulu: Asia Pacific Center for Security Studies, September 2003); "Noted Scholar Discusses 'New Thinking' in Sino-Japanese Relations," Beijing *Renmin Wang*, 1 January 2004 (Internet version); Liu Xiaobiao, "Where Are Sino-Japanese Relations Heading?" Beijing *Renmin Wang*, 13 August 2003 (Internet version). For background on these issues, see Sutter, *Chinese Policy Priorities*, 79-98.

15. Lyall Breckon, "Beijing Pushes 'Asia for Asians,'" *Comparative Connections*, October 2002.

206Chapter 7

16. Robert Sutter, "China's Regional Strategy," a paper presented to a conference at the George Washington University, Washington, D.C., 5 December 2003, 14. See also "U.S. Studying Possibility of Reestablishing Military Bases in Philippines," *Xinhua*, 15 August 2003; Hou Songling and Chi Diantang, "Southeast Asia and Central Asia: China's Geostrategic Options in the New Century," (Beijing) *Dangdai Yatai* no. 4 (15 April 2003): 9-15.

17. Thayer, "Regional Rivalries," *Comparative Connections*; Breckon, "Focus Is Elsewhere," *Comparative Connections*.

18. Sutter, *Chinese Policy Priorities*, 129; *China-Southeast Asia Relations*, CRS Report 97-553F, 3-6.

19. John Wong and Sarah Chan, "China-ASEAN Free Trade Agreement," *Asian Survey* 43, no. 3 (May-June 2003): 512; Dalpino and Juo-yu Lin, "China and Southeast Asia," *Brookings Northeast Asia Survey 2002-2003*, 82.

20. Figures from China's General Administration of Customs, cited in Shen Danyang, "ASEAN-China FTA" a paper presented to a conference in Singapore, 23 June 2004.

21. John Wong and Sarah Chan, "China-ASEAN Free Trade Agreement," *Asian Survey* 43, no. 3 (May-June 2003): 514.

22. Lyall Breckon, "China Caps a Year of Gains," *Comparative Connections*, January 2003.

23. Breckon, "SARS and a New Security Initiative From China," *Comparative Connections*, July 2003.

24. Wong and Chan, "China-ASEAN Free Trade Agreement," 517.

25. Wong and Chan, "China-ASEAN Free Trade Agreement," 519.

26. Robert Sutter, "Why China Matters," *Washington Quarterly* 27, no. 1 (Winter 2003-2004): 77-80.

27. China's Ministry of Commerce, cited in Shen Danyang, "ASEAN-China FTA," paper presented to a conference, Singapore, 23 June 2004.

28. Sutter, *Chinese Policy Priorities*, 115; "China-ASEAN Trade Volume Increases 45.3 Percent," *Xinhua*, 18 August 2003 (Internet version).

29. Eric Teo Chu Cheow, "A Southeast Asian Perspective on Cross-strait Relations," a paper presented to a conference at the East Asian Institute, National University of Singapore, June 21, 2004.

30. Eric Teo Chu Cheow, "A Southeast Asian Perspective on Cross-strait Relations."

31. Wong and Chan, "China-ASEAN Free Trade Agreement," 519.

32. Dalpino and Juo-yu Lin, "China and Southeast Asia," *Brookings Northeast Asia Survey 2002-2003*, 83.

33. Sutter, *Chinese Policy Priorities*, 115.

34. Sutter, *Chinese Policy Priorities*, 115.

35. "Text of Sino-Thai Joint Statement," *Xinhua*, 5 February 1999 (Internet version); Thayer, "China's 'New Security Concept,'" *Asia-Pacific Security: Policy Challenges*, 94.

36. Sutter, *Chinese Policy Priorities*, 116.

37. "PRC Expands Cooperation with ASEAN," *Xinhua*, 4 January 1998, carried by FBIS (Internet version).

38. *Declaration on the Conduct of Parties in the South China Sea*, November 2002, www.aseansec.org (accessed 15 December 2002); Breckon, "China Caps a Year of Gains," *Comparative Connections*.

39. "China Concerned Over Unilateral Oil Bidding in Disputed Waters," *Xinhua*, 20 January 2004 (Internet version).

40. Breckon, "China Caps a Year of Gains," *Comparative Connections*.

41. Zhang Xizhen, "Treaty Develops Relations with ASEAN," *China Daily*, 8 September 2003; Lyall Breckon, "SARS and a New Security Initiative From China," *Comparative Connections*, July 2003.

42. Sutter, "China's Regional Strategy," paper presented to a conference at The George Washington University, Washington, D.C., December 5, 2003, 14.

43. Lyall Breckon, "On the Inside Track," *Comparative Connections*, October 2003.

44. Breckon, "Focus Is Elsewhere," *Comparative Connections*.

45. Sutter, *Chinese Policy Priorities*, 116.

46. Carlyle Thayer, "ASEAN Ten Plus Three: An Evolving East Asian Community," *Comparative Connections*, January 2001.

47. Thayer, "ASEAN Ten Plus Three," *Comparative Connections*.

48. Lyall Breckon, "Gains for Beijing in an Otherwise Gloomy Quarter," *Comparative Connections*, January 2002.

49. Breckon, "Courtship and Competition," *Comparative Connections*, April 2002.

50. Carlyle Thayer, "China's 'New Security Concept' and ASEAN," *Comparative Connections*, October 2000.

51. Breckon, "Gains for Beijing," *Comparative Connections*.

52. Breckon, "Courtship and Competition," *Comparative Connections*.

53. Sutter, *Chinese Policy Priorities*, 116, 146, 150; "ASEAN Meetings Accomplish Results," *China Daily*, 21-23 June 2003, 1.

54. Sutter, *Chinese Policy Priorities*, 116.

55. Ba, "China and ASEAN," *Asian Survey*, 634-38.

56. Ba, "China and ASEAN," *Asian Survey*, 636; Lyall Breckon, "Inside Track," *Comparative Connections*.

57. Robert Marquand, "China Gains on Japan in Age-old Rivalry for Asian Influence," *Christian Science Monitor*, 29 October 2003, 1.

58. Ba, "China and ASEAN," *Asian Survey*, 638-44.

59. Lyall Breckon, "Former Tigers under Dragon's Spell," *Comparative Connections*, July 2002.

60. Breckon, "Tigers under Dragon's Spell," *Comparative Connections*.

61. Roy, *China and Southeast Asia*.

62. Jusuf Wanandi, *Southeast Asia-China Relations* (Taipei: Chinese Council of Advanced Policy Studies, December 1996): 6-10.

63. *Southeast Asian Security* (Washington, D.C.: Library of Congress), Congressional Research Service, Report 95-927S, 1 August 1995, 2-3.

64. Wanandi, *Southeast Asia-China Relations*, 7-8.

65. ASEAN states also modernized their own military forces and promoted military interaction with other powers, including New Zealand and Great Britain. See *Far Eastern Economic Review*, 24 April 1997. See also *China as a Security Concern in Asia* (Washington, D.C.: Library of Congress), Congressional Research Service, Report 95-46S, 22 December 1994.

66. Roy, *China and Southeast Asia*; Cindy Sui, "China Proposes New Asia Pacific Security Forum in Subtle Poke at U.S.," Hong Kong *AFP*, 18 June 2003; Breckon, "SARS and New Security Initiative for China," *Comparative Connections*; Breckon, "Courtship and Competition," *Comparative Connections*; Breckon, "Tigers under the Dragon's Spell," *Comparative Connections*; Carlyle Thayer, "Developing Multilateral Cooperation," *Comparative Connections*, October 2001; Thayer, "China's 'New Security Concept' and ASEAN."

67. Sutter, *Chinese Policy Priorities*, 119.

68. Dalpino and Juo-yu Lin, "China and Southeast Asia," *Brookings Northeast Asia Survey 2002-2003*, 82-84.

69. Sutter, *Chinese Policy Priorities*, 119.

70. Womack, "China and Southeast Asia," *Pacific Affairs*, 535.

71. Sutter, *Chinese Policy Priorities*, 119; Eddie Leung, "Southeast Asia: Threats, Opportunities," *Asia Times*, 2 August 2003 (Internet version).

72. Wong and Chan, "China-ASEAN Free Trade Agreement," *Asian Survey*, 507.

73. Dalpino and Juo-yu Lin, "China and Southeast Asia," *Brookings Northeast Asia Survey 2002-2003*, 80-82.

74. *China-Southeast Asia Relations*, CRS Report 97-553F, 20 May 1997.

75. Dalpino and Juo-yu Lin, "China and Southeast Asia," *Brookings Northeast Asia Survey 2002-2003*, 81.

76. Roy, *China and Southeast Asia*, 2-3.

77. Sutter, *Chinese Policy Priorities*, 120-21; Roy, *China and Southeast Asia*, 2-3; Hu Qihua, "Officials Trade Logistics Views," *China Daily*, 26 September 2002 (Internet version).

78. Maureen Aung-Thwin, "Burma," in William Carpenter, ed., *Asian Security Handbook 2000* (Armonk N.Y.: M. E. Sharpe, 2000), 146-53; Allen Clark, "Burma in 2002," *Asian Survey* 43, no. 1 (January-February 2003): 127-34.

79. Sutter, *Chinese Policy Priorities*, 121.

80. Clark, "Burma in 2002," 127-34.

81. *Cambodia in Crisis* (Washington, D.C.: Library of Congress), CRS Issue Brief 98036, 15 May 1999; Chanda, "China and Cambodia," *Asia-Pacific Review*, 1-11.

82. *Cambodia in Crisis*, CRS Issue Brief 98036; "PRC, Cambodia Sign Five Agreements," *Xinhua*, 26 July 1998, carried by FBIS (Internet version); "News Analysis Views Cambodia Election," *Xinhua*, 27 July 1998, carried by FBIS (Internet version).

83. Sutter, *Chinese Policy Priorities*, 122.

84. *Taiwan: Recent Developments and U.S. Policy Choices* (Washington, D.C.: Library of Congress), CRS Issue Brief 98034, 15 May 1999.

85. Wanandi, *Southeast Asia-China Relations*, 20-21.

86. Sutter, *Chinese Policy Priorities*, 123.

87. Breckon, "Focus Is Elsewhere," *Comparative Connections*.

88. Breckon, "China Caps a Year of Gains," *Comparative Connections*.

89. Thayer, "Regional Rivalries and Bilateral Irritants," *Comparative Connections*.

90. "China Says Indonesia's Ethnic Riots Internal Issue," *Reuters*, 13 April 1998; "China Pledges to Help Indonesia Overcome Financial Crisis," *Associated Press*, 12 April 1998; "Suharto Meets PRC Foreign Minister," *Jakarta Radio*, 13 April 1998, carried by FBIS (Internet version).

91. "Chinese Media Asked to Play Down Indonesia Riots," Hong Kong *Ming Pao*, 16 May 1998, A15; Sutter, *Chinese Policy Priorities*, 123-24.

92. Dalpino and Juo-yu Lin, "China and Southeast Asia," *Brookings Northeast Asia Survey 2002-2003*, 86-89; Tin Maung Maung Than, "Burma/Myanmar in 2001," *Asian Survey* 42, no. 1 (January-February 2002): 120-21.

93. In particular, the author held discussions with thirty government officials and nongovernment specialists in Singapore, June 21-24, 2004, and he benefited from the deliberations of the conference "ASEAN-China Forum 2004: Developing ASEAN-China Relations, Realities and Prospects" (Institute of Southeast Asian Studies, Singapore), June 23-24, 2004.

Chapter 8

Relations with Taiwan

Overview

In important respects, relations with Taiwan were an exception to the overall positive Chinese approach to surrounding governments. Chinese officials moderated their approach to surrounding areas in the 1990s, eventually extending by the early 2000s a moderate and accommodating approach to the United States, Japan, and other targets of previously harsh Chinese invective. Chinese officials and media recognized that harsh Chinese rhetoric regarding the "Taiwan issue" often worked against Chinese interests in conveying a good regional image and encouraging cross-strait ties. Nevertheless, the Chinese government was ruthless in applying diplomatic and other pressures to isolate Taiwan internationally; and it was unmoved by Taiwan, U.S., and other complaints regarding the increased tempo and scope of the Chinese military buildup opposite Taiwan.[1]

There were few signs of significant differences among Chinese leaders regarding policy toward Taiwan. Chinese leaders were at pains to balance the "sticks" of diplomatic and military pressure with "carrots" involving mutually beneficial cross-strait economic ties. The opportunities for trade and investment in the burgeoning Chinese mainland market proved irresistible to Taiwan entrepreneurs. Even the Democratic Progressive Party (DPP) leader with strong leanings toward Taiwan independence, Chen Shui-bian, shifted to a stance accommodating ever greater economic interchange with the Chinese mainland soon after his election as Taiwan's President in 2000.[2]

This positive interlude in cross-strait relations proved short-lived. Seeking reelection in a tight presidential election in March 2004, President Chen in 2003 shifted the terms of debate in Taiwan. This was partly in order to mobilize DDP supporters unhappy with his accommodating approach to trade, investment, and other interchange with mainland China, and partly to divert public attention away from the meager accomplishments of his first term in office. It also served to strengthen Taiwan's independence from China. In late 2003, the Chen administration outlined steps that would lead to a new constitution for Taiwan in the second term of the Chen government that would be ratified by a national referendum and would transform Taiwan into a "normal, complete, and great" country. The move was an unmistakable reminder for Beijing and others that the DPP for years had called for a referendum to determine whether or not the Taiwan people wanted to be independent of China—a stance consistently condemned by Beijing as a cause of war.[3]

Chen's maneuvers were well received in Taiwan in part because of deep Taiwan resentment over China's continued hard treatment of Taiwan. Notably, Beijing mishandled the SARS epidemic for months in early 2003, resulting in widespread infections in Taiwan that severely hurt Taiwan's efforts to recover from its most serious economic recession in fifty years. The SARS issue quickly involved the World Health Organization, an international organization where Taiwan for years had been seeking some form of representation but had been blocked at every corner by Chinese diplomats. At the height of the SARS epidemic, WHO specialists were eventually allowed to travel to Taiwan, but Chinese officials were blunt and dismissive of Taiwan's efforts to achieve any sort of formal interaction with the world body. The effect on Taiwan public opinion was unmistakably negative.[4]

Before taking on the issue of a new constitution, President Chen in mid-2003 called for a national referendum on Taiwan's representation in the WHO. Opposition from the Legislature controlled by his opponents eventually left President Chen with the sole option of calling a "defensive referendum" when the country faced a threat to sovereignty; in late 2003 he decided to pursue the option and focus that referendum on the Chinese missile buildup opposite Taiwan—the other main "stick" in the PRC repertoire of pressure and leverage against Taiwan in recent years.[5]

Alarmed by the Taiwan leader's repeated moves toward greater political separatism and independence despite growing cross-strait economic integration, PRC leaders nonetheless were loath to repeat the stern warnings and military exercises they used with poor results in trying to dissuade Taiwan voters in 1996 and 2000. In these circumstances Chinese leaders gave more attention to pressing the United States to take actions that would curb moves toward Taiwan independence. U.S. leaders were also alarmed by rising tensions in the strait and President Bush in December 2003 publicly rebuked Chen for disrupting the status quo.[6]

President Chen won reelection in a very close race in March 2004. He promised in his May 20, 2004 inauguration address to pursue a more moderate approach that would heal deep internal divisions in Taiwan, ease tensions with Beijing, and reassure the United States of Taiwan's continued support.[7] Taiwan officials were optimistic that the president would effectively implement these approaches, but seasoned observers in Taiwan had grave doubts. Beijing also remained deeply suspicious of Chen and his supporters. It was disinclined to make positive overtures to the Taiwan president, and it stepped up pressure on the United States to curb pro-independence moves by Taiwan. The Chen administration as well as Beijing and Washington focused on the lead-up to the important legislative elections in Taiwan in December 2004. If President Chen and his allies, as anticipated by many, were able to end the political opposition's control of the legislature, President's Chen's stature and power in Taiwan would grow substantially, presumably affecting China's considerations regarding policy toward Taiwan.

China and the Taiwan "Issue" under Lee Teng-hui

China's search for a stable and peaceful international environment prompted Chinese efforts to smooth over differences and emphasize common ground, especially with China's neighbors and major trading partners. This was broadly successful with most major powers and regional countries, but it never worked well with Taiwan. In part this was because the Taiwan government was not prepared to accept the PRC terms for establishing improved relations, especially demands that Taipei adhere to a "one-China" policy as defined by Beijing. And in part this was because Beijing was not nearly as accommodating with Taiwan as it was with other entities with which it has disputes.[8]

The so-called Taiwan issue enjoyed a unique status in Chinese foreign policy priorities in the 1990s.[9] Chinese leaders were unprepared for the rising sentiment in favor of greater separation from the mainland and a more prominent and distinctive role for Taiwan in world affairs that emerged with greater democracy on the island after the end of martial law in 1987. At first, Chinese leaders judged that the concurrent growth in cross-strait trade and other exchanges would hold these Taiwanese sentiments in check; but gradually they became deeply concerned about a perceived movement toward political independence, and deeply suspicious not only of avowed pro-independence activists in the then opposition Democratic Progressive Party but also of the president and chairman of the ruling Nationalist Party, Lee Teng-hui. China's concern reached fever pitch after Lee developed his successful flexible diplomacy in visiting countries that maintained official relations with the PRC and notably gained entry to the United States, ostensibly to visit his alma mater, Cornell University, in 1995.[10]

Beijing saw the Clinton administration's reversal of policy—first denying Lee a visa and then granting him one amid broad media and congressional pressure—as a major setback in Chinese foreign policy. President Jiang Zemin, Foreign Minister Qian Qichen, and others had to defend their handling of the issue in the face of strong criticism from other leaders. Not surprisingly, PRC policy hardened. On the one hand, China resorted to provocative military exercises designed to intimidate the people of Taiwan and their international supporters prior to important legislative and presidential elections on the island in December 1995 and March 1996, respectively. The military actions cowed Taiwan for a few months, though the United States eventually sent two carrier battle groups to observe PRC exercises—a sign that boosted Taiwan's morale and underlined for Beijing the potentially dangerous consequences of provocative military action against Taiwan. In the end, the crisis improved Lee Teng-hui's margin of victory in the 1996 Taiwan presidential election. On the other hand, Beijing further intensified its foreign policy efforts to isolate Taiwan, striving by this means to push Taiwan away from pursuing its independent posture in world affairs and, over the longer term, to prompt Taiwan to accept cross-strait talks on reunification on terms acceptable to Beijing. As the United States and other powers sought improved relations with China in the mid-1990s, reducing Taiwan's diplomatic stature was the most important issue of immediate concern to Chinese foreign policy makers.[11]

Well aware that Beijing's continued difficult domestic priorities meant that mainland China was unlikely to take rash assertive action against Taiwan, unless provoked, Taiwan leaders gave tit-for-tat in international competition with Beijing. Mainland Chinese leaders had expected that President Jiang Zemin's summit meeting with President Clinton in Washington in October 1997 would provide a springboard for Chinese public relations and international efforts to underscore Taiwan's vulnerability and isolation. Though Taiwan reacted to the summit with a calm visage, Taiwan's leadership was concerned that improved U.S.-PRC relations would come at Taiwan's expense. The Taiwan officials also had seen mainland China win away South Africa from recognizing Taiwan; South Africa was the last major state to maintain official diplomatic relations with Taiwan. Beijing was using aid, diplomatic pressure, and other means to whittle away Taiwan's shrinking band of diplomatic allies. Thus, China used its veto power to bar UN peacekeepers from Haiti until the government there modified its traditionally strong support for Taiwan.[12]

As the scope of the Asian economic crisis of 1997-1998 began to affect a wide range of Southeast Asia states, Taiwan government leaders jumped into action to improve Taiwan's diplomatic profile with high-level interchanges with Southeast Asian officials. Senior Singaporean, Malaysian, and other officials stopped briefly in Taipei for talks with senior Taiwan leaders. Taiwan loomed large in their economic calculus given its relatively strong economy, its large investment role in Southeast Asia, and its entrepreneurial middle class with many billions of dollars of foreign exchange reserves. Early in 1998, Taiwanese delegations led by the vice president, the premier, senior economic ministers, and even President Lee Teng-hui's wife traveled to Singapore, the Philippines, Thailand, and Japan for discussions on the Asian crisis. Taiwan officials from Lee Teng-hui on down also repeatedly warned of the danger of a possible devaluation of China's currency, urging Taiwanese investors to seek trade and investment opportunities in "safer" areas than mainland China.[13]

Not wishing to upset relations with Asian countries seeking financial help, the PRC at first adopted a low-key response to Taiwan's maneuvers, but senior leaders leveled increasingly tough warnings later in 1998. They harshly criticized Taiwan's motives; they castigated Taiwan for deliberately exacerbating the crisis by devaluing its currency in 1997 and spreading "rumors" about a Chinese devaluation in an effort to destabilize the Hong Kong and PRC economies and provide an opening for Taiwan diplomacy. Alluding to the possible United States support for a prominent Taiwan role in international efforts to relieve the Asian crisis, they reminded the United States of the primacy of the Taiwan issue in U.S.-China relations, calling for vigilance against Taiwan's efforts to make political gains during a period of financial turmoil.[14]

Beijing continued its pressure to isolate Taiwan further following South Africa's January 1, 1998, switch of official recognition from Taipei to Beijing. Despite preoccupation with the financial crisis, Beijing sent its Foreign Trade and Economics Minister to Fiji on January 15, 1998. Fiji had official relations with Beijing but maintained cordial unofficial ties with Taiwan. Fiji was a leader of the Pacific Island countries, four of which maintained official relations with Taiwan and supported Taiwan's role as a "special dialogue partner" with the South Pacific Forum, the main regional organization. The day before the Chinese minister arrived, Fiji television reported that Fiji's president had invited Lee Teng-hui to the island the next week.[15] Lee's visit, however, was postponed, presumably in deference to PRC sensibilities.

While the diplomatic guerilla war continued, neither side wanted to be seen, especially in Washington, as recalcitrant on cross-strait issues. The Clinton administration was anxious to see a reduction of tensions in the Taiwan Strait by reviving cross-strait talks that had been suspended as a result of Lee Teng-hui's visit to the United States in 1995. PRC and Taiwan leaders sought to improve cross-strait relations but on their own terms; they were also constrained by internal disagreements. Both sides viewed their competition in zero-sum terms, particularly with respect to U.S. support. Taiwan's effort to score political gains from the Asian financial crisis also soured the atmosphere. Little real progress was expected as formal high-level exchanges resumed in October 1998.[16]

Public statements during Chinese New Year in 1998 in Beijing and Taipei suggested that cross-strait shadowboxing was intended by both sides to prevent slippage rather than create a breakthrough. Former U.S. Defense Secretary William Perry reported to Taipei that Beijing was ready to resume talks between leaders of the respective cross-strait offices (Taiwan's Straits Exchange Foundation, SEF, and China's Association for Relations Across the Taiwan Strait, ARATS) from the point where they left off in 1995; Taipei indicated its receptivity. On the "one-China" sovereignty issue, both Taipei and Beijing were edging back toward the mid-1990s approach of setting aside differing interpretations to be dealt with later. Similarly, the issue of equality between parties—a Taiwan demand—could be bypassed for the time being by again using the quasi-official SEF/ARATS forum. China had insisted the next round be formal political negotiations on reunification; Taiwan wanted unofficial technical talks. Now both were saying unofficial talks could cover all issues: economic, administrative, and political.[17]

The give on both sides was minimal however, and intended mainly to gain time. A *People's Daily* editorial during the Chinese New Year period of 1998 repackaged old positions to project a leadership consensus on a peaceful settlement, but insisted Taipei must agree to eventual formal political negotiations, not merely to unofficial "preparatory" consultation. Similarly, Taiwan President Lee Teng-hui in a *Der*

Spiegel interview at the time reiterated his willingness to visit Beijing, but only as Republic of China (ROC) president. Beijing hoped that already planned low-level exchanges would build positive momentum. Not wanting to appear obstructionist, Taiwan went along but dragged its feet until it was in a stronger position.[18]

In the early 1990s, PRC leaders had appeared relatively confident of U.S. nonintervention in the Taiwan "issue" and concentrated on building relations with Taiwan political and economic leaders. This approach was based on Deng Xiaoping's premise that growing economic and cultural interdependence within a "greater China" (including Hong Kong as well as Taiwan) would provide a solid basis for staged reunification, beginning with unofficial technical talks and moving eventually to formal political negotiations. Beijing retained the option of using force as a hedge against independence. Lee Teng-hui's visit to the United States in 1995 undermined the PRC policy consensus and produced a more activist approach, using first military posturing and diplomacy aimed at checking separatist trends. The United States was again viewed as a major factor in the equation.

China's policy was to seek a negotiated agreement to end the civil war in accordance with the "one-China" principle. This assumed an activist strategy of confidence building with parallel pressure to end the U.S. commitment to Taiwan's security. In Beijing's thinking, U.S. distancing from Taiwan would weaken Taiwan's resistance to talks. This strategy did not allow for politically risky concessions to Taiwan's desire for an enhanced international stature. It did, however, include opening channels to other key constituencies on the island—in business, the military, and the political opposition—as well as continued planning and preparation for military contingencies.[19]

Lee Teng-hui's policy balanced efforts to upgrade Taiwan's international stature and defense capabilities with a go-slow approach to enhancing relations with the mainland. It began with confidence-building contacts by unofficial organizations and pointed vaguely toward closer, more official relations in the future. This gradualist approach reflected the strong popular desire in Taiwan to avoid early reunification without antagonizing China. In accordance with this strategy, Taiwan initiated the SEF/ARATS channel, which had conducted talks on and off since 1992. The principal officers of these organizations held formal talks in Singapore in 1993 and negotiated several practical cooperation measures. This was followed by staff negotiations and preparations for the next formal round of talks, scheduled for 1995 in Taipei. These talks were canceled by Beijing after Lee's U.S. visit. SEF/ARATS cultural exchanges continued however, and Taiwanese investments in mainland enterprises grew.[20]

U.S. initiatives to encourage both sides to resume talks were the main source of momentum in the late 1990s.[21] China wanted to take advantage of the high-profile U.S.-PRC summits of 1997 and 1998 to portray a common PRC-U.S. front. Taiwan feared lost leverage and realized the need to appear at least somewhat accommodating. Both sides focused on preventing a U.S. "tilt" toward the other; both worked hard to appear the more reasonable and aggrieved party. Beijing sought stronger U.S. pledges on Taiwan relations and arms sales. Taipei urged the United States to improve its relations with Taiwan in parallel with the warming of U.S.-PRC relations and emphasized the potential for instability in China as a strong rationale for caution.

Prior to President Clinton's trip to China in June 1998, agreement was reached to resume top-level SEF/ARATS contacts, albeit not formal negotiations. Beijing endeavored to turn to its advantage the U.S. president's affirmation in Shanghai on June 30, 1998, of the "three no's"—no support for two Chinas, one-China/one-Taiwan; no support for Taiwanese independence; no support for Taiwanese representation in international organizations where statehood is required. SEF/ARATS high-level contacts resumed with SEF leader Koo Chen-fun's October 1998 visit to Shanghai and Beijing, where, notably, he met with President Jiang. There was little substantive progress in cross-strait relations, however.[22]

Meanwhile, diplomatic skirmishing continued. The Taiwan prime minister visited Fiji and met with the Fijian prime minister in July 1998. In June 1998, the Taiwan foreign minister made a surprise visit to the Organization of African Unity meeting in western Africa, spoiling the first visit to the region by China's newly appointed foreign minister. In July 1998, Vice Premier Qian Qichen, who reportedly remained in charge of coordinating Chinese decision making on foreign affairs and Taiwan, led a delegation to five Caribbean countries with the aim of undercutting Taiwan. Qian retired as foreign minister in March 1998, but the Caribbean trip, the first he led abroad after his retirement, demonstrated the high priority the Beijing gave to combating Taiwan's flexible diplomacy, even among relatively small nations. Beijing succeeded in wooing Tonga away from Taiwan and established diplomatic relations with the Pacific Island state in November 1998. Taiwan wooed the Marshall Islands away from Beijing around the same time, and in early 1999 achieved diplomatic relations with Macedonia.[23]

In sum, diplomatic pressure, continued cross-strait economic exchanges, a PRC military buildup opposite Taiwan, and other actions had not lessened Taiwan's determination to remain separate and distinct from the PRC; successful elections in Taiwan in December 1998 underlined the island government's favorable democratic image in the United States and the West precisely when PRC leaders began cracking down on dissidents. Under pressure from Congress, the Clinton administration was boosting contacts with and military support for Taiwan, including possibly considering providing Taiwan with a means to counter the PRC ballistic missile threat. Beijing remained very sensitive about overt Taiwan moves to declare independence, or U.S. moves to notably upgrade military sales to Taiwan by possibly providing a "theater missile defense" for the island. It hoped that its longer-term strategy of positive and negative incentives would eventually create conditions that would persuade Taiwan to seek reunification with the mainland on terms acceptable to the PRC.[24]

The limits of PRC influence in Taiwan were once again evident when Lee Teng-hui, chafing under Chinese pressure and U.S. efforts to press for cross-strait talks that Lee saw as detrimental to Taiwan's future, announced in an interview in 1999 his view that the China-Taiwan relationship was one between two separate states and that the cross-strait relationship was actually a "special state-to-state relationship." Seeing a new and bold step toward Taiwan independence, Beijing reacted strongly, suspending formal exchanges through the cross-strait offices and escalating military pressures along the Taiwan Strait. Taken by surprise, U.S. officials endeavored to calm the situation. Lee's latest move solidified his reputation in the Clinton administration as a "troublemaker," though he retained important support in the Congress then in the midst of a white-hot debate with the president over various sensitive aspects of China policy, including policy toward Taiwan.[25]

The year 2000 was a presidential election year for Taiwan as well as the United States. The Taiwan election in March saw Chinese officials and senior leaders warn strongly against the DPP candidate, Chen Shui-bian. In the event, the Chinese rhetoric helped Chen improve his very narrow margin of victory against the runner-up candidate who was more acceptable to Beijing, once again demonstrating the unintended negative consequence of Chinese pressure tactics for Chinese interests regarding Taiwan.[26]

China and President Chen Shui-bian

The new political order in Taiwan under President Chen Shui-bian began in May 2001, ending fifty years of Nationalist Party (KMT) rule. At first, President Chen benefited from low expectations at home and abroad, especially in the PRC and the United States, on what he would likely do. Many in Taiwan, the PRC, and the United States linked him with the past, strongly pro-independence stance of his party, the Democratic Progressive Party (DPP), predicting an imminent crisis in cross-strait relations if he were elected. In fact, Chen appeared more moderate than was widely anticipated; his carefully worded inauguration speech (reportedly the work of fifty advisers) avoided serious provocations against Beijing while it gave no ground on Taiwan's separate status. Chen and his advisers also appeared to be working smoothly with the U.S. administration, and they established a government including officials from the political opposition, marking a democratic transition of national power—the first time in Taiwan's history.[27]

Though elected with less than 40 percent of the popular vote, President Chen's approval rating began at around 65 percent. He focused on an agenda of popular issues involving promoting domestic political reform while trying to ease cross-strait tensions without sacrificing core Taiwan interests. His record as mayor of Taipei municipality (1994-1998), where he also won only a minority election mandate, suggested that Chen was a pragmatic and careful deal-maker who would work hard and effectively to build support for key reform goals and more efficient and popularly accountable government.[28]

Success or failure of the new administration was influenced heavily by its ability to make progress on domestic reform and avoid increased difficulties with Beijing through 2001. The one-year time limit was determined by Taiwan's political clock. Taiwan was to hold important elections in late 2001 that would determine:

- The new Legislature, and
- The leaders of the twenty-plus counties in the rest of Taiwan, the most important organs of local government.

Through appointments and other administrative actions, President Chen and his administration hoped to move forward a popular reform agenda to some degree, but substantial progress required cooperation by the Legislature (the Legislative Yuan or LY) dominated by Nationalist (KMT) Party adherents and others not affiliated with Chen's DPP. Leaders in Chen's administration anticipated a hard time winning the support of the bureaucratic leaders and rank-and-file of the national administration. Many of these officials were KMT party members who for years followed the dictates of the KMT and the government as if they were the same. Though no widespread, organized sabotage effort was apparent, Chen and his entourage faced particular problems with KMT-dominated and hidebound practices in the Ministries of Foreign Affairs and National Defense, among others.[29]

The new president and his top aides favored continuing Taiwan's economic and development policies, but they also wanted to introduce certain changes, including some that would involve reallocation of resources, that were sure to generate controversy and opposition:

- They appeared less than clear regarding the DPP opposition to Taiwan's fourth nuclear power reactor;
- They favored efforts to support small and medium-sized enterprises rather than larger firms seen to have benefited from government policies in the past;
- They took a somewhat more global view of Taiwan's economic prospects, especially in information technology, a shift from the Asia-Pacific regional focus of past administrations; and
- They favored more social welfare for the elderly and the very young.[30]

Because of his own and the DPP's minority status in Taiwan politics, President Chen endeavored to reach out to opponents in the Legislature, and used the media and public opinion to win support and build coalitions for his reforms and changes. Continued DPP factionalism significantly hampered this effort, though its most immediate impact was to complicate the management of cross-strait relations. Vice President Annette Lu was notably more vocal than Chen in disputing PRC views of Taiwan.[31]

Beijing was unlikely to help the new Taiwan administration. Deeply suspicious of Chen and the DPP's perceived pro-independence leanings, and working to put together a coherent cross-strait policy following the end of Nationalist rule on Taiwan, PRC leaders persisted with a wait-and-see policy, showing little flexibility toward Chen.[32]

The outlook was heavily but not uniformly pessimistic. At one level, Chen Shui-bian appeared to Beijing as better than Lee Teng-hui; he seemed less personally committed to pushing toward independence, more concerned with keeping on good terms with both the mainland and the United States, and more preoccupied with domestic Taiwan affairs. Indeed, Chen was emphasizing less than past administration's competition with the PRC for formal international recognition by small countries or in the UN and other international organizations requiring statehood. The new Taiwan administration was emphasizing more Taiwan's human rights and democratic credentials in seeking broader recognition and positive media and other support through nongovernment channels and organizations. Also, unlike Lee Teng-hui, Chen was more open to direct economic exchange with the mainland.[33]

In his first year, Chen found that his domestic course was difficult and this hurt his ability to exercise leadership:

- His government had two premiers and three cabinet reshuffles.
- When he tried to discontinue Taiwan's fourth nuclear power plant, he initiated six months of sharp political conflict including an effort to recall him from office. He stayed in power but lost in court, and construction on the plant resumed in February 2001.
- Chen was widely criticized in the press for mishandling a natural disaster in 2000.
- Vice President Annette Lu routinely generated unwanted publicity by issuing controversial statements.
- Meanwhile, the Taiwan stock market declined substantially and during his term of office the unemployment rate rose to the highest level in over twenty years. Taiwan faced economic recession—unprecedented in recent decades.[34]

Moreover, Chen was not able to rally his party fully behind his cross-strait approach. Many in the DPP believed that Chen made too many concessions to Beijing, particularly when, in his inaugural address, Chen said that he would adhere to the Republic of China Constitution (which implies "one China") and otherwise disavowed formal independence for Taiwan.[35]

The two main opposition parties combined forces on occasion to challenge Chen on both his domestic policies and approach on cross-strait issues.

- The Kuomintang (KMT or Nationalist Party), which governed Taiwan continuously following World War II, took the lead in opposing Chen. It used its power in the Legislature to delay his budgets, force him to back down on the nuclear power project, and nearly recall him from office. The KMT also seemed to be altering its approach to Beijing. Few party leaders mentioned former President Lee's "state to state" formulation. Rather, several prominent KMT leaders traveled to Beijing and seemingly endorsed a "one-China" line.[36]
- The People First Party (PFP) was headed by James Soong (the former governor of Taiwan and member of the KMT who bolted the party to run in the March 2000 presidential election, thereby splitting the KMT vote and enabling Chen to win). Soong adopted positions different from the KMT and DPP on a broad range of issues.[37]

Chen's domestic political weakness constrained his cross-strait policy options. First, he tried to build public support to strengthen his leadership, but his ratings in the polls declined. Second, KMT and PFP opposition leaders criticized his cross-strait policies, working to deny him the cross-strait successes that would enhance his reelection chances. Third, he needed support from all wings of his party, including those hard-liners who probably would oppose his consideration of new, creative initiatives toward Beijing. Finally, Beijing, sensing that Chen could be discredited with Taiwan's voters and denied reelection in 2004, refused to deal with him.[38]

Chen, like his predecessors, was measured by Taiwan's electorate and politicians in part on how he dealt with mainland China. Taiwan's approach for dealing with Beijing included these key elements:

- Try to engage China, and persuade Washington that it is willing to do so, in an effort to ease military and political pressure from Beijing.
- Maintain, and if possible improve, Taiwan's international status.
- Secure healthy and mutually beneficial economic ties with the mainland.
- Use good ties with the United States to deflect Beijing's pressures for unification.[39]

During his inauguration speech, Chen used formulas designed to eschew independence for Taiwan while not accepting China's demand that he agree to adhere to a "one-China" policy. Specifically, he stated five "nos"—no declaration of independence, no change of national title, no inclusion of the "two-state" theory in the constitution, no holding of a referendum on reunification or independence, and no abolition of the National Unification Guidelines and the National Unification Council. Chen hoped this approach would reduce Chinese pressure on Taiwan, but it did not work. Rather, China held Chen to the five nos and continued to refuse to return to a dialogue with Taiwan's government (which was suspended following Lee Teng-hui's "state-to-state" comments in 1999). It increased strong efforts to isolate Taipei internationally, occasionally put pressure on Taiwan's business community located in mainland China, and reached out to opposition parties as a means of seeking to isolate Chen.[40]

Though Taiwan saw little prospect in the immediate future for a resolution of the political impasse over cross-strait talks, it quietly moved forward to approach the mainland in other ways, notably the easing of restrictions on investment and the expansion of trade. Beyond these, Taiwan increased the length of stays for mainland journalists on Taiwan. Taipei also moved to recognize academic degrees from mainland universities and relaxed restrictions on mainland educational and cultural visitors. Taiwan gaining membership in the World Trade Organization (WTO) immediately following China provided an opportunity for further economic interaction, but also increased chances for greater acrimony as Taiwan used the channel to achieve greater international recognition.[41]

Beijing's declaratory policy toward Chen initially was characterized as "wait and see," but was quickly superceded by a more active approach that sought to arrest greater moves by Taiwan toward independence and eventually to create momentum for reunification. Underlying Beijing's response to the new situation on Taiwan was a fundamental lack of trust in Chen. Beijing perceived that he and the DPP ultimately wanted Taiwan's separation from the mainland to become permanent. China perceived that it had to block this objective.[42]

Beijing undertook the following measures in dealing with Taiwan.[43]

- Following the election of Chen, Beijing began a campaign to criticize him and support his opponents, while wooing politicians and businesspeople from Taiwan. This "United Front" campaign to reach out to Chen's opposition gained some public statements by Taiwan politicians and businesspeople in support of "one China." Also, some Chinese officials perceived that Taiwan's growing economic interaction with the mainland provided leverage on Taiwan's political course.

- At the same time China was increasing pressure on Taiwan, it embarked on a diplomatic offensive toward the United States, which it held as bearing primary responsibility for Taiwan's continued separation from the mainland. This effort was dealt a setback when the Bush administration agreed in 2001 to sell a large arms package to Taiwan, allowed President Chen greater leeway during stop-overs in New York and Houston in mid-2001, and voiced top-level support for a U.S. military response if Taiwan were attacked by the mainland. The downturn in U.S.-PRC relations after the EP-3 incident in April 2001 also hurt PRC influence with the United States over Taiwan.

- Beijing's military modernization programs were designed particularly for a variety of Taiwan Strait contingencies. Many weapons acquisition priorities were aimed at countering U.S. forces in a strait conflict. Beijing hoped to deter the United States from intervening in the event of military conflict between China and Taiwan across the strait.

- China worked harder to limit Taiwan's membership in international organizations and to win diplomatic recognition from countries that maintained ties with Taiwan.

Beijing appeared reasonably satisfied with the results of these efforts in 2002. The Taiwan elections in December 2001 had strengthened the DPP in the Legislature and weakened the Nationalist Party, but Chen Shui-bian's opponents still held a narrow majority and seemed united in opposing any initiatives that might provoke the mainland. More important, Taiwan was mired in a serious economic downturn and saw trade and investment with the mainland as the immediate way out. The burgeoning mainland economy drew investments from half of the 1,000 top Taiwan companies by 2003. Taiwan government officials said the level of Taiwan investment in the mainland was over $100 billion. The PRC accounted for about three-quarters of Taiwan's total foreign investment in the previous decade. Bilateral trade amounted to over $40 billion in 2003, growing at an annual rate of 30 percent despite difficulties over SARS and cross-strait political issues. It was projected to be close to $50 billion in 2004, especially as PRC exports were being allowed to rise dramatically after being strictly curbed in the recent past. About one million Taiwan citizens were in mainland China, and there were 200,000 cross-strait marriages. Meanwhile, markedly improved China-U.S. relations were accompanied by strong U.S. affirmations of a "one-China" policy and repeated private assurances by President Bush that he "opposes" Taiwan independence.[44]

A turn for the worse in cross-strait relations came with Chen Shui-bian's shift to a much more assertive and pro-independence stance against China in 2003-2004. This new trend underlined the volatility of Taiwan politics and the deeply rooted tensions that continued to characterize relations between Taiwan and China. These ran up against the factors of stability in cross-strait relations including growing economic interdependence and personal interchange. Though more supportive of Taiwan in several respects, the United States under the Bush administration also remained strongly opposed to moves by either Beijing or Taipei that would disrupt the political status quo and risk serious confrontation or conflict. The overall mix of factors saw U.S. and other specialists agree that cross-strait relations would remain one of the most dangerous international hot spots for the foreseeable future. The chances of a repetition of the large-scale PLA exercises like those in 1995-1996, or of small military incidents between PLA and Taiwan forces, remained fairly strong, even though China probably would not be in a position to militarily coerce or defeat Taiwan for several more years, if then. Some observers warned that such demonstrations or incidents could escalate into broader military confrontation and combat, despite the intent of the leaders concerned to avoid such an outcome.[45]

The determinants of continued and probably rising tensions in cross-strait relations remained strong and would not be easily reduced. In recent years, Beijing viewed trends on Taiwan as moving in broad terms toward greater political separatism antithetical to China's core concern with national sovereignty and reunification. At first, Chinese officials tended to view President Chen Shui-bian as less provocative than the previous President Lee Teng-hui in pursuing Taiwan's independence from the mainland and in regional and world affairs. They remained deeply distrustful of President Chen, however. They tended to view him and his party as endeavoring to appear moderate on cross-strait issues in order to assuage U.S. and world opinion and to win favor in Taiwan, preparing to move toward greater independence when the time is ripe. They worried that Chen's moves toward a more assertive stance on Taiwan's separatism and his sharp rhetoric against China in 2003-2004 presaged an all-out move toward independence.[46]

Beijing officials at times viewed China's united front tactics as having weakened the Chen Shui-bian administration and helped to slow the movement toward political separatism on Taiwan. These tactics saw Beijing shun Chen and his party while warmly interacting with opposition party leaders willing to voice positions on cross-strait issues somewhat compatible with Beijing's "one-China" stance. The booming cross-strait economic relations also seemed for a while to brake independence sentiment on Taiwan as Taiwan's economy increasingly relied on trade and investment with the Chinese mainland.[47]

Nevertheless, the pattern of China's military modernization and buildup in the Taiwan area continued and intensified in recent years. This expensive multifaceted effort involved some extraordinary measures, notably the wide-ranging purchases of advanced Russian military equipment targeted to assist the PLA in dealing with military contingencies focused on Taiwan, including the possible intervention of U.S. forces to protect Taiwan. It demonstrated that senior Chinese leaders were relying on military means to halt Taiwan's move toward separatism and to press Taiwan to seek talks with China leading to eventual reunification. The military buildup probably did not mean that China was prepared to attack Taiwan—analysts pointed to continuing weaknesses and the dire consequences for Beijing leaders if they failed to win victory in the face of Taiwan and possible U.S. resistance. The military buildup nonetheless significantly added to regional tension and increased the danger of massive negative consequences for regional peace and stability if conflict were to break out on account of an unexpected escalation of cross-strait skirmishing or actions by Taiwan (e.g., declaration of independence) seen to fundamentally challenge China's vital interests. In the event of such an attack, U.S. defense specialists warned of a change in PLA doctrine emphasizing large-scale surprise attack that could neutralize Taiwan's defenses quickly before American forces would have an opportunity to intervene. Others warned that the danger of such an attack was increased as Taiwan leaders' willingness to support rigorous defense preparedness declined in recent years.[48]

Taiwan, meanwhile, seemed unready to give ground to Beijing on significant cross-strait political issues. The Chen Shui-bian administration's limited flexibility was due in part to its political base in the Democratic Progressive Party that long championed Taiwan's status independent of mainland control. The previous ruling party, the Nationalist Party, and the People's First Party of breakaway Nationalist Party leader James Soong, were more flexible in comments on cross-strait issues, discussing possible eventual reunification and appealing to Beijing's "one-China" sensitivities. While popular sentiment on the island remained cautious, President Chen Shui-bian appeared effective in gaining support during the 2003-2004 election campaign by taking steps that would pursue greater Taiwan independence in ways that seemed to antagonize Beijing.[49]

Chen Shui-bian's Reelection and the Outlook for PRC-Taiwan Relations

President Chen's narrow reelection victory in March 2004 saw the Taiwan leader tone down the harsh anti-China rhetoric used in the campaign. In his inauguration speech on May 20, 2004, he called for easing of severe political and social divisions in Taiwan that were exacerbated by the campaign, and promoted improved relations with Beijing. His stance was welcomed by many in Taiwan and by the U.S. government as conducive to stabilizing the situation in the Taiwan area, but Chinese officials rejected his overtures and complained about his refusal to meet Chinese conditions, notably regarding the need to accept the "one-China" principle acknowledging that Taiwan is part of China.

Consultations with officials and nongovernment specialists in Taipei, Kaohsiung, Beijing, and Shanghai in mid-2004[50] showed that Taiwan officials were optimistic that cross-strait relations would be improved as they said that the Chen administration would avoid renewed challenge to the cross-strait status quo and pursue an effective and responsible policy toward the mainland. Nongovernment Taiwan observers and U.S. and other foreign commentators were much less optimistic about the cross-strait situation and the overall competence of the Chen administration to manage sensitive issues involving relations with the Chinese mainland. Chinese officials and commentators, meanwhile, remained deeply distrustful of President Chen, resolved to firmly rebuff further Taiwan challenges to the status quo in cross-strait relations, and unlikely to move forward with positive incentives toward Taiwan, at least until after the important legislative elections in Taiwan in December 2004.

As explained by senior Taiwan officials, the overall approach of the Chen administration to deal with the challenges posed by cross-strait relations put a heavy emphasis on moderation and starting renewed dialogue with Beijing. The officials were hopeful that China's emphasis on "peaceful rise" and "peaceful development" in Chinese domestic and foreign policies would lead to a more peaceful and flexible PRC approach toward Taiwan. Though Taiwan officials foresaw little likelihood that the Chen Shui-bian administration would accept China's demand regarding the "one-China" principle, they were cautiously optimistic that other paths to improved relations could be pursued. To facilitate progress in cross-strait relations, they pledged to improve the atmosphere in relations with the PRC by toning down the sharp anti-China rhetoric seen during the Taiwan presidential campaign. They also promised to handle in a sober and incremental way sensitive issues involved in revising or remaking the Taiwan constitution. President Chen had raised the issue of constitutional revision prominently in the presidential election campaign, causing Beijing to react sharply to what it perceived as an important move toward dejure Taiwan independence.

Taiwan officials acknowledged that PRC officials deeply distrusted Chen Shui-bian and were unlikely to offer any significant overtures toward the Chen administration, at least until the elections for the Taiwan legislature in December 2004. Chen's opponents held a slim majority in the Legislature. If, as many expected, they were to lose to Chen's party and their political allies in the December 2004 elections, China would face a Taiwan political situation strongly controlled by President Chen and his allies. In these circumstances, Taiwan officials judged that Beijing might feel compelled to adjust the Chinese policy of refusing to deal with the Taiwan president until he accepted the "one-China" principle.

In the meantime, Taiwan government officials saw some possibilities of reaching understandings with Beijing over military behavior in the Taiwan Strait. The jet fighters of the two sides patrol close to each other in the strait and constructive communication could reduce the danger of an unintended military clash. Other possible confidence building steps included the announcement by both sides of the scope and purpose of military exercises, and a possible mutual understanding that the forces of both sides would be under orders not to fire first in the event of an encounter.

Taiwan officials emphasized strongly Taiwan's desire to reach some understandings with Beijing that would modify PRC pressure to isolate Taiwan internationally. They explained that such pressure prompted stronger anti-China reaction from Taiwan and Taiwan leaders' moves toward greater Taiwan assertiveness and independence. If Beijing wished to avoid such Taiwan actions in the future, the officials advised, they would be wise to reach some understanding with Taiwan that would allow Taiwan participation in organizations such at the World Health Organization, where Taiwan was seeking to participate for many years.

Taiwan officials saw a number of practical cross-strait issues that could be dealt with in pragmatic interaction with the mainland short of the formal dialogue, which Beijing refuses until President Chen accepts the "one-China" principle. These involved the active flow of trade and investments across the strait, the half million to one million Taiwan residents on the mainland, and the 200,000 PRC spouses of Taiwan citizens. The Taiwan officials also hoped that some progress could be made in implementing the "three links" involving proposed direct communication, transportation, and trade between Taiwan and the mainland.

To deal with the increasing mainland military threat and growing PRC pressure on Taiwan's international status, the Taiwan officials pledged to work hard to improve relations with the United States. In particular, they promised to adopt military measures and increase military spending as advocated by United States as U.S. officials deepened their advisory and supporting role in Taiwan's military preparation against the mainland threat.

Of most immediate importance in improving Taiwan's relations with the United States and creating a more positive atmosphere for cross-strait dialogue was the Taiwan officials' promise to avoid assertive rhetoric or pro-independence positions in the lead up to the December 2004 legislative elections. They judged that President Chen and his party were unlikely to repeat the kind of anti-China language and proposals for referenda and constitutional change that alarmed Beijing and Washington during the 2003-2004 presidential election campaign. They advised that the races in the legislative campaign focused more on local issues and personalities, and the national-level issues regarding relations with China and the future legal status of Taiwan were less important. Though pro-independence politicians would voice provocative positions regarding Taiwan's status and cross-strait relations, President Chen and the mainstream of his political supporters were said to be determined to avoid statements and positions that would disrupt relations with the PRC or the United States.

In contrast with the generally positive view of Taiwan government officials, nongovernment Taiwan observers and U.S. and foreign commentators tended to be much less optimistic that the Chen Shui-bian administration would manage the cross-strait relationship effectively and without serious disruption. Several judged that the president and his political allies used anti-China themes successfully in the 2004 presidential campaign and would be inclined to follow a similar approach to achieve victory in the legislative races in December 2004.

While some in the Chen government were seen likely to pursue the moderate and accommodating approach noted above, others were said to be inclined to pursue a much more assertive strategy designed to achieve dejure Taiwan independence relatively soon, by 2008. The latter were seen likely to make their views prominent in the lead up to the 2004 legislative elections, and if the DPP and its political allies were victorious in those legislative elections, to pursue a much more vigorous effort to establish the legal basis through constitutional change and other means of an independent Taiwan state.

Managing the consequences of such a radical approach for Taiwan's relations with the PRC and the United States, and Taiwan's overall security and unity, were said to be secondary concerns for many in the Chen Shui-bian camp; they were not likely to be dealt with effectively by the Chen administration, according to some Taiwan and U.S. observers. Thus, these observers warned that U.S. government officials seeking to keep the Chen administration from taking assertive positions on cross-strait issues would need to exert constant vigilance and pressure in an effort to hold off such steps. The wide political and social divisions in Taiwan would remain serious problems as the push toward greater assertiveness toward the mainland in the white-hot political competition in Taiwan severely strained Taiwan unity.

Meanwhile, the Chen administration's record on economic policy and defense policy was widely seen as inadequate. Nongovernment national security experts were alarmed by the government's provocative stance toward China at a time when the Taiwan administration's defense efforts were weak and its relations with the United States strained.

Well aware of the divisions in Taiwan and uncertain about the future course of the Chen administration on issues important to China, Chinese officials and specialists were cautious in dealing with the new situation. They reflected a PRC stance that appeared to offer little in the way of positive initiatives toward Chen, while they maintained and intensified the military and diplomatic pressure on Taiwan. They also encouraged U.S. pressure to keep Chen from moving toward greater independence and hoped to work closely with U.S. officials in constraining the Taiwan administration. They seemed intent on waiting to see what effect the U.S. pressure and China's firm stance might have on the Taiwan situation leading up to the legislative elections on December 2004. Presumably, any significant change in the PRC stance would await the results of those elections, unless Taiwan pursued more assertive or radical policies in the interim.

In the meantime, Chinese officials and commentators were uniform in emphasizing that China was prepared to resort to using force if Taiwan moved toward independence. They remained unclear what specific steps might lead to such action. One senior PLA officer was very firm in stating that despite China's recent emphasis on China's overall peaceful rise and peaceful development, Beijing was prepared at any time to launch a "short and strong" military strike that would "wake up" the Taiwan people to the negative consequences of their "pro-independence" actions.[51]

Behind the impasse in cross-strait issues lay several key factors[52] likely to stoke continued tensions:

- *Internal politics.* PRC leaders could not appear "soft" on Taiwan issues. They would otherwise run a serious risk of being attacked and replaced by other leaders appealing to strong nationalist sentiment prevalent in China. Taiwan politics encouraged continued emphasis on Taiwan's separate status and made meaningful compromise with the mainland difficult.
- *Legitimacy and respect.* Beijing went to extraordinary lengths in foreign affairs to ensure that its "one-China" stance and its leadership of China were accepted by the international community. Taiwan believed it deserved greater international legitimacy and respect as a democracy and an economic power, and ran up constantly against firm PRC opposition in its efforts to gain such recognition and respect.
- *Legacy.* Leaders on both sides of the Taiwan Strait sought progress in cross-strait relations as a means to enhance their respective political and historic legacies. The problem was that their objectives were fundamentally at odds; the push of legacy therefore led to greater friction.
- *Military preparations.* Beijing's military buildup opposite Taiwan received broad attention in international media. Taiwan's military response was less than many U.S. security planners wanted as the United States enhanced advice, support and offers of defense equipment to Taiwan. U.S. force enhancements to deal with Taiwan contingencies were also evident. This arms race added to tensions and could be viewed as increasing the chances of wider conflict.
- *U.S. policy.* Beijing tended to see U.S. policy supporting Taiwan's continued separate status from the mainland. The Bush administration's decisions on a large-scale arms package to Taiwan, and especially President Bush's strong personal pledge of U.S. military support for Taiwan if it were attacked by the mainland, reinforced this assessment. They were balanced to some degree by the U.S. president's subsequent affirmations of a "one-China" policy, of opposition to Taiwan independence, and of rebuke for Taiwan President's Chen Shui-bian for destabilizing cross-strait relations. Taiwan, meanwhile, endeavored to deepen the support it receives from the United States. It had strong backing from the U.S. Congress and media. It was pleased with the Bush administration support, and attempted to finesse differences with the president over Taiwan's insistence on referenda and other steps seen as destabilizing by the Bush administration. It remained wary of PRC efforts to use China's relatively much stronger strategic and economic importance to the United States to influence U.S. policy to move toward a cross-strait posture more acceptable to Beijing.

Notes

1. Denny Roy, "Returning Home or Selling Out? Taiwan's China Debate," in *Asia's China Debate* (Honolulu: Asia Pacific Center for Security Studies, 2003), chapter 13; Carol Lee Hamrin and Zhang Zheng, "The Floating Island: Change of Paradigm on the Taiwan Question," *Journal of Contemporary China* 13, no. 39 (May 2004): 339-50; Michael Swaine, "Trouble in Taiwan," *Foreign Affairs* 83, no. 2 (March-April 2004), www.foreignaffairs.org (accessed 29 December 2004).

2. David G. Brown, "Of Economics and Elections," *Comparative Connections* (Honolulu: CSIS/Pacific Forum), www.csis.org/pacfor (accessed 15 November 2001).

3. Brown, "Strains Over Cross Strait Relations," *Comparative Connections,* January 2004.

4. Brown, "The Shadow of SARS," *Comparative Connections,* July 2003.

5. Brown, "Pernicious Presidential Politics," *Comparative Connections,* October 2003.

6. Brown, "Cross Strait Relations," *Comparative Connections*; Glenn Kessler, "U.S. Cautions Taiwan on Independence," *Washington Post,* 22 April 2004, A22; Kenneth Lieberthal, "Dire Strait: The Risks on Taiwan," *Washington Post,* 8 January 2004, A23; Charles Snyder, "U.S. Unease Caused by Its Duty to Defend Chinese Threat," *Taipei Times* 8 February 2004, 3.

7. "President Chen Shui-bian's Inauguration Address," *China Post,* 21 May 2004, 6.

8. Denny Roy, *Taiwan: A Political History* (Ithaca, N.Y.: Cornell University Press, 2003), 146-50, 195-202, 212-22, 235-40; T. Y. Wang, "Taiwan's Foreign Relations Under Lee Teng-hui's Rule, 1988-2000," in Wei-chin Lee and T. Y. Wang, eds., *Sayonara to the Lee Teng-hui Era* (Lanham, Md.: University Press of America, 2003), 250-60; Hamrin and Zhang Zheng, "The Floating Island," *Journal of Contemporary China*; Swaine, "Trouble in Taiwan," *Foreign Affairs,* 83. See also chapters by Dennis Van Vranken Hickey and Kay Moller in Jean-Marie Henckaerts, ed., *The International Status of Taiwan in the New World Order* (The Hague: Kluwer Law International, 1996).

9. Charles Freeman, "Preventing War in the Taiwan Strait," *Foreign Affairs* (July-August 1998); Steven Goldstein, *Taiwan Faces the Twenty-first Century* (New York: Foreign Policy Association, 1997).

10. Nancy Bernkopf Tucker, "China-Taiwan: U.S. Debates and Policy Choices," *Survival* 40, no. 4 (Winter 1998-1999): 150-67.

11. Robert Ross, ed., *After the Cold War: Domestic Factors and U.S.-China Relations* (Armonk N.Y.: M. E. Sharpe 1998), 80-97; John Garver, *Face-Off* (Seattle: University of Washington Press, 1997); Harvey Feldman, "Cross Strait Relations With Taiwan" in Kim Holmes and James Przystup, eds., *Between Diplomacy and Deterrence* (Washington, D.C.: Hertitage Foundation, 1998), 141-62.

12. *Taiwan: Recent Developments and U.S. Policy Choices* (Washington, D.C.: Library of Congress), Congressional Research Service, Issue Brief 98034, 29 December 1999.

13. These developments are reviewed in Ralph Clough, *Cooperation or Conflict in the Taiwan Strait?* (Lanham, Md.: Rowman & Littlefield, 1999).

14. Robert Sutter, *Chinese Policy Priorities and Their Implications for the United States* (Lanham, Md.: Rowman & Littlefield, 2000), 106.

15. Fiji Television, 14 January 1998, carried in Foreign Broadcast Information Service (Internet version).

16. *Taiwan-Mainland China Talks* (Washington, D.C.: Library of Congress), Congressional Research Service, Report 98-887, 22 November 1998.

17. Sutter, *Chinese Policy Priorities*, 107.

18. Reviewed in *Taiwan: Recent Developments*, CRS Issue Brief 98034.

19. Beijing's approach is reviewed in Sutter, *Chinese Policy Priorities*, 107-8.

20. T. Y. Wang, "Taiwan's Foreign Relations Under Lee Teng-hui's rule, 1988-2000" in Wei-chin Lee and T. Y. Wang, eds., *Sayonara to the Lee Teng-hui Era*, 250-60.

21. Nancy Bernkopf Tucker, "China-Taiwan: U.S. Debates and Policy Choices," *Survival* 40, no. 4 (Winter 1998-1999): 150-67.

22. *Taiwan-Mainland China Talks*, CRS Report 98-887.

23. *Taiwan: Recent Developments*, CRS Issue Brief 98034.

24. Sutter, *Chinese Policy Priorities*, 109.

25. *Taiwan: Recent Developments*, CRS Issue Brief 98034.

26. Denny Roy, *Taiwan: A Political History*, 235.

27. Yu-Shan Wu, "Taiwan in 2000," *Asian Survey* 41, no. 1 (January-February 2001): 40-48; Denny Roy, *Taiwan: A Political History*, 235-36.

28. Nat Bellocchi, "Taiwan's New Government: The Domestic Political Climate," paper presented at *Taiwan's New Order and Cross Strait Relations, a Seminar*, Federal Research Division, Library of Congress, Washington, D.C., 9 June 2000.

29. Robert Sutter, *The United States and East Asia* (Lanham, Md.: Rowman & Littlefield, 2003), 156.

30. Yu-Shan Wu, "Taiwan in 2000," *Asian Survey*, 40-48; Shelly Rigger, "Taiwan's New Political Order: The Short-Term Outlook for A-bian's ROC," paper presented at *Taiwan's New Order and Cross Strait Relations, a Seminar*, Federal Research Division, Library of Congress, Washington, D.C., 9 June 2000.

31. David G. Brown, "Groping for a Formula for Cross-Strait Talks," in *Comparative Connections*, Honolulu, CSIS/Pacific Forum, www.csis.org/pacfor (accessed 25 July 2000).

32. Andrew Nathan, "Taiwan's New Political Order: Implications for Cross Strait Relations," a paper presented at *Taiwan's New Order and Cross Strait Relations, a Seminar*, Federal Research Division, Library of Congress, Washington, D.C., 9 June 2000.

33. Brown, "Groping for a Formula," *Comparative Connections*.

34. Brown, "A Fragile Calm," in *Comparative Connections*, Honolulu, CSIS/Pacific Forum, www.csis.org/pacfor (accessed 30 July 2001).

35. Rigger, "Taiwan's New Political Order," 9 June 2000; Roy, "Returning Home or Selling Out?" chapter 13.

36. Brown, "Economics and Elections," *Comparative Connections*.

37. Bellocchi, "Taiwan's New Government," 9 June 2000.

38. Brown, "Economics and Elections," *Comparative Connections*.

39. Nathan, "Taiwan's New Political Order," 9 June 2000; Sutter, *The United States and East Asia*, 159.

40. Brown, "Economics and Elections," *Comparative Connections*.

41. Roy, *Taiwan: A Political History*, 235-38; Brown, "Economics and Elections," *Comparative Connections*; Maureen Pao, "The Mainland Allure," *The Far Eastern Economic Review*, www.feer.com (accessed 4 October 2001); Elizabeth Olson, "Taiwan Is Cleared for Membership in WTO," *New York Times*, 19 September 2001; Bruce Gilley and Maureen Pao, "Defences Weaken," *The Far Eastern Economic Review*, www.feer.com (accessed 4 October 2001).

42. Gilley and Pao, "Defences Weaken," Yu-Shan Wu, "Taiwan in 2000," *Asian Survey*, 40-48.

43. Reviewed in Sutter, *The United States and East Asia*, 160.

44. Brown, "Cross Strait Relations," *Comparative Connections*; T. J. Cheng, "China-Taiwan Economic Linkage," in the forthcoming book *New Thinking on Cross Strait Relations*, Nancy Bernkoph Tucker, ed.

45. Thomas Christensen, "China," in Richard Ellings and Aaron Friedberg, eds., *Strategic Asia: Power and Purpose, 2001-2002* (Seattle, Wash.: National Bureau of Asian Research, 2001), 47-58; Brown, "Cross strait Relations," *Comparative Connections*; Hamrin and Zhang Zheng, "The Floating Island," *Journal of Contemporary China*; Michael Swaine, "Trouble in Taiwan," *Foreign Affairs* 83, no. 2 (March-April 2004); Kessler, "U.S. Cautions Taiwan," *Washington Post*; Lieberthal, "Dire Strait," *Washington Post*; Snyder, "U.S. Unease," *Taipei Times*.

46. Alan Romberg, "Support Democracy, Not Referendums, in Taiwan," *PACNET 10*, www.csis.org/pacfor (accessed 3 March 2003). See also Peng Guangqian, "The Reorientation and Development of China's Taiwan Policy," and "The Origins of the Policy to 'Pay Any Price to Contain Taiwan's Independence,'" both replayed in *China Strategy*, vol. 3, www.csis.org. (accessed 20 July 2004).

47. Wuu-Long-Lin and Pansy Lin, "Emergence of the Greater China Circle Economies: Cooperation Versus Competition," *Journal of Contemporary China* 10, no. 29 (November 2001): 695-710; Chong-pin Lin, "Goodwill and Proactive Exchange Policy: How Taipei Manages the Cross Strait Relations," *Journal of Contemporary China* 10, no. 29 (November 2001): 711-16.

48. U.S. Department of Defense, *Annual Report on the Military Power of the People's Republic of China, 2003*, www.defenselink.mil/pubs/20030730chinaex.pdf (accessed 1 November 2003); Denny Roy, *Taiwan's Threat Perceptions: The Enemy Within Asia*, Pacific Center for Security Studies, Occasional Paper, available at www.apcss.org (accessed 1 June 2003).

49. Brown, "Cross Strait Relations," *Comparative Connections*.

50. The author met with fifty government and nongovernment specialists in the PRC and forty such specialists in Taiwan during late May 2004.

51. Consultations, Beijing, 17 May 2004.

52. Reviewed in Sutter, *The United States and East Asia*, 204-5.

Chapter 9

Relations with South Asia

Slowly Improving Relations

China's leadership has worked assiduously in recent years to ease tensions and incrementally advance Chinese influence with countries along China's border with South Asia. The end of the Cold War and collapse of the Soviet Union opened opportunities for spreading Chinese interests. Beijing made considerable progress in improving relations with India, now devoid of a close strategic alignment with Moscow and more open to international economic and political exchange. The progress was made to some degree at the expense of traditionally close Sino-Pakistani relations, though Chinese leaders did their best to persuade Islamabad that Pakistan's interests were well served by a Sino-Indian rapprochement. China reportedly also continued its close support for Pakistan's nuclear weapons, ballistic missile, and other defense programs, at least until the Pakistanis had the ability to advance these sophisticated programs on their own. And Beijing continued its economic support for the sometimes crisis-prone Pakistani economy.[1]

Indian nuclear tests carried out in May 1998 by a newly installed nationalistic government in New Delhi posed the most serious challenge to China's strategy in the region since the end of the Cold War. Subsequently, Chinese officials demonstrated a carefully calculated reaction that endeavored to preserve Chinese interests in avoiding debilitating entanglements in South Asia while checking Indian nationalistic aspirations for greater regional and nationalistic prominence and preserving the close Chinese relationship with Pakistan. Beijing sought to work closely with the United States in the process, hoping to capitalize on their common interests and to avoid international publicity regarding China's role as a key supporter of nuclear weapons proliferation in Pakistan.[2]

Chinese leaders showed careful balance in China's approach to India and Pakistan during the Indian-Pakistani military confrontations over disputed territories in Kashmir. Seeking to avoid possible nuclear war in South Asia, China refrained from past rhetoric strongly supporting Pakistani interests against India. Its even-handed treatment of India-Pakistan differences during the so-called Kargil conflict of 1999 was followed by similarly balanced treatment during flare-ups of India-Pakistan tensions in 2001-2002.[3] China worked cooperatively with the United States, European powers, and others seeking to avoid war and limit instability in South Asia.

Chinese officials adjusted to the sharp rise in U.S. power and influence in South Asia as a result of the U.S.-led war against the Taliban regime in Afghanistan and the broader war on global terrorism. On the positive side as far as China was concerned, the more prominent U.S. commitment meant that Pakistan's government would once again enjoy strong support from the U.S. superpower. The U.S. material and military aid and strong political support would shore up shaky Pakistani government finances and enhance the Pakistani government's abilities to suppress militants and extremists promoting terrorism affecting China as well as others in the region. Growing U.S. involvement in India strengthened U.S. ability to influence New Delhi to ease tensions with Pakistan and to avoid war in South Asia.[4] At the same time however, the new U.S. presence and influence posed many negative implications for Chinese interests,[5] but PRC leaders played down these differences as they continued to pursue constructive Chinese approaches designed to improve incrementally Chinese interests and influence in South Asia.

Post-Cold War Chinese policy toward South Asia has generally been in line with broader efforts by China to reduce tensions around its periphery in order to stabilize the "peaceful international environment" needed for China's ambitious agenda of economic and other domestic changes and reforms. Using "dialogues," high-level visits, and other diplomatic measures, Beijing has publicly emphasized the positive and endeavored to minimize the negative with all its South Asian neighbors, including India. In this process, the Chinese authorities have avoided compromising core Chinese territorial, economic, political, and other interests, while they have sought to benefit through methodical and generally constructive interaction with the South Asian countries.[6]

China faced a difficult task in influencing India, the dominant regional power. India has long been at odds with China over territorial issues and over long-standing Chinese support for India's rival, Pakistan. Notably, China and India fought a border war in 1962; India was humiliated. But incremental efforts to ease tensions and improve relations moved forward in the 1980s and appeared to receive an added boost from the collapse of the Soviet Union. For many years, the latter had fostered a close strategic relationship with India based in part on their mutual suspicion of China. Prime Minister Rajiv Gandhi visited China in 1988; Premier Li Peng visited India in 1990; and President Jiang Zemin traveled there in 1996.[7]

As India and China improved relations, China modified its long-standing support for Pakistan.[8] It was already evident in the 1970s that China was unwilling to take significant military action against India in the event of an Indo-Pakistani war. During the 1965 Indo-Pakistani war, Chinese forces did take assertive actions along the Indian border in order to divert Indian forces and weaken their assault against Pakistan. But when India defeated Pakistan in the 1972 war, which saw the dismemberment of Pakistan and the creation of an independent Bangladesh, China took no significant military action.

In the 1980s and 1990s, China further modified its public stance in support of Pakistani claims against India over territorial and other issues. Beijing notably adhered to an increasingly even-handed approach over the sensitive Indo-Pakistani dispute over Kashmir. China continued its close military and economic support for Pakistan. Numerous reports and other evidence showed that China played a major role for many years in assisting Pakistan's development of nuclear weapons and related ballistic missile delivery systems, though Chinese officials deny this. President Jiang Zemin was asked in an interview published on June 3, 1998, "Has China helped Pakistan to make its nuclear bomb?" He replied, "No, China has not helped Pakistan. . . ."[9]

Continuing to benefit from Chinese military, economic, and political support, Pakistan chose to emphasize the positive in Sino-Pakistani relations and deemed counterproductive any significant show of irritation with Beijing's shift toward a more even-handed public posture in the subcontinent. Sino-Indian relations also improved, although both powers recognized significant areas of disagreement,[10] notably the following:

- *Border issues.* Large expanses of territory along India's northwestern and northeastern frontier remain in dispute. In many rounds of border talks since 1981, the two sides have made slow progress in their putative effort to delineate the so-called Line of Actual Control and other lingering problems. During Jiang Zemin's 1996 visit to India, the two sides codified many of the ad hoc confidence-building measures that had evolved over the years along the mostly quiet frontiers.
- *Chinese ties with Pakistan, Burma.* Long-standing close Chinese military ties with Pakistan and more recently with Burma are viewed by some Indian officials as a Chinese "pincer movement" to contain India. At times, some in India also have seen the United States playing a supporting role through its engagement policy toward China.
- *Tibet.* Beijing gives high priority to countering the efforts by the Dalai Lama and his supporters to seek a greater international profile for Tibet, and remains at odds with New Delhi over the issue of India's continued hosting of the spiritual leader and his government in exile.
- *Trade.* Recent Indian efforts to open the economy and increase exports led to nascent economic competition with China.

Chinese Reaction to the South Asian Crisis, 1998

Chinese officials were apparently surprised by the Indian tests and by New Delhi's emphasis on the so-called Chinese threat as a major rationale for its development of nuclear weapons. At first, Chinese officials had hoped that a strong international response to the Indian government might show the action to have been counterproductive for Indian interests, and might also have the effect of persuading Pakistan not to test. China reacted with strong rhetoric against the Indian tests. Chinese media also positively highlighted the U.S. response, including the imposition of sanctions, though Chinese officials made clear that Beijing would not impose sanctions of its own. (Having been subject to massive sanctions during the Cold War and more recently to milder sanctions after the 1989 Tiananmen incident, Beijing opposed international sanctions as, in principle, contrary to Chinese interests.)[11]

Privately concerned that other major powers (e.g., Russia, France) were less than forceful in their reaction to the Indian tests, Chinese officials were uncertain whether the international reaction would be sufficient to dissuade Pakistan from testing. Chinese leaders were asked by the United States and others to help persuade Pakistan not to test and they may have done so, but it was not publicly known how much emphasis they put on this effort. (It is probably true that without Chinese help, Pakistan would not yet have a bomb to test.) Chinese officials voiced their sympathy with Pakistan's situation, gave no indication of decreasing their ongoing economic and military assistance to Pakistan, and placed the full blame on India for starting the crisis. Meanwhile, Pakistan sought added assurances from China during high-level official exchanges, though there was no indication from either side of any significant increase in support for Pakistan in the face of the newly apparent Indian threat.[12]

Typical of China's public response to the crisis were Foreign Ministry, authoritative *People's Daily*, and other commentaries critical of the Indian tests. Beijing followed its strong condemnation of India, in a rare Foreign Ministry statement of May 13, with a harsh, authoritative party response in the *People's Daily (Renmin Ribao)*. A new wave of criticism appeared in two "commentator articles" in *Renmin Ribao* on May 15 and 19, and in a series of signed articles carried in the military daily *Jiefangjun Bao* on May 19. The commentator articles reiterated China's earlier call for international censure of New Delhi, but focused primarily on Beijing's ire over bilateral issues, security, and Beijing's claim that the tests had exposed India's drive to dominate South Asia. The articles also contained uncommonly strong personal criticism of India's leaders.[13]

Asserting that the weapons tests "aroused strong condemnation all over the world" and constituted a "serious situation," the May 15 commentator article reiterated China's call for the international community to "strongly demand" that "necessary measures" be taken against India, and that New Delhi "immediately" abandon its nuclear weapons program. Sharpening this criticism after Indian Prime Minister Vajpayee declared India a nuclear power, the May 19 commentator article denounced him as "brazen" for saying India would not sign the comprehensive test-ban treaty and attacked the "perverse" deeds of Indian authorities who, it said, "have no intention whatsoever to show restraint." As a result, it claimed, India had fallen into a state of unprecedented isolation.

Despite this attack on India for snubbing international opinion, the commentator articles made it clear that New Delhi's use of the "China threat theory" to justify its nuclear weapons program touched a very sensitive nerve in Beijing. Both articles, as well as the articles in the military paper, directed the bulk of their criticism to refuting this charge and amplifying Beijing's countercharge that the root cause of India's actions was a desire to bolster its alleged quest for hegemony in the region. The May 15 commentator article, for example, declared that the reason the Indian government had "disregarded the fundamental interests of the vast number of its people" and caused "serious unease among its neighbors" was "nothing less than a desire to threaten" those neighbors and "dominate South Asia." The article went on to attack the "even more disgusting" ploy of the Indian government of blaming Chinese military power for its actions, a tactic it said was "not at all clever" and "grossly underestimated the ability of people to judge things correctly." It also launched into a personal criticism of Indian Defense Minister George Fernandes, characterizing his allegations of China's military threat as "spouting nonsense" and sarcastically dismissing his recent "smiling" assurances to PLA Chief of Staff Fu Quanyou regarding the "peaceful and stable" Sino-Indian border as duplicitous. Fu had visited India prior to the Indian tests.

The May 19 commentator article attacked a letter reportedly sent by Prime Minister Vajpayee to U.S. President Bill Clinton tracing the Chinese threat to Chinese aggression in the 1962 Sino-Indian border war. Declaring that "nobody believes such preposterous logic" and "lies," the article went on to add a new charge against India for its "extremely ignominious role in the Tibet issue" in allowing the Dalai Lama to conduct "separatist activity" from Indian soil. The article concluded that "the Indian authorities owe the Chinese people an apology."

China's military leadership was not observed to take an official stance in PRC media on the Indian problem in May 1998. However, according to a Beijing press agency directed at overseas Chinese, the PLA's authoritative daily, *Jiefangjun Bao*, on May 19 devoted a full page to signed articles that "assailed" New Delhi's "military expansionism" and "ambition of seeking regional hegemony."[14] The articles, which detailed India's military spending and weapons programs, warned that these military developments warranted "more attention and vigilance." The press agency account called attention to a lengthy analytical piece in *Jiefangjun Bao*, claiming that since the end of the Cold War, India had "intensified" efforts to "make war preparation," rather than focusing on economic development. This effort, the article claimed, was a means of attaining New Delhi's strategic goal of "dominating South Asia, containing China, controlling the Indian Ocean, and becoming a major military power." The article also noted that India possessed intermediate-range nuclear-capable missiles that could reach the southern half of China.

Another commentary in the paper reportedly exposed Indian "double-dealing" as having "seriously damaged the security structure and political atmosphere in South Asia." Repeating a metaphor used by Beijing in the past to warn potential adversaries to change their ways, the article said that a country which "vainly hopes to dominate . . . a region," will "end up lifting a rock only to drop it on its own toes."[15]

Despite these acerbic attacks on the Indian government and its top leaders, the May 19 *Renmin Ribao* commentator article stopped short of threatening specific action and called on New Delhi to avoid further damage to bilateral ties—suggesting that Beijing still hoped to avoid a rupture in Sino-Indian ties. Following the pattern of China's earlier official protest, the articles called only for a strong international demand that India discontinue its nuclear weapons program. The commentator article of May 15, for example, noted the steady improvement in relations in recent years and went on to "advise" the Indian side to "treasure the fruit of the bilateral relations—which is not easy to come by—and refrain from saying anymore" that will "damage" relations. Repeating this admonition, the May 19 article stated that the common interests of the two countries are "far greater than their differences" and advised Indian authorities to "look to the future" and "not become the stumbling block obstructing" improvement in ties. It called the tests "an unwise move" by "a small number of Indian power-holders" acting against the people's wishes and disregarding the overall interests of "Sino-Indian friendship."

The Chinese commentary in May presaged the balanced Chinese approach to the crisis that emerged in mid-1998 and appeared to be aimed at maximizing Chinese advantages while avoiding complicating entanglements and costly involvements. Consultations with twenty Chinese and foreign officials as well as a careful review of China's statements on South Asian issues in 1998 helped to clarify the Chinese government's assessments and goals in the new situation.[16] The Chinese goals inclined Chinese leaders to continue close cooperation with the United States in the crisis, notably by issuing a joint statement on South Asia during President Clinton's June 1998 visit to Beijing.[17] In general, the Chinese goals could be reduced to the following points:[18]

1. *The situation was not yet a threat to China; therefore, avoid entanglements.*
    The South Asian situation was not yet a threat to China and therefore did not
    warrant substantial increases in military or other resources to deal with the
    problem. Chinese leaders' priorities remained focused on domestic issues.
    Beijing would revise its assessment if a major conflict broke out or India
    deployed nuclear weapons. For the present, Beijing intended to keep its lines
    open to New Delhi; it sent its new ambassador there after the Indian tests, and
    the Chinese media highlighted calls for improved relations by Indian politicians.
    Beijing registered strong concern for the future of international efforts to curb
    nuclear proliferation, with Chinese and foreign experts saying, unsurprisingly,
    that China's interests are best served by capping the number of members in the
    nuclear club at five.

2. *Work with the Perm-Five, especially the United States.* The United States was in the lead among world powers and the five permanent members of the UN Security Council (the Perm-Five) in taking strong action against India. China strongly supported the U.S. action,[19] while avoiding sanctions or other substantial commitments of its own. The two governments worked closely together to come up with a unified Perm-Five position at a meeting of the five powers in Geneva on June 4, 1998. China was much less enthusiastic about broader international efforts to deal with the crisis such as that of the G7 industrial powers who met on the issue on June 12, 1998. Beijing thought these might dilute the international pressure on India and diminish China's prominent international role.

3. *Press India, support Pakistan.* Though the Perm-Five statement of June 4, 1998, was critical of India and Pakistan, Chinese leaders continued to focus their criticism on India for "triggering" the crisis. They stressed strongly that India's perceived great power aspirations should in no way be rewarded by special consideration in joining the Nuclear Nonproliferation Treaty, the Comprehensive Test Ban Treaty, or the UN Security Council as a permanent member. For Pakistan, Beijing expressed understanding and continued active military and economic support. On Kashmir, Beijing was supportive of Pakistani-backed calls for greater international efforts to ease tensions; though it stuck to the long-standing Chinese position that the dispute should be settled by the parties concerned (Beijing opposed international involvement in its own territorial disputes with bordering countries, as well as with Taiwan).

4. *Highlight China's international role and avoid negative publicity on Chinese proliferation.* The Chinese media were replete with references to China's positive and constructive role in the Perm-Five meeting and other fora in dealing with the crisis. Beijing officials dismissed as "groundless" accusations by Indian officials and some in the West about China's reportedly deep involvement in Pakistan's nuclear weapons and ballistic missile programs. They hoped to emphasize China's constructive role and minimize its involvement in Pakistan's programs in part to create a positive atmosphere for the Sino-U.S. summit in late June 1998.

Kashmir

China demonstrated its careful balance on South Asian issues after the Indian and Pakistani tests by adhering to a nuanced and even-handed public posture on the sensitive issues of Kashmir. Many analysts judged that Indian-Pakistani tensions and the confrontation of their respective military forces in Kashmir would provide the spark for an escalating military conflict in the region.[20]

To calm the situation, Beijing urged moderation on both sides. During deliberations leading to a UN Security Council resolution on the South Asian tests, China's

UN Permanent Representative called on the two sides to seek a "mutually acceptable solution" in accordance with "relevant UN resolutions and the Simla Agreement."[21] The latter was an accord on differences between India and Pakistan reached in 1972.

Beijing had come to this even-handed position through a long process, where China no longer saw the advantages of a decided tilt toward Pakistan on this or other issues.[22] Reflecting its deep antagonism to India, and the nascent Indian-Soviet strategic alignment, China strongly supported Pakistan in the 1960s. Premier Zhou Enlai used a 1964 joint statement with Pakistan to underline Beijing's position in support of the Kashmir people's right to self-determination. This leaned toward Pakistan's preference for a UN plebiscite as called for by 1948-1949 UN declarations on Kashmir. During the 1960s and early 1970s, Beijing also used threats of military action against India and in support of Pakistan in ultimately unsuccessful efforts to prevent Indian-backed dismemberment of Pakistan. New Delhi, backed by the USSR, called China's bluff in supporting Bangladeshi independence, facilitating Pakistan's dismemberment in 1971-1972.

As Beijing sought to reduce tensions with New Delhi in the late 1970s, China grew sensitive to criticism by India's leaders that China's stance on Kashmir was complicating Sino-Indian relations. China's foreign minister in 1980 called for a just settlement in accordance with relevant UN resolutions and the 1972 Simla Agreement. The latter accord followed Islamabad's defeat in the third India-Pakistan war and (at India's insistence) called for bilateral negotiations to resolve the dispute. In further deference to India, China largely dropped public reference to Kashmir's self-determination, even during the late 1980s and early 1990s when rapprochement was severely threatened first by escalating military tension along the Sino-Indian border and then by friction between Islamabad and New Delhi after the outbreak of the Kashmir insurgency. China moved further away from the uncritical support for Pakistan during the 1990s by refusing to back Islamabad on Kashmir in the UN Human Rights Commission.

The balanced Chinese stance on Kashmir notified India of China's continued interest in improved relations despite sometimes heated Chinese commentary directed at the nationalistic Indian government. Indian policy makers, of course, had historic grievances regarding China and the Kashmir dispute. The Sino-Indian border war of 1962 confirmed Beijing's control of sixteen thousand square miles of disputed territory in Kashmir, which contains a strategic road connecting China's Xinjiang Autonomous Region with Tibet.

The altered Chinese stance on Kashmir was one of the disappointments Pakistan faced in watching its Chinese ally pursue its advantage in the new situation. Pakistani and Chinese officials alike emphasized the positive features of their relationship while soft-pedaling the reality that Pakistan, as the weaker party, needed to continue to cater to China and rely on Chinese support, even when Beijing's backing was notably less strong than in the past.

In sum, China's moderate and pragmatic approach to South Asia in the 1990s faced a major challenge as a result of India's nuclear tests and anti-China posture in 1998. Chinese leaders reacted calmly, hoping to encourage strong international pressure, led by the United States, to curb Indian ambitions. Beijing remained sensitive to perceived backsliding by the United States and Russia. Beijing refused Russian Prime Minister Yevgeni Primakov's suggestion in December 1998 that Russia, India, and China join forces to influence world politics.[23] Meanwhile, it solidified its relations with Pakistan, notably sending the Chinese defense minister there in February 1999.[24]

China soon joined the United States and other powers in resuming constructive relations with India in the years following the Indian nuclear tests. Beijing avoided siding with Pakistan during the India-Pakistani confrontation on disputed issues in Kashmir during the co-called Kargil war of 1999. It worked with the United States and other concerned powers in efforts to keep India-Pakistani tensions in dispute in 1990s and later from escalating into full-scale and possibly nuclear war.[25]

Sino-Indian leaders resumed exchanges. The emphasis the two powers placed on seeking normalization of their relations was diminished as a result of the major regional changes caused by the U.S.-led war against the Taliban regime in Afghanistan and the broader war against global terrorism. The United States quickly became the dominant outside power in both India and Pakistan, achieving an unprecedented situation of having improving relations with both New Delhi and Islamabad. After adjusting to the changed circumstances, China and India saw their interests well served by continued efforts to achieve greater cooperation, and they endeavored to pursue these interests through high-level contacts and other channels.[26]

China-India Relations

In general, Chinese-Indian relations have entered a path of limited cooperation that appears likely to continue with no major diversion for at least several more years. In general, Sino-Indian relations settled on a path of limited cooperation that appeared likely to continue with no major diversion for at least several more years.[27]

- The prospects for another military conflict between China and India appeared to be low.
- The chances that the two rivals would put aside their differences and become close partners also appeared to be low.

China and India were at odds over many issues that continued to make further rapprochement difficult. The relationship remained asymmetrical. The economic and strategic military disparities were wide and seemed to be widening in China's favor. Beijing regarded a more confident and prosperous India as a bothersome neighbor, a growing rival for influence in Asia, and a potential anti-China partner of the United States. Beijing, however, did not regard India as a major military threat or trade competitor. China, on the other hand, loomed larger in Indian calculations. Many

Indians saw China as an aggressive, undemocratic power that represented a long-term challenge to India's security.[28]

Key elements of the rivalry that do not seem likely to be resolved quickly or easily include:

- *The role of Pakistan.* Pakistan has remained India's traditional and most immediate rival and also one of China's closest strategic partners—relationships that have a long history. Despite Pakistan's steep economic and political decline in recent years, Beijing still values a stable and peaceful Pakistan that could assist in constraining India, protecting China's western flank from Islamic extremists, and facilitating Chinese entrée to the Islamic world. By contrast, Indian hostility toward Pakistan has been visceral. New Delhi has regarded China's conventional military, missile, and nuclear weapons support to Pakistan as a hostile act.
- *The border issue.* Border negotiations have been ongoing since the 1980s, but no major breakthrough has occurred. A border settlement that essentially formalized the status quo is increasingly likely but may take more years to realize due to deep-seated mutual suspicions and India's reluctance to set a precedent for settling the Kashmir dispute with Pakistan.
- *Competition for influence elsewhere in Asia.* China and India view one another as potential adversaries, and each is taking steps to counter the other's influence as they both expand power and influence in Asian affairs. China has a clear lead in spreading influence in Southeast Asia, but India competes with its own free trade agreements, diplomatic overtures to ASEAN, military deployments, and particularly efforts to improve ties with nearby Myanmar, and more strategically to foster closer cooperation in Asia with Japan and the United States.[29]

Limited but growing cooperation between China and India is occurring on a number of issues and seems likely to continue.[30] For a time during the post-Cold War period, both looked for ways to promote a multipolar world order against the dominance of the U.S. superpower; this effort flagged first in India and then in China in 2000-2001. Both opposed U.S. missile defense proposals, but India moderated its opposition in 2001. Both are cooperating in the U.S.-led antiterrorism campaign after September 11, 2001. China and India also seek to counter perceived Western infringements on state sovereignty that pose dangerous precedents for Tibet, Taiwan, and Kashmir. They also seek to share computer expertise and technology, and to expand bilateral trade. Trade grew from $350 million in 1993 to over $5 billion in 2003. Further rapid growth is forecast, possibly reaching $20 billion by the end of the decade. India has become China's largest trading partner in South Asia and China is India's largest trading partner in East Asia.[31]

Domestic politics are more important in determining possible shifts in India's policies than those of China, where the leadership seems in basic agreement about the outlines of China's policy toward India. Those in India benefiting from or advocating improved ties with China (e.g., bilateral trade flows that favor India) are offset by defense planners, economic strategists, and ruling coalition leaders who are very wary of Chinese power and intentions and resolved to maneuver effectively in order to protect Indian interests in anticipation of a shift toward a more assertive and less accommodating stance by Beijing.[32]

Certain catalytic events that appear less than likely would steer the relationship on to more cooperative or competitive paths than the path seen as most probable, above. More rapid movement toward a border settlement or a sharp deterioration of China-Pakistan relations could lead to closer relations between India and China. On the other hand, the coming to power of more hawkish leaders in India, or an India-Pakistan conflict in which Pakistan's survival is in jeopardy, would run the risk of another Sino-Indian military confrontation.[33]

President Clinton visited India in 2000 and the Bush administration followed with high-level consultations that markedly improved U.S.-Indian relations even before the marked upswing in U.S.-Indian cooperation after September 11, 2001. U.S. policy would be a more important determinant in a more competitive Sino-Indian relationship, where each Asian power—especially China—would tend to see movement by Washington to court the other as a U.S. attempt at containment. A deepening Sino-Indian rivalry also could evolve as a by-product of close Indo-U.S. strategic cooperation or renewal of strong U.S. cooperation with China-backed Pakistan.

Conversely, possible U.S. military operations to implement international sanctions—that China and India view as potentially threatening to their own freedom of action in handling sensitive issues of sovereignty such as Taiwan, Tibet, and Kashmir—could prompt closer Sino-Indian cooperation. A more cooperative Sino-Indian relationship probably would not preclude each side from pursuing advantageous economic and other bilateral relations with the United States.

Consultations with fifty foreign and defense policy specialists in New Delhi in mid-2004 clarified the state of play in India's reaction to China's approach to Asia and its implications for India. The consultations took place in conjunction with six formal presentations on Chinese foreign policy made by the author to groups of academic, diplomatic, military, and business representatives in New Delhi in June 2004. They reflected many different Indian perspectives regarding China and its intentions and approach toward India;[34] on the whole there continued to be mixed Indian views about China and Chinese leaders' intentions toward Asia and India in particular. Indian caution about negative aspects of China-India relations appeared to be offset to an increasing degree by perceived positive elements and opportunities in China's approach to Asia and India.

Elements of distrust and suspicion that long bedeviled Indian-Chinese relations remained strong. The perceived breach of trust by China in the 1962 war was not forgotten. Strong fears persisted concerning alleged Chinese ambitions to hobble India's rising power by using close Chinese support for Pakistan and developing Chinese relations with such regional nations as Myanmar. China's vibrant economy and active diplomacy were viewed as in competition with Indian interests. ASEAN was depicted as a key arena of Sino-Indian competition for economic benefit and political influence in a strategic area adjoining both powers. China was more advanced than India in interacting with Asia wide groups, and New Delhi was lagging behind China in seeking a leading position in these bodies. In Central Asia, China was seen behind continued refusal of the Shanghai Cooperation Organization to allow Indian participation, and it favored the protracted UN reform procedures that kept India from gaining a permanent seat in the UN Security Council.

The above issues, the broader historical experience of Sino-Indian relations, and especially the absence of substantial change in Chinese support for Pakistan tended to lean Indian specialists to reserve judgment about China's avowed benign intentions in the recent "peaceful rise" and "peaceful development" formulations. Many Indian specialists judged that the recent positive Chinese approach toward India and other Chinese neighbors could change as a result of changes in China or abroad. They were not reassured by what they viewed as the less than transparent Chinese decision-making process. They looked to improved or continued strong Indian relations with the United States, Japan, and Russia as assisting India in case China changed to a harder line toward New Delhi. They also favored a continuation of the status quo in the Taiwan Strait, which they viewed as keeping China occupied with strategic concerns on China's eastern frontier and reducing the likelihood of assertive Chinese behavior toward India on the West.

Among key barometers of Chinese intentions monitored by such Indian skeptics were Chinese missile and nuclear support to Pakistan and elsewhere in the region—China's Intermediate Range Ballistic Missile sales to Saudi Arabia in the 1980s continued to be viewed negatively. A Chinese resort to force against Taiwan would reinforce Indian wariness toward the PRC, while Chinese military modernization including missile developments threatening India or expanded naval forces in the South Asian region would be viewed with concern.

Weighted against elements of distrust and suspicion were growing positive conditions and perceptions in India regarding the status and outlook of relations with China and China's approach to Asian and world affairs. Heading the list was a perceived change in the asymmetry of power and influence between China and India. Until recently, it was argued, China tended to discount Indian power and influence, and India tended to fear Chinese power and influence. Several developments since the late 1990s changed this equation, giving Indian specialists a view that India was now dealing with China in a more equal way and from a position of improved strength. Key changes included India's demonstration of a nuclear weapons capability combined with a strong overall modernization of Indian conventional weapons and other military capabilities (e.g., ballistic missiles); India's vibrant economy, which attracted investment and other interchange from the West, Japan, and other developed economies; and India's improved military and other ties with the United States, along with continued close ties with Russia and improving relations with the European Union and Japan.

These perceived changes in power relations compelled China to "come to terms" with India, resulting in much greater positive Chinese attention to developing relations with India, according to some Indian specialists. Indian businesses were seen as able to compete with China's highly competitive manufacturers, who were feared in the past as a major threat to Indian industries. The fact that India ran modest trade surpluses with China was a positive indicator of India's ability to hold its own with Chinese competitors, a contrast from a few years earlier when Indian manufacturers were alarmed by the prospects of a wave of Chinese products surpassing Indian products in price and quality.

According to Indian specialists, a recently heightened threat of international terrorism to China prompted Chinese officials to deepen antiterrorism cooperation with India, while Chinese leaders also came to view Pakistan as a liability as far as the terrorist threat to China was concerned. Chinese officials were said to express to Indian officials their concerns of anti-Chinese terrorists remaining active inside Pakistan; Chinese officials also expressed concern about Pakistan nuclear weapons and weapons technology exports, and the possibility of such material getting into the hands of terrorists who were targeting China. Pakistan's weak economic conditions added to Chinese incentives to sustain close ties with India as a stable anchor of Chinese policy interests in South Asia, according to Indian specialists.

In the view of Indian officials and specialists, Indian Prime Minister Shri Atal Bihari Vajpayee's visit to China on June 22-27, 2003, captured many of the new positive elements in India's overall more forward-leaning approach to China. He signed a Declaration on Principles for Relations and Comprehensive Cooperation with his Chinese counterpart Premier Wen Jiabao on June 23. The declaration referred to the traditionally emphasized Five Principles of Peaceful Coexistence as well as to hard problems in Sino-Indian relations, and noted the two sides' expectations to advance relations.[35]

Nine Memoranda of Understanding, Executive Programs, and a protocol were signed during the visit that set the stage for greater bilateral cooperation. An agreement covering border trade between the previously independent and now Indian state of Sikkim and Tibet showed flexibility on territorial issues in the interests of promoting mutually advantageous economic exchange. The two leaders built on progress in dealing with border issues, notably the 1993 Agreement on the Maintenance of Peace and Tranquility along the Line of Actual Control (LOAC) in the India-China border areas, and the 1996 Agreement on Confidence Building Measures in the Military field along the LOAC in India-China border areas. They agreed "to each appoint a special representative to explore, from the political perspective of the overall relationship, the framework of a boundary settlement." The Indian side appointed the government's national security adviser while the Chinese side appointed its senior vice foreign minister—both officials had strong reputations as effective and influential representatives of their governments' interests.

The visit marked an increase in bilateral trade to a level of about $5 billion in 2003. The two leading Indian business bodies, the Federation of Chambers of Commerce and Industry and the Confederation of Indian Industries, mounted the largest-ever delegation of leading Indian entrepreneurs to accompany the prime minister abroad on this visit to China. This was seen as symbolizing the changed mind-set from a few years earlier of Indian businesses' fear of Chinese competition to one of confidence in the strengths of Indian entrepreneurship. This shift was underpinned by the large increases in bilateral trade and the experiences of some modest investments in each country. Trade was expected to increase rapidly in the next several years. Other areas of possible improved relations involved culture and education.

Indian observers were optimistic about closer Indian-China cooperation in ASEAN and other Asian forums as a result of the Indian prime minister's visit. The June 23 declaration said that "The two sides supported multilateral cooperation in Asia, believing that such cooperation promotes mutually beneficial exchanges, economic growth as well as greater cohesion among Asian countries. The two sides viewed positively each others' participation in regional and sub-regional multilateral cooperation process in Asia." It was deemed possible in light of the declaration to envision cooperation between India and China in various multilateral regimes—official and nonofficial—on a nonexclusive basis, for the common good of Asia and the world.

A balanced and comprehensive assessment of the status and outlook of Indian relations with China and Indian attitudes toward China and rising Chinese influence in Asia in 2004 showed momentum on the side of the positive aspects of India-China relations, while the negative aspects served as brakes slowing forward movement and precluding the kind of enthusiastic "China fever" seen in South Korea and among some in Southeast Asian states. Indian government representatives and nongovernment specialists showed greater confidence in India's ability to deal with Chinese policies and behavior in pragmatic ways that would preserve and enhance Indian interests. Compared to a few years earlier, there was less alarm and seemingly more realistic views of the dangers posed by Chinese manufacturers to their Indian counterparts. In security areas, Indian officials and specialists seemed similarly less alarmed and more realistic about Chinese activities in Pakistan, Myanmar, Nepal, and elsewhere in South Asia, which in the past had been viewed with deep concern as part of perceived Chinese efforts to encircle and contain Indian power and influence. The China-Pakistan tie remained a counterweight to Indian leadership in South Asia and Asian affairs, but Indian officials and nongovernment specialists seemed less concerned about Chinese activities in other nearby states. China also was seen as compelled by India's power and influence to deal pragmatically with the South Asian power in order to foster and develop Chinese interests in the region.

Looking out, Indian specialists tended to see more opportunities than challenges for India in China's recent emphasis on "peaceful rise" and "peaceful development," and the overall more accommodating and flexible Chinese approach to Asian affairs. They anticipated greater economic cooperation, cross-border trade, and perhaps greater progress on border issues. They averred that the change in Indian governments as a result of the parliamentary election in spring 2004 would not significantly affect the forward movement in Indian-China relations.

Indian officials and nongovernment specialists remained clear-eyed about Sino-Indian differences over Pakistan, the Sino-India border, competition for leadership in Asian and world bodies, and other issues. They valued Indian economic dynamism and close Indian relations with Russia, Japan, the European Union, and especially the United States as important factors causing China to treat India with more attention and respect.

Expanded U.S. Role in South Asia

The large and rapid increase in U.S. power, influence, and military presence in South Asia since 2001 has had a number of benefits for China and Chinese interests in South Asia. It has reduced the drain on Chinese resources as the U.S. superpower took the lead in supporting the shaky economic foundation of the Pakistani government. U.S. power drove out the terrorist harboring Taliban regime in Afghanistan and was instrumental in shifting Pakistani government policies away from extremists who threatened Chinese interests in stability in South and Central Asia. Stronger U.S. influence in both India and Pakistan helped to keep the peace in the region and avoided nuclear war, despite simmering tensions over Kashmir and other issues.[36]

At the same time, there was plenty of evidence that China viewed the expanding U.S. influences with suspicion. For years, Chinese strategists had sought to expand China influence throughout China's periphery and to weaken the standing of the U.S. superpower, encouraging the emergence of a multipolar world. China sometimes saw common ground with India, which also at times resisted U.S. dominance. Chinese leaders saw U.S. power and influence move quickly to tilt the overall strategic balance in South Asia decisively in favor of the United States. It appeared that the U.S. presence and dominance in the region, buttressed by closer U.S. strategic relations with both New Delhi and Islamabad, would remain for some years to come.[37]

Chinese officials showed unease with the expanded U.S. influence and presence. In 2002, the PLA's chief of staff warned the United States against using the war on terrorism to dominate global affairs—"counter terrorism should not be used to practice hegemony," he advised. Visiting Iran and Europe in April 2002, Jiang Zemin differed with the U.S. stance against Iran and Iraq, and highlighted Chinese differences with the United States in the war on terrorism.[38]

Particularly worrisome from Chinese leaders' perspective was the rapid and close convergence in U.S.-Indian strategic relations. New Delhi in early 2001 put aside past criticism of U.S. missile defense plans, responding more positively to President Bush's initiatives than most U.S. allies. At this time, China continued to view U.S. missile defense plans as a threat to core Chinese interests, including Taiwan, and a manifestation of U.S. "hegemonic" ambitions. In contrast to the slow pace of U.S.-China military exchanges, U.S. and Indian leaders saw broad common ground in improved military relations. The United States liberalized arms and technology transfers, cooperated closely with Indian forces in securing sea lanes in South Asia, and conducted a number of highly sophisticated military exercises with

Indian forces. Meanwhile, the main U.S. Asian ally, Japan, improved its strategic and defense relations with India along a parallel track.[39]

Chinese concern about the renewed U.S. strategic cooperation with Pakistan was more moderate as a strengthened Pakistan supported Chinese interest in South Asia. The changeable U.S. record of support for Pakistan also ensured that Islamabad was unlikely to favor Washington at the expense of Beijing. China remained a critically important and consistent backer of Pakistan, in contrast to seeming U.S. fickleness over the years. Emblematic of the more permanent features of Sino-Pakistani cooperation are large-scale infrastructure projects China has undertaken that involve Pakistan. China seems determined to use projects such as the Sino-Pakistan Friendship Highway—Gwadar Project to give its westernmost regions access to the sea and the global economy, via road and rail connections and enhanced Chinese-supported port facilities in Pakistan.[40]

Notes

1. John Garver, "China and South Asia," *Annals of the American Academy of Political and Social Science* 519 (January 1992): 67-85; J. Mohan Malik, "Chinese-Indian Relations in the Post-Soviet Era," *China Quarterly* 142 (June 1995): 317-55; Devin Hagerty, "China and Pakistan: Strains in the Relationship," *Current History* (September 2002): 284-89; J. Mohan Malik, "The China Factor in the India-Pakistan Conflict," *Parameters* (Spring 2003): 35-50; John Garver, *Protracted Contest: Sino-Indian Rivalry in the 20th Century* (Seattle: University of Washington, 2001); Vinod C. Khanna, "Review Article," (of Garver's *Protracted Contest)*, *China Report* (New Delhi) 39, no. 1 (2003): 87-97; Robert Wirsing, *The Enemy of My Enemy: Pakistan's China Debate* (Honolulu: Asia Pacific Center for Security Studies, December 2003); Li Shijia, "We Have Accomplished Something Significant: Experts Interpret China-India Declaration," *Xinhua*, 26 June 2003; Jay Solomon, Charles Hutzler, Zahid Hussain, "China Pursues India-Pakistan Peace," *Wall Street Journal,* 8 December 2003; Jay Solomon and David Murphey, "China-India Ties Strengthen," *Wall Street Journal*, 10 November 2003; Sanjeev Miglani, "India Says Mutual Suspicions of China Thing of the Past," *Reuters*, 23 June 2003; Faisal O. Al-Rfouh, "Sino-Indian Relations: From Confrontation to Accommodation" (1988-2001), *China Report* (New Delhi) 39, no. 1 (2003): 21-38; Song Mingjiang, "China-India-Russia Cooperation in Contemporary International Situation," *China Report* (New Delhi) 40, no. 2 (2004): 128-30; See also Mohan Malik, "India-China Relations," in *Asia's Bilateral Relations* (Honolulu: Asia Pacific Center for Security Studies, 2004); Francine R. Frankel and Harry Harding, *The India-China Relationship* (New York: Asia Society/Woodrow Wilson International Center, 2004).

2. "South Asian Crisis: China's Assessments and Goals" (Washington, D.C.: Library of Congress), Congressional Research Service, *CRS Memorandum*, 6 June 1998. This memorandum was based especially on twenty interviews conducted with Chinese and other official experts following the Indian nuclear tests.

3. Hagerty, "China and Pakistan," *Current History*, 289.

4. John Garver, "China's Influence in Central and South Asia," paper presented to a conference at The George Washington University, Washington, D.C., 6 December 2003, 13-15.

5. Wu Yixue, "U.S. Dreams of Asian NATO," *China Daily,* 18 July 2003, 4.

6. Abu Taher Salahuddin Ahmed, "India-China Relations in the 1990s," *Journal of Contemporary Asia* 26, no. 1 (1996): 100-15.

7. Denny Roy, *China's Foreign Relations* (Lanham, Md.: Rowman & Littlefield, 1998), 170-74.

8. Robert Sutter, *Chinese Policy Priorities and Their Implications for the United States* (Lanham, Md.: Rowman & Littlefield, 2000), 135.

9. Hong Kong *AFP* in English, 3 June 1998, carried by Foreign Broadcast Information Service (FBIS, Internet version).

10. Malik, "Chinese-Indian Relations," *China Quarterly,* 317-55. Ahmed, "India-China Relations," *Journal of Contemporary Asia,* 100-15; Garver, *Protracted Contest;* J. Mohan Malik, *Eyeing the Dragon: India's China Debate* (Honolulu: Asia Pacific Center for Security Studies, 2003).

11. "PRC on India Tests," FBIS *Trends,* 19 May 1998 (Internet version).

12. "South Asian Crisis," *CRS Memorandum,* 3.

13. Cited in "PRC on India Tests," *Trends.*

14. Cited in "PRC on India Tests," *Trends.*

15. Cited in "PRC on India Tests," *Trends.*

16. See review of these consultations in "South Asian Crisis," *CRS Memorandum,* 3.

17. "Sino-U.S. Joint Statement on South Asia," *Xinhua,* 27 June 1998, carried by FBIS (Internet version).

18. Reviewed in Sutter, *Chinese Policy Priorities,* 139-40.

19. Some Chinese officials privately encouraged the United States to take stronger action against India by asserting that such action was needed to counter Pakistani charges, echoed by some in China, that one of the reasons India carried out tests in the first place was that the United States tacitly "supported" India's rising power, partly as a check against China. The U.S. "failure" to detect and prevent the initial Indian test was seen as evidence of this alleged U.S. strategic plan for the region. Interviews, May-June 1998, summarized in "South Asian Crisis," *CRS Memorandum,* 3.

20. "Beijing Radio Comments on India's Foreign Policy," *Beijing Radio,* 28 May 1998, carried by FBIS (Internet version).

21. "Tang Jiaxuan on UNSC Meeting, South Asian Situation," *Xinhua,* 4 June 1998, carried by FBIS (Internet version).

22. Sutter, *Chinese Policy Priorities,* 140-41.

23. "Primakov Seeks Strategic Triangle," *International Herald Tribune,* 22 December 1998.

24. "Chi Haotian-led Chinese Delegation to Visit Pakistan, Islamabad," *The Nation* (Pakistan), 7 February 1999, 16.

25. Hagerty, "China and Pakistan," *Current History,* 289.

26. Shyam Bhatia, "George Warms Up to China," *Bangalore Deccan Herald,* 28 March 2002 (Internet version); "India and China Open Air Route," *BBC News,* 28 March 2002 (Internet version); Li Shijia, "We Have Accomplished Something Significant," *Xinhua,* 26 June 2003; Jay Solomon and David Murphey, "China-India Ties Strengthen," *Wall Street Journal,* 10 November 2003.

27. Robert Sutter, *The United States and East Asia* (Lanham, Md.: Rowman & Littlefield, 2003), 116.

28. See the review of Sino-Indian relations and the various documentary sources listed concerning Sino-Indian relations in *Access Asia Review,* July 2000, 3, no. 2 (Seattle, Wash.: The National Bureau of Asian Research, 2000); Malik, *Eyeing the Dragon.*

29. Malik, *Eyeing the Dragon.* See also Brahma Chellaney, "China Seeks to Stem India's Budding Military Ties With U.S.," *International Herald Tribune,* 9 January 2002 (Internet version); Feng Zhaokui, "China-Japan-India Axis Strategy: An All-round Economic and Political Cooperation," *People's Daily,* 29 April 2004 (Internet version).

30. Sutter, *The United States and East Asia,* 117.

31. Jay Solomon and David Murphey, "China-India Ties Strengthen," *Wall Street Journal,* 10 November 2003. See also Liu Limin, "China-India Relations Enter the Fast Lane of Development," replayed in *China Strategy,* vol. 3, www.csis.org (accessed 20 July 2004).

32. Stephen Cohen, *India: Emerging Power* (Washington, D.C.: Brookings Institution, 2001), 256-64.

33. Sutter, *The United States and East Asia,* 117.

34. (Retired) Brigadier Y. S. Desai, "Imperialist China," *Journal of the United Service Institution of India,* CXXXIV, no. 555 (January-March 2004): 55-61; Jairam Ramesh, "Vajpayee Goes to China: Time for Bold New Bilateral and Regional Initiatives," *Prime Minister Vajpayee's China Visit June 2003,* Occasional Studies, no. 1 (New Delhi: Institute of Chinese Studies, October 2003): 10-12. See discussion of "the Chinese Threat" and "Danger From China" in *Security Challenges of India in the Regional Context With Special Reference to Terrorism—Prognosis and Response* (New Delhi: United Services Institution of India, 4 September 2002): 14.

35. For a review of the major developments and detail of the visit, see C. V. Ranganathan, "India and China: 'Learning to Learn,'" in *Prime Minister Vajpayee's China Visit June 2003,* Occasional Studies, no. 1 (New Delhi: Institute of Chinese Studies, October 2003): 45-54.

36. Garver, "China's Influence in Central and South Asia,"13-15.

37. Cheng Ruisheng, "Some Observations on the International Situation Since September 11," *Foreign Affairs Journal* (Beijing) 67 (March 2003): 49-53; Shen Qiang, "Impact of U.S. Strategic Readjustments on International Relations," *Foreign Affairs Journal* (Beijing) 67 (March 2003): 54-62.

38. Malik, "The China Factor in the India-Pakistan Conflict," 43.

39. Malik, "The China Factor in the India-Pakistan Conflict," 44.

40. Garver, "China's Influence in Central and South Asia," 6-7.

Chapter 10

Relations with Central Asia

Advancing Ties with New Nations

China's leadership has worked assiduously to secure boundaries, curb terrorism and transnational crime, and incrementally advance Chinese influence with countries along China's border with Central Asia. The end of the USSR resulted in the creation of new states, reduced Moscow's influence, and opened opportunities for spreading Chinese interests. The collapse of the USSR also created a power vacuum that posed problems for Chinese security.[1]

Generally preoccupied with affairs at home, Chinese officials showed an interest in improving relations with newly independent Central Asian states as much for defensive reasons as for reasons of expanding Chinese influence and interests. Thus, Chinese comment was supportive of Russia's residual influence in the region and Moscow's efforts to preserve a strong position in the face of perceived encroachment from the West. During the 1990s, Beijing reportedly was keenly interested in getting Central Asian governments to take stronger actions against pan-Turkic, Islamic, and other radicals who were linked to bombings, insurrections, and other disturbances among Turkic minorities in Xinjiang Autonomous Region and other parts of China. At the same time, China wished to benefit from economic, military, and political exchanges, and took several notable steps to advance cooperation in joint ventures to exploit Central Asian oil resources.[2]

The U.S.-led global war on terrorism, the toppling of the Taliban regime in Afghanistan, and the stronger U.S. military presence and strategic influence in

Central Asia markedly changed the strategic environment for Chinese policies and initiatives in Central Asia. China's relative influence remained secondary to the United States and Russia, but it continued to grow as the broad outlines of China's policy toward Central Asia in the post-Cold War period persisted. China continued to expand its ties across Central Asia to stabilize its western frontier, gain access to the region's energy resources, and balance Western influence in an area Beijing traditionally viewed as Russia's reserve. Beijing has calculated that improved ties with Central Asian states, which are also concerned about problems arising from the linkage of religion and politics, can shield Xinjiang Province and its ethnically Turkic population from outside Muslim and pan-Turkic influence. Central Asian leaders assure Beijing they will not tolerate separatist groups targeting China, though China suspects its neighbors may lack sufficient resolve to eradicate the threat. In this context, U.S., Russian, and Chinese efforts to support antiterrorist initiatives in Central Asia seem to reflect important common ground among the three powers.[3]

China's Central Asian energy projects reflect PRC efforts to obtain secure supply lines and avoid overdependence on a few sources of energy. Among various agreements and arrangements, Beijing has an agreement to develop two major Kazakhstan oil and gas fields and construct pipelines to Xinjiang, and reportedly is exploring gas and other pipeline links with Kyrgyzstan, Turkmenistan, and others. But the projects are expensive, logistically difficult, and complicated by inadequate energy-processing and transport systems in western China.[4]

China and Kazakhstan on September 24, 1997, signed two agreements worth $9.5 billion for the development of two major oil and gas fields and the construction of two pipelines in Kazakhstan, according to press reports. One pipeline was to cover three thousand kilometers from Kazakhstan into western China and take an estimated five years to build; the other would extend two hundred fifty kilometers to the Turkmen border and be connected to a pipeline into Iran.[5]

Political and economic factors may have tilted Almaty toward China rather than toward competing U.S. companies. President Nazarbayev was presumably sensitive to Chinese political concerns, including pressure to clamp down on Uighur exiles that provide support to dissidents in Xinjiang and complaints about Almaty's increasing cooperation with the United States, including cooperation on NATO expansion.[6]

Kazakhstan officials were also aware that Beijing's large foreign exchange reserves could help it win bids it was prepared to pay for. Moreover, China's proposal to build a pipeline eastward—and thereby link the eastern Kazakhstan cities with the country's oil resources, before joining a planned trans-China pipeline, also favored the PRC.

However, even under the best of circumstances these projects are fraught with difficulties. The China national petroleum corporation was regarded within the industry as lacking world-class technology and experience in managing such complex international construction projects. Moreover, regional politics—including energy politics—remain complicated. Such uncertainties reinforce a prevailing pattern of many signed agreements but only slow progress toward pipelines and other expensive infrastructure needed to get the oil and other energy to the consumer.[7]

In the 1990s, China carefully monitored the growing Western commercial presence in Central Asia and viewed expanding NATO activities as indicative of U.S. efforts to extend its influence to the region, squeeze out Russia, and, with the U.S.-Japan military alliance, contain China. Beijing sharply criticized a September 1997 Partnership for Peace (PFP)-sponsored exercise in Kazakhstan and Uzbekistan, which involved the Central Asian Peacekeeping Battalion and contingents from four other countries, including Russia. The exercise featured the record-setting long-distance air transport of five hundred U.S. troops to Kazakhstan. Despite its participation, Russia was at best ambivalent about the exercise and its NATO connection.[8]

China's expanding influence in Central Asia has prompted little adverse reaction from Moscow, which heretofore jealously guarded the region's resources. For its part, Beijing regards a Central Asian power balance favoring Russia as advantageous to its own interests, but believes the Russian leadership may be too weak to guarantee security in the former Soviet territories. China nonetheless pursues its interests in Central Asia cautiously, presumably in part to avoid provoking its strategic partner into discontinuing the steady supply of Russian arms to China and possible risking a strong nationalist backlash from Russia's leadership.[9]

The complex range of factors influencing Chinese policy in the region was revealed in the Chinese relationship with Turkey, an influential actor in Central Asian diplomacy. The visit to Beijing by the Turkish deputy prime minister in June 1998 reflected these factors as it marked ongoing efforts to strengthen economic ties and play down differences, especially over the treatment of Turkic Uighurs in Xinjiang.

Relations had remained somewhat chilled between these two generally low-key competitors for Central Asian markets and political influence since the PRC crackdown against Xinjiang's assertive Uighurs following a violent post-Ramadan uprising in early 1997. The Turkish Foreign Ministry at that time issued a statement deploring the "bloody developments" while respecting China's territorial integrity and stating that the people of Xinjiang should be a "bridge of friendship" between the two countries.[10]

In Beijing in June 1998, Turkish Deputy Prime Minister Ecevit again acknowledged PRC sovereignty over Xinjiang but suggested that Ankara was limited in its ability to prevent demonstrations in Turkey by Uighur separatist elements, according to Turkish press reports.[11] Turkey, unlike the Central Asian states, had resisted Chinese pressure to issue public assurances that separatist activities will not be tolerated or otherwise crack down on such groups.

Turkey's NATO ties were also, presumably, problematic for PRC hard-liners, who perceived Turkey as a U.S. bridgehead for expanding NATO into Central Asia to squeeze out Russia and contain China. Beijing also closely monitored U.S.-Turkish collaboration on negotiations for a Central Asian pipeline, owing to concerns that China's own energy security might be affected if Central Asian oil flows predominantly westward. Chinese leaders viewed two additional developments—Turkey's growing military ties with Israel and Turkish incursions into Northern Iraq in pursuit of Kurdish insurgents—as threats to regional stability with serious implications for China's friends in the Arab world and Iran.[12]

Both countries saw increased trade and economic ties as one means of smoothing over their differences. This was consistent with China's emphasis on this approach in its foreign relations to secure a stable environment for its domestic reform program. Turkey in recent years sought stronger ties with Central and East Asia, and showed particular interest in gaining access to the Caspian region's energy resources.

A Turkish state minister during an April 1998 visit to Beijing underscored the need for more balanced trade and announced an agreement with Chinese officials to increase the annual bilateral trade volume to more than $1.2 billion. Turkish imports from China, primarily manufactured goods, totaled about $560 million in 1997; exports to China amounted to just over $64 million.[13]

Typical of China's frequent diplomatic and high-level exchanges with Central Asian states was President Jiang Zemin's hosting of Kyrgyzstan President Askar Akayevich Akayev in April 1998.[14] Chinese media recalled that Jiang and Akayev had signed, along with Russian and other Central Asian leaders, a 1997 agreement on trust-strengthening measures and on cutting military forces in border areas. Jiang explicitly thanked Akayev for his government's opposition to "national separatism"—a presumed allusion to radical movements in Xinjiang. Akayev said that the Kyrgyz Republic opposes separatism and religious extremism, and "has learned from Chinese experiences on handling relations among ethnic groups." After pledging to improve trade and promote regional prosperity and peace, the two presidents witnessed the signing of four documents providing the following:

- An agreement on economic cooperation and trade;
- A framework for providing loans with reduced interest to the Kyrgyz Republic by China;
- Exchanges of the ratification certificates of a Chinese-Kyrgyz boundary agreement; and
- An agreement on extradition.

Meanwhile, Beijing adopted a typically even-handed public stance on the most contentious political issue in Central Asian politics in the 1990s—the continuing civil war in Afghanistan. In China's view, all warring parties were urged to stop fighting and to discuss their problems among themselves without any outside interference. China was willing to support international proposals for peace, but typically supported a major role for the UN, where China has a permanent seat on the Security Council. The Chinese were also reported to suspect the Taliban faction in Afghanistan of being supportive of radicals in Xinjiang.[15] The Chinese Foreign Ministry sent a delegation to the Taliban regime in early 1999, reportedly seeking to build relations.[16]

The record of China's approach toward Central Asia in the post-Cold War period clearly reflected key Chinese interests discerned by a U.S. study group sponsored by the Washington think tank the Center for Strategic and International Studies.[17] They were:

- *Strategic position.* China's engagement with Central Asia, and specifically the Shanghai Cooperation Organization (SCO), is part of China's overall diplomatic strategy to foster stable and productive international environment around China's periphery while fostering a more widely accepted Chinese leadership role. Beijing's relations with Central Asia also aim to legitimate Chinese positions on major international issues, strengthen relations with Russia, and serve as a counter to U.S. power and influence. China's diplomacy in Central Asia aimed to prevent the region from becoming a distraction from China's internal development and more important foreign policy goals.
- *Security.* China seeks to curb outside support to separatists in Xinjiang province. It sees common ground with regional governments in working against terrorist and criminal elements.
- *Borders.* China's seeks to demarcate, demilitarize, and stabilize borders with Russia, Kazakhstan, Kyrgyzstan, and Tajikistan. Border stability is central to Chinese development plans and foreign policy priorities.
- *Economic.* China's main economic interest in the region is energy—China seeks growing amounts of oil and gas abroad and in Central Asia—especially Kazakhstan appears as a promising partner.

As John Garver has highlighted recently, Chinese development of economic, military, and transportation links strengthened China's regional approach.[18] Following agreement with the Soviet Union in 1984 to build the first direct-rail link between Xinjiang and Soviet Central Asia (what is now Kazakhstan), the two sides agreed to broaden the cooperation on this "Eurasian land bridge." China double tracked some of its rail links leading to the cross-border line. It also built a line in the late 1990s into southwestern Xinjiang, and used this line as the basis for plans to build a new rail link between Xinjiang and Kyrgyzstan. China also proposed building another rail link in northern Xinjiang, with a different crossing point into Kazakhstan. Highway links between Xinjiang and Central Asia improved markedly beginning in the 1990s, with five hard-surface roads linking China and Kazakhstan and a new road to Kyrgyzstan. The China Kazakhstan pipeline agreement continued to encounter difficulties but the Chinese government appeared committed to the project.

Mongolia

Closer proximity to Chinese population centers and long-standing experience in dealing with its massive neighbor to the south have made Mongolia much more wary than states in Central Asia in dealing with China. Without its Soviet ally and determined to make its own way with a vibrant and sometimes confusing drive toward a market economy and democratic system, the Mongolian government watched carefully for signs of Chinese dominance while seeking reassurances from other powers, especially the United States. Beijing demonstrated little concern over trends in Mongolia, well aware that Ulan Bator, among all regional capitals, was more sensitive than most to possible adverse Chinese reactions if they are seen to align themselves in ways contrary to basic Chinese interests.[19]

Situated between Central and East Asia, Mongolia has sought to become more economically and politically integrated into East Asia. A more well-integrated Mongolia would play a larger regional role that would enable Mongolia to try to balance its relations with China and Russia, without depending too heavily on the United States. Mongolia publicly stated that enhanced cooperation with the United States remains a major pillar of its foreign policy and a means of preserving its independence and security.

Mongolia has supported the U.S. role in Asian security, in particular in northeast Asia. Mongolia sent a token force in support of the U.S.-led military effort in Iraq. Senior U.S. foreign and defense officials visit Mongolia. The Mongolian government has worked hard to maintain good relations with other regional actors—Russia, China, both Koreas, Japan—but Mongolian officials have expressed concern privately about potential Russian and Chinese rivalry over Mongolia. As part of its regional security strategy, Mongolia also has sought deeper trade and economic links with East Asian countries.

The Mongolian government has tried to expand its international contacts beyond its two neighbors. The leadership tends not see Mongolia as a part of Central Asia for cultural, religious, and political reasons, and has sought to identify the country as part of northeast Asia. It has aspired to participation in Asia Pacific regional organizations.[20]

Historic animosity and distrust of China's intentions toward Mongolia have continued to be factors in Mongolia's relations with its southern neighbor. The cornerstone of the Mongolian-Chinese relationship is a 1994 Treaty of Friendship and Cooperation, which codifies mutual respect for the independence and territorial integrity of both sides. Mongolian leaders in private have said that they continue to fear political forces in China that question Mongolian independence.

Despite their concerns, Mongolian leaders have recognized that a return to economic prosperity in their country depends upon maintaining and improving Mongolia's economic ties with China and Russia. Mongolia has been encouraged that both Russia and China are moving rapidly to integrate with the world politically and economically. Mongolia beat both its neighbors into the WTO with its January 1997 accession.

The issue of Tibet is one of some sensitivity in Mongolian-Chinese relations. Mongolia shares with Tibet its brand of Buddhism and in recent years received visits from the Dalai Lama, despite Chinese protests. Mongolians sympathize with the plight of Tibet, recognizing that but for the backing of the Soviet Union they might have suffered a similar fate. Realistically, however, they know there is little they can do for Tibet.

The positive aspects of Sino-Mongolian cooperation were on display when newly selected Chinese President Hu Jintao stopped in Mongolia in June 2003 during his first trip abroad as Chinese president. According to Chinese and Western press reports,[21] Hu told Mongolian counterparts that a stronger China was not a threat to the rest of Asia (and by implication neighboring Mongolia) and he proposed closer economic cooperation between China and Mongolia. He said that China would encourage large local companies to invest in Mongolia and would seek greater bilateral cooperation, especially in industries such as mining and infrastructure. Chinese reports noted that China was the largest foreign investor in Mongolia, accounting for nearly 40 percent of capital inflows into the country. China was also Mongolia's largest trade partner, accounting for 40 percent of its trade volume. To boost economic cooperation the Chinese and Mongolian leaders proposed several large-scale projects that would push forward the development of both countries.

Regional Multilateral Cooperation

China's interest in using multilateral organizations to pursue Chinese interests around its periphery in the post-Cold War period showed first in Central Asia. Building on a burgeoning "strategic partnership" with Russia, China hosted in Shanghai in April 1996 the first meeting of representative leaders of what became known as the Shanghai Five, consisting of China and Russia and the three other former Soviet republics that border on China, Kazakhstan, Kyrgyzstan, and Tajikistan. The group focused at first on finalizing border settlements between China and the four Soviet Republics, demilitarizing their frontiers, and establishing confidence-building measures. These issues were dealt with in a 1996 Shanghai Five "agreement on confidence building in the military field along the border areas," and a 1997 "agreement on reducing each other's military forces along the border regions."[22] At their summit in July 2000, the Shanghai Five declared success in building a border belt of trust and transparency.[23] They also had begun collaborating against terrorism, arms smuggling, and a range of illegal transnational activities affecting their common interests. They agreed in 1999 to set up a joint antiterrorist center in Kyrgyzstan.

Agreements in the late 1990s saw many steps to institutionalize the procedures of the Shanghai Five in dealing with border and security matters, and regularized meetings of the group's defense ministers and foreign ministers were established. Uzbekistan joined the group in July 2001, establishing the Shanghai Cooperation Organization with six members: Russia, China, Kazakhstan, Kyrgyzstan, Tajikistan, and Uzbekistan. The declaration on the creation of the Shanghai Cooperation Organization showed strong attention to regional security issues involving terrorism, drug trade, and other transnational crimes affecting the countries. Work in subsequent annual summit meetings of the group saw efforts to establish a charter and small budget for the organization, to start the small antiterrorism center in Kyrgyzstan, and to set up an SCO secretariat headquartered in Beijing and paid for by China to foster cooperation on terrorism and other transnational issues. Chinese leaders showed strong interest in broadening the scope of the SCO to include strong economic development efforts, notably Chinese interest in building transportation infrastructure that would benefit western China.[24]

Russia and China predictably used the Shanghai Five summit meetings and other occasions to issue statements and make speeches against U.S. domination and to call for a multipolar world, though such rhetoric dropped off once Russia and then China moderated toward the Bush administration by mid-2001. Until mid-2001, Chinese officials and media were uniform in calling attention to the Shanghai Five and the SCO as a model of the type of mutually respectful, consultative, and equal state relationships favored by China's New Security Concept, in contrast to the "power politics" and "hegemonism" practiced by the United States.[25]

Developing the SCO

The April 26, 1996, Shanghai summit meeting was the first meeting of the Shanghai Five, and was initiated by China. China proposed the meeting in part to address and stabilize the sometimes tense 7,000-kilometer border China shares with the former states of the USSR. The "treaty of deepening military trust in border regions" signed at the summit called on the signatories to invite the others to observe military drills and inform about any military activities within 100 kilometers from the border. It also forbade attacks on each other and restricted the scope and frequency of military maneuvers in border areas.[26] The next year, the "treaty on reducing military forces in border regions" was signed in Moscow. This agreement proposed to reduce the total number of military forces along the border to less than 130,400.[27] At a 1999 Shanghai Five summit in Bishkek, Kyrgyzstan, both the 1996 and 1997 agreements were seen as successful and the borders were said to be secure and stable.[28]

The Shanghai Five summit in Dushanbe, Tajikistan, in 2000 moved beyond previous emphasis on border security to stress a variety of regional issues of mutual concern. The gathered leaders discussed treaties to fight separatism, extremism, and terrorism—three "evils" stressed repeatedly by Chinese leaders. They also talked about dealing with drug trafficking and illegal immigration. In this context, the leaders agreed to hold regular meetings of officers from their justice, border control, customs, and public security departments.[29] They judged that developments and problems in the region had become more complicated and that the existing mechanisms under the Shanghai Five needed upgrading.[30]

At the summit in Shanghai in 2001, Uzbekistan was added to the group, prompting the Declaration of the Establishment of the Shanghai Cooperation Organization. The summit created a Council of State Coordinators to write a charter for the SCO and to establish regular meetings schedules.[31] The representatives of the six countries also signed the "Shanghai Convention on combating terrorism, separatism, and extremism"—China's so-called three evils or three vices. The convention established a legal foundation for combating these problems.[32]

Since then, SCO activities have developed. In addition to the annual head of state meetings, regular meetings occur at the levels of head of government, foreign minister, defense minister, and heads of law enforcement, energy, and trade departments. At the SCO summit in St. Petersburg in 2002, the group endorsed the SCO charter. It provides a legal basis of the principles, purpose, and tasks of the organization, the procedures for adopting new members, the legal effects of SCO decisions, and the means of cooperation with other multilateral organizations.[33] Reflecting China's strong role as a driving force behind the SCO's creation and development, Chinese Foreign Minister Tang Jiaxuan said at the summit that the SCO was no longer a "club for empty discussion but a viable institution capable to make an important contribution to the international war on terror."[34]

In January 2004, the SCO opened two permanent bodies, a secretariat in Beijing and a regional antiterrorism structure based in Tashkent. Chinese media highlighted UN General Secretary Kofi Annan announcing at the opening of the secretariat that "an institutionally strengthened SCO has been evolving into an increasingly important regional security organization. The secretariat represents the logical extension of that process and the UN looks forward to multi-faceted cooperation with our new regional partner."[35] Mongolia's foreign minister was present at the secretariat opening, and Iran, India, Pakistan, and Turkey expressed interest in joining. At the June 2004 SCO summit in Tashkent, Uzbekistan, the SCO Regional Anti-terrorist Structure was officially launched. Mongolia was admitted to the SCO as an observer, and Afghanistan was accepted under guest status. Among other agreements at the summit were a development fund and an entrepreneurs committee. Russia's bid to have India join the SCO was turned down. Chinese President Hu Jintao offered $900 million in preferential buyer's credit loans to the other SCO members.[36]

Chinese Security Interests. Chinese media were particularly insistent that the success of the SCO had to do with its "new security view." The 2000 Summit declared that "a new security view that is built on mutual trust, equality, and cooperation are conducive to enhancing mutual understanding and good neighbor relations."[37] Chinese president Jiang Zemin called the new view the "Shanghai spirit." At the 2001 summit, he declared that "the new model of regional cooperation represented by the 'Shanghai spirit' is a partnership not an alliance. It is an open mechanism not targeting any third party. In dealing with state to state relations it advocated the principle of equality and mutual benefit for the sake of win-win results and mutual development."[38] Of course the ideas seen in this SCO development had their roots in China's "Five Principles of Peaceful Coexistence" of the 1950s which emphasize respect for sovereignty, nonaggression, and noninterference, as well the use of those principles seen in China's "New Security Concept" of the 1990s, which advocates greater dialogue and mutual development and security.[39]

China's stronger support for multilateral security mechanisms in the SCO show that Chinese officials recognize that internal security issues cannot be met only with confidence building and other such measures among sovereign states. Chinese rulers historically viewed Central Asia as a source of threats to Chinese national security. The dissolution of the Soviet Union, the civil wars in Tajikistan, Afghanistan, and Chechnya, and the rise of Islamic unrest in western China created a tense and unstable regional situation of great concern to Chinese leaders. The rise of Islamic extremism in Central Asia and the Taliban regime in Afghanistan were related to militant attacks in Xinjiang. CSIS reported over 200 militant attacks resulting in 162 deaths in Xinjiang over a decade after the Cold War.[40]

Home of a large ethnic Turkish Muslim population of Uighurs who have periodically resisted Chinese rule, Xinjiang remained central to Chinese concerns. Unrest and insurrection there would be especially troubling for Beijing given Xinjiang's large size, vast resources, and vital strategic location. There are considerable Uighur populations in many Central Asian states including 120,000 in Kazakhstan and 50,000 in Kyrgyzstan. Suppressing dissidents in Xinjiang affects China's relations with these neighboring governments. Nonetheless, rising militant activism directed against China and other SCO government caused them to band together against the threat posed by militant Islam and the associated three evils.[41]

The 2001 SCO summit in Shanghai pledged a collective response from all the members in defense of a government attacked by militants. In one sense, this agreement created a basis for China to project power abroad through a multilateral mechanism.[42] This was followed by an agreement at the 2002 SCO foreign minister's meeting that endorsed Chinese actions fighting the "East Turkestan terrorists," along with Russian suppression of terrorists in Chechnya.[43] At a subsequent SCO defense ministers' meeting in Moscow, the SCO representatives issued a communiqué on military cooperation and established a senior defense official commission and a joint expert group responsible for coordinating military exercises among SCO participants.[44]

In addition to cooperating against terrorists, the SCO participants agreed to cooperate more regarding more-general emergency situations. In October 2002, Chinese and Kyrgyzstan militaries cooperated in a joint exercise in southern Kyrgyzstan, and in August 2003, five SCO members (not Uzbekistan) collaborated in a military exercise known as "Coalition 2003."[45] That exercise had two parts consisting of a mock hijacking of an airliner and a bus.[46] Meanwhile, it remained unclear in 2004 what would come from the Regional Antiterrorism Structure established in Tashkent in January 2004.

Chinese Economic Interests. China has also seen the SCO and broader regional cooperation as helpful in expanding Chinese economic growth and influence in the region. Chinese and Central Asian economies are complementary as Central Asian states have raw materials China needs (notably oil and gas), while China has consumer goods sought by the consumers in these states. Chinese leaders focused on Xinjiang are well aware that the province gets the bulk of its foreign trade with

Central Asian states. As Xinjiang's economic development is part of Beijing's strategy to calm unrest in the area, Chinese leaders pay special attention to Central Asian trade. In 1992-1997, China's total trade with Central Asia doubled to $872 million. In 2004, China was the second-largest trading partner (after Russia) of Kazakhstan and Kyrgyzstan.[47]

Russia endorses closer trade relations with China with President Putin saying at the SCO summit in Shanghai that "cooperation in economics, trade and culture is far more important than military cooperation."[48] A statement from a meeting of SCO trade ministers in 2002 said that "the SCO is different from the 'Shanghai Five' because regional economic cooperation is its main task."[49] A 2003 meeting of SCO prime ministers issued the "Outline for multilateral economic and trade cooperation of the SCO," furthering economic progress among the members.[50]

A key driver in China's economic interest in Central Asia is energy. The rapid growth of China's economy has seen China become a net importer of oil for over a decade and greatly increased Chinese government interest in securing reliable supplies of foreign oil and natural gas. By 1997 China had become the world's second-largest energy-consuming country, accounting for 9.6 percent of global energy consumption. It was projected that by 2020 China would account for 16.1 percent of global consumption.[51] While China has large reserves of coal, coal's inefficiencies and pollutants have made oil and natural gas more appealing and heightened China's search for overseas supplies.[52]

Though China is the world's fifth-largest oil producer, it became a net importer of petroleum in 1993. In 1999 it imported 18 percent of its oil consumption and imported twice as much in 2000 as it did in 1999. Though large, Chinese oil fields are mature and production has leveled off. The annual growth of domestic oil supply during the past decade was 1.67 percent while China's oil consumption grew at an annual rate of 5.77 percent. The deputy director of China's State Economic and Trade Council judged that China might have to rely on international markets for 50 percent of its oil by 2020. In this context, China's involvement in energy projects in Russia, Kazakhstan, and Kyrgyzstan are part of a broader Chinese effort planning for the future.[53]

China's Strength in Central Asia

Chinese foreign policy in Central Asia has been effective in promoting border security, curbing transnational crime and terrorism, and supporting greater economic interaction. Chinese active participation in the Shanghai Five and the Shanghai Cooperation Organization mark clear advances in Chinese government willingness to engage vigorously with multilateral organizations and to put aside past Chinese suspicions that such international groups would invariably be influenced by forces hostile to Chinese interests. As President Jiang Zemin said in reference to the SCO at the St. Petersburg summit in 2002, "facts have proven that the establishment of this organization was correct and I am fully confident of its future."[54]

Nevertheless, the shortcomings and relative weakness of the SCO and of China's overall influence in Central Asia have also been evident in recent years. China and its Central Asian allies did little of consequence in dealing with the Taliban and the problems in Afghanistan, while after September 11, 2001, the U.S.-led Operation Enduring Freedom accomplished more in the area in five months than the Shanghai grouping had accomplished in five years. The SCO members remain wary of one another and there are numerous obstacles to greater economic, political, and military cooperation. By contrast, many of these governments—including Russia and China—were willing—and several were eager—to cooperate with the sharp increase in U.S. military activity and presence in Central Asia after 2001.[55]

Economically, China's trade with the post-Soviet Central Asian republics expanded while Russia's trade with them generally declined. Yet, Russia is still a far more important trading partner than China. Moreover, the Central Asian countries quickly turned their trade attention to the European countries, which became leading trading partners for these states.[56] As Central Asia was rapidly transformed after September 11, 2001, from a peripheral area of U.S. concern to a front line in the war on terrorism, China saw its increased influential position in Central Asia, built incrementally over the previous decade, greatly diminished. U.S. military, economic, technological, and political capabilities offered far more to the Central Asian states that they could hope to obtain from China. China was pushed into a secondary role in Central Asia. Its persistent drive to incrementally improve its stature and work with the SCO in the process are part of an apparent longer-term effort to sustain Chinese interests and relevance in regional political, economic, and security trends.

Notes

1. Bates Gill and Matthew Oresman, *China's New Journey to the West* (Washington, D.C.: Center for Strategic and International Studies, CSIS Report, August 2003); John Garver, "China's Influence in Central and South Asia," conference paper, December 2003; Stephen Blank, "Central Asia's Strategic Revolution," *NBR Analysis* 14, no. 4 (November 2003): 51-76; Guangcheng Xing, "China and Central Asia," in Roy Allison and Lena Jonson, eds., *Central Asian Security* (Washington, D.C.: Brookings Institution, 2001); Kathleen Collins and William Wohlforth, "Defying 'Great Game' Expectation," in Richard Ellings and Aaron Friedberg, eds., *Strategic Asia 2003-2004* (Seattle, Wash.: National Bureau of Asian Research, 2003); Tang Shiping, "Economic Integration in Central Asia," *Asian Survey* 40, no. 2 (March/April 2000): 360-76; Ted Weihman, "China Making Diplomatic Push in Central Asia," *Eurasianet.org*, 9 June 2003; Philip Andrews-Speed and Sergei Vinogradov, "China's Involvement in Central Asian Petroleum," *Asian Survey* 40, no. 2 (March/April 2000): 377-97; Deng Hao, "China's Relations with Central Asian Countries: Retrospect and Prospect," (Beijing) *Guoji Wenti Yanjiu* (13 May 2002): 8-12; Christopher Pala and Keith Bradsher, "Beijing Struggles with Caspian Oil," *New York Times* (Internet version), 1 April 2003; Bates Gill and Matthew Oresman, "NATO's Border with China," *PACNET 50*, www.csis.org/pacfor

(accessed 1 December 2002); Thomas Woodrow, "The New Great Game," Jamestown Foundation *China Brief* III, no. 3 (11 February 2002): 1-3.

2. Lillan Craig Harris, "Xinjiang, Central Asia, and the Implications for China's Policy in the Islamic World," *China Quarterly* 133 (March 1993): 111-29; "The Ethnic Tinderbox Inside China," *Business Week* 31 (March 1997): 57; Li Peng, "China's Basic Policy Toward Central Asia," *Beijing Review* 39 (22 July 1996): 8-9; Ross Munro, "Central Asia and China," in Michael Mandelbaum, ed., *Central Asia and the World* (New York: Council on Foreign Relations, 1994).

3. Gill and Oresman, *China's New Journey*, viii-ix.

4. Bernard Cole, *Oil for the Lamps of China—Beijing's 21st-Century Search for Energy* (Washington, D.C.: National Defense University, 2003), 19-20.

5. Robert Sutter, *Chinese Policy Priorities and Their Implications for the United States* (Lanham, Md.: Rowman & Littlefield, 2000), 142.

6. Guang Wan, "The U.S. New Central Asian Strategy," Beijing *Xiandai Guoji Guanxi*, no. 11 (November 17, 1997): 13-16.

7. Cole, *Oil for The Lamps of China*, 19-20.

8. Guang Wan, "The U.S. New Central Asian Strategy," 13-16.

9. Sutter, *Chinese Policy Priorities*, 143.

10. Dru Gladney, "Rumblings from the Uighur," *Current History* (September 1997): 287-90; "Ecevit Comments on Demonstrations in Xinjiang Province," Ankara TRT Television, 1 June 1998, carried by FBIS (Internet version).

11. "Turkey Willing To Expand Ties with China," *Xinhua,* 29 May 1998, carried by FBIS (Internet version).

12. Sutter, *Chinese Policy Priorities*, 144.

13. Sutter, *Chinese Policy Priorities*, 144.

14. "Roundup on Chinese-Kyrgyz Ties," *Xinhua*, 25 April 1998, carried by FBIS (Internet version); "Jiang Zemin Holds Talks with Kyrgyz Counterpart," *China Daily*, 28 April 1998; "China, Kyrgyzstan Sign Joint Statement," *Xinhua,* 28 April 1998, carried by FBIS (Internet version).

15. "Year Ender on Peace in Afghanistan," *Xinhua,* 8 December 1997, carried by FBIS (Internet version).

16. "Chinese Foreign Ministry Delegation Arrives in Afghanistan," *Kabul Radio* 31 January 1999, carried by FBIS (Internet version).

17. Gill and Oresman, *China's New Journey*, viii-ix. See also Gao Qiufu, "U.S. Wishful Thinking Omits Military Presence in Central Asia and Real Purpose," *Liaowang* no. 18 (29 April 2002): 57-59; Hou Songling and Chi Diantang, "Southeast Asia and Central Asia: China's Geostrategic Options in the New Century" (Beijing) *Dangdai Yatai* no. 4 (15 April 2003): 9-15.

18. John Garver, "China's Influence in Central and South Asia," conference paper, December 2003, 2-6. See also Matthew Oresman, "The SCO Summit and Criteria for Analysis," and "News," in *China Eurasia Forum*, www.chinaeurasia.org (accessed 15 September 2004); Marat Yermukanov, "A Thorny Road to Sino-Kazakh Partnership," *China Brief*, Jamestown Foundation, 8 July 2004, 1-4.

19. Michael Mitchell, "Mongolia," in William Carpenter, ed., *Asian Security Handbook* (Armonk, N.Y.: M. E. Sharpe, 1996): 184-91; "Stronger China No Danger to Asia, Hu Tells Mongolian Lawmakers," *AFP*, 5 June 2003 (Internet version). See also "China Shuts Mongolia Border as Dalai Lama Visits," *Reuters*, 7 November 2002; "Mongolia Agrees Not to Participate in Military Alliance Against China," *Chinacom military*

news, 6 June 2004 (Internet version); James Brooke, "Mongolia's Shifting Ties: More China, Less Russia," *New York Times*, 9 July 2004 (Internet version).

20. See among others, Sutter, *Chinese Policy Priorities*, 145-46.

21. "Stronger China No Danger to Asia, Hu Tells Mongolian Lawmakers," *AFP*, 5 June 2003 (Internet version).

22. "China: Reproducing Silk Road Story," *China Daily*, 5 June 2001 (Internet version).

23. Gill and Oresman, *China's New Journey*, 7.

24. Gill and Oresman, *China's New Journey*, 6-10.

25. Gill and Oresman, *China's New Journey*, 10-12.

26. "Silk Road Story," *China Daily*.

27. "Silk Road Story," *China Daily*.

28. Jyotsna Bashki, "Sino-Russian Strategic Partnership in Central Asia: Implications for India," *Strategic Analysis* 25, no. 2 (May 2001): 4.

29. "Silk Road Story," *China Daily*.

30. "*People's Daily* Editorial Hails SCO Founding," *Xinhua*, 15 June 2001 (Internet version).

31. "China: Regional Co-op Boosted," *China Daily*, 15 June 2001 (Internet version).

32. "*People's Daily* Editorial Hails SCO Founding," *Xinhua*, 15 June 2001 (Internet version).

33. "SCO Charter Adopted," *China Daily*, 8 June 2002 (Internet version).

34. Sergei Blagov, "Shanghai Cooperation Organization Prepares for New Role," *Eurasianet.org*, 29 April 2002.

35. "SCO Opens Permanent Secretariat in Beijing," *Xinhua* 15 January 2004 (Internet version).

36. Yu Bin, "Party Time," *Comparative Connections*, www.csis.org/pacfor (accessed 2 September 2003); Yu Bin, "Geoeconomics for Geopolitics," in *Comparative Connections*, www.csis.org/pacfor (accessed 30 August 2004).

37. Gill and Oresman, *China's New Journey*, 7.

38. "'Shanghai Spirit'—New Banner of International Cooperation," *Xinhua*, 15 June 2001 (Internet version).

39. Robert Sutter, "China's Recent Approach to Asia: Seeking Long Term Gains," *NBR Analysis* 13, no. 1 (Seattle, Wash.: National Bureau of Asian Research, March 2002): 19.

40. Gill and Oresman, *China's New Journey*, 17.

41. Gill and Oresman, *China's New Journey*, 18; Yu Bin, "Coping with the Post-Kosovo Fallout," *Comparative Connections*, www.csis.org/pacfor (accessed 30 September 1999).

42. Stephen Blank, "Central Asia's Strategic Revolution," *NBR Analysis* 14, no. 4 (November 2003): 58.

43. "SCO Officials Vow to Pursue Peace," *China Daily*, 8 January 2002 (Internet version).

44. "SCO Defense Ministers Sign Communiqué on Military Cooperation," *Xinhua,* 15 May 2002 (Internet version).

45. "Shanghai Five Fight Terrorism," *China Daily*, 12 August 2003 (Internet version).

46. "Feature: Hijacked Airline Tests SCO's Anti-terror Skills," *Xinhua* , 7 August 2003 (Internet version).

47. Guangcheng Xing, "China and Central Asia," in Roy Allison and Lena Jonson, eds., *Central Asian Security* (Washington, D.C.: Brookings Institution, 2001): 156; Tang Shiping, "Economic Integration in Central Asia," *Asian Survey* 40, no. 2 (March/April 2000): 367-70.

48. Yu Bin, "Treaties Scrapped, Treaties Signed," *Comparative Connections*, www.csis.org/pacfor (accessed 2 September 2001).

49. "Roundup: Economic Cooperation to Add New Light to SCO," *Xinhua*, 28 May 2002 (Internet version).

50. Yu Bin, "The Russian-Chinese Oil Politik," *Comparative Connections*, www.csis.org/pacfor (accessed 2 November 2003).

51. Cole, *Oil for the Lamps of China*, vii.

52. Cole, *Oil for the Lamps of China*, 7.

53. Cole, *Oil for the Lamps of China*, viii, 70.

54. "SCO Charter Adopted," *China Daily*, 8 June 2002 (Internet version).

55. Matthew Oresman, "The SCO: A New Hope or a Graveyard of Acronyms," *PACNET*, www.csis.org/pacfor (accessed 22 May 2003).

56. John Garver, "China's Influence in Central and South Asia," conference paper, December 2003, 11.

Conclusion

China's "Peaceful Approach" to Asia and Its Implications for the United States

China's Recent Approach

In 2003, Chinese leaders marked a new stage in China's efforts to define China's approach toward its neighboring countries and what China's approach meant for the United States and U.S. interests in Asia and the world. Premier Wen Jiabao addressed the topic of China's peaceful approach in a speech in New York on December 9, 2003. He pointed out that "the Chinese nation has always cherished peace and harmony. The rise of China is peaceful. It relies on itself for its progress. . . . China is a developing country and will remain so for many years to come. China has a population of 1.3 billion which is the primary factor of its national conditions. China's GDP ranks sixth in the world, however its per capita GDP ranks 111th. China is still faced with such problems as unemployment, poverty, and uneven development, which we cannot afford to ignore. These problems are enough to keep us busy. It calls for arduous endeavors of generations for China to catch up with developed countries. China will never seek hegemony and expansion, even when it becomes fully developed and stronger."[1]

Despite such high-level pronouncements, the exact purpose and scope of the new emphasis on China's "peaceful rise" remained less than clear to Chinese and foreign specialists. There seemed to be debate among Chinese leaders in 2004 over whether or not Chinese officials should use the term "rise" to define China's approach to Asia and the world. Some Chinese officials and specialists voiced concern that this could be interpreted as a challenge to the United States and other powers, and should be avoided. They favored a more neutral term such as China's "peaceful development."[2] As the year wore on, Chinese officials and official media referred less to China's peaceful rise, preferring to focus on China's peaceful development.

Consultations in 2004 with fifty Chinese officials and nongovernment specialists closely involved in this issue helped to clarify the state of play in Chinese decision-making circles regarding China's peaceful approach and what it meant for China's policy to Asia and for U.S. interests and policy in the region. Those consulted included officials in the Central Party School and other party organs, government ministries, and the PLA, and a variety of government and party think tank, academic, and other nongovernment specialists. Debate and discussion among these officials and specialists continued as to the precise meaning and importance of peaceful rise, and the word "rise" gradually dropped from use late in 2004, but a number of findings and conclusions were evident.

There appeared to be agreement among those consulted that it was premature to expect a definitive view of China's peaceful rise to emerge soon. What had begun was a process of discussion among leaders and elites regarding how China should define its policy positions at home and abroad during the next two decades. The process received impetus from the new party leaders appointed at the sixteenth Chinese Communist Party Congress in 2002.

As described by senior party officials concerned with planning and strategy, the "peaceful rise" approach was based on a careful consideration of China's moderniza-tion experience of the past twenty-five years, and represented an effort to set forth a vision of China's future development that would be compatible with China's interests and those of its neighbors and concerned powers, notably the United States. Its emphasis was as much or more on Chinese domestic development as on China's approach to foreign affairs. Thus, it stressed Chinese economic modernization through an embrace of globalization and an emphasis on China developing on the basis of its own resources and abilities without seeking control of others or expan-sion. A focus was placed on dealing with contradictions and difficulties inside China that result from Chinese modernization. These included gaps between the rate of development in rural and urban China, and gaps between coastal and interior regions in China; environmental issues; unemployment problems; revamping weak state-owned enterprises, and other problems. The peaceful rise also was used to deal with social, ideological, and cultural questions, attempting to ensure that Chinese modern-ization does not disrupt social welfare and provides a good ideological and cultural atmosphere for Chinese people as they modernize and advance economically.

In Asian and world affairs, the Chinese approach built on the moderation and flexibility shown in Chinese foreign policy in recent years. According to senior party strategists and other officials, Chinese leaders reviewed the negative experiences of China's past confrontations with neighbors and other powers, and the negative experiences of earlier rising powers, such as Germany and Japan in the twentieth century, to conclude that China cannot reach its goals of economic modernization and development through confrontation and conflict. As a result, they incorporated the moderate features of China's recent approach to Asia and the world into their broader definition of China's peaceful rise.

Thus, China was expected to become even more active in economic, political, and security interaction with nearby countries, attempting to reassure them that China's rise is not a threat to their interests. China will pursue mutually beneficial economic schemes that will assist the economic rise of China's neighbors as well as China. Such "win-win" approaches also will be applied to political and security issues. Chinese participation in various regional and global multilateral organizations will advance, allowing China to become more fully integrated into the prevailing regional and global order, and in the process permitting Chinese officials to interact more closely in moderate and flexible ways with neighboring governments and concerned powers.

A central feature of the Chinese approach was a very clear and carefully balanced recognition of the power and influence of the United States. In the post-Cold War period, the Chinese leadership often worked against and confronted U.S. power and influence in world affairs. China resisted the U.S. superpower-led world order, seeking a multipolar world of several powers where China would enjoy more influence and room for maneuver. In recent years, Chinese leaders reevaluated this approach. Adopting a more pragmatic attitude to the continued unipolar world led by the United States, they acknowledged and gave more prominence to the fact that U.S. power and influence actually served many important Chinese interests. For example, it guaranteed the sea lines of communication so important for oil imports coming to China, it helped keep stability in the Korean peninsula, and it provided important leadership in the war on terrorism.

Greater pragmatism and a strong desire to offset views in the United States that saw rising China as a competitor and a threat prompted Chinese leaders and officials to narrow sharply their view of areas of difference with the United States. They avowed that most differences with the United States now would center on the Taiwan issue and U.S. continued support for Taiwan. The wide range of other Chinese complaints about U.S. "hegemonism" in the post-Cold War period was said to be reduced. This seemed to conform to actual Chinese practice in recent years, though at times there were strong rhetorical attacks in the Chinese media against U.S. policies and practices not related to Taiwan.

In this more improved atmosphere, Chinese leaders sought to build closer ties with America. They wished to integrate China more closely in the Asian and world system, which they saw as likely to continue to be dominated by U.S. power for many years to come. They pursued closer partnership with the U.S. leaders and wanted to avoid taking steps that would cause the U.S. leaders to see China as a danger or threat that would warrant a concerted U.S. resistance to Chinese development and ambitions. At the same time, they were not abandoning their past differences with U.S. hegemonism. They still disapproved of perceived U.S. domination and unilateralism seen in U.S. practices in Iraq, U.S. missile defense programs, U.S. strengthening alliance relations with Japan, NATO expansion, and other areas that were staples in the repertoire of Chinese criticism of U.S. post-Cold War practices. But Chinese officials were not prepared to raise such issues as significant problems in U.S.-China relations, unless they impinged directly on core Chinese interests. As a result, most important Chinese criticism of U.S. policy focused on issues related to disputes over Taiwan.

Issues of Debate and Concern

Consultations with Chinese officials and specialists concerned with the process of defining the purpose and scope of China's peaceful approach showed several areas of concern and debate. Inside China, the new approach was not well understood. The decision to articulate this new posture with its moderate and pragmatic approach toward the United States and China's neighbors was done at high levels. As a result, it took middle- and lower-level specialists by surprise. In general, the latter adjusted and followed the party line. Thus, the elites in China concerned with Asian affairs and relations with the United States and other concerned powers went along with the new more moderate and flexible approach.

They differed among themselves on some issues, however. For one thing, some specialists averred that the main motives behind the new Chinese approach were "tactical," designed specially to offset the widely held view in the United States, parts of Asia, and elsewhere of rising China as a threat. By contrast, the prevailing Chinese Communist Party rationale behind the recent emphasis on China's peaceful rise was a strategic one, designed to meet a broad array of Chinese leaders' concerns and to last well into this century.

Meanwhile, some officials insisted that China's new emphasis on peaceful rise reflected greater "confidence" among Chinese leaders and people. Their argument was that China's impressive economic growth, continued political stability after a major leadership transition at the sixteenth Party Congress, and greater acceptance in the international community seen in China joining the WTO and hosting the 2008 Olympics provided a sound foundation for Chinese leaders to initiate a dramatic new foreign policy concept. Some officials averred that China muting past opposition to U.S. hegemonism and China's approach to the Taiwan situation also reflected confidence despite obvious difficulties posed by perceived U.S. unilateral and domineering behavior and Chen Shui-bian's pro-independence maneuvers.

In contrast, more common was the view voiced by Chinese officials and specialists that Chinese leaders pursued their current peaceful approach because they needed the appropriate environment to deal with massive internal difficulties and to avoid creating foreign opposition as China developed greater economic and other power and influence. In this context, there also was some disagreement as to whether the current Hu Jintao leadership was seeking the more prominent international spotlight sought by Jiang Zemin, or was reverting to the more low profile approach associated with Deng Xiaoping. If the formula of peaceful rise was to be changed to the more neutral formula of peaceful development, specialists in China judged this would be a signal that the Hu Jintao leadership was more comfortable with a lower international profile than that sought by Jiang Zemin in the post-Deng Xiaoping period. As it turned out, by late 2004 Chinese officials and media muted reference to "rise," referring to China's peaceful development.

A major domestic Chinese problem for the moderate Chinese approach to the United States, Japan, and other neighbors and concerned powers was seen posed by Chinese public opinion and domestic politics. In general, the public in China was said to have attitudes toward many of these powers that were less flexible and more hard-line. Conditioned by years of education and media coverage emphasizing past and present injustices against China carried out by these governments, Chinese public opinion constrained the flexibility of Chinese leaders as they dealt with sensitive foreign policy issues. In the more pluralistic decision-making procedures used by post-Mao Chinese leaders to carry out foreign policy, public opinion and its related influence on Chinese domestic politics was said to have an important influence in foreign policy making.

In addition to issues inside China, Chinese specialists also saw complications and issues for China's peaceful approach posed by forces outside China. In general, they expressed concern that the viability of the new peaceful approach depended greatly on the reaction of concerned powers and developments in sensitive areas. Heading the list was Taiwan where President Chen Shui-bian's strongly assertive posture toward redefining Taiwan's legal status through constitutional revision elicited Chinese warnings of war. Chinese officials and specialists were uniform in warning that China would put aside its peaceful approach and resort to force if necessary to prevent Taiwan independence. Some believed that a resort to force over Taiwan could be done without major adverse impact on China's regional interests, but most were more pessimistic about the consequences for China's broader interests even as they reaffirmed determination to use force if necessary.

Chinese officials expected the United States to take a direct role in curbing Chen Shui-bian's pro-independence leanings. They were pleased with U.S. statements warning Chen not to disrupt the status quo, but were skeptical such moves would be enough. They pressed for curbs in U.S. military support for the Taiwan leader. This lead to a brief upsurge in Chinese public complaints about U.S. arms sales to Taiwan at the time of National Security Advisor Condoleeza Rice's visit to China in July 2004. Continued strong U.S. support for Taiwan—a core concern for Chinese leaders—underlined Chinese worry that their peaceful approach would not elicit appropriate U.S. responses. Continued strong U.S. opposition to Chinese interests on Taiwan could prompt a Chinese reevaluation of the viability of the recent peaceful approach, they averred.

Japan posed a special impediment to China's approach to Asia. Unlike in the case of the United States, Chinese leaders did not mute most differences with Japan. Though media coverage of differences in Sino-Japanese relations was less than in the 1990s, it was much more prevalent than in the case of the United States. Reasons offered by Chinese specialists included the Japanese prime minister's continued visits to the Yakasuni Shrine, Japan's refusal to acknowledge past aggression in ways acceptable to China, and domestic politics in both Japan and China. In general,

Chinese specialists recognized that continued friction in China-Japan relations complicated the attractiveness of China's peaceful strategy in Asia, but they were pessimistic that there would be any diminishment of such differences in the near future.

Though China was seen to have had considerable success in improving relations with South Korea and ASEAN, there was concern among some Chinese specialists about the reactions of Russia and India to China's rise. Though Chinese relations with both Moscow and New Delhi were good, there were perceived tendencies by these powers to maneuver with the United States, Japan, and in other ways to ensure that their power and influence relative to China was not seriously diminished as a result of China's greater power and influence. Such perceived "balancing" of China was said to be a secondary concern to Chinese officials, though it represented an adverse trend that worked against Chinese interests in Asia.

Because of its perceived power and influence, the United States loomed large in Chinese specialists' calculation of possible problems for China's peaceful approach. In general, the success or failure of the Chinese initiative depended on the reaction of the United States. If U.S. policy turned from the recent trend of seeking convergence with China and resumed an approach viewing China as a strategic competitor, Chinese leaders' were thought likely to reevaluate their foreign policy and adopt a more confrontational posture in return. This was seen as especially likely if U.S. hardening affected Chinese interest in Taiwan.

Chinese specialists duly acknowledged that there remained broad segments of U.S. opinion and interest groups disposed to be negative and suspicious of China and its policies.[3] Many American groups had participated actively in the vocal debates over U.S. China policy after the Cold War and saw a wide range of continuing differences between China and the United States over political, economic, security, and other issues. In the view of these Americans, the U.S.-China relations remained the most complicated and contentious U.S. bilateral relationship after the Cold War. The major shift in U.S. strategic attention to the war on terrorism and the conflicts in Iraq and Southwest Asia had distracted attention away from China, but had not ended suspicion and wariness by many Americans.

These Americans were not inclined to accept without careful verification Chinese assurances of peaceful intent. The Chinese peaceful approach played down Chinese negative treatment and criticism of the United States on most issues, with the notable exception of Taiwan, but this did not necessarily assuage American critics of China. For example, U.S. security planners and related specialists in intelligence and other departments in the U.S. government and supporting nongovernment agencies had been compelled to devote extensive and continuing attention to potential or real threats from China. This came particularly in response to the Chinese military buildup after the Taiwan Strait crisis of 1995-1996, and the accompanying stream of rhetoric and articles by Chinese strategists and other commentators pointing to China's willingness and ability to resort to various means of asymmetrical warfare in order to defeat U.S. forces should they intervene in a Taiwan contingency. As a result, the willingness of these U.S. government and nongovernment specialists to take at face value Chinese assertions that peaceful intent in 2003-2004 were balanced by their continued awareness that Chinese military forces continued to add sophisticated capabilities to PLA forces targeted at Taiwan and at U.S. forces that would intervene in a Taiwan contingency. Without explicitly addressing China's military doctrine, force structure, and increased military capabilities, China's new peaceful approach to the United States and others was not very meaningful to these Americans. They judged it was hard for the United States to be a true partner of a country that continued to develop and expand military capabilities targeted at Americans.

Among other areas of concern involving the United States and China's peaceful approach, according to several Chinese specialists, the Chinese leaders saw their peaceful approach as very much in U.S. interests and expected the United States to reciprocate with steps that would assist Chinese interests. Taiwan was mentioned in this regard—that is, Chinese leaders were looking for signs of U.S. support for China's position on Taiwan and a diminution of U.S. support for separatist tendencies on the island. Moreover, over the longer term, some Chinese specialists with a "realist" international-relations perspective wondered if there could ever be strong compatibility and convergence between a rising power such as China and a dominant, hegemonic power such as the United States. From their viewpoint, these two powers seemed destined to have friction and conflict.

Implications for U.S. Interests

In the short term, over the next year or two, the Chinese emphasis on peaceful approach seems generally advantageous for the United States. It continues to reduce important areas of friction with a major power at a time when the U.S. administration seeks broader international support as it deals with protracted international problems, notably the problems in Iraq and other parts of Southwest Asia. The Bush administration by 2003 confronted a variety of charges from European, Middle Eastern, and other governments complaining about U.S. "hegemonism" and power politics in Iraq and elsewhere; but China, a previous leader in the campaign against U.S. domination and hegemony, chose this time to curb invective and avoid sharp criticism—an important "bright spot" for Bush administration diplomacy.[4]

Indeed, the U.S. government saw common ground with China as it endeavored to deal with North Korea's provocative nuclear weapons development and the crisis this caused in 2002-2004. The facilitator of multilateral talks on this issue and the main international power capable of exerting pressure to constrain North Korean provocative behavior, China became a key partner of the United States in managing tensions on the peninsula and working to deal with the nuclear issue through negotiations. The Bush administration entered office with little inclination to rely on China to deal with North Korea, choosing instead to work with allies and rely on U.S. strength. But Chinese support continues to be very important at a time when U.S.

strength is diverted to Southwest Asia, and U.S. allies, notably South Korea, are in the midst of political and foreign policy realignments that make South Korean policy diverge in often unpredictable ways from U.S. interests on the peninsula.

Though Taiwan remains the key area of Sino-U.S. differences, trends in 2003-2004 saw a convergence in U.S. and PRC interests based fundamentally on the two powers' desire to avoid confrontation and conflict brought on by assertive policies and positions by Taiwan. President Bush's public rebuke of the Taiwan president during a meeting with the visiting Chinese premier on December 9, 2003, was emblematic of a growing if still-limited convergence of Sino-U.S. policies to deal with this important East Asian trouble spot.[5]

Among the many challenges posed by China's peaceful approach are those posed by the fact that China is rising in influence in Asia and that it does tend to compete with U.S. interests and influence. This happens in specific ways, notably Chinese competition with U.S.-led security initiatives in Southeast Asia and efforts to curb U.S. naval freedom there, and in more general ways. Regarding the latter, China's approach to Asia tends to be more geoeconomic, whereas U.S. policy, particularly in the war on terrorism, is more geopolitical and geostrategic. Since many of the governments in Southeast Asia and other parts of China's periphery have strong economic concerns and seem to prefer China's approach to that of the United States, this poses some difficulty for U.S. relative power and influence. Also, China's growing involvement in multilateral organizations is warmly welcomed by many of China's neighbors and seems to stand in contrast with U.S. continued emphasis on bilateral alliances and relationships and U.S. impatience with many multilateral organizations that appear to accomplish little. Finally, China's "win-win" approach to its neighbors helps to mute competitive power relations, while the United States is seen as following a more traditional view that holds power and influence as limited things; when one gains power, another tends to lose. Again, many of the smaller states around China's periphery seem to prefer the Chinese approach to the more "realist" orientation of the United States, which is seen to force them to choose or balance between various powers and interests.[6]

Meanwhile, as noted earlier, U.S.-China conflict over Taiwan is real, tangible, and dangerous. In particular, the respective buildups of Chinese, U.S., and Taiwan military forces, and the emotionalism attached to this issue, especially in Beijing and Taipei, mean the danger of serious conflict will persist and may become critical.

Over the longer term, reaching into the next decade, there is considerable debate on what China's peaceful standing in Asia means for U.S. interests. A group of U.S.-China specialists and some others have set forth the view that there is likely to be ever greater convergence in U.S.-China relations. The initiatives that China is taking in Asian and world affairs regarding greater involvement, taking more responsibility, and seeking mutual benefit support U.S. goals of regional stability and prosperity. Though American officials and opinion leaders have a legacy of mixed views of China at best, they will be persuaded by Chinese behavior and come to accept ever more fully China's role as a partner and collaborator in seeking greater world order for the broad benefit of all.[7]

On the other hand are a range of skeptics. Some see the latest Chinese initiative as little more than a tactical maneuver designed to reduce U.S. and other countries' concerns over the China threat and to disguise actual Chinese intentions to dominate Asia and push the United States away from Chinese borders and nearby spheres of influence.[8]

Others, including this author, see mixed motives in the Chinese initiatives in the recent Chinese approach to Asia, and also see so many possible and real obstacles to them being carried out that the outlook for U.S.-China cooperation appears more mixed than the optimists would expect.[9] The obstacles have been reviewed earlier in this chapter. Perhaps the most important will be the likely unwillingness of the United States to reciprocate for Chinese moderation in their peaceful strategy in ways sufficient to satisfy China. The depth and breadth of U.S. antipathy and suspicion of the Chinese government seem sufficient to curb any significant diminution of U.S. wariness of China any time soon. This is likely to remain the case so long as there are concrete signs that China's peaceful approach is not all it is said to be. In particular, the PLA buildup opposite Taiwan is inconsistent with the peaceful approach and has direct negative consequences for U.S. interests. It will be hard for many Americans in and outside of government to accept China's peaceful approach wholeheartedly until China makes clear how the peaceful approach will curb Chinese military buildup focused on Taiwan and possible U.S. intervention in a Taiwan contingency. They will watch carefully for shifts in Chinese military doctrine and force posture for hopeful signs that show the Chinese buildup is indeed becoming less of a threat to the United States.

China's Peaceful Approach in Asia—A Hedging Strategy

A balanced U.S. judgment of Chinese behavior and a U.S. middle-range view on China's peaceful approach is that China's new posture in Asian and world affairs is a form of hedging that broadly has characterized Chinese and other powers' behavior in Asia since the end of the Cold War.[10] Hedging in this regard involves pursuing various paths to secure a nation's interests in an uncertain environment. Thus, while pursuing détente with a former adversary, a nation may continue to pursue military modernization and improved relations with the adversary's neighbors as a means to keep the adversary in check should the détente fail. It also means that a country's ostensible foreign policy approach may have varied and sometimes hidden objectives, allowing the country to benefit under varied circumstances in a fluid regional context.

With the collapse of the Soviet Union, the break in U.S.-China relations following the Tiananmen incident, and the rise of Taiwan's perceived importance and approval in the United States as a result of the democratization of the Taiwan regime, Chinese leaders faced an uphill struggle to preserve the U.S. relationship so important to China's development and regime survival. They did so by trying to accommodate U.S. demands, but they also broadened contacts to European and Japanese business interests and government leaders and tried to use these ties to offset U.S. pressure on human rights and trade issues; they also began the process of building extensive contacts with Russian military leaders in order to get equipment and technology needed to build up China's military in order to offset perceived U.S.-backed pressure and adverse developments, especially over Taiwan. Later in the decade, Chinese leaders used initiatives like strategic partnerships and the New Security Concept to offset U.S. pressure and perceived efforts to "contain" China's rise.

Chinese leaders were not alone in these kinds of hedging efforts. The environment of post-Cold War Asia lent itself to hedging on the part of all regional powers, including the United States. The tendency to hedge had its roots in prevailing security, economic, and political trends prompted by five categories of factors influencing regional dynamics. Those categories were:

1.   Changing regional power relationships and trends. Since 1990, this included the rise of China, Japan's stagnation, Indonesia's declining power and influence, and the more active role in regional affairs played by Russia, India, the EU, and other powers outside the region.
2.   The changing dynamics on the Korean peninsula, characterized by the off-again, on-again thaw in North-South Korean relations and North Korea's nuclear weapons programs and its varying engagement in international affairs.
3.   Economic concerns. These focused on the difficulty in sustaining economic growth in the highly competitive global economic environment.
4.   The challenge of freer information flows to both authoritarian regimes and non-authoritarian governments.
5.   Uncertainty in the region over U.S. policy. At times, regional leaders saw signs of U.S. withdrawal or preoccupation elsewhere. At other times, they saw evidence of U.S. unilateralism and intervention. Both were viewed as disruptive to regional stability.

These five categories of factors influencing regional dynamics led to several important trends that created an uncertain regional security environment. It was not so uncertain that countries felt a need to seek close alignment with a major power or with one another to protect themselves. But it prompted a wide variety of hedging, with each government seeking more diverse and varied arrangements in order to shore up its security and other interests. For example, all powers wanted generally positive relations with the United States, but sought diversified ties to enhance their options. They continued to differ on a strong U.S. regional security presence, with China notably encouraging a gradual weakening of the U.S. position as it sought expanded regional influence, while most others backed a strong U.S. presence.

The United States was in the lead in this hedging behavior. Regarding China, on the one hand the United States sought closer engagement and cooperation, especially in economic relations, but on the other it took repeated political, economic, and military steps designed to pressure China to change its political system and conform to international norms supported by the United States. The Clinton administration revitalized U.S.-Japan security ties at a time of greater Chinese assertiveness in East Asia, and also pursued improved U.S.-India ties that benefited the U.S. standing vis-à-vis China. The Bush administration followed through and further developed these initiatives as it structured an order in Asia that initially played down China's role as the United States endeavored to deter Chinese assertiveness and aggression, especially regarding Taiwan. At the same time, the Bush administration welcomed closer economic ties with China and responded positively to Chinese efforts to broaden common ground between the two powers.

Japan remained tied to the United States for concrete security and economic reasons, and yet it pursued independent weapons development efforts and promoted Asia-only economic groupings seen at odds with U.S. interests. South Korea under President Kim Dae Jung tried to solidify relations with the United States but took dramatic steps to broaden South Korea influence with China and Russia in support of an asymmetrical normalization policy that led to the dramatic breakthrough in North-South Korea summit in Pyongyang in 2000. India welcomed the increased U.S. security cooperation and high-level attention as it pursued arms sales with Russia, slow normalization with China, and improved economic ties with Japan. Russia worked with China to tilt against U.S. pressure and hegemonism, but pragmatically came to terms with the United States and the West over such contentious issues as the intervention in Kosovo, NATO expansion, and abrogation of the ABM treaty.

Against this background, it would be surprising if Chinese policy in Asia—including the new emphasis on peaceful development—were an exception to this prevailing pattern of hedging. Indeed, close examination of China's new approach shows ample evidence of hedging, notably keeping Chinese options open in case the United States and other powers do not respond as positively as China would like to the new Chinese initiatives or other complications arise. In particular, the PLA buildup is an obvious hedge in case developments in Taiwan under U.S. influence move in the wrong direction from China's point of view. Enhanced military power also is something to fall back on in case the U.S.-Japan security relationship and U.S. security presence around China's periphery seeks to pressure or contain China.

China's markedly improved relations with South Korea help to ensure that Seoul will be a reluctant participant at best in any possible U.S.-led effort to pressure or constrain China, and that U.S. ability to establish a future order on the Korean peninsula contrary to Chinese interests also will be curbed.

Chinese improvement of relations with smaller countries of Southeast Asia and elsewhere along China's periphery, and its greater participation in various economic, political and security regional multilateral groups, also serve Chinese interests by providing a buffer against possible U.S. pressure. Chinese specialists are frank in admitting that improved Chinese relations with such groups help to ensure that

China's interests will be protected in case the United States reverses its current policies and seeks to dominate China in some way. The "Gulliver" strategy that ASEAN has applied to China in seeking to constrain PRC assertiveness and aggression also applies to the use of regional groupings by China to hold in check U.S. assertiveness.

The growing Chinese involvement in regional and other multilateral organizations seen notably in the 1990s represents a significant change in Chinese foreign policy. Previously, Chinese officials generally were wary of many international organizations. They were concerned that such groupings might be influenced by powers opposed to Chinese interests, might require costly commitments of Chinese resources, and might constrain Chinese maneuvering in pursuit of important Chinese interests. These suspicions waned in the 1990s as Chinese officials became more adroit in working constructively with Asian and other multilateral organizations in seeking goals that benefited China. Chinese influence in Asian organizations grew in tandem with the growth of the Chinese economy and the even more rapid growth of Chinese trade with Asian economic partners. China's increasing economic and strategic importance saw Asian leaders seek closer Chinese involvement with regional groupings, and Chinese leaders saw such organizations as consistent with their foreign policy goals emphasizing regional stability and favorable economic exchanges.

Chinese leaders also saw Asian regional groups as useful means to constrain the United States and possibly other powers that might be inclined to take actions contrary to Chinese interests in the prevalent order in Asia. Chinese officials and specialists made clear in consultations in mid-2004 that Chinese leaders viewed deeper Chinese involvement in Asian multilateral organizations as providing a defense against possible revival of U.S. efforts to pressure or contain China. The ever-growing webs of Chinese connections with an increasing array of Asian multilateral organizations and groups provided the basis of a strategy that would tie down and impede possible U.S. efforts to engage in sharp pressure or containment of China.

Meanwhile, China continues to pursue some efforts at "soft balancing" U.S. power and influence in Asia that it sees as contrary to Chinese interests. It uses such paths as promoting Asia-only economic, political, and security groupings where China is in the lead, endeavoring to persuade regional states to work against U.S. naval activities China opposes, seeking assurances that Russian military supplies will be forthcoming despite improvement in U.S.-Russia relations, and competing with the United States and other regional powers for prominence in ASEAN.

Recommendations for U.S. Policy

The rise of China in Asia—"peaceful" or otherwise—poses both opportunities and challenges for U.S. policy. There appears little question that the Chinese leadership's recent determination to reduce conflict with the United States and seek common ground in ways compatible with U.S. regional leadership and interests in peace, stability, and prosperity works well for U.S. policy and should be supported by the United States. To try to resist China's "peaceful" ascendancy would appear both foolish and unpopular in much of Asia. China's smaller neighbors have been working for decades to get the Chinese leaders to commit to a peaceful and cooperative approach toward the region, and would not welcome U.S. efforts that might upset this trend.

Chinese influence in Asia will grow as a result, but there is little preventing the U.S. influence from growing in tandem, from a much more powerful base. U.S. officials need to consider methods to use America's dominant regional role as the economic partner of choice and security guarantor to enhance a positive U.S. profile in the region. The U.S. intervention in Iraq resulted in chaos, violence, and repression that undermined U.S. stature, especially in Asian Islamic states, but the war on terrorism has enhanced the U.S. profile in several previously neglected Asian states and if handled effectively could redound to U.S. influence in the region.

U.S. observers, like many in China, have been surprised by the marked shift toward the positive in China's approach toward the United States in Asia. At best, it will take time and further proof of Chinese intentions to convince many Americans, deeply suspicious of Chinese intentions as a result of the repeated U.S.-China conflicts especially since 1989, that China's intentions are benign. Many will assume that Chinese moves are the latest in a series of Chinese efforts to "bide time" as Deng Xiaoping advised, preparing to pursue Chinese interests more assertively once Chinese power is greater. A key indicator of Chinese intentions in this regard will be Chinese military doctrine, force structure, and deployment in areas of concern to the United States.

U.S. policy also will need to take account of the importance of U.S. policy to China's approach to Asia. Chinese specialists have made clear that an overly assertive U.S. stance, especially on the Taiwan issue, could challenge core Chinese interests and derail China's peaceful approach. They warn that unspecified "hard-liners" are prepared to assert their influence on Chinese policy under these circumstances. A case also can be made that without sufficient U.S. power and attention to Asia, China would be more inclined to pursue a more assertive approach to Asia in order to fill the vacuum left by U.S. inattention or decline.

U.S. policy needs a clear awareness of how the United States might disappoint Chinese leaders with a less forthcoming U.S. stance than Beijing would like, or how issues involving U.S. relations and policies regarding Taiwan, Korea, Japan, and other sensitive areas could prompt adjustments or even reversal of China's benign approach. There is plenty of evidence that Chinese leaders have designed their peaceful policy with ample hedges in case the U.S. response is unacceptable or other contingencies arise. The spread of Chinese influence to neighboring countries as a result of China's recent active and accommodating approach has the effect of setting up a buffer against possible future U.S. pressure or containment of China.

In response, U.S. policy would be wise to pursue a similar hedging strategy. Most useful would appear to be U.S. efforts to broaden and deepen American influence in Asia in ways that have wide appeal among the various regional states. U.S. economic and security leadership in Asia provide a good foundation for such efforts. The importance of the recent rise of China probably should not be exaggerated to the point of prompting the United States to compete overtly with China, seeking to pressure Asian countries to choose between China and the United States. From one perspective, the challenge posed to U.S. leadership in Asia by China's rising power and influence can be viewed as about the same as the challenge faced by U.S. leadership in Asia during the 1980s, when Japan's rising economic and political power saw commentators predict the demise of U.S. leadership in the region and the emergence of a Japanese-dominated regional order.

Asian countries have avoided choosing the United States against China in the past, partly for fear of prompting harsh Chinese actions against them. Now, these same nations likely would avoid siding with the United States against China out of concern over losing the many benefits they now derive from closer relations with a friendly and economically dynamic China. Thus, while one can conclude today that China's rising influence limits U.S. ability to resort to pressure in order to contain China, this option for U.S. policy already had been limited by prevailing and long-standing concern among Asian countries that they not provoke China by siding with the United States in such a containment effort. Under such circumstances, a more sensible U.S. policy would reflect confidence in and take steps to deepen the essential role the United States plays as the leading security and major economic actor in the region.

Meanwhile, Japan, Russia, and India show various degrees of concern about China's rise and what it means for their respective power and influence in Asian and world affairs. In contrast with many in South Korea and perhaps some Southeast Asia governments, they have not been won over by the strong charm offensive of China's soft power, though they duly pursue economic and other advantageous relations with China. They have tended to view regional power relations realistically and have reservations about prevailing China-centered trends in the region. They presumably would welcome U.S. efforts to improve relations with them that had no overt anti-China connotation; that such relations could provide a hedge against China at some point appears fairly obvious.

In sum, a prudent U.S. welcoming of China's peaceful and rising influence in Asia seems likely to work well for U.S. interests. More U.S. energy and attention to Asia will be required, but this need not be onerous given U.S. leadership and economic and military power, despite the likely continued U.S. preoccupation with Iraq and Southwest Asia. A clear awareness that China's peaceful posture in Asia and its relatively benign approach to the United States in Asia could change—both dramatically and sharply—should prompt U.S. efforts to sustain sufficient power and useful international contacts to deal with such an outcome should it arise.

Notes

1. The speech is available at www.fmprc.gov.cn/chn/zxxx/t55972.htm. See also Zheng Bijian, "New Path for China's 'Peaceful Rise,'" (Shanghai) *Wen Hui Bao*, 21 March 2004 (Internet version); Zheng Bijian, "Globalization and the Emergence of China," opening remarks at a conference hosted by the Center for Strategic and International Studies, Washington, D.C., 13 November 2003.

2. This chapter is based heavily on consultations with Chinese officials and specialists carried out in 2004, notably during a research trip to Beijing and Shanghai in May 2004.

3. U.S.-China Security Review Commission, *Report to Congress July 2002*, www.uscc.gov/anrp02.htm (relevant sections); U.S. Department of Defense, Annual Report on the Military Power of the People's Republic of China, 2003, www.defense-link.mil/pubs/20030730chinaex.pdf (accessed 3 September 2003).

4. Kerry Dumbaugh, *China-U.S. Relations: Current Issues for the 108th Congress* (Washington, D.C.: Library of Congress), Congressional Research Service, Report RL 31815, 25 May 2004.

5. For more on U.S.-China convergence on Korea and Taiwan, see Robert Sutter, *Bush's Korea Policy Gravitates Toward China. Will Taiwan Policy Follow?* PACNET 13, www.csis.org/pacfor (accessed 1 April 2004).

6. The above line of analysis was offered by an American affairs specialist in Shanghai, 21 May 2004.

7. Consultations at an Asia Foundation daylong meeting on "America's Role in Asia," Washington, D.C., 14 May 2004.

8. Bruce Klingner, "'Peaceful Rising' Seeks to Allay 'China Threat,'" *AsiaTimesonline*, 12 March 2004.

9. Consultations at an Asia Foundation daylong meeting on "America's Role in Asia," Washington, D.C., May 14, 2004.

10. For more details on how China and other powers in Asia engaged in hedging in order to protect their interests, see Robert Sutter, *The United States and East Asia* (Lanham, Md.: Rowman & Littlefield, 2003).

Appendix

Australian Perspectives on China's Approach to Asia and Implications for the United States

Key Findings

Consultations with groups of Australian government and nongovernment specialists on China, Asian affairs, and the United States were conducted in four Australian cities in June 2004. They included formal presentations by the author of the outline and main findings of this study, in order to solicit guidance from the Australian specialists, who were knowledgeable about China, Chinese policy in Asia, and its implications for the United States. Such sessions were conducted with fifteen specialists in the Australian government's Office of National Assessments, and with a similar number of academic specialists in the Australian National University in Canberra, and with ten such specialists in Griffith University in Brisbane. A variety of other consultations were held with Australian government and nongovernment experts on aspects of China, China's policy toward Asia, and implications for the United States and other countries, including Australia, in order to assess how Australian specialists assessed the overall importance of China's recent approach to the region.

The findings of these meetings are presented here in order to amplify and present other perspectives on the main findings and arguments in this study, and to provide additional information on how China's foreign policy approach is affecting Chinese relations with Australia, an important country that is a close ally of the United States and adjoins states along the periphery of China.

Reactions by Australian Specialists to the Key Findings of This Study

The Australians consulted were in agreement that most of the findings in the book about the methods and goals of China's approach to Asia were straightforward and noncontroversial. China clearly sought to secure China's periphery in order to focus better on domestic issues, to calm China's neighbors regarding any threatening implications of China's rising power, to seek advantageous economic contacts and exchanges, and to isolate Taiwan. The main issues of controversy about Chinese motives and methods in Asia focused on what China's approach meant for the position and influence of the United States in Asia.

The Australian specialists duly acknowledged that there were divergent views about the latter question, with some scholars in the United States viewing the Chinese approach negatively as part of a longer-term effort to displace the United States as the leader of Asia; and others in the United States viewing the Chinese approach in benign terms, seeing Chinese leaders determined to put aside differences in search of a long-term cooperative relationship with the United States as the dominant power in Asian and world affairs.

In general, they judged that the argument of the study that China's approach was more uncertain and dependent of circumstances that could change was more sensible than the two above views. They acknowledged long-standing constraints and differences in both China and the United States that were described in the book and that continued to impede close Chinese relations with the United States; they acknowledged that a change in circumstances in the recent China-U.S. relationship—for example, further tension over Taiwan, new tension over Korea, or a major bilateral incident—could prompt a different and less moderate Chinese approach toward the United States. They agreed that the United States was less than likely to respond in a fully positive way to China's recent "peaceful rise" approach of extraordinary moderation on issues and differences with the United States, with the exception of Taiwan-related questions. The United States was different than China, which remained an authoritarian state with an ability to curb expressions of differences over sensitive issues. While the debate over China policy in the United States declined after the start of the war on terrorism, the many differences in U.S. relations with China over values, security, sovereignty, and economic issues remained and could not be silenced by the U.S. government. The Australian experts also understood that U.S. defense officials and officials who work with them in Congress and in the U.S. intelligence apparatus would continue to view China's "peaceful" approach warily; this wariness would continue at least until such time as Chinese officials began to reduce the active defense preparations in recent years seen as focused on intimidating U.S. forces from entering a Taiwan conflict and attacking them if they do.

There was little disagreement among the Australian specialists with the judgment noted in the study that even if China were not successful in persuading the United States to fully embrace China's "peaceful" approach to Asia, China still gained greatly in Asian influence with its current moderate approach. In this regard, they agreed with the book's finding that with increasingly positive relations with countries around its periphery, and with increasing close involvement with multilateral groupings involving China's periphery, China was in a better position to curb or neutralize U.S. pressure, should the United States at some point in the future shift its policy toward a hard-line stance such as that which appeared in early defense strategy documents in the Bush administration.

Several Australian specialists questioned whether Chinese officials actually suspected or feared such a possible reversion to a hard-line by the United States against China. They also judged that the U.S. ability to contain or pressure China had long been weakened by the regional countries' unwillingness to choose between the United States and China. In the recent past, if Asian countries joined the United States in pressing China, they feared a hostile or aggressive Chinese response. With more recent benign Chinese approaches to Asian countries, regional governments feared the loss of benefits they derived from recent relations with China. In either case, these Australian experts argued, U.S. ability to gain regional support for a tougher stance designed to pressure China was low.

One implication for the United States seen in the view of these Australian specialists was that the United States was not losing very much as a result of China's rising in Asia. As the study pointed out, many of the implications for the United States of China's moderate approach to Asia were good for U.S. interests. On the negative side, there was a danger that with China's rising influence, the United States would be less able to gain support in the region if the United States chose to reverse its current policy and try to deal with China in a more confrontational way. In the view of these Australians, the U.S. option to contain China with the cooperation of regional countries ended long ago. The moderate Chinese approach to Asia and its rising influence in Asia merely served to reinforce a situation which existed for some time, in the view of these Australian specialists.

Australia's Response to China's Approach to Asia

The mood of business representatives and politicians on the whole tended to be very positive about China, with China's role as an increasingly important importer of Australian raw materials looming very large in business and government calculations.[1] Nonetheless, large portions of Australian manufacturing industry were fearful of added competition from China, and the Australian government officials had a carefully balanced approach to China that avoided excessive enthusiasm as Australia sought to capitalize on new opportunities seen in the China market and other areas.

According to Australian government officials, the government of Prime Minister John Howard, in power since 1996, endeavored to strike a careful balance between his well-known emphasis on close cooperation with the United States, and Australia's strong interests in Asia. In economics, Japan remained Australia's largest trading partner, with the United States second, and China third. If one included services trade, the United States was Australia's largest trading partner. China was a fast-growing market and was expected to overtake the United States as the second-largest, after Japan, export market for Australian goods. China seemed very important for large sectors of the Australian economy that export raw materials. A deal involving billions of dollars of Australian liquefied natural gas for China was a recent highlight in a burgeoning Australian export trade with China. Australian government and business representatives judged that Australia had the widest range in world markets of the types of raw materials (gas, iron ore, etc.) that China needed, and Australia had advantages of being a stable supplier relatively close geographically to China.

Against this background, Australian government officials gave higher priority to China, though they did so in the context of continuing to develop close ties with Japan and the United States. Thus, the Howard government endeavored to follow up on its free trade agreement with the United States with a similar agreement with Japan. This was said not to have worked well. At the same time, the Australian government began the process of seeking a free trade agreement with China. Chinese officials were responsive and the process was under study, with some officials and business observers foreseeing an agreement sometime in 2005. The free trade agreement with China was seen as a means to consolidate Australian relations with China's increasingly important market for Australian goods. Australia also tried in vain to foster free trade arrangements with ASEAN, meeting resistance especially from Malaysia's government. A free trade agreement with China would provide access to ASEAN through the China-ASEAN Free Trade arrangement, and might add some incentive to ASEAN to "catch up" with China in developing ties with Australia, according to U.S. officials in Australia.

The growing economic relationship with China added to reasons for the Howard government to improve relations with China. According to Australian government officials, Prime Minister Howard found that his strong support for the United States in the Taiwan Straits crisis in 1996 hurt Australian relations with China. Since then, Australia endeavored to improve ties with China in a variety of ways. Australia employed more nonconfrontational dialogues rather than pressure tactics in order to encourage China to engage with the region and the world in more constructive ways. Australian officials believed that China's increasingly moderate approach to Asia was in part the result of and underlined the wisdom of the moderate Australian approach.

Australian officials were impressed by China's flexibility and effectiveness in dealing with regional, especially Southeast Asian, neighbors. For example, they viewed Chinese efforts over the previous year to promote an Asian regional security conference based on the ASEAN Regional Forum (ARF) as directed in part to counter the U.S.-backed Shangri-La forum of Asian defense leaders that met in Singapore annually. At a senior ministers' meeting of the ARF in Jakarta in May 2004, China proposed that the chairmanship of the proposed new security conference involve a representative of ASEAN and a representative of a non-ASEAN state. According to Australian officials, ASEAN objected, and China withdrew its plan; in the Australian view, this showed great flexibility and won goodwill from ASEAN participants.

While expressing admiration for China's maneuvering and flexibility, and expressing optimism about China's approach to Asia over the short term, Australian officials were cautious about the future. They were especially watchful for signs that China would use regional groupings and its growing stature in regional affairs to try to exclude the United States and Western interests and influence from Asia.

In this context, Australian officials were careful to show that their positive approach to China was part of a balanced approach that included a continued close relationship with the United States. In 2003, the Australian and Western media widely reported the positive welcome for the Chinese president by the Australian Parliament, the day after President Bush spoke to the Parliament and met with some protests. Relevant background provided by Australian officials showed that the Chinese president's visit was scheduled well in advance and his stay in the Australian capital had to be delayed by a day in order to accommodate President Bush's visit. As a means to assuage Chinese irritation, the opportunity to speak to the Parliament was offered to the Chinese president, whose officials insisted strenuously that all signs of protest be avoided during the visit.

Australian officials were positive about China's role in dealing with the North Korean nuclear crisis. They said that Australia was joining with the United States in praising China's role in the talks, using such public demonstrations to appeal to Chinese pride and international recognition as a means to reinforce China's resolve to pursue a responsible approach to dealing with the North Korean nuclear issue. They judged that Chinese officials were still "sitting back" too much to suit Australian and American officials, and they awaited a more active Chinese stance to deal with the North Korean issue.

On Taiwan, Australian officials indicated that the Australian government was tilting against Taiwan in recent years. It responded positively to China's calls on the United States and other international actors in 2003-2004 to criticize the moves by the Taiwan government of President Chen Shui-bian to assert a more independent posture in world affairs. Australia instituted in recent years greater restrictions governing Taiwan officials visiting Australia, and refrained for four years from sending an Australian minister-level official to Taiwan—something that had been an annual occurrence before. Australia also came down harder on Taiwan than China in condemning the use of money and payoffs to top Pacific island officials in order to garner diplomatic support among small Pacific island states. Australia had great influence among these states and saw Taiwan and China "money diplomacy" adding to regional corruption and poor governance. Meanwhile, Australia voted as China wished and against a U.S.-backed effort in 2004 to help Taiwan gain entry into the World Health Assembly, according to Australian officials.

Australia faced a national election in 2004, and there was much speculation about the policy toward China of the opposition Labor Party should it gain power. The opposition leader was a widely known protégé of the Australian prime minister who normalized diplomatic relations with China in the early 1970s. Since then, the Labor Party gave special positive attention to relations with China, and it was widely assumed that it would do so were it to win the 2004 national election.

Nonetheless, the Labor Party, and also political leaders representing Australian business, faced strong crosscurrents in the wave of Australian interest in China, and especially the Chinese economy. According to Australian business representatives, officials, and political activists, Australian manufacturers represented 13 percent of the Australian economy and employed one million workers. By and large, these constituencies—manufacturing business and labor—were fearful of China and opposed to the liberalizing of the Australian market to Chinese competition that would come with the proposed Australian-China free trade agreement. The liberalizing measures in the proposed agreement likely were relatively small in the already very open Australian economy, but these Australian groups saw the changes as the death knell or at least a heavy blow for the employee-heavy Australian textile industry, car-parts industries, and many other sectors. Often, these groups judged it was inevitable that Australian manufacturers would face the "threat" of massive competition from Chinese manufacturers, but they did not want to expedite the process through a free trade agreement with China. These groups were uncertain whether their opposition would offset the enthusiasm of Australian raw materials exporters and political leaders for the positive fallout expected from closer economic ties with China seen in the proposed free trade agreement.

Australia-U.S.-China Relations

The general enthusiasm over China among Australian politicians, business leaders' and others came in the context of public frictions in U.S.-Australian relations and substantial debate in Australia over the wisdom of recent policy aligning Australia closely with the United States. The Labor Party leader strongly criticized U.S. President Bush, and called for the withdrawal of the small contingent of Australian soldiers in Iraq. Meeting with Prime Minister Howard in June 2004, President Bush strongly attacked the proposed troop withdrawal, and senior U.S. officials followed up with criticism of the Labor leader's position.[2] In this context, there was widespread speculation that if elected in Australia's 2004 election, the Labor leader might tilt Australian policy away from the U.S. alliance and use the party's long-standing emphasis on close relations to China as a counterweight in Australian foreign policy. Observers in Australia differed on the likelihood of this turn of events. Though the debate in Australia over close ties to the United States had roots going back to the Vietnam War, and was clearly exacerbated by the Bush administration's handling of the war in Iraq, the more accommodating U.S. approach and the success in gaining UN approval for the Iraq situation in June 2004 seemed to reduce the salience of the Iraq issue to some degree. Meanwhile, unlike in the case of South Korea where the relationship with China posed a seemingly viable security option for some and possibly many South Koreans, few in Australia were said to view China relations this way. In short, according to career Australian government officials, a Labor Party victory was unlikely to prompt any substantial shift in Australia's emphasis from the United States to China. Relations with the United States may be less close, and relations with China probably will continue to improve, but Australians seeing the two as either/or options was deemed unlikely. They advised that Australia continued to stay close to the United States while it developed relations with China.

Notes

1. The author had roundtable discussions with business groups in Sydney, Melbourne, and Canberra, June 2004, and he made at that time ten talks to public affairs groups that involved interaction with local and national politicians.

2. For background, see interviews with U.S. Deputy Secretary of State Richard Armitage replayed in *The Australian,* 9 June 2004, 1, and *The Sydney Morning Herald*, 11 June 2004, 1.

Index

Bangladesh, 233
basic principles, 115, 140
Boao Forum for Asia (BFA), 82,
    191
bridge of friendship, 251
Brunei, 177
Buddhism, 254
Burma, 178, 179, 182, 187, 188,
    195, 233
Bush, George W., 5, 8, 12, 53, 79,
    83, 99, 120, 135, 162, 180
Bush administration, 5, 8, 12, 13,
    27, 53, 66, 83, 85-99, 120, 126,
    128, 129, 172, 180, 220, 221,
    226, 241, 256, 271, 275, 283

Cambodia, 6, 40, 41, 45, 109, 110,
    177-79, 182, 188, 192, 196,
    203
Cambodian People's Party (CPP),
    196
Canada, 190
Caspian, 252
Central Asian Peacekeeping
    Battalion, 251
Central Military Commission, 55,
    60
Chan, Sara, 182
Chechnya, 117, 118, 121, 258
Chen Shui-bian, 99, 209-11, 216-
    26
Chernomyrdin, Viktor, 115
"China card," 117
China Democracy Party, 62
"China fever," 146, 166, 200, 202,
    244
"China threat," 81, 164, 180, 235,
    273
Chinese Communist Party (CCP),
    8, 27, 52, 55, 60
Chinese Empire, 108, 136
Chinese New Year, 213
Clinton, William, 13, 29, 31, 44,
    85, 86, 91, 92, 99, 143, 162,

211-13, 215, 216, 235, 241,
    275
"Cobra Gold" military exercises,
    81, 181
Cold War, 2-4, 11, 12, 15, 16, 25,
    26, 29, 30, 32, 33, 39, 43, 46,
    64-66, 79, 91, 92, 99, 107, 110,
    112, 116, 120, 125-27, 129,
    132, 133, 135-37, 140, 155,
    156, 165, 169, 170, 177-81,
    184, 189, 199, 231, 232, 234,
    235, 240, 250, 252, 255, 258,
    267, 270, 273, 274
"Cold War thinking," 32, 79, 165,
    180
Commonwealth of Independent
    States (CIS), 111
containment, 9, 12, 15, 26, 29, 36,
    57, 241, 276-78
Cornell University, 52, 211
"correct historical perspective,"
    143
Cultural Revolution, 37, 39, 43, 54,
    131

Dalai Lama, 28, 180, 181, 197,
    233, 235, 254
Davos, 82, 191
defense cooperation treaty, 143
"defensive referendum," 210
demarcation, 114, 115, 189
demobilization, 42
democracy, 43, 62, 91, 189, 198,
    200, 211, 226
Democratic Progressive Party
    (DPP), 209, 210, 216-20, 225
democratization, 43, 273

Deng Xiaoping, 7, 11, 36, 40, 44,
    52, 53, 55, 65, 78, 111, 268,
    269, 277
Diaoyu Islands, 136
East Asian Economic Caucus
    (EAEC), 190

State Peace and Development
Council (SPDC), 187
State Planning Commission (SPC),
56
Straits Exchange Foundation
(SEF), 213-15
Straits of Malacca, 3
strategic partnership, 66, 107, 120,
122, 255
strategic unions, 116
Suharto, 198
Sukarnoputri, Megawati, 89, 189,
198

Taepo Dong missile, 132, 133
Taiwan Strait, 7, 30, 34, 63, 69, 96,
133, 140, 167, 196, 202, 213,
216, 220, 223, 226, 242, 270
Tajikistan, 8, 253, 255, 256, 258
Taliban, 120, 232, 239, 245, 249,
252, 258, 260
Tang Jiaxuan, 198, 257
terrorism, 4, 6, 7, 28, 34, 45, 46,
65, 66, 70, 86, 87, 89, 91, 93,
95, 97, 99, 127, 134, 172, 179,
193, 199-201, 232, 239, 243,
245, 249, 255-57, 259, 260,
267, 270, 272, 277, 282
Thailand, 82, 177, 178, 182, 183,
185, 190-92, 197, 199-202,
212
Thaksin, Thai Prime Minster, 197
Than Shwe, 187
theater missile defense (TMD), 144
Third World, 2, 3, 37-42, 70, 71,
85, 178
"three no's," 215
"three obstacles," 109
Tiananmen, 11, 12, 26, 30, 34, 37,
43, 44, 46, 52, 78, 107, 110,
111, 126, 127, 130, 134, 141,
178, 234, 273
Tibet, 28, 31, 43, 65, 66, 87, 117,
197, 233, 235, 238, 240, 241,

243, 254, 255
Tonga, 215
Turkestan, 258
Turkey, 251, 252, 257
Turkmenistan, 250
"two Chinas," 140, 142, 215

"unequal treaties," 118
UN Human Rights Commission,
150, 238
"unilateralism," 82, 121, 122, 267,
274
unipolarity, 30, 32
united front, 33, 38, 196, 220, 221
United Nations (UN), 65, 70, 89,
93, 94, 116, 120, 126, 138,
140, 150, 212, 218, 237, 238,
242, 252, 257, 287
UN Security Council, 94, 116, 138,
150, 237, 242
U.S. "imperialism," 33, 131
Uzbekistan, 8, 111, 122, 251, 255-
58

Vajpayee, Shri Atal Bihari, 234,
235
Vietnam, 3, 14, 27, 32, 40-42, 109,
110, 177, 179, 186, 188, 189,
192, 196, 199, 200, 287
Vietnam War, 27, 192, 287
Vladivostok, 112

"war maniacs," 108
weapons of mass destruction
(WMD), 27, 69, 77, 95, 147
Wen Jiabao, 96, 185, 243, 265
Western Pacific, 32, 46, 109
Wong, John, 182, 183
World Bank, 45, 46, 64, 66
World Health Assembly, 286
World Health Organization, 150,
210, 224
World Trade Organization (WTO),
6, 31, 34, 45, 53, 56, 58, 59,

About the Author

Robert Sutter became a visiting professor of Asian Studies, a full-time position of teaching and research, in the School of Foreign Service at Georgetown University in 2001. Sutter specialized in Asian and Pacific Affairs and U.S. foreign policy, with a focus on China and Chinese foreign policy, in a U.S. government career of thirty-three years. Working in the legislative branch, he directed for many years the Foreign Affairs and National Defense Division of the Congressional Research Service of the Library of Congress and served as the Service's senior specialist in international politics. In the executive branch, he worked for many years in the Central Intelligence Agency, dealing with China, and also served as the director of the China Division in the State Department's Bureau of Intelligence and Research. He finished his government career as the national intelligence officer for East Asia and the Pacific at the U.S. government's National Intelligence Council.

Sutter received a Ph.D. in history and East Asian languages from Harvard University. For thirty years, he taught regularly as an adjunct professor at Washington-area universities including Georgetown, George Washington, Johns Hopkins Universities, and the University of Virginia. He has published thirteen books, numerous articles, and several hundred government reports dealing with China, contemporary East Asian and Pacific countries, and their relations with the United States. His most recent book is *The United States and East Asia: Dynamics and Implications* (Rowman & Littlefield, 2003).